Stephen Kershaw is a Classics Tu... Department for Continuing Educat... Art for the European Studies Program of Rhodes College and The University of the South, and a Guest Speaker for Swan Hellenic Cruises, and as such he has spent much of the last thirty years travelling extensively in the world of the ancient Romans both physically and intellectually. His *Brief Guide to the Greek Myths* (2007) and *Brief Guide to Classical Civilization* (2010) are both published by Robinson.

Highlights from the series

A Brief History of the Roman Empire

STEPHEN KERSHAW

ROBINSON

ROBINSON

First published in Great Britain in 2013 by Robinson

3 5 7 9 10 8 6 4

A CIP catalogue record for this book
is available from the British Library.

ISBN 978-1-78033-048-8

Printed and bound in Great Britain by
CPI Group (UK) Ltd, Croydon CR0 4YY

Papers used by Robinson are from well-managed forests
and other responsible sources

MIX
Paper from
responsible sources
FSC® C104740

Robinson
An imprint of
Little, Brown Book Group
Carmelite House
50 Victoria Embankment
London EC4Y 0DZ

An Hachette UK Company
www.hachette.co.uk

www.littlebrown.co.uk

To my First Triumfeminate: Lal, Mum and Hebe
Uxor venustissima, mater optima, canis fidelissima.

Contents

List of Maps

Genealogy Tables

BRITANNIA

Portus Itius

COLONIA AGRIPPINA

BELGICA

GERMANIA INFERIOR (17 BCE)

Moguntiacum

LUGDUNENSIS

Alesia

GERMANIA SUPERIOR (17 BCE)

RAETIA (15 BCE)

NORICUM (15 BCE)

PANNONIA SUPERIOR

PANNONIA INFERIOR (10 BCE)

Lugdunum

AQUITANIA

NARBONENSIS

P

C

M

Aquileia

ILLYRICUM

Mutina

Adriatic Sea

Nemausus

River Rubicon

Massilia

Lucca

Perusia

ITALY

Scodra

TARRACONENSIS

Tarraco

Rome

Velitrae

Dyrrhacium

LUSITANIA (c.27 BCE)

Apollo

Corduba

Munda

BAETICA

Naulochus

Gades

SICILY

Carthage

MAURETANIA

Thapsus

AFRICA

Naval victory over Sextus Pompeius 36 BCE

	Imperial frontier as in 14 CE
	Provincial frontiers
ASIA	Senatorial provinces

ALPINE PROVINCES (15–14 BCE):

M Maritimae
C Cottiae
P Poeninae

Client Kingdoms

0   250   500 miles

0   250   500   750   1000 km

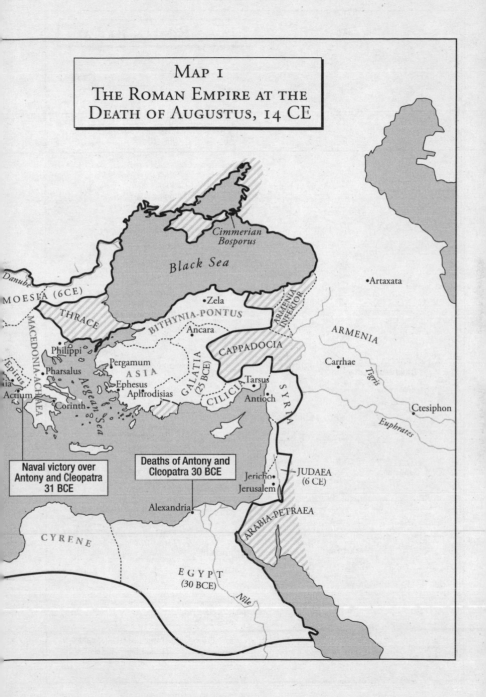

MAP 1
THE ROMAN EMPIRE AT THE DEATH OF AUGUSTUS, 14 CE

Danube

MOESIA (6CE)

THRACE

MACEDONIA-ACHAEA

Cimmerian Bosporus

Black Sea

•Zela

BITHYNIA-PONTUS

Ancara

•Artaxata

ARMENIA INFERIOR

ARMENIA

Philippi•

Pergamum

Pharsalus

ASIA

Epirus•

Ephesus

Aphrodisias

GALATIA (25 BCE)

CAPPADOCIA

CILICIA

Tarsus•

Antioch•

Carrhae•

SYRIA

Tigris

ia

Actium•

Corinth•

Aegean Sea

Ctesiphon•

Euphrates

Naval victory over Antony and Cleopatra 31 BCE

Deaths of Antony and Cleopatra 30 BCE

Jericho•

JUDAEA (6 CE)

Jerusalem•

Alexandria•

ARABIA-PETRAEA

CYRENE

E G Y P T (30 BCE)

Nile

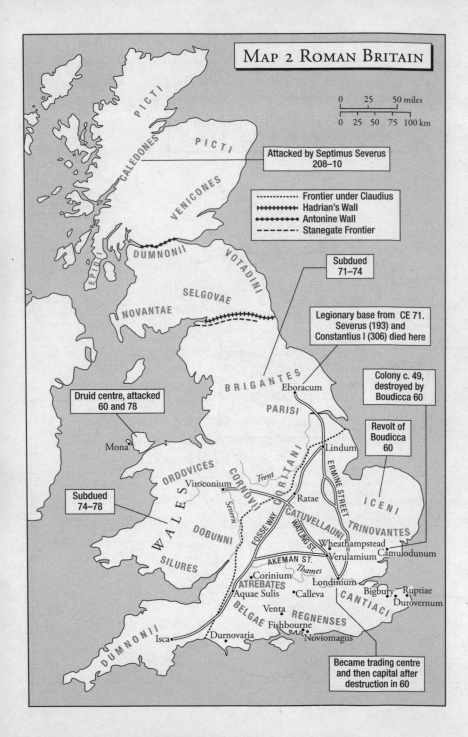

MAP 2 ROMAN BRITAIN

0   25   50 miles
0   25   50   75   100 km

PICTI

CALEDONES

PICTI

VENICONES

Attacked by Septimus Severus
208–10

·········· Frontier under Claudius
+++++++ Hadrian's Wall
•••••••• Antonine Wall
- - - - - Stanegate Frontier

EPIDI

DUMNONII

VOTADINI

SELGOVAE

NOVANTAE

Subdued
71–74

Legionary base from CE 71.
Severus (193) and
Constantius I (306) died here

BRIGANTES

Eboracum

PARISI

Colony c. 49,
destroyed by
Boudicca 60

Druid centre, attacked
60 and 78

Mona

Lindum

Revolt of
Boudicca
60

ORDOVICES

Viroconium

Trent

CORNOVII

Ratae

ERMINE STREET

ICENI

Subdued
74–78

W A L E S

Severn

CORITANI

FOSSE WAY

CATUVELLAUNI

TRINOVANTES

DOBUNNI

WATLING ST.

Wheathampstead

Camulodunum

SILURES

AKEMAN ST.

Thames

Verulamium

Corinium

Londinium

Aquae Sulis

Calleva

Bigbury

Ruptiae

ATREBATES

CANTIACI

Durovernum

Venta

REGNENSES

BELGAE

DUMNONII

Isca

Durnovaria

Fishbourne

Noviomagus

Became trading centre
and then capital after
destruction in 60

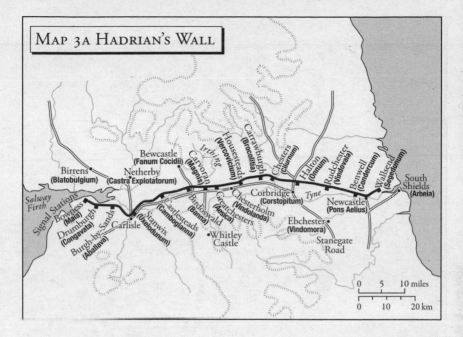

MAP 3A HADRIAN'S WALL

Signal Stations

Birrens
(Blatobulgium)

Bewcastle
(Fanum Cocidii)

Netherby
(Castra Explotatorum)

Solway
Firth

Bowness
(Maia)

Drumburgh
(Congavata)

Burgh-by-
Sands
(Aballava)

Carlisle

Stanwix
(Uxellodunum)

Castlesteads
(Camboglanna)

Birdoswald
(Banna)

Carvoran
(Magnis)

Irthing

Greatchesters
(Aesica)

Chesterholm
(Vindolanda)

Whitley
Castle

Housesteads
(Vercovicium)

Carrawburgh
(Brocolitia)

Chesters
(Cilurnum)

Corbridge
(Corstopitum)

Halton
(Omnum)

Rudchester
(Vindovala)

Benwell
(Condercum)

Wallsend
(Segedunum)

South Shields
(Arbeia)

Newcastle
(Pons Aelius)

Tyne

Ebchester
(Vindomora)

Stanegate
Road

| 0 | 5 | 10 miles |
| 0 | 10 | 20 km |

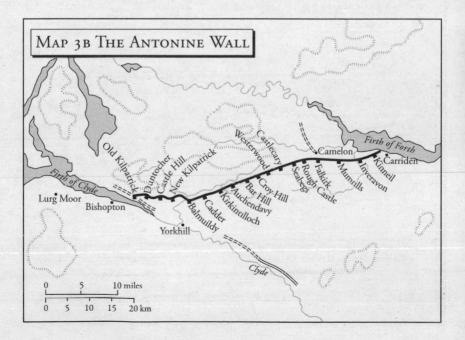

MAP 3B THE ANTONINE WALL

Old Kilpatrick

Firth of Clyde

Lurg Moor

Bishopton

Dunrocher

Castle Hill

New Kilpatrick

Balmuildy

Yorkhill

Cadder

Kirkintilloch

Auchendavy

Bar Hill

Croy Hill

Westerwood

Castlecary

Seabegs

Rough
Castle

Falkirk

Camelon

Mumrills

Inveravon

Kinneil

Carriden

Firth of Forth

Clyde

| 0 | 5 | 10 miles |
| 0 | 5 | 10 | 15 | 20 km |

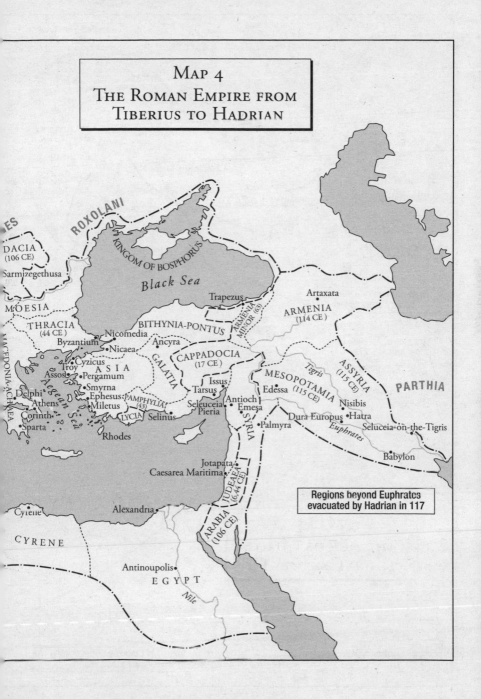

MAP 4
THE ROMAN EMPIRE FROM
TIBERIUS TO HADRIAN

ROXOLANI

DACIA
(106 CE)

Sarmizegethusa

MOESIA

THRACIA
(44 CE)

Byzantium

MACEDONIA-ACHAEA

Delphi
Athens
Corinth
Sparta

Troy
Assos
Pergamum
Smyrna
Ephesus
Miletus

Aegean Sea

Rhodes

Cyrene

CYRENE

KINGOM OF BOSPHORUS

Black Sea

Nicomedia
Nicaea
Cyzicus

ASIA

PAMPHYLIA
(43)

LYCIA

Ancyra

GALATIA

Trapezus

ARMENIA MINOR (63)

ARMENIA
(114 CE)

Artaxata

BITHYNIA-PONTUS

CAPPADOCIA
(17 CE)

Issus
Tarsus

Selinus

Seleuceia
Pieria

Antioch
Emesa

Edessa

SYRIA

Palmyra

Tigris

MESOPOTAMIA
(115 CE)

ASSYRIA
(115 CE)

PARTHIA

Nisibis
Hatra

Dura Europus

Euphrates

Seluceia-on-the-Tigris

Babylon

Jotapata
Caesarea Maritima

JUDAEA
(6, 44 CE)

Alexandria

ARABIA
(106 CE)

Regions beyond Euphrates
evacuated by Hadrian in 117

Antinoupolis

EGYPT

Nile

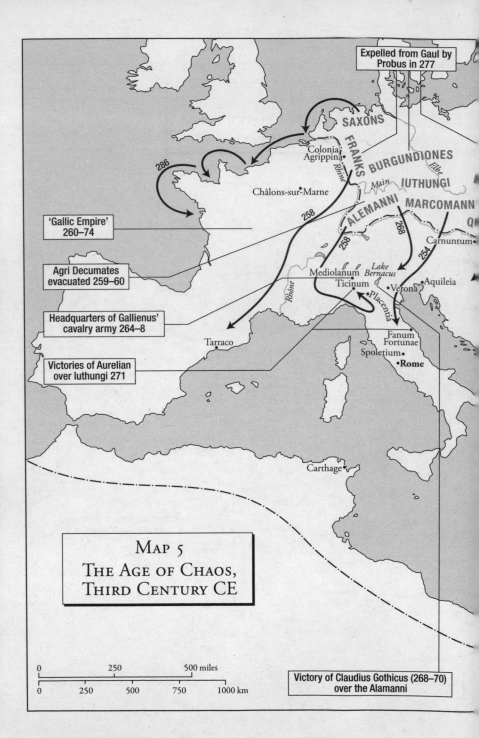

Expelled from Gaul by Probus in 277

SAXONS

FRANKS

BURGUNDIONES

Colonia
Agrippina

Rhine

IUTHUNGI

Main

MARCOMANN

Châlons-sur-Marne

286

ALEMANNI

Q

258

258

268

254

Carnuntum

'Gallic Empire'
260–74

Mediolanum
Ticinum

Lake
Bernacus

Verona

Aquileia

Agri Decumates
evacuated 259–60

Rhône

Placentia

Headquarters of Gallienus'
cavalry army 264–8

Tarraco

Fanum
Fortunae

Spoletium

Rome

Victories of Aurelian
over Iuthungi 271

Carthage

MAP 5
THE AGE OF CHAOS,
THIRD CENTURY CE

0	250	500 miles

0	250	500	750	1000 km

Victory of Claudius Gothicus (268–70)
over the Alamanni

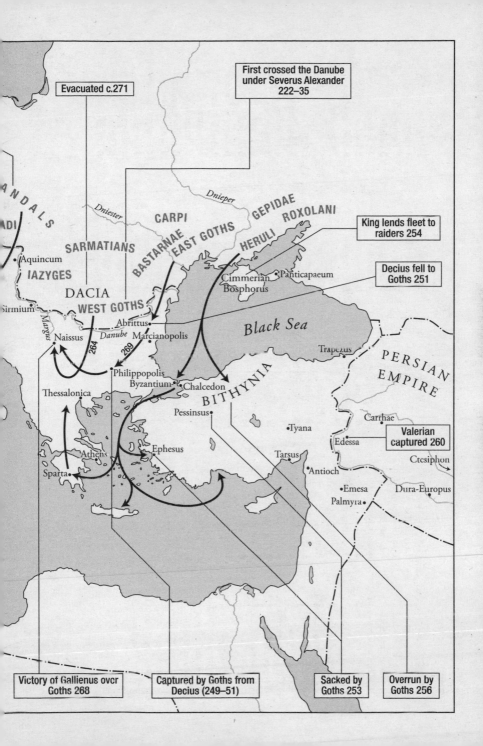

First crossed the Danube
under Severus Alexander
222–35

Evacuated c.271

King lends fleet to
raiders 254

Decius fell to
Goths 251

Valerian
captured 260

Victory of Gallienus over
Goths 268

Captured by Goths from
Decius (249–51)

Sacked by
Goths 253

Overrun by
Goths 256

Dnieper

Dniester

CARPI

GEPIDAE

ROXOLANI

SARMATIANS

BASTARNAE

EAST GOTHS

HERULI

IAZYGES

•Aquincum

DACIA

WEST GOTHS

Cimmerian
Bosphorus

•Panticapaeum

Sirmium•

Margus

Naissus•

Danube

264

269

Abrittus•

Marcianopolis

Black Sea

Trapezus•

PERSIAN
EMPIRE

Thessalonica•

Philippopolis•

Byzantium•

Chalcedon•

BITHYNIA

Pessinsus•

Carrhae•

Edessa•

Ctesiphon•

•Tyana

Tarsus•

Athens•

•Ephesus

Sparta•

•Antioch

•Emesa

Palmyra•

Dura-Europus•

ANDALS

MDI

Key

Brittaniae

1 Britannia Prima
2 Britannia Secunda
3 Flavia Caesariensis
4 Maxima Caesariensis

Galliae

1 Lugdunensis Prima
2 Lugdunensis Secunda
3 Belgica Secunda
4 Belgica Prima
5 Germania Secunda
6 Germania Prima
7 Sequania

Viennensis

1 Aquitanica Secunda
2 Aquitanica Prima
3 Novem Populi
4 Narbonensis Prima
5 Viennensis
6 Narbonensis Secunda
7 Alpes Maritimae

Hispaniae

1 Gallaecia
2 Tarraconensis
3 Lusitania
4 Carthaginiensis
5 Baetica
6 Mauretania Tingitana

Africa

1 Mauretania Caesariensis
2 Mauretania Sitifensis
3 Numidia Cirtensis
4 Numidia Militaris
5 Proconsularis
6 Byzacena
7 Tripolitania

Italia

1 Alpes Grainae
2 Alpes Cottiae
3 Raetia Prima
4 Raetia Secunda
5 Aemilia
6 Venetia and Histria
7 Liguria
8 Flaminia
9 Corsica
10 Tuscia and Umbria
11 Picenum
12 Sardinia
13 Campania
14 Samnium
15 Lucania and Bruttii
16 Apulia and Calabria
17 Sicilia

Pannoniae

1 Noricum Ripense
2 Noricum Mediterraneum
3 Savia
4 Pannonia Prima
5 Pannonia Secunda
6 Valeria
7 Dalmatia

Moesia

1 Moesica Prima
2 Dacia
3 Praevalitana
4 Dardania
5 Epirus Nova
6 Epirus Vetus
7 Macedonia
8 Thessalia
9 Achaia
10 Insulae

Thraciae

1 Scythia
2 Moesia Secunda
3 Thracia
4 Haemimontus
5 Rhodope
6 Europa

Asiana

1 Hellespontus
2 Asia
3 Lydia
4 Phrygia Prima
5 Phrygia Secunda
6 Caria
7 Lycia and Pamphylia
8 Pisidia

Pontica

1 Bithynia
2 Paphlagonia
3 Galatia
4 Diospontus
5 Pontus Polemoniacus
6 Armenia Minor
7 Cappadocia

Oriens

1 Libya Superior
2 Libya Inferior
3 Aegyptus Iovia
4 Aegyptus Herculia
5 Thebais
6 Arabia Secunda
7 Arabia Prima
8 Palestina
9 Phoenicia
10 Augusta Libanensis
11 Syria Coele
12 Augusta Euphratensis
13 Osrhoene
14 Mesopotamia
15 Cicilia
16 Isauria

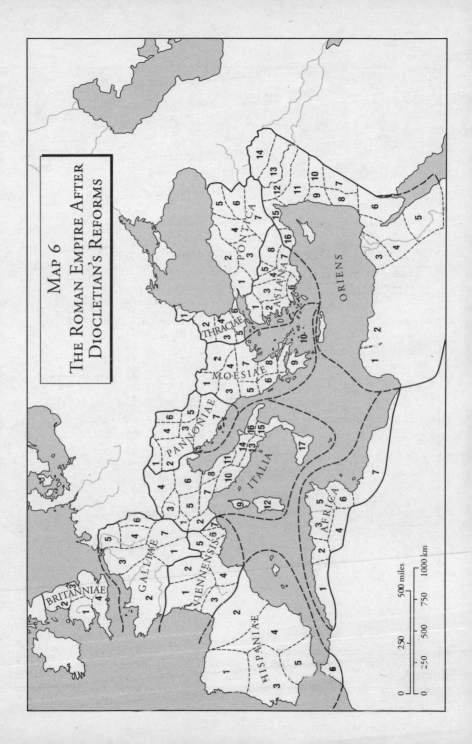

MAP 6

THE ROMAN EMPIRE AFTER
DIOCLETIAN'S REFORMS

BRITANNIAE

Londinium

Evacuated
c.259–60

Rhine

Colonia Agrippina

Moguntiacum

Augusta
Treverorum

Argentoratum

AGRI
DECUMATES

GALLIAE

ITALIA

PANNONIAE

Residence of Constantius I
(Maximian's 'Caesar')

VIENNENSIS

Mediolanum

Verona

Aquileia

Cibalae

Augusta
Taurinorum

Ticinum

Patavium

Siscia

Mons Seleuci

Arelate

Salonae

Spalato

SUBURBICARIA

Hispellum

Interamna

Rome

HISPANIAE

Residence of Maximian

AFRICA

Lepcis Magna

0   250

500 miles

0   250   500   750   1000 km

Line of division between the East
(Diocletian) and the West
(Maximian) parts of the empire

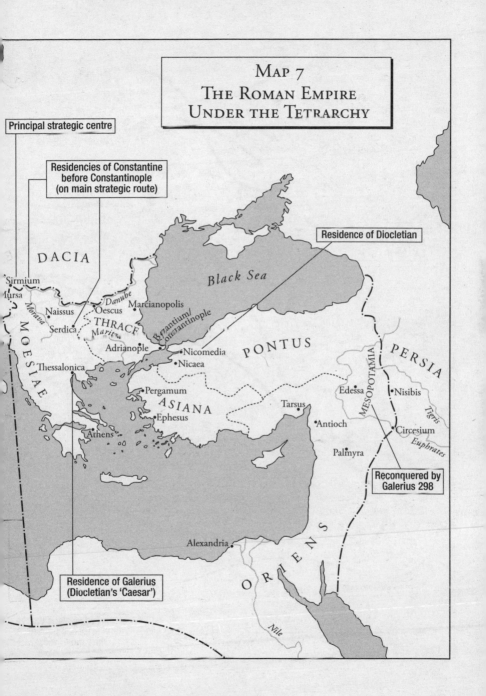

MAP 7
THE ROMAN EMPIRE
UNDER THE TETRARCHY

Principal strategic centre

Residencies of Constantine
before Constantinople
(on main strategic route)

Residence of Diocletian

DACIA

Black Sea

Sirmium
Mursa

Moravia

Danube

Naissus

Oescus

Marcianopolis

THRACE

Serdica

Marica

Byzantium/
Constantinople

Adrianople

Nicomedia

PONTUS

PERSIA

Nicaea

MOESIAE

Thessalonica

MESOPOTAMIA

Edessa

Nisibis

Pergamum

ASIANA

Tigris

Ephesus

Tarsus

Antioch

Circesium

Athens

Euphrates

Palmyra

Reconquered by
Galerius 298

ORIENS

Alexandria

Residence of Galerius
(Diocletian's 'Caesar')

Nile

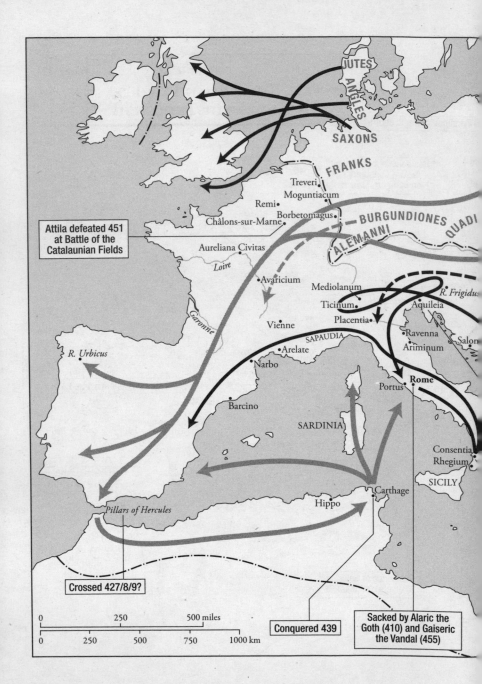

JUTES

ANGLES

SAXONS

FRANKS

BURGUNDIONES

ALEMANNI

QUADI

Treveri

Moguntiacum

Remi

Borbetomagus

Châlons-sur-Marne

Attila defeated 451
at Battle of the
Catalaunian Fields

Aureliana Civitas

Loire

Avaricium

Mediolanum

R. Frigidus

Ticinum

Aquileia

Vienne

Placentia

Ravenna

Salon

Garonne

SAPAUDIA

Ariminum

Arelate

Rome

R. Urbicus

Narbo

Portus

Barcino

SARDINIA

Consentia

Rhegium

SICILY

Pillars of Hercules

Hippo

Carthage

Crossed 427/8/9?

0   250   500 miles

0   250   500   750   1000 km

Conquered 439

Sacked by Alaric the
Goth (410) and Gaiseric
the Vandal (455)

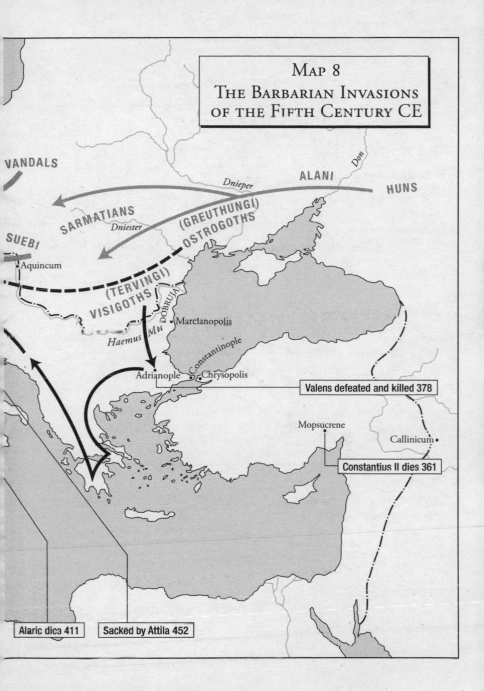

MAP 8
THE BARBARIAN INVASIONS
OF THE FIFTH CENTURY CE

VANDALS

Don

Dnieper

ALANI

HUNS

SARMATIANS

(GREUTHUNGI)

Dniester

OSTROGOTHS

SUEBI

Aquincum

(TERVINGI)

VISIGOTHS

DOBRUJA

Marcianopolis

Haemus Mts

Constantinople

Adrianople

Chrysopolis

Valens defeated and killed 378

Mopsucrene

Callinicum

Constantius II dies 361

Alaric dies 411

Sacked by Attila 452

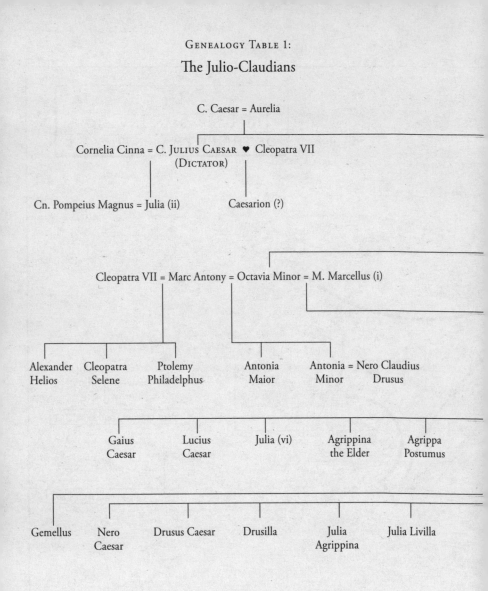

GENEALOGY TABLE 1:

The Julio-Claudians

C. Caesar = Aurelia

Cornelia Cinna = C. JULIUS CAESAR ♥ Cleopatra VII
(DICTATOR)

Cn. Pompeius Magnus = Julia (ii)   Caesarion (?)

Cleopatra VII = Marc Antony = Octavia Minor = M. Marcellus (i)

Alexander   Cleopatra   Ptolemy   Antonia   Antonia = Nero Claudius
Helios   Selene   Philadelphus   Maior   Minor   Drusus

Gaius   Lucius   Julia (vi)   Agrippina   Agrippa
Caesar   Caesar   the Elder   Postumus

Gemellus   Nero   Drusus Caesar   Drusilla   Julia   Julia Livilla
            Caesar   Agrippina

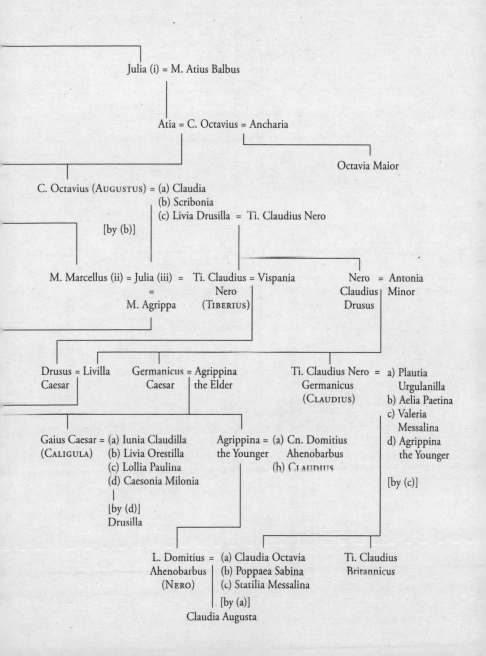

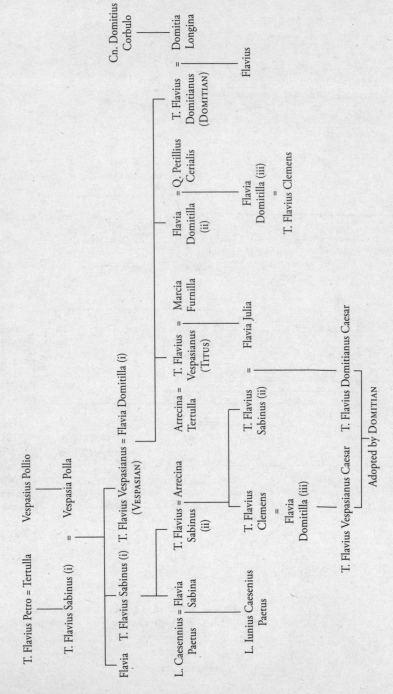

GENEALOGY TABLE 2:
The Flavians

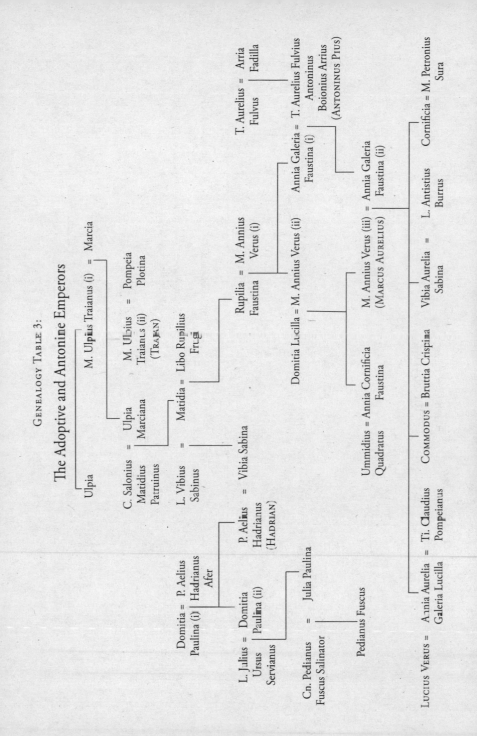

GENEALOGY TABLE 3:

The Adoptive and Antonine Emperors

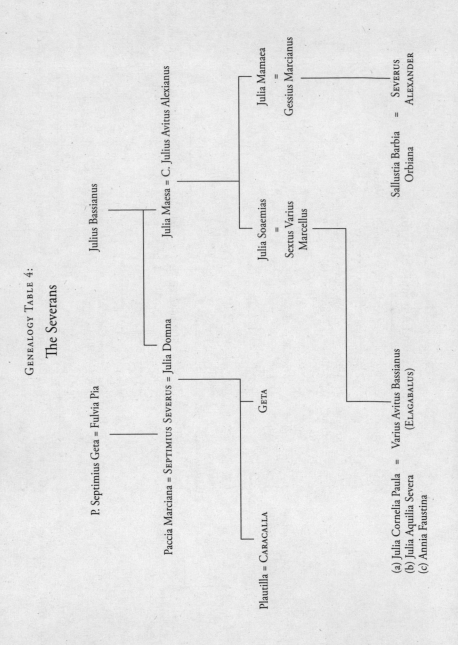

GENEALOGY TABLE 4:
The Severans

GENEALOGY TABLE 5:

Diocletian and the Tetrarchy

DIOCLETIAN = Prisca

GALERIUS = Valeria

Unknown = MAXIMIANUS = Eutropia

Helena = CONSTANTIUS I = Theodora

MAXENTIUS = Valeria Maximilla

Fausta = CONSTANTINE I THE GREAT

CONSTANTINE I
THE GREAT
=
(a) Fausta
(b) Minervina

Flavius Dalmatius   Julius Constantius   Hannibalianus   Constantia
=
Licinius

Eutropia   Anastasia

Constantine, his Heirs and the Houses of Valentinian and Theodosius

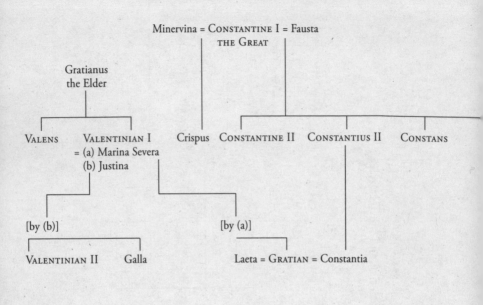

Minervina = CONSTANTINE I = Fausta
THE GREAT

Gratianus
the Elder

VALENS   VALENTINIAN I   Crispus   CONSTANTINE II   CONSTANTIUS II   CONSTANS
= (a) Marina Severa
(b) Justina

[by (b)]   [by (a)]

VALENTINIAN II   Galla   Laeta = GRATIAN = Constantia

Aelia Eudoxia = ARCADIUS

? = MARCIAN = Aelia Pulcheria

Aelia Euphemia = ANTHEMIUS

Alypia = Ricimer

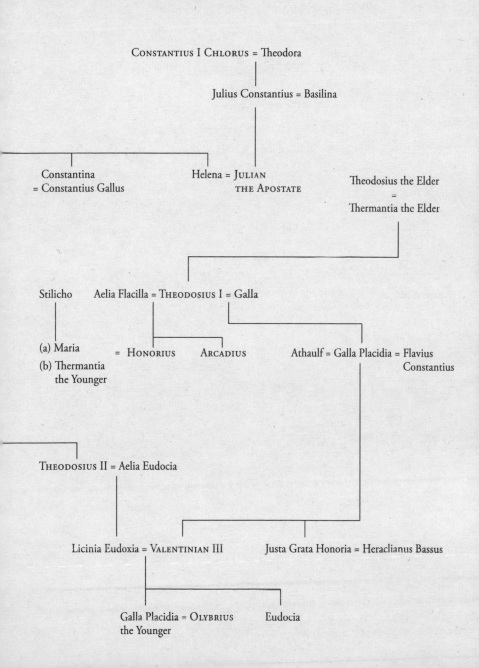

Acknowledgements

I owe a tremendous debt of gratitude to a great many people without whom this book could never have come into existence. In no particular order I would like to thank Richard Sanderson, 'Big Jimmy Feesh', Alan 'Froggy' Guy and Philip 'Smiley' Highley for igniting and sustaining my interest in Roman History; J. G. McQueen, Richard Jenkyns, Brian Warmington, Thomas Weidemann, Nial Rudd, Jim Tester, John Betts and Richard Buxton for their enormous expertise; Pam Perry, Paul Carter and Hugh Lesley at Swan Hellenic; all the fine people at OUDCE; Sally Dormer, Graziella Seferiades, Hakan Özel, Brian Masters, Peter Cocconi and Stevens Anderson from European Studies; Leo Hollis, Duncan Proudfoot, Alison Tullett, Nicky Lovick, Jan McCann and Stephen Dew at Constable & Robinson; all my students, both 'live' and 'virtual'; Philip and Dorothy Kershaw for all their unstinting support over so many years; Lal Jones for her love and understanding; Hebe for her unwavering companionship; and all the inhabitants of the Roman Empire, past and present.

1

External Expansion, Internal Implosion

'This is Rome.' Our city is a cesspool of humanity, a place of deceit, plots and vice of every imaginable kind. Anywhere you turn you will see arrogance, stubbornness, malevolence, pride and hatred. Amid such a swirl of evil, it takes a remarkable man with sound judgement and great skill to avoid stumbling, gossip and betrayal.

[Q. Cicero] *A Short Guide to Electioneering*, 54[1]

Trojans, Kings and Republicans

The history of the Romans stretches well in excess of a millennium on even the shortest calculation, and their mythology extends the time frame even further. They traced their origins back to Troy via the mythical Trojan prince Aeneas, who escaped from the carnage inflicted by the Greeks after they had used the trick of the Wooden Horse. He and a small band of survivors made their way to Italy, where they fought, and then united with, the native inhabitants to form the future Roman race. Legend has it that the city of Rome was founded by Romulus in 753 BCE, and was then ruled by seven kings until 510 BCE, when the populist but tyrannical King Tarquinius

---

1 Tr. Freeman, P., in *Q. Tullius Cicero, How to Win an Election: An Ancient Guide for Modern Politicians,* translated and with an introduction by Philip Freeman, Princeton, NJ and Oxford: Princeton University Press, 2012. 'Q.' is the Roman abbreviation for Quintus.

Superbus was expelled by Brutus the Liberator. Rome became a Republic the year after, and the Romans always remained acutely sensitive to the difference between a Kingdom (*Regnum*) and a Republic (*Res Publica*, literally 'the Public Thing'). During the Republican period (509–27 BCE), when the government was (theoretically) controlled by elected magistrates, Rome gradually became the dominant power in Italy, and then in the Mediterranean (see Map 1). However, they seemed 'to have conquered and peopled half the world in a fit of absence of mind',[2] and the acquisition of these overseas territories had opened a Pandora's box of unforeseen domestic problems. From around the late second century BCE, Rome started to implode in a series of violent internal struggles.

The Year 63 BCE

In the midst of those struggles, the year 63 BCE – or 'the consulship of Gaius Antonius and Marcus Tullius Cicero', as the Romans called it – was a critical one for the history of the world, and not purely because a child was born in that year who would become the first Emperor of Rome. The situation that Rome was in often elicits comments of the 'History is always repeating itself' variety:[3] there was a domestic crisis centred around debt and credit; recent elections had been sullied by bribery, corruption and political sleaze; the world's superpower to the West had recently witnessed the demise of one in the East, but had just become embroiled in troubles with people living in what are now Iraq, Iran, Palestine/ Israel, Syria and Lebanon; Arabs were fighting with Jews; Jews were fighting among themselves; and Rome was struggling not only to keep all this under control, but, on the domestic front, desperately needed to reconcile the competing interests of a number of very powerful personalities, the State and the people.

---

2 The phrase comes from the Victorian historian J. R. Seeley, *Expansion of England: Two Courses of Lectures,* Boston: Roberts Brothers, 1883, p. 8. He is talking about the British Empire.

3 History, of course, never repeats itself: see p. 223 below.

At the heart of this was an up-and-coming politician called C. Julius Caesar,[4] who belonged to an aristocratic family that traced its descent to Aeneas and the goddess Venus. Caesar had a particularly good year in 63 BCE, managing not only to get himself appointed *Pontifex Maximus* (Chief Priest), but also, thanks to some lavish and well-targeted bribery, securing Rome's second-highest elective office, the praetorship, for the following year. He wasn't yet bestriding the world like the colossus he was to become, but his career was definitely on an upward trajectory.

The real big beast of Roman politics that year was Cn. Pompeius Magnus[5] ('Pompey'). His meteoric rise to power and fame had violated many of Roman politics' most hallowed protocols (he was both too young and unqualified for the posts he held), but he had successfully solved a number of Rome's nagging issues. In 67 BCE he had been appointed to eradicate the Mediterranean's endemic pirate problem. This was not a case of the odd swashbuckling, parrot-wearing buccaneer: entire communities were involved, and even Caesar had once been captured by pirates. However, the legislation that granted Pompey the wherewithal to take on the pirates made his opponents feel uneasy about the potential security ramifications, even though Pompey himself was a good choice for the job. He ended up with 500 ships, 125 000 troops, numerous high-ranking subordinates, vast financial resources, and a three-year *imperium* (command) whose power applied throughout the Mediterranean and extended 80 kilometres inland of its coasts.[6] Pompey justified his appointment not only by defeating the pirates in just three months, but by putting them into 'rehab'

---

4 'C.' is the Roman abbreviation for Gaius.
5 'Cn.' is the Roman abbreviation for Gnaeus.
6 Cicero, *pro lege Manilia* 59; Sallust, *Histories* 5.24; Velleius Paterculus 2.32.1; Valerius Maximus 8.15.9; Dio 36.31 ff.. There is dispute about whether it was '*maius*', i.e., greater than that of the other governors, or '*aequum*', equal, at this stage. On balance it was most likely *aequum*: see Seager, R., *Pompey: A Political Biography*, Oxford: Basil Blackwell, 1979, p. 35 f.

and attempting to repair some of the desolation caused by the fighting. He was so successful that many pirates actually turned towards agriculture and depopulated areas were reinvigorated.

The following year Pompey had been given the command versus King Mithridates VI of Pontus on the southern coast of the Black Sea, whom Velleius Paterculus described as:

> Ever eager for war, of exceptional bravery, always great in spirit and sometimes in achievement, in strategy a general, in bodily prowess a soldier, in hatred of the Romans, a Hannibal.[7]

Mithridates had been a thorn in the eastern side of Rome's interests ever since he had imprisoned his mother, killed his younger brother, married his sister and taken the throne in 120 BCE. Pompey's *imperium* was probably upgraded to *maius*, and he certainly had the hugely significant power of making war and peace on his own initiative. Cicero, whose speech survives,[8] spoke in favour of the measures, and by 63 BCE Mithridates was blockaded in the Crimea, albeit still alive and taking a daily regime of antidotes to safeguard himself from would-be poisoners.

One significant knock-on effect of this conflict was to sour Rome's relations with the Parthian Kingdom, which at its greatest extent stretched from the Euphrates to the Indus (thus encompassing both modern Iraq and Iran), with its capital at Ctesiphon (near what is now Baghdad). Its king, Phraates III, felt short-changed by Pompey for the help he had given him in dealing with Mithridates. Another ramification of the Mithridatic Wars was Rome's annexation of Syria, once the focal point of the proud and mighty Seleucid Kingdom, carved out of the remains of Alexander the Great's empire by Seleukos I Nikator. However, the Seleucid Empire was now merely a faded memory,

---

7 Velleius Paterculus, 2.18.1, tr. Shipley, F. W., in *Velleius Paterculus, Compendium of Roman History*, Cambridge, MA.: Harvard University Press, 1924. His name is spelled either Mithridates or Mithradates.

8 *Pro lege Manilia.*

and Syria was ravaged by extortion and war. It was ripe for picking. Pompey marched through the region imposing order and discipline, giving the Syrian king, Antiochus XIII Asiaticus, short shrift at a meeting at Antioch (modern Antakya, Turkey), annexing his territory to secure it from incursions by Jews and Arabs, and ultimately bringing Syria under Rome's direct rule. Egypt, under the dissolute, arrogant King Ptolemy XII Neos Dionysos, whose addiction to music had earned him the derisory title of 'Auletes' ('Flute Player'), was now the only surviving autonomous remnant of Alexander's empire.

In 63 BCE Pompey had made his way into Judaea, where he got involved in the Hasmonean Civil War. Two brothers, Aristoboulus and Hyrcanus, were contesting the Jewish throne. Pompey seemed to back Hyrcanus, and Aristoboulus ultimately withdrew to Jerusalem. When Pompey had reached Jericho in his pursuit, he received news of the death of Mithridates: faced by a rebellion from one of his sons, the old king had taken poison, but since the daily antidotes had pretty well immunized him, a loyal servant duly dispatched him, providing the inspiration behind the famous verses written by A. E. Housman in *A Shropshire Lad*:

> I tell the tale that I heard told.
> Mithridates, he died old.

Things now moved quite quickly in Judaea: Aristoboulus fortified Jerusalem; Pompey laid siege to it; Aristoboulus was arrested when he tried to negotiate; further internal strife arose among the Jews, as the factions of Aristoboulus and Hyrcanus were confronted by those who wanted a theocracy (the *Psalms of Solomon* represent the Roman conquest as the 'reward' for Jewish impiety);[9] the three-month siege of Jerusalem ended with

9   2.3ff., 8.8ff., 25ff. Some scholars think that the Kittim mentioned in the Commentary on Habakkuk (Pesher Habakkuk, 1Q p Hab), one of the seven original Dead Sea Scrolls, may well be the Romans under Pompey and his predecessor Lucullus.

horrendous bloodshed; Pompey desecrated the sanctuary of the Temple, although he didn't plunder it; Hyrcanus was established as High Priest, but not King; and Pompey made his so-called Eastern Settlement.

Pompey had exceptional organizational skills, and his Eastern Settlement of 62 BCE laid the foundations for the later *Pax Romana* in the region by means of a three-faceted arrangement that involved: creating a virtually continuous ring of provinces from the southern shore of the Black Sea to Syria/Palestine; founding about forty new cities; and organizing and promoting independent 'client' states as a kind of firewall outside the ring of provinces. On the whole, the new cities began to flourish, bringing Rome a 70 per cent increase in revenue from the region. The client states, many of whose rulers owed their position to Pompey, were nominally independent and maintained friendly relations with Rome in an arrangement modelled on that between a high-ranking Roman *patronus* ('patron') and his *clientes* ('dependents'). Pompey's administrative talents were indisputable, but what really mattered to Rome was that he was a *conqueror*. He was now an incredibly powerful man: he received divine cult on Delos; his eye-watering wealth made him the richest man in Rome; kings were in his debt, both literally and figuratively; his client base encompassed individuals, cities, provinces and kingdoms; and he commanded vast military resources.

Throughout this period, Pompey's interests back in Rome had been promoted by M. Tullius Cicero.[10] Cicero was a *Novus Homo* ('New Man'), in other words from a family new to the political scene at Rome. A man like Cicero could regularly enter the lower echelons of the political hierarchy, but he had his heart set on holding the consulship, Rome's highest elective office. This was an incredibly ambitious aspiration. Every Roman citizen could vote in this election, and also on legislation in Rome's Assemblies, but he (they were all male) had to do so in person at Rome. The Romans therefore had a 'direct' democracy, rather than the

---

10   'M.' is the Roman abbreviation for Marcus.

'representative' systems that most Western democracies now use, and this had worked effectively enough while Rome was just a small town, but in Cicero's time many Roman citizens couldn't exercise this right because they didn't live anywhere near Rome. There was no local voting, so Cicero would have to go to Rome and canvass personally, and do so in the *toga candida*, a specially whitened toga that gives us our word 'candidate'. He could expect vigorous political opposition, and indeed was warned in the pamphlet known as the *Commentariolum Petitionis* (*Short Guide to Electioneering*) to expect deceit, plots, vice, arrogance, stubbornness, malevolence, pride, hatred and betrayal.[11] The underlying reason for this atmosphere was that Rome had become the venue for ruthless power struggles between factions within a ruling elite that Cicero was trying to break into.

SPQR

In Cicero's day, Rome's governmental system combined a Senate, various magistrates and several Popular Assemblies, into what was designated *Senatus Populusque Romanus* (SPQR), 'the Roman Senate and People'.

The magistrates were usually elected for a one-year term and progressed through a series of offices known as the *Cursus Honorum*. After a spell of military and/or legal service, you would hope to be elected as Quaestor, with *potestas* (the power, which all the magistrates had, to enforce the law by the authority of your office), along with financial and administrative duties.

After this you might take an optional spell as Tribune of the Plebs, when you would benefit from personal sacrosanctity, the power of *veto* (= 'I forbid' in Latin), and the right to summon the *Concilium Plebis* (Assembly of the Plebs) and put resolutions (*plebiscita*) to it. The social divide between the plebs and the patricians was most fundamental at Rome: the patricians were a hereditary aristocracy of exceptionally wealthy

---

11 See [Q. Cicero] *A Short Guide to Electioneering*, 54, quoted above, p. 1.

landowners, and for a great part of Rome's history they had held all the legal, political and religious posts. Patrician rank was normally inherited, and the non-patricians, who were the vast majority of Rome's population, were known as plebeians (Latin *plebs* = multitude). Tribunes were supposed to act as champions of the lower classes, but this happened far less often than it should have. You might, on the other hand, stand for the post of *Aedilis* ('Aedile'), which would entail an obligation personally to finance things like the upkeep of the streets, the water supply or the arrangement of public games and festivals. Either way, you would hope that your burgeoning fame and popularity might win you the office of Praetor.

As Praetor you received *imperium*, which took your power to a whole new level. *Imperium* gave you the right to command an army, interpret and carry out the law, and to issue orders and expect them to be obeyed. You would be attended by six *Lictors*, who carried the *fasces*, a bundle of rods, to which an axe was added whenever they left the city precincts, symbolizing the right to inflict corporal and capital punishment that *imperium* conferred, although magistrates were not allowed to execute Roman citizens without trial. As Propraetor (*pro* in Latin = 'on behalf of') you would then take up a provincial governorship with *imperium* for one year. The provinces were Rome's dependent territories (*provincia* = 'a sphere of duty assigned to a magistrate'), and now you could start to recoup the money you had spent on your election campaigns: a provincial governorship could be very lucrative even if you were honest; if you weren't, you could make an absolute fortune.

The ultimate achievement was to secure one of the two consulships. Your *imperium* was limited by your colleague's right of veto, but you now held twelve *fasces*, and would become Commander-in-Chief of the army, preside over the Senate, organize the community religion, conduct the main elections and implement the Senate's decisions, before moving on to a 'better' provincial governorship as Proconsul.

There were three Popular Assemblies at Rome at this time: the

Comitia Centuriata, arranged into 193 Centuries (constituencies) in which the richer ones dominated, that could pass *leges* (laws, sing. *lex*) and elect magistrates with *imperium*; the *Comitia Tributa*, which was based on Rome's thirty-five tribes and acted as a law-making body and elected magistrates known as Curule Aediles and Quaestors; and the *Concilium Plebis*, comprising only plebeians, which could pass *plebiscita* binding on the whole community, and elected Tribunes of the Plebs and Plebeian Aediles.

Technically and traditionally speaking, the Senate (*senes* = 'old men') was an advisory body, composed of ex-magistrates who did unpaid public service as legal advisers, judges, diplomats, military officers and priests. Its membership generally ranged between 300 and 600 men, who had to possess a minimum property qualification of one million *sestertii* in the time of Augustus – an enormous amount, given that in around 50 BCE a rank-and-file soldier was paid 900 *sestertii* a year. Two Censors had the power to remove anyone guilty of misconduct. Members of the Senatorial order (Latin *ordo* = 'class'/'rank') wore a broad purple stripe (*latus clavus*) on their togas and occupied prominent seats on major religious and public occasions. As Cicero put it,

> a Senator has many privileges [. . .] rank, position, magnificence at home, reputation and influence abroad, the embroidered robe, the chair of state, the badges of rank, the lictor's rods, armies, commands, provinces.[12]

The Roman belief in tradition was so incredibly strong that over the centuries the Senate's *advice* had acquired the force of *law*. Fundamentally the Senators felt that their wealth and status justified their right to control Rome. They were ambitious and individualistic, had a strong sense of their own self-worth (*dignitas*), and for a very long time their control over domestic and

---

12 Cicero, *Pro Cluentio* 154, tr. Grose Hodge, H., in *Cicero in Twenty-eight Volumes, IX, Pro Lege Manilia, Pro Caecina, Pro Cluentio, Pro Rabirio Perduellionis, with an English Translation by H. Grose Hodge*, Cambridge, MA.: Harvard University Press, 1929.

foreign policy had seldom been questioned: Rome might have called herself a Republic, but in fact she was ruled by a closely circumscribed group of families. Furthermore, within the Senate itself there was an exclusive inner clique called the *nobiles* (nobles), who were either ex-Consuls or men who could boast a Consul among their ancestors. The elitist nature of the system is shown by the fact that over a period of 300 years only fifteen non-nobles had held the office of Consul.

'New men' like Cicero tended to be 'Equestrian' (Latin *equites* = 'horsemen'/'knights'). The key qualification for admission to the order was possession of 400 000 *sestertii*. Distinguished by a narrow purple stripe on their togas, the Equites were not a middle class (Rome did not really have one in the modern sense): what distinguished them from the Senators was participation in politics; what distinguished them from the plebs was an absolutely enormous financial gulf that made upward social mobility extremely difficult. The standard of living of the majority of Rome's population was far lower than that of the modern British, European or American working classes, and the notion of 'poverty' at Rome needs to be used with care: even the 'poor' still had to have a reasonably secure means of support, be this a trade, craft or some kind of connection with a prosperous family; if by 'the poor' we mean 'the destitute', there were hardly any – if you were destitute, you died.

Within the Senate there were also two factions, the *Optimates* and the *Populares*. According to Cicero:

> Those who wanted everything they did and said to be pleasing to the masses were considered *Populares*; but those who conducted themselves so as to win for their policies the approval of all the best citizens were considered *Optimates* [. . .] All are *Optimates* who are neither malevolent, nor shameless in behaviour, nor insane, nor embarrassed by family problems.[13]

---

13   Cicero, *Pro Sestio* 45, 96, tr. Shenton, J. A., in *As the Romans Did: A Source Book*

Actually, the *Optimates* were a powerful, determined, cohesive, ruthless and more or less permanent group who made up the majority in the Senate and defended the established traditions because it was in their interests. The *Populares* felt that they could achieve quicker results by whipping up popular feeling and side-stepping the Senate in order to gain personal advancement. They were not instinctive 'democrats', and although some *Populares* had genuine concerns about social justice, many were merely demagogues. Political idealism was rare at Rome.

The Consulship of M. Tullius Cicero and C. Antonius Hybrida (63 BCE)

Against all the odds, Cicero was elected Consul for 63 BCE alongside C. Antonius 'Hybrida', beating a colourful, disaffected aristocrat called L. Sergius Catilina ('Catiline')[14] in the process. Contemporary sources, Cicero included, describe Catiline as a perverted, destructive, extravagant, over-ambitious traitor, although they do acknowledge his mental and physical energy, toughness and ability to win friends and influence people. With a shady political past and a string of unsuccessful election campaigns behind him, Catiline had found himself badly in debt, and when his wealthy backer M. Licinius Crassus withdrew his support, he opted to stand again for the consulship of 62 BCE on a platform of cancellation of debts. This was attractive to a wide range of people: the indebtedness of the poor was a big issue, but many wealthy property owners would also have benefited from Catiline's programme.

However, Catiline was not elected, so he turned to violence. Amid armed risings and terrorism, Cicero exposed Catiline's conspiracy in the Senate on 21 October 63 BCE, and the *Senatus Consultum Ultimum* (*SCU*, the Final Decree of the Senate,

---

in Roman History, New York and Oxford: Oxford University Press, 1988, p. 299.
14   'L.' is the Roman abbreviation for Lucius.

empowering the Consuls to see to it that the State came to no harm) was passed, yet Catiline stayed in Rome, plotting Cicero's murder and trying to face him down. Cicero responded by making his *First Catilinarian Speech* in the Senate on 8 November, which forced Catiline to quit Rome and join his henchman Manlius in Etruria. Their co-conspirator Lentulus remained in the capital, though, and on 9 November Cicero's magnificent *Second Catilinarian* was delivered to the people. The key moment came at the end of the month, when the conspirators tried to get some Gallic envoys to join them. But the Gauls chose instead to pass the details on to Cicero. With incontrovertible written proof of the conspiracy, he had the conspirators at Rome arrested, and on 3 December he made the *Third Catilinarian* to the people. Two days later the Senate discussed the conspirators' fate, with Cicero making his *Fourth Catilinarian* in favour of the death penalty. He got his way and oversaw their execution, famously responding to the question of what had happened to them with an elegant use of Latin's perfect tense: *vixerunt* = 'they have lived'. Catiline himself was run to ground, defeated and killed early in 62 BCE; Cicero was proclaimed 'Father of the Fatherland'; yet he had become vulnerable to accusations of having executed Roman citizens without trial.

Cicero was extremely pleased with himself: to many people's irritation he referred endlessly in his speeches to how he had 'restored the Republic'. However, he too became entangled in Rome's factional infighting, and the 'Republic' was ultimately 'restored' (the inverted commas are significant) by a man who was probably born in a house on the north-east slopes of the Palatine Hill in Rome just before sunrise on 23 September in the year of his consulship: Gaius Octavius, who legend had it was the son of Apollo, and who would ultimately become Rome's first Emperor.

Octavius came from a family of small-town big men from Velitrae (modern Velletri), just to the south-east of Rome. The historian Suetonius tells us that:

An 'Octavian Street' runs through the busiest part of the city, and an altar is shown there consecrated by one Octavius, a local commander [. . .] King Tarquinius Priscus admitted the Octavians, among other plebeian families, to the Roman Senate, and though Servius Tullius awarded them patrician privileges, they later reverted to plebeian rank until eventually Julius Caesar made them patricians once more.[15]

Some of Octavius' ancestors had held high office at Rome; others had followed Equestrian career paths; and his great-grandfather had fought in the Second Punic War. Octavius' enemies, Mark Antony for instance, wrote that his great-grand-father had been an ex-slave and a rope-maker, and that his grandfather had been a money-changer. There were also jibes that his father, also called Gaius Octavius, was a money-changer who distributed electoral bribes. But whatever his day job, C. Octavius senior became a Senator, held the praetorship in 61 BCE, and went on to govern Macedonia, courageously and justly by all accounts.

Little Octavius' future prospects derived more from his mother Atia's side of the family (See Genealogy Table 1). She was the daughter of M. Atius Balbus and Julius Caesar's sister Julia (making Octavius Caesar's great-nephew). Mark Antony also tried to besmirch Octavius' maternal line by alleging that his great-grandfather Balbus had been born in Africa, and ran a perfumery and then a bakery, and Cassius of Parma also sneered at him as the grandson of a baker and a money-changer:

Your mother's flour came from a miserable Arician bakery, and the coin-stained hands of a Nerulian money-changer kneaded it.[16]

---

15 Suetonius, *Augustus* 1–2, tr. Graves, R., in *Suetonius: The Twelve Caesars*, 2nd edn., Harmondsworth: Penguin Books, 1979.
16 Quoted by Suetonius, *Augustus* 4, tr. Graves, R., op. cit.

However, when Atia's husband died suddenly on his return to Rome (Octavius was four at the time), she remarried to L. Marcius Philippus, who proved to be a safe pair of hands for the upbringing of the rather sickly Octavius and his two siblings, Octavia Maior and Octavia Minor.[17]

The First Triumvirate: Pompey, Crassus and Caesar

On the political front at Rome, no sooner had Catiline been dispatched than another scandal broke. P. Clodius Pulcher[18] was in love with Julius Caesar's wife, Pompeia, who was, apparently, amenable to his advances. As the wife of the *Pontifex Maximus*, her public duties included presiding over the all-women festival of *Bona Dea* ('the Good Goddess'), which was celebrated in Caesar's house. Clodius took advantage of Caesar's absence to infiltrate the event by dressing up as a woman in order to enjoy some 'quality time' with Pompeia. Unfortunately, his voice betrayed him and he was indicted for sacrilege. Other allegations were made against him, one of which was incestuous adultery with his notoriously promiscuous sister Clodia, who could well be the lover of the poet Catullus, under the literary name of Lesbia. Caesar insisted that Pompeia was innocent, but still divorced her: 'I considered that my wife ought not to be even suspected,' he said.[19] At the trial Cicero annihilated Clodius' alibi, but still didn't secure a guilty verdict, and Clodius never forgave Cicero.

Pompey now arrived back from the East. To considerable relief he disbanded his army before celebrating a magnificent triumph. But then he ran into a brick wall. He had two needs and one want: land for his veteran soldiers as their pension on demobilization, ratification of his Eastern Settlement and marriage into the family of the arch-*Optimate* M. Porcius Cato. However, the *Optimates*

---

17 The mother of Octavia Maior was C. Octavius' first wife Ancharia; the other two were Octavius Senior's children by Atia.

18 The 'P.' is the Roman abbreviation for Publius.

19 Suetonius, *Caesar* 10.

closed ranks against him and prevented him achieving any of these, and he wasn't the only man to be frustrated.

Prior to Pompey's Eastern conquests, M. Licinius Crassus had been Rome's richest individual, gaining the nickname *Dives* (= 'the Rich'). His dealings had made him the spokesman for a syndicate of Equestrian tax-farmers. The *Pax Romana* was expensive to maintain, and the Romans expected that their Empire should 'happily pay for this continual peace and tranquillity, which benefits her'.[20] Rome had a privatized tax-collection system, administered by ruthless syndicates who would guarantee to collect a certain amount from a given province, but who were free to retain any surplus that they could exact. To make things worse, provinces that struggled to pay their taxes frequently resorted to borrowing. Unfortunately for them, the Equestrian businessmen who lent them the money (an APR of 48 per cent was not unknown) were often the selfsame people who collected the tax. However, on this occasion Crassus' syndicate had made a bad deal over the taxes of Asia, and they faced the prospect of merely breaking even. They wanted to renegotiate, but the *Optimates* would have none of it.

The third man to fall foul of the *Optimates* was Julius Caesar. He wanted both to celebrate a triumph for his recent campaigns in the Iberian Peninsula and to stand for the consulship of 59 BCE. The rules on this were clear: you had to wait outside the city boundaries of Rome for a triumph, but appear in the city in person to submit your candidacy for election. Caesar wanted to do both by standing for election *in absentia*, but the *Optimates*, who had never liked him, blocked his attempt. He completely wrong-footed them by giving up the triumph and arriving in Rome, whereupon they decreed that, should he be elected, his *Provincia* would be the third-rate post of Commissioner for the Forests and Cattle Drifts of Italy: this was blatantly insulting – it would not be acceptable to any Proconsul, let alone Julius Caesar.

---

20   Cicero, *Letters to His Brother Quintus* 1.1.11.

Pompey, Crassus and Caesar were by no means good friends, but they knew that their combined political leverage could secure their individual short-term ambitions. So they formed an *amicitia* (an informal political deal), which later became known as the First Triumvirate. They could now dominate Roman politics.

The *triumviri* secured Caesar's election as Consul for 59 BCE. However, his colleague was L. Calpurnius Bibulus, an *Optimate* who not only vetoed Caesar's bill for Pompey's veterans, but also, in a cynical piece of manipulation of religion for political ends, declared a 'sacred period', and went home to take the auspices – for the rest of the year. This meant that no legislation could now legally be passed, although Caesar pressed on regardless, securing the land for Pompey's veterans, distributing 20 000 allotments of public land in Italy to the urban poor (and gaining 20 000 guaranteed votes for himself in the process), ratifying Pompey's Eastern Settlement, securing Crassus' tax renegotiation, and arranging for the patrician Clodius to be adopted into a plebeian *gens* so that he could stand as Tribune of the Plebs and attack Cicero.[21] Caesar took Cisalpine Gaul and Illyricum as his *Provincia* for five years, along with three legions, and when the governor of Transalpine Gaul died at a convenient (though not suspicious) juncture, he added this and one more legion to his area of control and embarked on the conquest of Gaul. To cement the *amicitia*, Pompey married Caesar's beautiful and virtuous daughter Julia.

Clodius was elected Tribune for 58 BCE and immediately made a proposal that any magistrate (obviously Cicero) who had put Roman citizens to death without trial should be exiled. The spineless Pompey, cowed by the violence of Clodius, who was perhaps being financed by Crassus, abandoned Cicero and kept a very low profile until it became obvious to him that Cicero was actually a very valuable asset. Pompey then sought to neutralize

---

21   Suetonius, *Tiberius* 2. His original name was Claudius: see Allen, W. jnr., 'Claudius or Clodius?', *The Classical Journal,* vol. 33, no. 2 (1937), 107–110.

Clodius by organizing a gang under T. Annius Milo,[22] and getting Cicero recalled (by a majority of 416 to 1 – Clodius).

Yet amid all the acrimony the three amigos still needed one another: Crassus hankered after military prestige, Caesar wanted to complete his campaigns in Gaul, which was conquered but not totally pacified; and Pompey was not guaranteed the support of the *Optimates* even if he broke away from the others. So before the campaigning season of 56 BCE they hammered out a deal at Lucca in Italy that gave them total control of Rome: Pompey and Crassus became joint Consuls in 55 BCE; Crassus then took Syria for five years; Pompey got Spain for five years but could stay in Rome; Caesar's *Provincia* was extended for five years; and impressive building projects that included Caesar's Forum and Pompey's Theatre (Rome's first permanent stone theatre) were initiated at Rome.

Caesar's Invasions of Britain

Things were looking good for the Triumvirate, and Caesar now took the opportunity to invade Britain. His pretext was not to stamp out the Druids, as is sometimes asserted, but, in his own words, because he 'knew that in almost all the Gallic campaigns the Gauls had received reinforcements from the Britons'.[23] This military justification stems from the fact that Caesar was technically exceeding his powers by campaigning outside his *Provincia*, and so running the risk of prosecution. Unspoken motives may have included a desire to assess Britain's mineral wealth, tap into the island's production of wheat in order to supply his troops in Gaul, and, of course, to win prestige. Britain was regarded as a distant, exotic, triangular land across the Ocean, near the ends of the earth, whose west side faced Spain (!) and Ireland, and whose inhabitants dyed themselves with blue woad

---

22 'T.' is the Roman abbreviation for Titus.
23 Caesar, *Bellum Gallicum* 4.20, in *Caesar: The Conquest of Gaul*, tr. Handford, S. A., London: Penguin Books, revised with a New Introduction by Jane F. Gardner, 1982.

and shaved all their bodies apart from their heads and the upper lips: conquest would match Pompey's achievements in the East (see Map 2).

Towards the end of summer 55 BCE, Caesar detailed an officer called C. Volusenus to assess potential landing sites, and dispatched Commius, a pro-Roman chieftain of the Gallic Atrebates tribe, to persuade as many British tribes as possible to accept Rome's 'protection'. Neither man was particularly successful: Volusenus only found a series of open beaches rather than a suitable harbour, and Commius was taken prisoner.

Undeterred, Caesar requisitioned eighty transport vessels and a number of warships at Portus Itius (identified as modern Boulogne), plus eighteen transports for the cavalry 13 kilometres along the coast. He set sail around midnight on 24 August with *Legio* VII and his favourite *Legio* X. Unfortunately, the cavalry were slow off the mark, and were carried back to land by the tide. Caesar himself reached Britain at about 9 a.m. on the 25th, but with hostile forces on the hills ready to oppose him he rode at anchor until 3 p.m., when the wind and tide turned in his favour. He ran his ships aground on a sloping beach, but finding themselves shoulder-deep in the waves and weighed down by their weapons, his men struggled to establish a beach-head until, in an iconic moment in British history, the eagle-bearer of *Legio* X (subsequently called *Equestris*) yelled:

> Jump down, comrades, unless you want to surrender our eagle to the enemy; I, at any rate, mean to do my duty to my country and my general![24]

He leaped out of the ship; the Romans rallied round him and drove the Britons from the beach; the British chieftains released Commius and sued for peace; Caesar reproached them for making war on him 'without provocation',[25] and took hostages.

---

24   Ibid. 4.25.
25   Ibid. 4.27.

When the cavalry eventually sailed, they immediately ran into a gale that forced them back to the continent. The storm, combined with a full moon and a particularly high tide – 'a fact unknown to our men', according to Caesar[26] – severely damaged the Roman fleet, which was drawn up on the beach or riding at anchor. Caesar had never intended to winter in Britain, and his men had not provided themselves with a stock of grain with this in mind. The British chieftains knew that Caesar had no cavalry, ships or corn, and that his force was not large, and so decided to renew hostilities: if they repulsed the Romans now, it might deter anyone from invading Britain again.

As Caesar repaired his ships and sent out foraging parties, the Britons responded by ambushing *Legio* VII using their expert chariot fighters:

> They combine the mobility of cavalry with the staying power of infantry; and by daily training and practice they attain such proficiency that even on a steep incline they are able to control the horses at full gallop, and to check and turn them in a moment. They can run along the chariot pole, stand on the yoke, and get back into the chariot as quick as lightning.[27]

Caesar's timely intervention saved the day, but when some typical British weather curtailed the fighting, the Britons took the opportunity to assemble a large force in order to eradicate the Roman menace once and for all. However, this played into Caesar's hands: the natives were no match for the Romans in formal warfare and were totally routed; the Romans devastated a wide area before returning to camp; British envoys sued for peace; Caesar demanded twice as many hostages (though only two tribes actually delivered them), and made a safe night-crossing back to the continent.

---

26 Ibid. 4.29.
27 Ibid. 4.33.

Modern scholarly assessments tend to regard the outcomes of this expedition with circumspection. Objectively it had not been a spectacular success, and Caesar had been in considerable jeopardy, but on the other hand he had crossed the ocean and the barbarians of Britain had capitulated. Seen from Caesar's perspective, it had ticked all the necessary boxes:

> On the conclusion of these campaigns and the receipt of Caesar's dispatches, the Senate decreed a public thanksgiving of twenty days.[28]

The fact that Caesar had unfinished business in Britain is shown by the events of 54 BCE. He returned having learned important lessons: a purpose-built fleet of 600 extra transport ships was constructed; Gallic troublemakers were dealt with; and the invasion force was increased to five legions (about 25 000 men: *Legio* VII is the only one mentioned by name in Caesar's account, but X was probably used, and also XIV (later called *Gemina*, which was commanded by Cicero's brother Quintus, who wrote letters home from Britain) plus 2 000 auxiliary cavalry. Other lessons had not been learned: again he was driven far off course by the tidal current, but when he did finally land at about midday on 6 July, he was able to do so unopposed – his 'invincible armada' had frightened the Britons away.

Caesar struck hard and fast. A night march of about 32 kilometres brought him within sight of the enemy, who confronted him from across the River Stour. When the Roman cavalry drove them back they occupied the hill-fort of Bigbury, but assaulting this type of defence was meat and drink to Roman legionaries: the soldiers of the *Legio* VII locked their shields together in the *testudo* ('tortoise') formation and captured the place with relative ease.

So far so good. But then came news that a gale had severely damaged the Roman fleet, and that forty ships were a total

---

28   Ibid. 4.38.

right-off. Again Caesar was paying the price for not finding a suitable harbour, and for misreading the local weather conditions. During the ten days that it took him to enclose the ships in a fortified camp, a numerous British force had been assembled by Cassivellaunus of the Catuvellauni, a bellicose tribe whose territory lay north of the River Thames, with their capital at Wheathampstead.

The hit-and-run tactics of the British cavalry and charioteers made life difficult for the Romans as they advanced northwards, but when the Britons tried a more forceful onslaught Caesar routed them. This proved so demoralizing that the various tribes that had assembled to help Cassivellaunus dispersed, allowing Caesar to forge ahead to the Thames. Where he made the crossing into Cassivellaunus' territory is disputed (Tilbury and Brentford are the favoured suggestions), but despite large enemy forces on the opposite bank using sharp stakes fixed along the edge and concealed in the river bed, his combined cavalry and infantry assault drove the Britons off.

Cassivellaunus reverted to guerrilla tactics with his charioteers, while Caesar received envoys from the Trinovantes, a rival tribe from Essex, whose young prince Mandubracius was a personal enemy of Cassivellaunus. Caesar agreed to protect Mandubracius from Cassivellaunus in return for his people's support, and other tribes surrendered too. They gave Caesar the intelligence he needed to locate Cassivellaunus' stronghold at Wheathampstead. Once found, this was easily captured, and Cassivellaunus sued for peace, using Commius as an intermediary. By now, Caesar was keen to return to Gaul, and he was relatively lenient: he demanded hostages, fixed an annual tribute to the Roman government, banned Cassivellaunus from harassing Mandubracius or the Trinovantes, and then took advantage of calm seas to take the fleet safely back to Gaul.

Caesar never divulges what his objectives really were, but as far as the Senate was concerned Britain had been conquered, and that was all that mattered. However, the mere fact of

Caesar's departure may indicate a moral victory for Cassivellaunus, and Tacitus tells us that a century or so later the British chieftain Caratacus

> invoked their ancestors, who by routing Julius Caesar had valorously preserved their present descendants from Roman officials and taxes – and their wives and children from defilement.[29]

Even if history is written by the victors, as it literally was in Caesar's case, not everyone always accepts their version of events.

---

29 Tacitus, *Annals* 12.34. tr. Grant, M., in *Tacitus: The Annals of Imperial Rome, Translated with an Introduction by Michael Grant, rev. edn.*, Penguin Books: Harmondsworth,1989.

2

Civil Wars, the Dictator and the 'Egyptian Woman'

Rome, who had never condescended to fear any nation or people, did in her time fear two human beings. One was Hannibal, the other was a woman.

W. W. Tarn[1]

Descent into Civil War

By the mid-50s BCE the First Triumvirate was starting to unravel. When Julia, whom Pompey genuinely loved, died in childbirth in 54 BCE, he spurned another marriage alliance with Caesar in favour of one with the *Optimate* Q. Caecilius Metellus Pius Scipio. With Clodius controlling much of the 'Urban Mob', Rome descended into anarchy, and the violence reached a spectacular climax when Milo murdered Clodius on the Appian Way on 18 January, although Clodius might have smiled at the irony when the Senate House became his funeral pyre. To make matters considerably worse, in 53 BCE Crassus started a needless war with King Orodes II of Parthia, only to find himself defeated by Orodes' general Surena at Carrhae in the Mesopotamian desert with the loss of 20 000 dead, 10 000 prisoners, and the Roman legionary standards. Ten thousand Romans escaped, but not Crassus.[2]

1 In Cook, S. A., Adcock F. E. and Charlesworth, M. P. (eds.), *The Cambridge Ancient History: Volume X, the Augustan Empire 44 BC–AD 70*, Cambridge: Cambridge University Press, 1934, p. 111.
2 Plutarch, *Crassus* 16–33.

Civil war was looking increasingly likely. Caesar's military successes were putting him on a par with Pompey, despite the fact that he had become occupied with a serious Gallic rebellion led by Vercingetorix that was only put down after an enormous siege at Alesia in 52 BCE. Yet Pompey had no desire needlessly to provoke Caesar, and Caesar still needed Pompey for his political survival. The *Optimates* also needed Pompey to uphold law and order, and amid an escalating crisis of violence and anarchy at Rome in 52 BCE, he was appointed sole Consul. He took the opportunity to extend his own command over Spain for another five years.

In the end, Caesar's political survival became the deal breaker. In 50 BCE, proposals were made for Pompey and Caesar to relinquish their commands, to which the Senate eventually assented by a margin of 370 to 22. However, when the Consul C. Marcellus spread rumours that Caesar was marching on Rome, Pompey openly sided with the *Optimates*. Caesar offered simultaneous disarmament while threatening war, and although moderate opinion favoured the peace option, Lentulus (Consul, 49 BCE) was implacably opposed, as was Pompey's father-in-law Metellus Scipio, who insisted that Caesar should demobilize his army or be outlawed. The pro-Caesar tribunes Mark Antony and C. Cassius Longinus vetoed this, and Cicero worked hard to achieve some sort of reconciliation, but the hardliners were intransigent: the *SCU* was passed; Caesar's tribunes were 'run out of town' (although this might have been staged); Pompey took command of the Republican forces; and in January 49 Caesar crossed into Italy over the River Rubicon.

A post-civil-war inquiry would probably have reached the following conclusions: legally speaking, Caesar had started it, but he would have preferred not to fight; Pompey's behaviour hadn't helped, but he probably felt that the threat of force would have made Caesar climb down; the Senate's voting record indicates that the majority wanted peace; the *Optimate* hawks wanted Caesar destroyed whatever the cost; and everyone saw war as preferable to compromise.

The ensuing civil war came to be etched on the Roman consciousness in a very painful way. In Virgil's *Aeneid* the ghost of Anchises shows Aeneas the souls of Caesar and Pompey awaiting reincarnation:

> What battles and what carnage will they create between them -
> Caesar descending from Alpine strongholds, the fort of Monoecus,
> His son-in-law Pompey lined up with an Eastern army against him.
> Lads, do not harden yourselves to face such terrible wars!
> Turn not your country's hand against your country's heart!
> You, be the first to renounce it, my son of heavenly lineage,
> You be the first to bury the hatchet![3]

But the only place where Caesar would have buried a hatchet was in Pompey's head. He overran Italy, then, moving via Spain and Massilia (modern Marseilles), he laid siege to Pompey's forces at Dyrrhachium (in modern Albania), and crushed them at the battle of Pharsalus in central Greece on 9 August 48 BCE. Pompey fled to Alexandria in Egypt.

Caesar and Cleopatra

Egypt was ruled by the Ptolemaic dynasty that had carved its realm out of the remnants of Alexander the Great's empire. In 48 BCE, the young King Ptolemy XIII was involved in a struggle for power with his sister–wife Cleopatra VII.[4] They had ruled Egypt jointly since the death in 51 BCE of their feckless father Ptolemy XII Auletes (ironically Cleopatra means 'of a

---

3   Virgil, *Aeneid* 6.828 ff., tr. Day Lewis, C., in *The Eclogues, Georgics and Aeneid of Virgil*, Oxford: Oxford University Press, 1966. Monoecus is modern Monaco.
4   She was born in 69 BCE.

noble father'), whose position had at one stage been secured thanks to a massive bribe to Julius Caesar. According to Dio Cassius, Cleopatra was

> brilliant to look upon and to listen to, with the power to subjugate every one, even Julius Caesar, a love-sated man already past his prime.[5]

Plutarch is somewhat circumspect about her physical attractiveness, but he still endorses her charisma:

> Her own beauty [. . .] was not of that incomparable kind which instantly captivates the beholder. But the charm of her presence was irresistible, and there was an attraction in her person and her talk, together with a peculiar force of character which [. . .] laid all who associated with her under its spell.[6]

Even though Cleopatra was of Macedonian descent and had no Egyptian blood (despite some rather desperate, politically motivated, 'popular archaeological' attempts to prove otherwise), she was loved by her Egyptian subjects. She faced a number of challenges as queen: Egypt was in a bureaucratic mess, riddled with insurgency, its currency was weak, her sister Arsinoë coveted the throne, and her brother–husband Ptolemy XIII was being manipulated by three advisers antagonistic to her: a eunuch, Photinus; a soldier, Akhillas; and a rhetorician, Theodotus. Her siblings fomented a revolt against her, and early in 48 BCE she was forced to flee from Alexandria. She had just raised an army of mercenaries to fight back when Pompey, with whose son she had allegedly once had an affair, arrived. Ptolemy's henchmen in Alexandria debated what to do:

---

5   Dio, 42.34.4. tr. Cary, E., *Dio Cassius Roman History with an English Translation by Earnest Cary on the Basis of the Version of Herbert Baldwin Foster,* Cambridge, MA., and London: Harvard University Press, 1924.
6   Plutarch, *Antony* 27, tr. Scott-Kilvert, I., in *Plutarch, Makers of Rome: Nine Lives by Plutarch,* Harmondsworth: Penguin, 1965.

Theodotus felt that Caesar would be grateful if they killed Pompey, and that 'dead men don't bite',[7] and the mighty Roman was stabbed in the back as he stepped ashore on 28 September.

Caesar reached Alexandria a few days later and was presented with Pompey's signet ring and severed head. He summoned Cleopatra and Ptolemy XIII, at which point, in order to secure a private audience, Cleopatra pulled off one of history's sexiest tricks:

> She stretched herself out at full length inside a sleeping bag, and Apollodoros, after tying up the bag, carried it indoors to Caesar.[8]

This stunt captivated the Roman, and the ensuing relationship suited both parties: he was after money and she wanted power. Caesar ended up taking military action against Ptolemy XIII, who lost his life by drowning on 27 March 47 BCE, and the collateral damage included a fire that devastated the great library at Alexandria. Caesar and Cleopatra then enjoyed a fortnight's amorous relaxation, and the poet Lucan described how Cleopatra – beautiful, brazen and very sexy – entertained Caesar: the price for Caesar's support was a night of 'unspeakable shame', so unspeakably shameful that he didn't describe it.[9]

Caesar had to go to deal with Pharnaces II, the son of Mithridates VI, whom he defeated at his famous *veni, vidi, vici* battle at Zela (modern Zile, Turkey). He left Cleopatra firmly installed as ruler of Egypt, and she now took her other brother, the eleven-year-old Ptolemy XIV, as her husband and co-Pharaoh. Some say she was also pregnant with a son whom she called Ptolemy XV Philopator Philometor Caesar, but who is better known as Caesarion ('Little Caesar'). Whether Caesar

---

7 Plutarch, *Pompey* 77.
8 Plutarch, *Caesar* 49, tr. Warner, R., *The Fall of the Roman Republic: Six Lives by Plutarch*, rev. edn., Harmondsworth: Penguin, 1972.
9 Lucan, *Pharsalia* 10.5.

was in fact the father is hard to tell, but since Caesarion was born on 23 June 47 BCE, it seems unlikely.

Shifting his focus back to Roman affairs, Caesar eradicated the Pompeian opposition in Africa by scoring a major victory at Thapsus (in modern Tunisia), and as soon as he returned to Rome in 46 BCE he celebrated a four-day triumph in which Cleopatra's sister Arsinoë was paraded as a prisoner. Cleopatra and Caesarion followed him to Rome, and Caesar had a golden statue of her erected in the temple of Venus Genetrix, while she herself was installed in one of Caesar's villas. But 'the Egyptian woman' was virulently unpopular – the Romans could hardly bring themselves to utter her name:

> I hate the Queen [. . .] And another thing – I can't recall the Queen's insolence without intense indignation, at the time when she was in the pleasure-gardens across the Tiber.[10]

Even at this stage the Pompeian opposition refused to lie down, and it took yet another huge victory for Caesar, this time at Munda in Spain (45 BCE), to bring the Civil War to a conclusion.

Dictator for Life

Caesar had been amassing ever-increasing powers throughout the Civil War, and early in 44 BCE he became *dictator perpetuo* or *dictator in perpetuum* (= 'dictator for life'), and his head appeared on Roman coins. Whether he ever wanted to be King of Rome is endlessly debated. Mark Antony certainly offered him the crown, but it is unclear whether this was a way of testing public opinion, or simply a PR stunt designed to show that Caesar really didn't want it: *non sum Rex, sed Caesar*, he quipped.[11] Still, he exercised unprecedented powers but

---

10   Cicero, *Ad. Att.* 15.15, 13 June 44 BCE, tr. Kershaw, S.
11   'I'm not King, but Caesar': Rex was a Roman name, just like King is an English surname.

without any overarching vision for Rome: citizenship was granted to Transpadane Gaul; overseas colonies were promoted, notably Corinth; the Senate's membership was increased to 900; traffic problems in Rome were addressed; the courts were allocated to the Senate and in Equites in equal numbers; and the astronomer Sosigenes of Alexandria was employed to sort out the calendar, which was in a total mess because of the mismatch of the solar and lunar years. With one important modification we use this calendar today, and July is still named after Caesar.

There was no doubting Caesar's popularity with the plebs and the army, but Rome's old-school Senators hated him: they felt emasculated by the perpetuity of his dictatorship; the fact that Caesar's statue was placed in the temple of the deified Romulus rankled; they loathed the subtext behind the erection of a temple to *Clementia Caesaris* ('Caesar's Clemency') because *clementia* was a kingly virtue – indeed Cato the Younger committed suicide rather than receive Caesar's *clementia*; Caesar was planning a campaign to avenge Crassus' defeat, and the Sibylline Books prophesied that the Parthian Empire could only be destroyed by a king; and if the idea of Caesar as King of Rome was alarming, the thought of Cleopatra as Queen was utterly disgusting. For his part, Caesar seems to have felt that Rome needed to face up to new political realities, but this was a catastrophic error of judgement. On 15 March 44 BCE (the 'Ides of March'), he was assassinated.

The murder was perpetrated openly on the steps of Pompey's theatre in Rome. The conspirators were led by M. Iunius Brutus (to whom, according to Suetonius, Caesar spoke the Greek words *'kai su teknon?'* = 'You too, my son?'[12]) and C. Cassius Longinus. The motives of the participants varied, yet they all badly misread the true state of the Roman system. Their idealism blinded them to the hard political realities; they ran into the streets shouting 'Liberty!', only to find that they had precipitated an even more ghastly series of civil wars.

---

12   Suetonius, *Caesar* 82.2: he did *not* say, '*Et tu, Brute?*'

More Civil Wars; the Second Triumvirate

The man who assumed the leadership of the Caesarean faction was Caesar's roué and ruthless friend Mark Antony. Cicero later bewailed the fact that the assassins had ignored him in the misguided belief that they simply had to kill Caesar to restore the Republic:

> I could wish that you had invited me to the banquet of the Ides of March: there would have been nothing left over! As it is, your leavings give me much trouble.[13]

But Antony was not the only man with his sights set on power. Out of left field appeared a rival in the shape of the eighteen-year-old C. Octavius. Caesar had clearly seen his potential: he had got him elected to the priestly college of the *pontifices*, let him participate in his African triumph for his victories in the Civil War, and enrolled him into the patrician aristocracy. Health issues had prevented Octavius from accompanying Caesar to Spain in 46 BCE, although he followed on later 'along roads infested by the enemy, after a shipwreck, too, and in a state of semi-convalescence'.[14] Soon after this, Caesar made Octavius his heir in his will (although he didn't tell him), and having appointed the young man to his staff for the projected Parthian campaign, had sent him to Macedonia to finish his studies and get some military training. It was there, at Apollonia (now in Albania), that he heard that Caesar had died, adopted him as his heir, and made him the beneficiary to three-quarters of his estate. Conflict with Antony was inevitable.

Octavius' adoption allowed him to change his name. Historians call him 'Octavian', but he was officially Gaius Julius Caesar

---

13   Cicero, *Letters to His Friends* 12.4 (written to C. Cassius Longinus in Syria, from Rome on 2 February 43 BCE), tr. Shuckburgh, E. S., in *Cicero. The Letters of Cicero; the whole extant correspondence in chronological order, in four volumes*, London: George Bell and Sons, 1908–1909.
14   Suetonius, *Augustus* 8. 1, tr. Graves, R., op. cit.

Octavianus. 'You, boy, owe everything to your name,'[15] sneered Antony, but in a sense he was right. Moreover, the appearance at Julius Caesar's funeral games of what was possibly the brightest daylight-visible comet in recorded history,[16] the *sidus Iulium* ('Julian Star') or *Caesaris astrum* ('Caesarean Star'), was widely taken to prove that Caesar had been deified:

> Then Jupiter said to [Venus]
> You must rescue [Caesar's] soul from his cut-ridden body and make him a comet [. . .]
> [Venus] caught the soul of her Caesar up as it passed from his body [and] carried it straight as it was to the stars in the heavens.
> During her journey, she felt it glowing and catching fire, so she let it escape from out of her bosom and fly right upwards.
> Higher far than the moon it soared, displaying a sweeping trail of flame in its wake, till it finally took the form of a gleaming star.[17]

A Temple of the Deified Julius, also known as the Temple of the Comet Star,[18] was duly constructed by Octavian. It featured a huge image of Caesar that had a flaming comet attached to its forehead.

Octavian also raised an army of 3 000 veterans and secured a considerable amount of funding, but Antony refused to hand over Caesar's legacy. Octavian responded by attaching himself to Cicero, who managed to get the Senate to declare Antony a

---

15 Antony, quoted by Cicero, *Philippics* 13.11.24.

16 See Ramsey, J. T. and Licht, A. L., *The Comet of 44 BC and Caesar's Funeral Games*, Chicago: Scholars Press (Series: APA American Classical Studies, No. 39.), 1997.

17 Ovid, *Metamorphoses* 15.807 ff., tr. Raeburn, D. in *Ovid Metamorphoses*, London: Penguin Classics, 2004. Cf. Suetonius, *Caesar* 88. Coins minted around 19–18 BCE show the laureate head and carry the legend *CAESAR AVGVSTVS* on the obverse, and show a comet (star) of eight rays, tail upward, with the legend *DIVVS IVLIV[S]* on the reverse.

18 Pliny the Elder, *Natural History* 2.93–94. It was built in 42 and dedicated in 29 BCE.

public enemy and order the Consuls A. Hirtius[19] and C. Vibius Pansa Caetronianus to expel him from Italy. When the rival forces engaged near Mutina (modern Modena), it worked out perfectly for Octavian: not only was Antony defeated, but both the Consuls were killed. Cicero's scheme was to use Octavian against Antony to restore the Republic and then dispense with him – 'He is a young man to be praised, honoured and removed', he said[20] – but the reality would be the other way round.

Octavian exploited Cicero's eloquent attacks on Antony in the *Philippic Orations*, and got himself made a Senator in 43 BCE. Additionally, the deaths of Hirtius and Pansa had left him in sole command of the consular armies, which he used as leverage to secure the consulship itself, despite being just twenty years old. To confound the Republicans still further, Octavian promptly struck a deal with Antony, and they had Brutus and Cassius declared outlaws. Caesar's assassins had to leave Italy.

Cool, calculating and opportunistic, Octavian met up with Antony and M. Aemilius Lepidus (another important friend of Caesar) near Mutina, where the three men formed a power-sharing agreement called the Second Triumvirate (November 43 BCE). They sliced up the Roman world between them: Antony took Gaul; Lepidus Spain; Octavian Africa, Sicily and Sardinia. Then they published proscription lists in order to eliminate their enemies and replenish their funds:

> Marcus Lepidus, Marcus Antonius, and Octavius Caesar, chosen by the people to set in order and regulate the Republic, declare as follows:
> [...] Let no one harbour anyone of those whose names are appended to this edict, or conceal them, or send them away anywhere, or be corrupted by their money. [...] Let those who kill the proscribed bring us their heads and receive the following rewards: to a free man 25 000 Attic drachmas per head, to a

---

19   'A.' is the roman abbreviation for Aulus.
20   Cicero, *Letters to his Friends*, 11.20 (24 May 43 BCE).

slave his freedom and 10 000 Attic drachmas and his master's right of citizenship. Informers shall receive the same rewards.[21]

There was no *clementia* this time. Some 300 Senators and 2 000 Equites fell victim to this, and on Antony's insistence the man at the top of the list was Cicero. Plutarch tells us that his head and hands were cut off and fixed to the speaker's platform in the Roman Forum:

> It was a sight to make the Romans shudder. They seemed to see there, not so much the face of Cicero, but the soul of Antony.[22]

Antony's wife Fulvia took macabre pleasure in stabbing the great orator's lifeless tongue with a gold hairpin.

Octavian, who thanks to Julius Caesar's deification was now the 'son of a god', set off for Greece with Antony to fight Brutus and Cassius. The decisive battle was contested at Philippi in north-east Greece in 42 BCE. Brutus routed Octavian's forces and captured his camp, while Antony made an audacious onslaught and achieved the same result against Cassius. But in the confusion neither side was aware of what the other had done, and Cassius retired to Philippi under the mistaken assumption that Brutus has also been defeated. He ordered a slave to kill him (though some think that the slave didn't wait to be asked). When Brutus heard the news he wept and called his comrade

> The last of the Romans, meaning that his equal in virtue would never exist again.[23]

A three-week stand-off then ensued during which Octavian and Antony started to experience logistics difficulties. It was

---

21 Appian, *Civil Wars* 4.2.8 ff., tr White, H., *Appian's Roman History with an English Translation by Horace White, M.A., LL.D, in Four Volumes, IV,* London: William Heinemann, 1913.

22 Plutarch, *Cicero* 49, tr. Warner, R., op. cit.

23 Appian, *Civil Wars* 4.114, tr. White, H., op. cit.

therefore in Brutus' interests to delay as long as possible, but his troops grew restive and eventually he yielded to pressure from his officers and led his men out.

Both sides divined equally that this day and this battle would decide the fate of Rome completely; and so indeed it did.[24]

Antony and Octavian prevailed after a titanic tussle; Brutus' retreat turned to flight; flight turned to slaughter; Brutus spent the night in the mountains quoting lines from Euripides' *Medea*; and in the morning he called upon his friend Straton to kill him. It had unquestionably been one of the world's most politically significant battles:

The Romans' form of government was decided by that day's work chiefly, and they have not gone back to democracy yet.[25]

There would no longer be any question of civil war in defence of the Republic – any future conflict could only be about who would rule Rome.

Octavian now undertook to put down Sextus Pompeius (the son of Pompey), whose piratical activities were menacing Rome's grain supply, and accepted the controversial job of settling the demobilized soldiers. This entailed the summary dispossession of thousands of Italian farmers, but he felt it was worth it because he became the soldiers' patron: soldiers were more powerful than farmers. In Virgil's first *Eclogue*, the rustic Meliboeus articulates the trauma that this caused:

To think of some godless soldier owning my well-farmed fallow,
A foreigner reaping these crops! To such a pass has civil
Dissension brought us: for people like these we have sown
    our fields.[26]

---

24   Ibid. 4.127.
25   Ibid. 4.138.
26   Virgil, *Eclogues* 1.70 ff., tr. Day Lewis, C., op. cit.

Such grievances were exploited by Antony's wife, Fulvia, and his brother, Lucius Antonius, who raised eight legions and occupied Rome. Octavian managed to dislodge them and drove them to Perusia (modern Perugia). Acorn-shaped lead slingshots (*glandes*) used in the fighting there carry some lurid sexual insults: 'Hey, Octavian! You suck cock!'; 'I'm aiming at Fulvia's clitoris'; 'bald Lucius Antonius and Fulvia, open up your arse'.[27] It seems that the slingers missed those particular targets, since Fulvia and Lucius Antonius escaped, but Perusia itself fell in 41 BCE, and Octavian was merciless to the POWs: they were told simply, 'You must die!' and some sources say that 300 Equestrian and Senatorial prisoners were offered as human sacrifices on the Ides of March at the altar of the Divine Julius.

Although Fulvia was fighting on Antony's behalf, she is not always portrayed as the dutiful wife. Octavian supposedly wrote an obscene epigram, quoted verbatim by the poet Martial, in which he claimed that Fulvia, wanting to punish Antony for his extra-marital liaison with the Cappadocian Queen Glaphyra, told Octavian 'Either fuck me or let's fight' at Perusia.[28] Plutarch dubbed Fulvia

> a woman who [. . .] wanted to rule a ruler and command a commander – and consequently Cleopatra owed Fulvia the fee for teaching Antony to submit to a woman.[29]

Antony and Cleopatra

Antony resurrected Caesar's plans to invade Parthia and summoned Cleopatra to Tarsus (modern Cumhuriyet Alani in Turkey). She was now in her late twenties, 'the age when a woman's

---

27   *CIL* 11.6721.9; 11.6721.5; 11.6721,14, tr. Kershaw, S. See also Degrassi, A. (ed.), *Incsriptiones Latinae Liberae Rei Rublicae*, Florence: La Nuova Italia, 1963. There is an extra double entendre in that the shape of a *glans* is quite phallic.
28   Martial, *Epigrams* 11.20.7.
29   Plutarch, *Antony* 10, tr. Scott-Kilvert, I., op. cit.

beauty is at its most superb and her mind at its most mature',[30] and arrived fashionably late, sailing up the River Cydnus in an astonishingly opulent barge, reclining beneath a canopy of cloth of gold, attired as Venus, with her most beautiful waiting women dressed as Nereids and Graces, in a cloud of exotic perfume. This achieved the desired result: Antony postponed the Parthian expedition and went with her to Alexandria where they began to host incredibly extravagant banquets – a student doctor at Alexandria once saw eight wild boars being roasted to serve only about a dozen guests. The 'Inimitable Livers' wallowed in this kind of extravagant debauchery until Antony's deteriorating relations with Octavian forced him to return to Italy in 40 BCE, leaving behind new-born twins, Alexander Helios and Cleopatra Selene.

The triumvirs smoothed over their differences by signing the Treaty of Brundisium, which in effect gave the East to Antony, the West to Octavian and excluded Lepidus. The boundary line was fixed at Scodra (modern Shkoder in Albania), and the pact was sealed by a marriage alliance. Fulvia had recently died, and Antony married Octavian's newly widowed, virtuous and serenely beautiful sister Octavia. Octavia was the perfect antidote to 'bad women' like Cleopatra and Fulvia, and within three years she had given birth to two daughters, Antonia Maior and Antonia Minor, whom she raised alongside her son and two daughters from her first marriage, as well as her two stepsons from Antony's marriage to Fulvia. Antony went straight back to the East with his new bride in tow, and minted coins depicting the two of them – the first time a clearly identifiable living woman had appeared on official Roman coinage in her own right.

Octavian's first wife was Fulvia's daughter Claudia, but the marriage was short-lived and, so he said, unconsummated, although this gave rise to slurs against his manly prowess. His second was Scribonia, ten years his senior, who was the mother of his only daughter Julia (see Genealogy Table 1). 'I could not bear the way she nagged me,' he complained, although Antony

---

30   Ibid. 25.

accused him of being so lecherous that he had once dragged off a dinner host's wife before returning her to the party dishevelled and pink-faced.[31] Antony would later taunt Octavian about the times when his friends would arrange 'showcases' of naked women and girls for his inspection, as though they were up for sale. However, the new arrangement saw Octavian divorce Scribonia and marry the beautiful, dignified, intelligent and possibly previously dishevelled and pink-faced Livia Drusilla, who in turn was forced to divorce her husband-and-cousin Tiberius Claudius Nero, by whom she was already the mother of the future Emperor Tiberius. She was also six months pregnant with Nero Claudius Drusus (father of the Emperor Claudius), and mischievous verses were soon doing the rounds:

How fortunate those parents are for whom
Their child is only three months in the womb![32]

But Livia's fertility was an asset, and her lineage combined two of Rome's greatest families – the Claudii and the Livii. Although her marriage to Octavian would be childless, it would be strong.

In the spring of 37 BCE, Octavia helped to iron out some further differences between the triumvirs, which were settled by the Treaty of Tarentum, which renewed the triumvirate for five more years. She was hailed as 'a marvel of womankind',[33] and appeared again on coins, this time with both her husband and her brother. Antony headed east in the autumn to continue the Parthian campaign, but this time he left Octavia at Rome.

With the help of the highly capable M. Vipsanius Agrippa, Octavian eliminated Sextus Pompeius in 36 BCE, discharged around 20 000 men from the forty or so legions that he now had at his disposal, and returned to Rome, where he squeezed the maximum psychological advantage out of Antony's absence in

31 Suetonius, *Augustus* 62; 69.
32 Quoted by Suetonius, *Claudius* 1, tr. Graves, R., op. cit.
33 Plutarch, *Antony* 31.

the East. While Octavian campaigned in Illyricum, cleared the Adriatic of pirates and initiated major public projects in Rome, Antony renewed his liaison with Cleopatra (another child, Ptolemy Philadelphos, was born in 36 BCE) and saw his Parthian expedition end in a costly failure.

All this allowed Octavian to present Antony as debauched and emasculated, and the contemporary poet Horace brilliantly captured the Roman horror at what his relationship with Cleopatra implied:

> Now Roman soldiers – lies, you'll say in later times –
> Made over to a woman, bear
> Weapons and stakes for her, can bring themselves to do
> Whatever wrinkled eunuchs bid.
> While, reared among our battle-standards – shameful sight! –
> The sun can see mosquito-nets.[34]

His point is that a Roman soldier should take his insect bites like a man: nothing could be more effete, more appalling or more un-Roman than this.

Cleopatra herself came to be portrayed as 'the harlot queen of impious [or incestuous] Canopus',[35] the polar opposite of the virtuous, betrayed, matronly Octavia. Antony told Octavian that this was utterly hypocritical:

> What's changed you? Because I'm fucking the Queen like a beast? [. . .] So you're only boning Drusilla, then? Good health to you, if when you read this letter, you haven't shagged Tertullia, or Terentilla, or Rufilla, or Salvia Titsenia – or all of them. Does it make any difference where or in which woman you get a hard-on?[36]

---

34   Horace, *Epodes* 9.11 ff., tr. Oakley, M., in *Horace: the collected works translated by Lord Dunsany and M. Oakley*, London: Dent, 1961.
35   Propertius, *Elegies* 3.11.39. He also speaks of Cleopatra spreading her 'foul mosquito-nets' over Roman landmarks.
36   Quoted by Suetonius, *Augustus* 69, tr. Kershaw, S.

But it was the event known as the 'Donations of Alexandria' (34 BCE) which provided the biggest propaganda gift to Octavian: Antony and Cleopatra held a ceremony where they sat on golden thrones, along with Caesarion and their own three children; Cleopatra was hailed as Queen of Kings, Caesarion as King of Kings; and Antony granted to Cleopatra and her children huge tracts of territory in the East that was not his to give. Cleopatra also supplanted Octavia on coinage that Antony issued after he finally scored some military success in Armenia, but placing a foreign female monarch on official Roman coinage was utterly monstrous in Roman eyes.

Historians struggle for first-hand evidence concerning Cleopatra's life, but there is one document that provides a wonderful exception. This is a royal ordinance on papyrus, granting duty-free tax privileges to Antony's right-hand man P. Canidius, dated to 23 February 33 BCE. Below the main text, written by a scribe, Cleopatra signs off the document, and if it is the only word she left to posterity, it is a wonderfully appropriate one: γινέσθοι (= 'make it happen').[37]

The Second Triumvirate officially lapsed at the end of 33 BCE, but Octavian deliberately didn't renew it. This was another smart propaganda coup, since it left Antony holding the title of triumvir purely on his own authority. Even so, not everyone backed Octavian, and events moved swiftly: both Consuls and over 300 Senators left Rome to join Antony early in 32 BCE; Octavian nominated fresh Consuls; Antony divorced Octavia; completely illegally Octavian published Antony's will, which allegedly showed that he wanted to relocate the centre of Roman government to Egypt; Antony crossed

---

37   *P. Berolinensis* 25.239. It comes from the Roman cemeteries at Abusir el-Melek, where it was reused as mummy cartonnage, and is now in the Ägyptisches Museum und Papyrussammlung, Berlin. See Van Minnen, P., 'An Official Act of Cleopatra (with a Subscription in her Own Hand)', *Ancient Society* (30), 2000, 29–34. *Ginesthoi* is a phonological variant of *ginestho*, that was used in the Greek of Cleopatra's day. See Teodorsson, S., *The Phonology of Ptolemaic Koine*, Studia Graeca et Latina Gothoburgensia 36, Lund: Berlingska Boktryckeriet, 1977, 163 ff., 235.

into Greece with Cleopatra; Octavian secured a declaration of war against Cleopatra (it was essential that it was not seen as a Civil War), and crossed to Greece for the final showdown.

The history of the ensuing events was almost entirely concocted by the winning side, who were masters of spin and distortion. Octavian's propaganda tells us that

> the whole of Italy of its own accord took an oath of allegiance to me and demanded that I should be its leader in the war [. . .] The same oath was taken by the provinces of Gaul and Spain, and by Africa, Sicily, and Sardinia.[38]

He had a slight superiority in forces (possibly 600 ships and 80 000 infantry v 500 ships and 70 000 infantry), and an excellent admiral in M. Agrippa, whereas Cleopatra's presence among Antony's troops was disruptive. Quite what happened at the crucial Battle of Actium, fought on 2 September 31 BCE, is hard to pinpoint in detail, but the end result was that Cleopatra's squadron escaped, Antony followed in her wake, and the remainder of his forces surrendered. Virgil imagined that Aeneas had the battle prophetically emblazoned on his shield, and presents it as a conflict between virtuous Romans and obscene barbarians:

> On one side Augustus Caesar, high up on the poop, is leading
> The Italians into battle, the Senate and People with him . . .
> On the other side, with barbaric wealth and motley equipment,
> Is Antony [. . .]
> Egypt, the powers of the Orient and uttermost Bactra
> Sail with him; also – a shameful thing – his Egyptian wife.[39]

---

38   Augustus, *Res Gestae* 25, tr. Lentin, A., in Chisholm, K. and Ferguson, J. (eds.), *Rome: The Augustan Age*, Oxford: Oxford University Press, 1981.
39   Virgil, *Aeneid* 8.678 ff., tr. Day Lewis, C., op. cit.

Antony and Cleopatra fled to Egypt, and the final denouement came when Octavian took possession of Alexandria around a year later. The historical accounts tell us that Cleopatra barricaded herself into the mausoleum that she had constructed for herself, and then sent messengers telling Antony that she was dead. He made a botched suicide attempt, but when he discovered that Cleopatra was still alive he ordered his slaves to carry him to the mausoleum, from which Cleopatra let down ropes and pulled him up with the help of her two waiting women. Plutarch describes Antony, covered with blood, struggling in his death throes, and stretching out his hands towards Cleopatra as he swung helplessly in the air. When she had got him up, she laid him on a bed, tore her dress and spread it over him, beat and lacerated her breasts, and smeared her face with the blood from his wounds.

With Antony dead, Cleopatra still had to meet Octavian. Dio says that

> She preferred to die bearing the title and majesty of a sovereign rather than live in a private station. At any rate she kept ready fire to destroy her treasure, and asps and other reptiles to end her life; she had experimented before on human beings to discover how these creatures caused death in each case.[40]

The asp is the Egyptian cobra. Plutarch adds that she had discovered that its bite caused a kind of drowsy lethargy and numbness, and that its sufferers resisted any attempt to revive them, like people do when they are in a deep natural sleep.

> It has four fangs, their underside hollow, hooked, and long, rooted in its jaws, containing poison, and at their base a covering of membranes hides them. Thence it belches forth poison unassuageable on a body [. . .] No bite appears on

---

40   Dio 51.11, tr. Scott-Kilvert, I., in *Cassius Dio, The Roman History: The Reign of Augustus*, London: Penguin Books, 1987.

the flesh, no deadly swelling with inflammation, but the man dies without pain, and a slumberous lethargy brings life's end.[41]

The sources unanimously assert that Octavian wanted her alive. She used all her sexy tricks:

> She dressed herself with studied negligence – indeed her appearance in mourning wonderfully enhanced her beauty – and seated herself on [a richly ornamented] couch. Beside her she arranged many different portraits and busts of Julius Caesar, and in her bosom she carried all the letters Caesar had sent her.[42]

Octavian remained impervious to her seduction attempts, but she did convince him that she wanted to live. He departed, smugly convinced that he would soon be parading her through the streets of Rome.

In Plutarch's account of her death (17 August 30 BCE) she bathes and eats an exquisite meal, after which an Egyptian peasant arrives carrying a basket, and when the guards ask him what is in it, he strips away the leaves at the top to reveal a load of figs. Cleopatra then sends a sealed writing tablet to Octavian, dismisses all her attendants except for her two faithful waiting women, and closes the doors of the monument.

There is no certainty about how Cleopatra died. Our sources mention the asp (or asps) in the figs, or in a pitcher, perhaps covered beneath some flowers, or a comb filled with poison, or a pin smeared with it. They also say that the asp was never discovered, and that her body showed no symptoms of poisoning, although there were two tiny punctures on her arm.

The Roman propaganda machine did its best to demonize

---

41   Nicander, *Theriaka* 182 ff., tr. Gow, A. S. F. and Scholfield, A. F., *Nicander: The Poems and Poetical Fragments Edited with a Translation and Notes*, New York: Arno, 1979. Nicander wrote somewhere between 241 and 133 BCE.
42   Dio, 51.12–13, tr. Scott-Kilvert, I., op. cit.

Cleopatra, but it never really succeeded. Horace wrote of the mood of celebration that followed Octavian's victory over the Egyptian Queen and her 'squalid pack of diseased half-men':

> Today is the day to drink and dance on. Dance, then,
> Merrily, friends, till the earth shakes.[43]

Yet Horace's triumphalism is tempered by respect and admiration:

> She did not, like a woman, shirk the dagger
> Or seek by speed at sea
> To change her Egypt for obscurer shores,
> But [. . .]
> With a calm smile, unflinchingly laid hands on
> The angry asps until
> Her veins had drunk the deadly poison deep,
> And, death-determined, fiercer then than ever,
> Perished. Was she to grace a haughty triumph,
> Dethroned, paraded by
> The rude Liburnians? Not Cleopatra![44]

Octavian spared her children by Antony, but had his eldest son by Fulvia put to death, and, of course, Caesarion. Egypt was annexed by Rome, ending 300 years of Ptolemaic rule, but because it was a major producer of grain, Octavian took it under his own personal administration, although he fudged the issue in his propaganda: 'I added Egypt to the Empire of the Roman people.'[45] The Roman Empire had just extinguished the last embers of Alexander the Great's.

---

43 Horace, *Odes* 1.37.1 ff., tr. Michie, J., in *The Odes of Horace*, Harmondsworth: Penguin, 1964.
44 Ibid. 1.37.22 ff.
45 Augustus, *Res Gestae* 27, tr. Kershaw, S.

3

Augustus: From Teenage Butcher to Father of the Fatherland

Let the soldier carry arms only to repress arms.
Let the trumpet sound only for ceremony.
Let the ends of the earth stand in awe of the men of Rome:
if not fear, let there be love.

Ovid, *Fasti* 1.715 ff.[1]

The Augustan Settlements

Octavian had become the master of Rome. In secure possession of all the powers of the State, he returned to Italy in mid-29 BCE. The gates of the Temple of Janus Quirinius were ceremonially closed for the first time in 200 years as a sign of 'peace with victory throughout the empire of the Roman people'.[2] Contemporary historians sang his praises:

> There is no boon that men can desire of the gods or gods grant to mankind, no conceivable wish or blessing which [Octavian] did not bestow on the Republic, the Roman people, and the world.[3]

---

1   Tr. Ferguson, J., in Chisholm, K. and Ferguson, J. (eds.), op. cit.
2   Augustus, *Res Gestae* 13. This event had only ever taken place twice before.
3   Velleius Paterculus, 2.89, tr. Lentin, A., in Chisholm, K. and Ferguson, J. (eds.), op. cit.

Later commentators have not been so generous: Ronald Syme famously described him as 'a chill and mature terrorist',[4] and even his wife warned him that

> although it is impossible for a man to guide so great a city from democracy to monarchy [. . .] without bloodshed, if you continue in your old policy, you will be thought to have done these unpleasant things deliberately.[5]

So Octavian began to work on his statesmanship. He was unquestionably an autocrat, yet unlike Caesar he never rubbed people's noses in it, and he would give the world 'a large measure of peace and stable government for the next two hundred years'.[6]

Octavian knew how to manipulate all the acclaim that came his way, and did so in traditional Republican style: he celebrated a triple triumph; the Senate voted him a triumphal arch inscribed '*re publica conservata*' ('the Republic saved'); he still held the consulship, sometimes with Agrippa as his colleague; he distributed largesse to the people of Rome and to his soldiers; he carried out the first census of the people since 70 BCE, and, under a special grant of *Censoria Potestas* (the powers held by a Censor), he downsized the Senate to around 800 members. This purge of the Senators was intended to re-establish their traditional respect and prestige, and Octavian was acutely aware of what had happened when Julius Caesar disrespected them. In any case, he would need their experience and expertise. The acceptance of his power by the Equites, the acquiescence of the plebs of Rome and the loyalty of the military were also essential.

In 28 BCE he declared a general amnesty, annulled any illegal/unjust orders that he had previously given, and had all

---

4   Syme, R., *The Roman Revolution*, Oxford: Oxford University Press, 1939, p. 191.
5   Dio 55.21, tr. Cary, E., op cit.
6   Scullard, H. H., *From the Gracchi to Nero: A History of Rome from 133 BC to AD 68*, 5th edn., London and New York: Methuen, 1982, p. 208.

his acts ratified by the Senate. The designation Imperator ('General'), an accolade given to a victorious commander by his troops, which he had been using as a personal title (preceding his name instead of after it as under normal practice), now became an official honorific title. Only an Imperator was allowed to wear the purple robe that went with that title.

Octavian did not want to step down, but neither did he want to be *dictator perpetuo*. He constantly downplayed the irregularity of his position, and placed great emphasis on the *restitutio* (restoration/repair/revival) of the Republic. His principal challenge was to find a way of combining discipline with liberty without the overt use of military force. It would be no easy assignment.

The big moment came on 13 January 27 BCE when, sensationally, in Octavian's own words:

> After I had put an end to the civil wars, having by universal consent acquired control of all affairs, I transferred government from my own authority to the discretion of the Senate and people of Rome.[7]

After a storm of protest, heartfelt or otherwise, he agreed to retain control of Spain, Gaul and Syria – and therefore the bulk of the legions – for ten years, along with Egypt, which was crucial to Rome's grain supply. He also assumed the rights of war and peace and treaty-making, and the power of directly appointing all senior army officers and the governors of key provinces. However, he always ensured that (ostensibly) his powers were granted by the SPQR and followed Republican precedents, and he made great play of pointing out just how many (excessive) honours he did *not* accept.

One honour that he did take, however, was the name 'Augustus'. This was a brilliantly chosen epithet, rather than a title,

---

7   Augustus, *Res Gestae* 34, tr. Lentin, A., in Chisholm, K. and Ferguson, J. (eds.), op. cit.

which had quasi-religious overtones of reverence and fruitful increase: *augeo* = 'I increase/enlarge/enrich/embellish', and *augustus* = 'holy/majestic/august/venerable/worthy of honour/ associated with the gods'. As Dio Cassius put it:

> All the most precious and sacred objects are termed *augusta*. For this reason when he was addressed in Greek he was named *Sebastos*, meaning an august individual: the word is derived from the passive form of the verb *sebazo*, I revere.[8]

Livia had no official title at this stage: our word 'empress' (= 'the woman married to the Emperor of Rome') has no Latin equivalent.

The way Augustus presented the total package is most illuminating:

> Henceforth, I exceeded all men in authority (*auctoritas*), but I had no greater power (*potestas*) than those who were my colleagues in any given magistracy.[9]

This was crucial: people simply obeyed him because of who he was – a discrete hint would usually make things happen. And the acclaim kept on coming:

> A golden shield was set up in the Julian Senate house [. . .] in honour of my fortitude, clemency, justice, and piety.[10]

He now styled himself 'Imperator Caesar Divi Filius Augustus' ('General Caesar Son-of-a-God Venerable'), but additionally he was to be known as *Princeps* ('first citizen'/'first among equals'). Historians conventionally call this new phase of Roman history the Principate, so in a sense they have

8 Dio 53.16.6, tr. Scott Kilvert, L., op. cit.
9 Augustus, *Res Gestae* 34, tr. Lentin, A., in Chisholm, K. and Ferguson, J. (eds.), op. cit.
10 Ibid.

swallowed Augustus' propaganda: Augustus developed 'new truthful narratives about the past'[11] and many contemporaries bought into them:

> Thus the ancient time-honoured constitution of the Republic was revived.[12]

The *Fasti Praenestini* for 27 BCE tell how

> The Senate decreed that an oak-leaf crown be placed above the door of the house of Imperator Caesar Augustus because he restored the Republican Constitution to the People of Rome.[13]

Even so, Augustus wasn't able to pull the wool over everyone's eyes: Tacitus characterized him as a power-crazed autocrat hiding behind a veneer of Republicanism, and Dio Cassius stated that 'all the power of the people and that of the senate reverted to Augustus, and from his time there was a genuine monarchy'.[14]

The overall package, known nowadays as the First Settlement of 27 BCE, was not an unqualified success, and a conspiracy against him by Fannius Caepio and A. Terentius Varro Murena, combined with a potentially life-threatening illness, made him reassess his position. In 23 BCE he vacated the consulship and only held it twice more for limited, specific purposes. But to offset this loss he received *tribunicia potestas* – the powers of a Tribune of the Plebs – which crucially included the right of veto and of putting legislation to the people. From

---

11   Rohrbacher, D., *The Historians of Late Antiquity*, London and New York: Routledge, 2002 p.11.
12   Velleius Paterculus, 2.89 tr. Kershaw, S.
13   *Fasti of Praeneste*, 27 BCE, tr. Kershaw, S.
14   Dio 53.17.1, tr. Foster, H. B., *Dio's Rome: An Historical Narrative Originally Composed in Greek During the Reigns of Septimius Severus, Geta and Caracalla, Macrinus, Elagabalus and Alexander Severus: Now Presenterd in English Form*, New York: Pafraet's Book Company, 1905.

now on, Rome's Emperors would count their reigns from the year when they acquired *tribunicia potestas*.

The loss of his consular powers was counterbalanced by the grant of *imperium proconsulare* (the command associated with a Proconsul). This was renewed automatically at (usually) ten-year intervals, and was valid both in Italy and inside the city of Rome itself. The icing on the cake was that his *imperium* was made *maius* – superior to that of any other Proconsul. Augustus could now legally intervene in whatever province he liked, whenever he liked.

Honours still came his way, of course: in 19 BCE his *imperium* was re-defined so that he held the power of a Consul without having to hold the consulship; when Lepidus died, he became *Pontifex Maximus*, taking control of the State Religion; in 8 BCE the month of August was named after him; and six years later he was designated *Pater Patriae* ('Father of the Fatherland').

All this was underpinned with irregular, but exceptionally generous, handouts of money and grain:

> In [23 BCE] I made twelve distributions of corn from grain purchased at my own expense; and in [11 BCE] for the third time I gave every man 400 *sestertii*. These gratuities of mine reached never fewer than 250 000 persons. In [5 BCE] I gave to 320 000 of the common people of Rome 60 *denarii* apiece.[15]

Running the Empire (Easy); Running the Family (Not so Easy)

There was no way that Augustus could run the Roman Empire single-handedly. The Senate, whose leading member he had now become, had effectively controlled Rome for half a millennium, and it remained at the heart of his new order. Although in reality it lacked real power, its dignity, authority and ego were

---

15 Augustus, *Res Gestae* 15, tr. Lentin, A., in Chisholm, K. and Ferguson, J (eds.), op. cit.

carefully massaged; its members still occupied Rome's highest offices; its decrees had the force of law; it became a High Court; it supervised the 'safer' provinces, which contained relatively few troops (see Map1); in theory it handled the State finances; and Augustus adopted a non-confrontational stance towards it whenever possible.

Many less glamorous posts came to be allocated to the Emperor's freedmen or slaves, while important new positions like the Prefects of the corn supply, the Praetorian Guard, the fleet, the *vigiles* (fire brigade) and of Egypt, were allotted to the Equites. Given that it was possible for an *Eques* to become a Senator, subject to being elected and possessing the appropriate property qualification, and because the Equites were not exclusively Roman, the Senate slowly started to become more representative of the Roman Empire's geographical and ethnic make-up.

Augustus was also meticulous about keeping the plebs onside, guaranteeing the grain supplies, and alleviating unemployment by monumentalizing Rome's urban environment. He bragged that Rome was a city of sun-dried brick before him, but clothed in marble afterwards, and he claimed to have restored, repaired or built a vast number of temples, theatres, aqueducts and roads. Coinage and dedicatory inscriptions rammed the message home:

> The Senate and the people of Rome in honour of Imperator Caesar son of the divine Julius, consul for the fifth time, consul designate for the sixth [29 BCE], hailed as Imperator for the seventh, for having saved the Republic.[16]

Augustus may also have felt some desire for racial 'purification'. For much of the Republican era slaves had come from Greek, Semitic and Asiatic backgrounds, but because freed slaves became Roman citizens, over the years the citizen body

---

16   *CIL* 6.873 = *ILS* 81, on the triumphal arch of Augustus next to the temple of divine Julius, tr. Kershaw, S.

steadily became more multicultural. Naturally the *Princeps* wanted these new citizens to be culturally attuned to the political requirements of his regime, and although various laws[17] still imposed restrictions on freedmen, who were ineligible for the Senatorial and Equestrian Orders, these conditions did not apply to sons born after manumission (Horace is a prime example) or to grandsons.

Central to Augustus' thinking was a 'back to basics' moral policy that sought to return family life to the (imaginary and idealized) morals and virtues of the 'Good Old Days', and Augustus sounds quite smug about the ethical qualities of his regime:

> I brought back many exemplary ancestral traditions that were dying out.[18]

Laws were passed to strengthen marriage, encourage larger families and punish adultery. Under the *lex Julia de maritandis ordinibus*, freeborn persons were forbidden to marry prostitutes, adulteresses or actresses. The *lex Julia de adulteriis coercendis* made adultery[19] a public crime in which the woman was punished by exile or hard labour and the loss of a third of her property and half her dowry. A wronged wife could not prosecute an adulterous husband, but her father could, and a man was compelled to divorce a guilty wife. The unmarried and childless were penalized by the loss of inheritance rights, and ludicrously long engagements that enabled men to evade marriage by becoming betrothed to very young girls were outlawed. The *ius trium liberorum* (Law of Three Children) rewarded parents of large families: the father got improved status and promotion prospects, and a mother of three children (four if she was a freedwoman) gained the right to choose whom

---

17 Notably the *lex Fufia Caninia* and *lex Aelia Sentia*.

18 Augustus, *Res Gestae* 8, tr. Kershaw, S.

19 Latin *ad ulteriis* = 'to other places': it has nothing (etymologically) to do with adults.

to include in her will. The upshot of this was the development of 'legacy hunting', as Roman women's property became highly sought after:

Gemellus wants to marry Maronilla:
He sighs, pleads, pesters, sends a daily present.
Is she a beauty? No, a hideous peasant.
What's the attraction, then? That cough will kill her.[20]

Ironically, the *lex Papia Poppaea*, which completed the *lex Julia de maritandis ordinibus* in 9 CE, was proposed by two Consuls who were both unmarried and childless.

Augustus' new legislation didn't necessarily engender new attitudes. His own reputation was hardly beyond reproach, and the lifestyle choices of some women in his household didn't help. He had certainly insisted on a strict upbringing for his daughters and granddaughters:

He prevented them from meeting strangers so strictly that he once wrote to L. Vicinius, a young man of good character and family, that he had acted improperly because he had come to call on [Augustus' daughter] Julia at Baiae.[21]

This fashionable resort at Baiae has been described as 'a place to which men came and left broken-hearted or women came chaste and left as adulterers',[22] and some of this seems to have rubbed off on Julia. Macrobius records a story of her wearing slutty clothes (*licentiore vestitu*) and offending Augustus, but appearing the following day with an entirely different dress and attitude, to his great delight. Her comment was, 'Today I am

---

20   Martial, *Epigrams* 1.10, tr. Michie, J., *The Epigrams of Martial*, London: Hart-Davis, MacGibbon Ltd., 1973. Cf. Pliny, *Letters* 10.20.
21   Suetonius, *Augustus* 64, tr. Graves, R., op. cit.
22   Laurence, R., *Roman Passions: A History of Pleasures in Imperial Rome*, London, New York: Continuum, 2009, p. 74; cf. Ovid, *Ars Amatoria* 1.283; Martial, *Epigrams* 1.62; Propertius 1.11.30.

dressed to meet my father's eyes: yesterday it was for my husband's.'[23] Julia was married first to Augustus' nephew M. Marcellus; then to Agrippa by whom she had five children in among numerous alleged infidelities; and, following Agrippa's death, to her stepbrother Tiberius (see Genealogy Table 1). At this juncture things then went badly awry. Julia was in her late thirties, 'a time of life approaching old age',[24] although Ovid said that thirty-something women were the ones who got the most pleasure from sex. Perhaps too clever for a conventional Roman woman, witty, popular, long since not sleeping with Tiberius,[25] she became the focus of a notorious pleasure-loving clique. As a mother of five she should have been the perfect model for Augustus' family legislation, but in 2 BCE he banished her to the island of Pandateria, where she was forbidden both wine and male company:

> She had been accessible to scores of paramours; in nocturnal revels she had roamed about the city; the very forum and the rostrum, from which her father had proposed a law against adultery, had been chosen by the daughter for her debaucheries; she had daily resorted to the statue of Marsyas, and, laying aside the role of adulteress, there sold her favours.[26]

Julia and her circle might have been engaged in political intrigue rather than (or as well as) sexual debauchery, since one of her lovers was said to be Iullus Antonius, who was Mark Antony's son by Fulvia.[27] Either way, Augustus was devastated and he never forgave her.

---

23 Macrobius, *Saturnalia* 2.5.5.
24 Macrobius, *Saturnalia* 2.5.2. Julia was born in 39 BCE.
25 Suetonius, *Tiberius* 7. He was in self-imposed exile on the island of Rhodes at this time.
26 Seneca, *On Benefits* 6.32.1, tr. Basore, J. W., *Lucius Annasus Seneca. Moral Essays*. London: Heinemann, 1928–1935.
27 See Ferrill, A., 'Augustus and his Daughter: A Modern Myth', in Deroux, C. (ed.), *Studies in Latin Literature and Roman Society,* vol. II, 1980, 332–66. Julia was allowed to return to Italy, but remained confined to Regium. She was disinherited, and died in 14 CE.

Julia's fate didn't seem to deter her daughter, also called Julia, who was accused of adultery with the Senator D. Iunius Silanus[28] and banished in 8 CE. This may also have covered a political offence, since her husband L. Aemilius Paullus was executed for treason. To add spice to the affair, Rome's then premier poet Ovid was also exiled to a cultural wilderness on the Black Sea, for what he describes as *carmen* ('a poem', the *Ars Amatoria*, 'Art of Love', a didactic work about how to conduct adulterous liaisons), and *error*, an 'indiscretion' that may have involved Augustus' family.[29]

Out on the Wild Frontiers

Augustus had a grand design both to consolidate the areas within the Empire that were not properly pacified or organized and to push the Empire out to its 'natural' boundaries, and he boasted that he had 'extended the frontiers of all the provinces of the Roman people where the neighbouring peoples were not subject to our rule'.[30] These boundaries were essentially deserts, rivers and the ocean (see Map 1). Where subjugation was likely to be challenging, client kings, dependent on Augustus' goodwill but under an obligation to provide military aid, were the preferred option, since they removed the necessity for risky expansionist warfare or maintaining strong defences over a wide area.

The south of Rome's empire was relatively trouble free. The area north of the Sahara and the Atlas Mountains was secured (*c.*25 BCE) by annexing the client kingdom of Numidia and placing Juba, who was the son of its last king and who had married Antony and Cleopatra's daughter Cleopatra Selene, on the throne of Mauretania. *Legio* III *Augusta* policed Africa and

28   'D.' is the Roman abbreviation for Decimus.
29   Ovid, *Tristia.* 2.133f.; 4.10.99. See, e.g., Norwood, F., 'The Riddle of Ovid's Relegatio', *Classical Philology* (1963), 154; Thibault, J. C., *The Mystery of Ovid's Exile*, Berkeley, CA: University of California Press, 1964.
30   Augustus, *Res Gestae* 26.

by 23 BCE *Legiones* III *Cyrenaica* and XXII *Deiotariana* oversaw Egypt. To the south of Egypt a military zone was established between the territories of Rome and the Queen of Ethiopia.

In the East, Augustus retained Pompey's ring of buffer client kingdoms, although Judaea was incorporated as an imperial province in 6 CE. Parthia was always the big worry here, and Augustus stationed four legions in Syria and envisaged the River Euphrates and the Arabian Desert as the frontier. Armenia, across the Euphrates, became the key to Romano-Parthian relations, and when dynastic problems broke out both in Parthia and in Armenia, the future Emperor Tiberius joined Augustus in the East in 20 BCE, installed the thoroughly Romanized Tigranes on the Armenian throne and

> compelled the Parthians to give back [. . .] the booty and the standards of three Roman armies and to seek the friendship of the Roman people as suppliants.[31]

This was a massive propaganda coup.

There was no obvious natural frontier to the north of Armenia, but north of the Black Sea the client kingdom of the Cimmerian Bosporus provided some protection for Asia, Bithynia et Pontus, Cilicia and Galatia, which was a large new province in central Anatolia carved out of a client kingdom that Augustus annexed in 25 BCE.

The northern frontier, several thousand kilometres long, was the most concerning. In a 'just' war[32] from 16 to 15 BCE, Augustus' stepsons Tiberius and Nero Claudius Drusus conquered the territory north of the Alps as far as the River Danube, which was then organized into the provinces of Raetia and Noricum. An inscription from the triumphal arch in La Turbie on the French Riviera commemorates this:

---

31 Ibid. 29, tr. Kershaw, S. The reference is to the eagles lost by Crassus at Carrhae.
32 So says Augustus, *Res Gestae* 26.

To the Emperor Augustus, son of the late lamented Caesar,
[. . .] erected by the Senate and People of Rome, to commemorate that under his leadership and auspices all the Alpine
races stretching from the Adriatic Sea to the Mediterranean
were brought under the dominion of the Roman people.
Alpine races conquered – [a list of 46 tribes follows].[33]

In 14 BCE the area between Gaul and Italy was made into
the province of Alpes Maritimae, and Augustus boasted that

the peoples of Pannonia, where no army of the Roman people
had ever been before my Principate, [were] completely
defeated through Tiberius Nero [. . .] and brought under the
rule of the Roman people.[34]

Further to the East, Moesia was organized as a province in 6
CE. The effect of all this was to make the frontier follow the
Danube, but since Europe's major rivers tend to unify adjacent
peoples rather than separate them, and since political, cultural,
linguistic, religious and economic frontiers seldom coincide, the
frontier was always relatively permeable, with much movement
across it in both directions. This naturally made it vulnerable,
too, and it took Tiberius three years, fifteen legions and an equal
number of auxiliary forces to quell a major uprising among the
Pannonians and Dalmatians in Illyricum that broke out in 6 CE.
    The Rhine frontier was so problematical that Nero Claudius
Drusus tried to extend it as far as the River Elbe (12 to 9 BCE),
before being killed in a fall from his horse. Tiberius then continued the process until the outbreak of the Pannonian and
Dalmatian revolts. All remained well from the Roman perspective until 9 CE, when P. Quinctilius Varus' arrogant attitude
towards the Germans provoked a chieftain called Arminius to

---

33   Pliny, *Natural History* 3. 136–8, tr. Rackham, H. A., *Pliny: Natural History in Ten
Volumes, II, Books 3–7*, Cambridge, MA.: Harvard University Press, rev. edn. 1949.
34   Augustus, *Res Gestae* 30, tr. Lentin, A., in Chisholm, K. and Ferguson, J.
(eds.), op. cit.

lure three legions, XVIII, XIX and possibly XVII, into difficult terrain at Kalkriese near the *saltus Teutoburgiensis* (Teutoburg Forest), where they were annihilated:

> They put out the eyes of some men and cut off the hands of others. They cut off the tongue of one man and sewed up his mouth, and one of the barbarians, holding the tongue in his hand, exclaimed, 'That stopped your hissing, you viper'.[35]

Archaeologists have excavated pits that contained dismembered human remains whose bones show deep cuts: these are probably the mass graves of the Romans.[36]

Varus committed suicide and Augustus apparently used to bang his head against a door and cry, 'Quinctilius Varus, give me back my Legions!' Although Tiberius effectively shored up the Rhine fortifications, the lost territory was never recovered. On the Rhine itself the military districts of Germania Superior and Germania Inferior were created, and Augustus left a recommendation that the Empire should be kept within the existing confines of the Rhine, Danube and Euphrates.

At the Western end of the Empire, on the conclusion of a seven-year campaign by Agrippa in 19 BCE, Spain now became three provinces: Baetica, Lusitania and Tarraconensis, overseen by *Legiones* III *Macedonica*, VI *Victrix* and X *Gemina*. Gaul now comprised four provinces: Narbonensis, Aquitania, Belgica and Lugdunensis.

Questions arise as to whether Augustus intended to invade Britain – and, if so, why he didn't. Dio Cassius suggests that as early as 34 BCE he had serious thoughts about a British expedition in emulation of Julius Caesar,[37] but had to put things on

---

35 Florus, *Epitome* 2.30.37, tr. in Pollard, N. and Berry, J., *The Complete Roman Legions*, London: Thames & Hudson, 2012. Cf. Tacitus, *Annals* 1.60.3.

36 See Harnecker, J., *Arminius, Varus and the Battlefield at Kalkriese: An Introduction to the Archaeological Investigations and their Results*, Bramsche: Rasch Verlag, 2004.

37 Dio 49.38.2.

hold until after the First Settlement of 27 BCE. He then revived his plans, and chose a commander:

> Wherever earth is bounded by Ocean, no part of it, [C. Valerius] Messalla [Corvinus], will raise arms against you. For you is left the Briton, whom Roman arms have not yet vanquished.[38]

Horace knew about it too:

> Augustus will be recognized as a god upon earth when he has added the Britons [. . .] to the empire.

> I pray that you may protect Caesar on his expedition against the Britons, the furthest nation of the world.[39]

However, the plans were again shelved because of revolts in other more strategically sensitive areas of the Empire. Strabo tried hard to justify the non-intervention:

> Although the Romans could have possessed Britain, they scorned to do so [. . .] For at present more seems to accrue from the customs duties on their commerce than direct taxation could supply, if we deduct the cost of maintaining an army to garrison the island and collect the tribute. [And anyway] some of the kings have gained the friendship of Caesar Augustus by sending embassies and paying him deference. They have not only dedicated offerings in the Capitol, they have also more or less brought the whole island under Roman control.[40]

---

38   [Tibullus] 3.7.147 ff, tr. in Mann, J. C. and Penman, R. G. (eds.), *LACTOR 11: Literary Sources for Roman Britain*, 2nd. edn., London: London Association of Classical Teachers, 1985. Cf. the *Panegyricus Messallae* 147–9; Dio 53.22.5.
39   Horace *Odes* 3.5.2 ff.; 1.35.29 f., tr. in Mann, J. C. and Penman, R. G. (eds.), op. cit.
40   Strabo 2.5.8; 4.5.3, tr. in Mann, J. C. and Penman, R. G. (eds.), op. cit.

This is ludicrously optimistic, as is Horace's talk of the 'whale-burdened sea' that batters the 'exotic' British coast 'venerating' Augustus.[41] But perception mattered more than reality.

The Augustan Peace

Within the borders of Rome's empire there was a clear-cut distinction between Italy and the provinces. After the First Settlement there were two main types of province: the Senatorial provinces, whose Proconsuls (governors) were selected by lot and commanded no troops, and the Imperial provinces, which were quite heavily garrisoned and controlled by *legati Augusti pro praetore* ('legates of Augustus with authority of a Praetor') appointed directly by the Emperor (see Map 1). The fiscal affairs of the provinces were handled by *procuratores Augusti*, usually Equestrian, although some were imperial freedmen. Some smaller imperial provinces where no legions were stationed were governed by Equestrian *praefecti* (later designated *procuratores*). The governor of Egypt (*praefectus Aegypti*) was an Equestrian, and he was in the unique position of being the only Equestrian to command legions. Yet he still had to know his place: C. Cornelius Gallus put self-congratulatory inscriptions on the pyramids, only to be recalled and commit suicide in 27/6 BCE.

All these layers of administration raise the question of exactly what the Romans were trying to achieve by controlling their provinces. One answer comes in Virgil's *Aeneid*, where the ghost of Anchises talks about the 'Roman mission':

> But, Romans, never forget that government is your medium!
> Be this your art: to practise men in the habit of peace,
> Generosity to the conquered, and firmness against aggressors.[42]

---

41 Horace, *Odes* 4.14.47 ff.
42 Virgil, *Aeneid* 6.851 ff., tr. Day Lewis, C., op. cit.

'Firmness' in this context can extend as far as ethnic cleansing, and given that Roman 'defensive' warfare covered the elimination of any *potential* threat, the definition of 'aggressors' was somewhat loose. On the other side, the provincials did not always swallow the propaganda. One British chieftain says of the Romans:

> They are the robbers of the world [. . .] If their enemy is opulent, they are greedy for wealth; if he is poverty-stricken, they are eager for glory [. . .] They alone out of everyone lust for wealth and want with equal passion. They call plunder, murder and rape by the spurious names of 'empire', and where they make a desert they call it 'peace'.[43]

However, if the Romans did seek military domination, either as the 'plunder of the world' or as 'firmness against aggressors', and even if some provincial governors 'completely filled their territories with the irreparable evils of openness to bribery, rapes, injustices, evictions and banishments of the innocent, and executions without trial of men of rank and influence',[44] the provinces were generally better off now than they had been under the Republic. Dozens of inscriptions survive expressing gratitude towards Augustus:

> Whereas the divine providence that guides our life has displayed its zeal and benevolence by ordaining for our life the most perfect good, bringing to us Augustus, whom it has filled with virtue for the benefit of mankind, employing him as a saviour for us and our descendants, him who has put an end to wars and adorned peace.[45]

---

43 Tacitus, *Agricola* 30.4, tr. Kershaw, S. The speaker is Calgacus of the Caledones, although it is notable that his speech is written by a Roman historian. See below p. 165.
44 Philo *Against Flaccus* 105, tr. Kershaw, S.
45 *OGIS* 458, ll. 32 ff., tr. Jones, A. H. M., in Ehrenberg, V. and Jones, A. H. M. (eds.), *Documents Illustrating the Reigns of Augustus and Tiberius*, Oxford: Clarendon Press, 1955, p. 94.

One of the best expressions of this comes in a delicious parody in Monty Python's *Life of Brian*, in a hilarious scene where the leader of the People's Front of Judaea famously asks, 'What have [the Romans] ever given us?' He receives a variety of positive responses that he doesn't want to hear, and explodes in exasperation:

> All right! But apart from the sanitation, the education, the medicine, wine, public order, the fresh water system and public health, what have the Romans ever done for us?

Someone pipes up, 'Brought peace!' This is quite accurate, and Augustus wanted everyone to know it.

Symptomatic of the positive provincial response is the monumental complex known as the Sebasteion (Temple of the Emperors) at Aphrodisias in modern Turkey. Funded by leading local families, its superb sculpture depicts fifty personified peoples and places in a visual catalogue of Augustus' Empire. Livia is there too, as are Augustus' grandsons Gaius and Lucius Caesar, Augustus himself depicted as Zeus with Victory, and various mythological scenes, notably featuring Aeneas.[46]

As part of the same process at Rome, on 4 July 13 BCE the Senate decreed that the *Ara Pacis Augustae* (Altar of the Peace of Augustus) should be consecrated on the Campus Martius at the place where a returning general would make the transition between military and civilian dress. Ovid wrote about it:

> Peace, be present with the wreath of Actium on your head
> and stay in kindness through the world.
> Let there be no reason for a triumph – and no enemies:
> you will bring more glory than war!
> [. . .]

---

46   See Smith, R. R. R., Ilgım, M. and Özguven, H., *Aphrodisias Sebasteion Sevgi Gönül Hall*, Istanbul: Yapı Kredi Publications, 2008.

May the house which guarantees peace, in peace last for ever.[47]

Officially inaugurated on 30 January 9 BCE, the Ara Pacis formed part of a complex that came to include Augustus' mausoleum, the *ustrinum* where he would be cremated, the Pantheon, and the *Horologium* or *Solarium Augusti*, an immense monumental sundial whose symbols indicated Augustus' dominion over time and the heavenly bodies. The sundial's gnomon was an obelisk brought back from Egypt, and its base still bears an inscription celebrating the victory over Antony and Cleopatra:

> The Emperor Caesar, son of a god, Augustus, *Pontifex Maximus*, Imperator for the 12th time, in his 11th consulship, with tribunician power for the 14th time, gave [this obelisk] as a gift to the sun [i.e., Apollo, Augustus' patron divinity] when Egypt had been placed under the power of the Roman People.[48]

The sculptural decoration of the Ara Pacis itself shows Augustus' desire to disseminate a family-man image. For the first time ever, women and children were depicted on a Roman state monument, in a procession that included Augustus, Livia, Agrippa, maybe Julia (despite her disgrace and exile), probably her sons Gaius and Lucius Caesar and her daughter Julia, Iullus Antonius (despite his possible involvement with Julia), Tiberius, Augustus' sister Octavia, and numerous significant others. Elsewhere Augustus' mythical ancestor Aeneas makes a sacrifice; Romulus and Remus are suckled by the she-wolf; personified Rome appears in an ensemble that symbolizes *Pax Romana*; and a figure who may be Mother Earth, Italy, Venus Genetrix,

---

47   Ovid, *Fasti* 1.711 ff., tr. Ferguson, J., in Chisholm, K. and Ferguson, J. (eds.), op. cit.
48   *CIL* 701 and 702, tr. Davies, P. J. E., *Death and the Emperor: Roman Imperial Funerary Monuments from Augustus to Marcus Aurelius*, Cambridge: Cambridge University Press, 2000, p. 76.

Augustan Peace personified, or Ceres symbolizes the happiness of the Golden Age of Augustus.

Peace was an expensive commodity, though. As Cicero put it:

> Asia should bear in mind that the calamity both of foreign war and of internal strife would befall her if she were not part of our Empire [. . .] and she should therefore happily pay for this continual peace and tranquillity.[49]

The provinces funded their peace through two direct taxes paid to their *procurator*: *tributum soli*, levied on land and fixed property, and *tributum capitis*, paid on other forms of property. There were also indirect taxes (*vectigalia*) collected by *publicani* (private contractors), such as harbour dues, levies on the sale and manumission of slaves, death duties, and so on. In order to monitor the resources of the Empire, Augustus carried out several censuses, and it was during one of these that Jesus Christ was born:

> There went out a decree from Caesar Augustus that all the world should be taxed. (And this taxing was first made when Cyrenius was governor of Syria.)[50]

P. Sulpicius Quirinius (the Latin Quirinius becomes *Kyrenios* in Greek, and finds its way into English as *Cyrenius*) actually became governor of Syria in 6 CE, but Matthew writes:

> Jesus was born in Bethlehem of Judaea in the days of Herod the king.[51]

---

49   Cicero, *Letters to His Brother Quintus* 1.1.11, written in December 60 BCE, tr. Shuckburgh, E. S., op. cit.
50   Luke 2:1.
51   Matthew 2:1; cf. Luke 1:5, which also places the Nativity story in the context of Herod's reign.

Now Herod died in 4 BCE, shortly after he (allegedly) perpetrated the 'Massacre of the Innocents' to prevent losing his throne to a newly born King of the Jews.[52] Interestingly, this is mentioned neither by Luke nor by any contemporary historian, nor by Josephus, who does record other examples of Herod's atrocities, and modern scholars tend to be sceptical about its historicity. Nevertheless, because the massacre is said to have happened within two years of the appearance of the Star of Bethlehem, Jesus would have been aged about two at the time, and therefore born around 6 BCE.[53] Other calculations work back from an estimate of the start date of Jesus' ministry and place the Nativity between 6 and 4 BCE, or use astronomical data to pinpoint a spectacular conjunction of Venus and Jupiter over Bethlehem on 17 June 2 BCE.

The precise date of Jesus' birth matters less than the impact of the religion that eventually crystallized around him: from this moment on, the Roman Empire and Christianity would be inextricably linked. But the burgeoning new religion would still have to compete with the fact that both individuals and communities across the Roman Empire worshipped Augustus and his successors as gods, and that viewed from their subjects' perspectives, this was perfectly logical. In essence, the cults of the gods provided the perfect template for a response to something/someone that (1) had power over you, (2) exercised that power from outside your city, and (3) was culturally like you. So you responded in exactly the same way – you worshipped the Emperor as a god.

---

52   Matthew 2:16–18. Some recent attempts have been made to place the lunar eclipse related to Herod's death on 10 January or 29 December 1 BCE, or 15 September 5 BCE, with consequent re-calculations for Jesus' birthday: see Pratt, J. P., *The Planetarian**, vol. 19, no. 4, Dec. 1990, 8–14.

53   He might have been older: Matthew suggests that he may have already been aged two at the time of the Magi's visit. For the thoughts of the current Pope, see Ratzinger, J., Pope Benedict XVI, *Jesus of Nazareth: The Infancy Narratives*, London, New Delhi, New York and Sydney: Bloomsbury, 2012, pp. 58 ff.

Augustus' Death and the Transfer of Power

Augustus, of course, knew that he was not immortal, and making arrangements for what happened after his death took up a great deal of his energy. Nobody wanted a return to the horrendous violence that had followed Julius Caesar's death, and Augustus was well aware that the Principate would not become a permanent system unless he was succeeded by someone who was as committed to it as he was. On the other hand, any hint of 'dynasty building' would destroy the illusion that his position was merely based on his *auctoritas*. Then again, the next incumbent would have to be acknowledged as having a legitimate claim to power by the SPQR, and in that respect, a member of Augustus' family would do nicely. The main problem with this, however, was that unfortunately Augustus didn't have a son: his only child was Julia, by his first wife Scribonia (see Genealogy Table 1).

M. Agrippa started in pole position at a time when Julia was unmarried and Augustus' stepsons, Livia's children Tiberius and Nero Claudius Drusus, had not yet come of age. In 23 BCE, Augustus became so ill that he gave Agrippa his signet ring, but then he recovered, and when Julia was married off to Augustus' nephew M. Claudius Marcellus, Agrippa left Rome. But not for long. Marcellus died suddenly in 23 BCE, so Agrippa divorced his wife, returned to Rome, and married Julia. Augustus duly adopted their sons Gaius (b. 20 BCE) and Lucius (b. 17 BCE), gave them the name Caesar, and in 13 BCE he struck coins depicting himself on the obverse ('heads') and Julia, Gaius and Lucius on the reverse ('tails'). But Agrippa died the year after, whereupon Augustus turned to Livia's sons, forcing Tiberius to divorce Agrippa's daughter Vipsania (whom he loved very genuinely) and to marry Julia (whom he didn't love at all, but who had come on strongly to him on occasion). When Nero Claudius Drusus died in 9 BCE Tiberius looked like the heir apparent, but he retired to Rhodes for the next seven years. 'Disgust at his wife'[54] may have been one reason, but Augustus was now again showing favour towards Gaius and Lucius, who were coming of age. In 5 BCE Gaius was appointed Prince of Youth and 'destined' to become Consul in 1 CE; three years later Lucius was accorded the same privileges.

Then there was another twist in the saga:

> Lucius Caesar [2 CE] and then Gaius Caesar [4 CE] met with premature natural deaths – unless their stepmother Livia had a secret hand in them.[55]

So the focus shifted back onto the elder Julia and her other children, Julia and Agrippa Postumus.[56] But with Postumus' brutishness making him a non-starter, and various sex scandals enveloping both Julias, Augustus banished them all, and Tiberius, who had returned to Rome in 2 CE, became Augustus' successor by default. On 27 June 4 CE, to his mother Livia's delight, he was adopted as the Emperor's son. Augustus also made Tiberius adopt Nero Claudius Drusus' son, his nephew Germanicus, and in 13 CE he procured a law giving Tiberius unlimited *imperium proconsulare*, thereby making him virtually co-ruler. There was now no doubt about who would be Rome's second Emperor.

Augustus died in August 14 CE, shortly before he turned seventy-eight. His health had been deteriorating, and Tacitus hints darkly of foul play on Livia's part, since Augustus had recently visited Agrippa Postumus, whose return would confound her aspirations for Tiberius' succession:

> Tiberius was recalled from [. . .] Illyricum [. . .] by an urgent letter from his mother [. . .] At intervals, hopeful reports were published – until the steps demanded by the situation had

---

54   Suetonius, *Tiberius* 10.1.
55   Tacitus, *Annals* 1.3, tr. Grant, op. cit.
56   Her other daughter was Agrippina the Elder, mother of Caligula.

been taken. Then two pieces of news became known simultaneously: Augustus was dead, and Tiberius was in control.[57]

Augustus was cremated in the Campus Martius and his ashes were placed in his Mausoleum. His will nominated Tiberius and Livia as his principal heirs, and the Senate deified him. Suetonius quotes an edict in which Augustus outlined his mission statement:

May I be privileged to build firm and lasting foundations for the Government of Rome. May I also achieve the reward [...] of carrying with me, when I die, the hope that these foundations will abide secure.[58]

In many ways he succeeded. The Roman Republic was effectively cremated along with Augustus, but the Roman Empire would abide for another four and a half centuries at the very least.

---

57 Tacitus, *Annals* 1.5, tr. Grant, op. cit.
58 Suetonius, *Augustus* 282, tr. Graves, R., op. cit.

4

The Pervert and the Madman: Tiberius (14–37) and Gaius 'Caligula' (37–41)[1]

The reigns of Tiberius, Gaius, Claudius and Nero were described during their lifetimes in fictitious terms, for fear of the consequences; whereas the accounts written after their deaths were influenced by still raging animosities.

Tacitus, *Annals* 1.1[2]

The Second Emperor of Rome

The historian Tacitus insinuates that Augustus only chose Tiberius to make himself look good against Tiberius' cruelty and arrogance, and Suetonius writes that, on his deathbed, Augustus moaned, 'O woe for the Roman people, destined to be chomped by such slowly grinding teeth!'[3] But despite the fact that Tiberius had spent so much time out of the political loop that he had acquired the nickname 'the Exile', he had still accumulated some first-hand experience of government, and his military achievements, notably the recovery of the eagles that Crassus had lost to the Parthians at Carrhae, were not to be trifled with.

This rather enigmatic man, now called Tiberius Julius Caesar Augustus, was arguably the most powerful ruler that had ever

---

1 All dates from here on are CE, unless indicated otherwise.
2 Tr. Grant, M., op. cit.
3 Suetonius, *Tiberius* 21.2.

controlled Rome. He was now in his mid-fifties, of ultra-noble lineage, highly intelligent, equipped with a trenchant sense of irony, and avidly interested in Greek mythology.[4] He was tall, powerfully built and in rude health. Suetonius tells us that he had a fair complexion and wore his hair rather long, whereas Tacitus says his head had no trace of hair and that his face was pockmarked with ulcers, which, needless to say, do not feature in his official portraits. These use an image modelled on that of Augustus, showing him with a high, broad forehead, large eyes, an aquiline nose and a small curved mouth with a protruding upper lip, but with the whole image tweaked to make him look younger than he really was. Both writers agree, though, that he was a brusque, misanthropic, suspicious, miserly, bloodthirsty, perverted tyrant.

However, when the SPQR, magistrates and, crucially, the army swore an oath of allegiance to him in 14, he appeared shy of assuming power and complained about the 'miserable and oppressive servitude being imposed upon him'.[5] His powers were conferred by a *lex de imperio* ratified by the people, but he spurned the *praenomen* of Imperator and the *cognomen* of Father of his Country, rejected having a civic crown in the vestibule of his house, and only used the name of Augustus in letters addressed to kings and princes. His default approach to government was hands-off, and he got frustrated with the Senate when they wouldn't act on their own initiative, but irritated with them when they did. He never won the hearts and minds of the SPQR, and an atmosphere of reciprocal fear and mistrust developed: he often quoted the Greek proverb that he was 'holding a wolf by the ears'[6], but also derided the Senate as 'men fit to be slaves'.[7]

Despite providing generous disaster relief when a major earthquake devastated a dozen cities in Asia in 17, and when

---

4   Philo, *Legatio ad Gaium* 142; Tacitus, *Annals* 6.6. See also Kershaw, S., *A Brief Guide to the Greek Myths*, London: Robinson, 2007, p. 241.
5   Suetonius, *Tiberius* 24.2. Cf. Tacitus, *Annals* 1.10–13.
6   Terence, *Phormio* 506; Suetonius, *Tiberius* 25.1.
7   Tacitus, *Annals* 3.65. He said this in Greek, apparently.

serious fires gutted wide swathes of Rome in 27 and 36, he found it hard to shake off his reputation for stinginess. The historian Velleius Paterculus, who did military service under Tiberius, was gushing in his praise:

> What public buildings did he construct in his own name or that of his family! With what pious munificence, exceeding human belief, does he now rear the temple to his father! For a feeling of kinship leads him to protect every famous monument.[8]

Yet Suetonius states that he never erected any noble edifice during his entire reign, never entertained the people with public spectacles, and was seldom present when others did so, and the archaeological evidence tends to endorse this perspective, suggesting that the only major project in Tiberius' reign was the Temple to the Deified Augustus, which he either never finished or didn't bother to consecrate.

Yet however tight-fisted Tiberius may have been, his subjects often sought to bestow extravagant honours on him. For example, in 15 the Greek city of Gythium decreed that one of its public officials should erect statues of 'his father the deified Augustus Caesar, the Emperor Tiberius Caesar Augustus and Julia Augusta' (i.e., Livia), and that the councilmen and magistrates should offer sacrifice for the preservation of all three of them, plus the Victory of Germanicus Caesar and the Venus of Drusus Caesar. Tiberius immediately replied indicating his unease about this:

> I commend you [. . .] and consider it fitting that [. . .] your city [. . .] should reserve special honours befitting the gods in keeping with the greatness of my father's services to the whole world; but I myself am content with the more modest honours appropriate to men. My mother, however, will

---

8   Velleius Paterculus 2.130.1, tr. Shipley, F.W., in *Velleius Paterculus and Res Gestae Divi Augusti*, Cambridge, MA, and London: Harvard University Press, 1924.

answer you herself when she learns from you your decision about honours to her.[9]

Tiberius' relationship with Livia, whom her great-grandson Caligula described as '*Ulixem stolatum*' ('Ulysses in a female toga') – a backhanded compliment if ever there was one – was often fractious. Suetonius tells that she claimed equal shares of the power with him, but although she became the first woman ever to be made 'Augusta' ('Femmeperor' – a feminized version of Augustus), Tiberius denied her the title 'Mother of her Country' and instructed her 'to keep out of important affairs, and ones that were inappropriate for a woman'.[10]

Livia was not the only family member that posed a threat to Tiberius' authority: Agrippa Postumus was permanently 'eliminated', and there was always the possibility that Tiberius' adoptive son Germanicus might try to oust him.

Tiberius and the Army

Tiberius' supremacy ultimately depended on the loyalty of the army. One of Augustus' great achievements had been to convert the army's vested interest in unrest into an interest in stability, mainly by making it a fully professional institution with fixed terms and conditions. Tiberius inherited a standing army of twenty-five legions: eight on the Rhine, three in Spain, two each in Africa and Egypt, four in the territory stretching from Syria to the Euphrates, two in Pannonia, two in Moesia, and two in reserve in Dalmatia (see Map 4).

Each individual legion was commanded by a *legatus Augusti legionis* or *legatus legionis* ('legionary legate') directly appointed by the Emperor. It comprised ten cohorts of roughly 500 soldiers, each divided into six centuries of (despite their name)

---

9   *AE*, 1929, no 99–100, ll. 17 ff., tr. Lewis, N. and Reinhold, M. (eds.), *Roman Civilization: Selected Readings Edited by Naphtali Lewis and Meyer Reinhold, Volume II, The Empire*, New York: Columbia University Press, 1990, 3rd edn, p. 522.
10   Suetonius, *Tiberius* 50.3, tr. Kershaw, S.

about eighty men. Beneath the *legatus* were six military trib-unes, one *tribunus laticlavius* ('broad stripe') of Senatorial rank but usually in his twenties and lacking any prior military experi-ence, and five *tribuni angusticlavii* ('narrow stripes'), normally of Equestrian rank, who did have some previous experience. Between the *tribunus laticlavius* and the *tribuni angusticlavii* in the hierarchy, and so third in command, was the fully profes-sional *praefectus castrorum* (camp prefect/quartermaster). Below the Senatorial and Equestrian officers came the centurions, the senior of which was the *primus pilus*.

Some lower-ranking soldiers received extra pay. These '*prin-cipales*' included the *signifer* (standard-bearer), *optio* (orderly) and the *tesserarius* (guardian of the daily watchword). Every legion had an *aquilifer*, who carried the legionary eagle, and an *imaginifer*, who carried the emperor's portrait. Next down the pecking order came the *immunes*, on basic pay (225 *denarii* per annum under Augustus) but with specific skills that exempted them from everyday fatigues: arrow makers, blacksmiths, carpenters, grooms, medical orderlies, surveyors, veterinaries, and so on. The rank-and-file soldiers were simply called *milites*, and would hope to progress as far as possible along this career path. Clerical staff of varying rank handled the extensive logisti-cal demands of the legion, and since the legionaries were often used for peacetime building projects their transferable skills were invaluable.

Rome's legions were supported by the *auxilia* (auxiliaries), recruited from different communities who possessed useful fighting qualities: archers from Crete, slingers from the Balearic Islands, first-rate cavalry from Gaul, Germany and Numidia, etc. Auxiliary units were of three types: infantry *cohortes* with a normal strength of 480 (quingenary) or 800 (milliary);[11] cavalry *alae* ('wings') numbering 512 (quingenary) or 768 (milliary); and *cohortes equitatae* of, probably, 480 (or 800) infantry and 120 (or 240) cavalry combined. They might be

---

11 The names imply 500 or 1000, but in practice there were fewer.

commanded by their own chiefs, but regular auxiliary regiments were normally commanded by Roman Equestrian tribunes or prefects.

Rome also had naval bases at Misenum (modern Miseno) and Ravenna in Italy, Forum Julii (modern Fréjus) in Gallia Narbonensis, Alexandria in Egypt and Seleucia Pieria in Syria, as well as flotillas on the Rhine and Danube, all under the command of Equestrian prefects.

By around the end of the first century the majority of 'Roman' soldiers were non-Italian, and by the second century they were all being rewarded on discharge with Roman citizenship for themselves and their children. In Tiberius' day Roman soldiers below centurion level could not legally marry, but many had mistresses whose children, though technically illegitimate, were brought up around the forts, or even in the barracks, and then followed their fathers into the military. So the Roman army became a kind of cultural glue binding the empire together: its language was Latin, its culture was Roman, and retired soldiers frequently settled in the provinces where they had served and acquired families and Roman citizenship.

At Rome itself the garrison consisted of the elite Praetorian Guard, the urban cohorts and the *vigiles*, making a total force under Tiberius of around 7 500 men. The Praetorian Guard, commanded by two Equestrian prefects (each called *Praefectus Praetorio*), was the permanent imperial bodyguard and consisted of twelve cohorts (around 6 000 men) with a small cavalry contingent.[12] Its soldiers were hand-picked from Italy and the adjacent provinces, and they enjoyed far superior pay and conditions (750 *denarii* per annum under Augustus) and wore more ornate kit. The Emperor also had a personal German bodyguard, the *Germani corporis custodes*, and there were three paramilitary *cohortes urbanae* (urban cohorts), who formed a city police under the control of a Senatorial *Praefectus Urbi*

---

12 Tiberius had increased it from nine cohorts under Augustus. It went up to sixteen under Vitellius, then back to nine under Vespasian.

(City Prefect), plus seven cohorts of 500 (later 1 000) *vigiles*, a fire-brigade-cum-nightwatch.

In normal circumstances it was the Emperor, a close family member or a *legatus Augusti pro praetore*[13] who led the army in wartime. But Augustus' death was not a normal circumstance, and Tiberius immediately had to face mutinies by four of the Rhine legions and three on the Danube. Tacitus narrates the tale of a soldier called Percennius from the Danube force, who was an ex-professional applause-leader in the theatre, manipulating the soldiers' uncertainty and anger over pay and conditions, and of Tiberius having to dispatch a substantial force under L. Aelius Sejanus, the newly promoted *Praefectus Praetorio*, and his own son Drusus Caesar. Drusus took an uncompromising line, intimidated the soldiers, executed Percennius, and put the rebellion down. In Germany, where the mutiny was much more serious, Germanicus' soldiers wanted him to seize the throne. He was having none of this, but when he unsheathed his sword and threatened to commit suicide unless the men returned to their loyalty, one wag offered him his sword instead, saying that it was sharper. However, some last-ditch negotiations over pay and conditions defused the situation. Germanicus had effectively cemented his uncle's position as Emperor.

Tiberius' Early Years: Germanicus and Drusus

Most sources agree that Tiberius conducted the first phase of his reign pretty successfully and 'with a reasonable regard for the public good'.[14] Much would depend on whether or not Tiberius had any real appetite for the job, and at this stage problems including revolts by Tacfarinas in Africa, the Gallic Treveri and Aedui led by Iulius Florus and Iulius Sacrovir, and the Frisii, along with unrest in Thrace, were dealt with effectively, and Arminius, destroyer of Varus' legions, was killed by

---

13   See above, p. 59.
14   Suetonius, *Tiberius* 33.

his treacherous relatives. When some of Tiberius' governors proposed increasing provincial taxation, he told them, 'It is the part of a good shepherd to shear, not flay, his sheep,'[15] and he halved Augustus' unpopular 1 per cent sales tax in 17.[16] Suetonius credits him with saying that freedom of speech and thought was the test of a Free State.

The Emperor's real and adoptive sons, Drusus and Germanicus Caesar, were prominent early on. Germanicus' campaigns in Germany in 14, 15 and 16 brought home two of Varus' lost legionary eagles, but Tiberius, possibly uneasy about his rising popularity, recalled him to Rome, although he still awarded him a triumph in 17 and shared the consulship with him the year after. Germanicus was looking like the next Emperor-in-waiting, while his prolific wife Agrippina the Elder bore nine children, notably Caligula and Nero's mother Agrippina the Younger (see Genealogy Table 1).

Germanicus' next assignment was to reorder the eastern part of Rome's Empire. This involved crowning Artaxias III (aka Zeno-Artaxias) as King of Armenia and bringing Cappadocia and Commagene (at the intersection of Cilicia, Syria and Cappadocia) into provincial status. But when he made an unauthorized visit to Alexandria in 19, he had to dampen down some over-enthusiastic acclamations:

> They are appropriate only to him who is really the saviour and benefactor of the whole human race, my father [Tiberius], and to his mother [Livia], my grandmother.[17]

Soon after this, however, Germanicus fell ill and died at Antioch (10 October 19). The finger of suspicion pointed at Syria's ex-governor and Germanicus' personal enemy Cn. Calpurnius

---

15   Suetonius, *Tiberius* 32.2, tr. Rolfe, J. C., op. cit.
16   He put it back to 1 per cent in 31, though.
17   Mitteis, L. and Wilcken, U., *Grundzüge und Chrestomathie der Papyruskunde*, Leipzig and Berlin: Teubner, B. G., 1912, no. 413, ll. 31–45, tr. in Lewis, N. and Reinhold, M. (eds.), op. cit. p. 523.

Piso, and circumstantial evidence suggested that Piso had poisoned Germanicus on Tiberius' orders. However, when Piso returned to Rome to face trial, he was found to have 'committed suicide' just before the verdict was delivered, and immediately after a visit from Sejanus. The court's finding, that Piso was implicated in Germanicus' death, is preserved on the *Senatus Consultum de Pisone patre*, a bronze tablet that is complemented by inscriptions known as the *tabula Hebana* and the *tabula Siarensis*, which outline the funerary honours that Germanicus received, including a marble arch in the Circus Flaminius complete with an inscription recording that Germanicus avenged the 'deceitful destruction of an army of the Roman people'.[18]

The Piso case was symptomatic of a worrying shift in ethos in Tiberius' reign: treason trials, often brought by informers (*delatores*), were becoming frequent. Treason came under an extremely vague law that covered anything that might 'diminish the majesty of the Roman people', and under which a successful accuser was rewarded with a share of the convicted person's property. Some 'crimes' were unbelievably frivolous, as when Tiberius allegedly executed a Senator for taking a coin with his likeness on it into a toilet:

> With my coin in your bosom you turned aside into foul and noisome places and relieved your bowels.[19]

With Germanicus' death, Drusus became the heir apparent, but he too encountered an untimely end. There were no rumours at the time (he died on 14 September 23), but for some years previously his wife Livilla[20] (who was Germanicus' sister) had been having an affair with Sejanus. This was clearly about power as well as sex: doubtless Sejanus fancied Livilla, but he also

---

18   *AE,* 1984, no. 508, tr. Lewis, N. and Reinhold, M., (eds,) op. cit., p. 524.
19   Dio 58 fr. 2, tr. Cary, E., op. cit. However, see Seneca *On Benefits* 3.26.1–2, where the man is saved by a quick-witted slave.
20   Tacitus calls her Livia; Suetonius often gives diminutive names like this to women.

fancied himself in relation to Tiberius as Agrippa had been to Augustus. His perfect outcome would be for Drusus to die and him to marry his widow, and some eight years later it was duly discovered that Drusus had been poisoned by Livilla . . .

Sejanus: His Rise and Fall

Sejanus' star was very much in the ascendant. As *Praefectus Praetorio* he had amalgamated all the urban cohorts into one camp, and his control of this concentrated military force, combined with his adept social-networking skills, enabled him to become Tiberius' 'partner of his labours'.

But Sejanus wanted more. The heirs to the throne were now Agrippina the Elder's teenage sons, Nero Caesar and Drusus Caesar (see Genealogy Table 1), but they and their mother seem to have alienated Tiberius. Sejanus then threw his own hat into the ring in 25 by seeking Tiberius' permission to marry Livilla. Tiberius refused, telling the Equestrian Sejanus not to have ideas above his station, although he still had statues of Sejanus erected all over Rome.

Sejanus' powers increased further when Tiberius left Rome for Campania in 26. The Emperor had a near-death experience at a seaside residence called 'the Cavern' (modern Sperlonga), where a cave decked out with a collection of important and very impressive sculptures depicting scenes from Homer's *Odyssey* functioned as a banqueting hall. There Tiberius survived a rock fall that killed several guests. He then continued on to the isle of Capri. This effectively meant that from the year 27 the running of the state, and access to the Emperor, devolved onto Sejanus with, according to Suetonius, dangerous and dishonourable results: Spain and Syria were left without suitable governors for years; the Parthians overran Armenia; the Dacians and Sarmatians ravaged Moesia; and the Germans invaded Gaul. In addition, the animosity between Tiberius and Livia worsened until she died in 29 at the grand old age of eighty-six. Her son refused to attend the funeral, forbade her deification, and disregarded the provisions of her will.

That same year Agrippina the Elder and her eldest son Nero Caesar were arrested for plotting against Tiberius and deported. Tiberius

> ordered a centurion to give her a good flogging, in the course of which she lost an eye. And when she resolved to starve herself to death, he ordered her mouth to be forced open, and meat to be crammed down her throat.[21]

But Agrippina stayed resolute and died soon afterwards; Nero Caesar was driven to suicide when an executioner showed him various halters and hooks; and his brother Drusus was already in Hades following his arrest and conviction two years earlier.

The fate of his mother and brothers placed Gaius Caesar (aka Caligula) in pole position for the imperial succession, at least if Livilla and Drusus' son, Tiberius Julius Caesar Nero 'Gemellus', born in 19, didn't beat him to it. Both were favoured by Tiberius, both were living on Capri, but both had to face the rivalry of Sejanus.

Matters came to a spectacular climax in 31. Sejanus' power was a potential threat to Tiberius, and Germanicus' mother Antonia Minor warned the Emperor of a conspiracy. Tiberius' response was utterly devious: Q. Naevius Cordus Sutorius Macro, prefect of the *vigiles*, was promised Sejanus' command, and the Praetorian Guard was transferred to his control; Tiberius delivered a letter to the Senate charging Sejanus with plotting against Caligula; and Sejanus was 'tried' and executed. A brutal witch-hunt brought about the murders of Sejanus' children and supporters, who possibly included the historian Velleius Paterculus. Sejanus' wife Apicata committed suicide, but not before she had accused Livilla of complicity in Drusus' death. Sejanus' corpse was thrown to the Roman mob. They tore it to pieces.

---

21   Suetonius, *Tiberius* 532, tr. Graves, R., op. cit.

Capri, Perversion, Crucifixion and Death

It was not just the Roman mob who displayed barbarity now. While Tiberius hid away at the Villa Jovis on Capri for nine months, the Senate lived in perpetual terror of the ever more frequent treason trials. The Emperor surrounded himself with astrologers and academics, and continued the literary interests that had always given him pleasure, but the rumour mill went into overdrive with tales of alcohol, sex and violence: Tiberius was such a hard drinker that his name, Tiberius Claudius Nero, was mutated into Biberius Caldius Mero, 'Drunkard Hot-wine Unmixed-wine', in his aptly named 'latrines' groups of specially selected girls and young men, known as *spintriae* – so perverted that new vocabulary had to be invented to describe their activities – would perform threesomes completed by *exoleti*, 'adult' prostitutes;[22] there were pornographic artworks and manuals everywhere; he went swimming with his 'little fishes', boys who would get between his thighs to lick and nibble him; suckling babies would be made to fellate him; a fisherman who gave him an enormous mullet had his face rubbed with it, and when he yelled 'Thank Heaven, I did not bring Caesar that huge crab I also caught!' Tiberius used the crab in the same way; men were tricked into drinking huge amounts of wine, and then had cords tied round their genitals to prevent them from urinating; and people were thrown from the cliffs of Capri, and battered to death with boat hooks if they survived. All this came from the man who notoriously said: 'Let them hate me, so long as they accept me!'[23]

There is absolutely no way of corroborating any of this, but it shows the growing odium and disrespect in which the Emperor, now in his seventies, was held: what mattered was not the truth of the rumours, but their existence.

---

22 See Williams, C. A., *Roman Homosexuality*, 2nd edn., Oxford: Oxford University Press, 2010, pp. 90–93, 258.
23 Suetonius, *Tiberius* 59.2, tr. Kershaw, S. A very similar phrase (where 'fear' replaces 'accept') is attributed to Caligula (Suetonius, *Caligula* 20.1). See p. 91.

While on Capri, Tiberius would probably have been informed of a world-changing event. A long-serving Prefect of Judaea called Pontius Pilatus ('Pilate'), whose period of office had not always been a comfortable one, was relieved of his post in 36, shortly after authorizing the crucifixion of Jesus of Nazareth. As with Jesus' birth, the precise dating of this event is controversial: the Gospels, endorsed by Josephus and Tacitus, say that the Crucifixion took place during Pilate's tenure, although they mistakenly call him *procurator*, not *praefectus*. Governors of Judaea were only known as *procurator* from 44, starting with Cuspius Fadus, and an inscription found at Caesarea Maritima, known as the 'Pilate Stone', which dates from Tiberius' reign, calls him *praefectus Iudaeae*:

> To the Divine Augusti [i.e., Augustus and Livia] [this] Tiberieum [probably a complex of buildings in honour of Tiberius] . . . Pontius Pilatus . . . Prefect of Judaea . . . has dedicated [this].[24]

Jesus was pretty certainly crucified on a Friday,[25] probably on or near Passover (this falls on Nisan 15 in the Hebrew calendar and is calculated from the appearance of the new moon), but the year, and hence the month, is heavily disputed. Differing theories have been constructed from the accounts in the Canonical Gospels, from the chronology of St Paul's conversion (around 33–36,[26] just after the Crucifixion), and from astronomical calculations going back to Sir Isaac Newton that take into account solar or lunar eclipses (some accounts say that a period of darkness occurred at the Crucifixion). A Friday in April 33 or 34

---

24   Israel Museum, Jerusalem, *AE* 1963 no. 104, tr. Kershaw, S. See Vardaman, H., 'A New Inscription Which Mentions Pilate as "Prefect,"' *Journal of Biblical Literature* 81 (1962) 70–71.

25   *Mark* 15:42; *John* 19:14; 19:31; 19:42.

26   He was tried by Junius Annaeus Gallio, the Proconsul of Achaia, in around 51–52 (*Acts* 18:12–17), met Priscilla and Aquila who were expelled from Rome about 49, and spent some fourteen years on his missions (*Acts* 11:25–26; *2 Corinthians* 11:23–33) before he returned to Jerusalem (*Galatians* 2:1).

comes out as the favourite (but by no means the only) option, although there are those who regard the darkness as bogus or supernatural.

Around the same time there were other crucifixions at Rome when Tiberius pulled down the temple of Isis, had her image thrown into the Tiber and crucified her priests for dishonouring a noble Roman lady; earlier, in 19, when another Roman matron had been swindled by a gang of Jewish con men, Tiberius forced 4 000 Jewish youths into military service in the bandit-infested, fever-ridden island of Sardinia, and expelled all the other Jews from Rome on pain of slavery. Astrologers received similar threats, although he revoked the decree when they promised to renounce their profession.

Somewhat inconsistently, though, Tiberius allowed astrology to influence his thinking when it came to the succession. Gaius 'Caligula' was now in his twenties, and Gemellus was around ten years younger, but Tiberius had an inkling that the latter was the product of Livilla's adultery with Sejanus, rather than his own grandson, and although he had serious reservations about Gaius' suitability, stating that he was 'bringing up a water-snake for the Roman people, and a Phaethon for the world',[27] the stars suggested that Gaius' accession was inevitable.

In March 37 Tiberius fell ill following an abortive attempt to return to Rome. Put off by the frightening portent of the death of a pet snake, and warned by a soothsayer to 'Beware the power of the mob',[28] he headed back to Campania. He tried to disguise his ill health by attending the Games at Circeii in Latium, but he strained his side while throwing javelins at a wild boar, aggravated things by sitting in a draught, and then moved on to Misenum, where he continued to party as hard as ever. Sickness and inclement weather prevented him getting to Capri, and on

---

27 Suetonius, *Gaius* 11, tr. Kershaw, S. In Greek mythology, Phaethon lost control of the chariot of the sun and almost destroyed the world. See Kershaw, S., op. cit., 2007, p. 263 f.

28 Suetonius, *Tiberius* 72.2.

16 March he died in a villa at Misenum. Inevitably there were conspiracy theories: one that he had been poisoned by Caligula, another that believing Tiberius to be dead, Caligula took the signet ring off his finger and was acclaimed as Emperor, only to find Tiberius recovered and asking for food. The *Praefectus Praetorio* Macro calmed Caligula's panicked response by smothering the ageing Emperor with a cushion.

There was general rejoicing at Tiberius' death. At Rome people shouted, '*Tiberium in Tiberim*' (= 'to the Tiber with Tiberius!' – the fate of a common criminal's corpse), and prayers were said to Mother Earth and the Infernal Gods to give his spirit no residence except among the damned. However, Caligula arranged for the cadaver to be taken to Rome under armed escort and properly cremated. Tiberius' ashes were put in Augustus' Mausoleum, but he was not deified.

Caligula's Honeymoon Period

Tiberius' death might have generated unbridled celebrations among the SPQR, but he had still left behind an Empire with relatively secure borders and a massive treasury surplus of some 2.7 billion *sestertii*. The young man who succeeded him has grabbed the popular imagination in a way that is out of all proportion both to the shortness of his Principate and to the quality of the source material. The section of Tacitus' *Annals* that covered his reign has been lost, and much of the other material that survives tends to be anecdotal, sensationalist and clichéd: similar or even identical prurient tales of his sexual deviances and crazy antics are told about many of Rome's unpopular Emperors. He is portrayed as the ultimate in 'mad, bad and dangerous to know' (especially if you were related to him), but the ancient accounts actually make it hard to get to know him.

Born on 31 August 12 at Antium (modern Anzio),[29] and very

---

29 There were other traditions about his birthplace, but Suetonius quotes the *Gazette* to certify the point: Suetonius, *Gaius* 8.2.

touchy about his maternal grandfather M. Agrippa's plebeian roots, Gaius had accompanied his parents on Germanicus' campaigns on the Rhine when he was a child, and had been displayed to the troops dressed up in a miniature military uniform, from which he acquired the affectionate nickname 'Caligula', meaning 'A Small Military Boot'.[30] He was highly intelligent and had a rapier-sharp (and rapier-cruel) wit. He had delivered Livia's funeral oration at the age of seventeen, and spent his late teens and early twenties with Tiberius on Capri. His relationships with his three sisters were so close that stories arose about him regularly committing incest with all of them, and Suetonius adds the rumour that he also violated Drusilla's virginity. But this might just be scurrilous falsehood: the equally unpopular Commodus, who shared his birthday with Gaius, was accused of practically the same things.[31] Caligula's first wife Iunia Claudilla died in childbirth soon after their wedding in 33, after which he seduced Macro's wife Ennia Naevia, whom he falsely promised to marry once he became Emperor.

With Macro's aid, the minor inconvenience of Tiberius' will, which named Gaius and Gemellus as joint heirs, was side-stepped by declaring it invalid on the grounds of Tiberius' insanity, and on 18 March 37 the SPQR conferred sole power on a man who was only twenty-four, barely had any hands-on experience of government, and who, by all accounts, was not a good-looking person:

> He was very tall and extremely pale, with an unshapely body, but very thin neck and legs. His eyes and temples were hollow, his forehead broad and grim, his hair thin and entirely gone on the top of his head, though his body was hairy.[32]

---

30 Tacitus, *Annals* 1.41.3; Suetonius, *Gaius* 9.1. The word is a diminutive of *caliga* = a leather hobnailed sandal of the type worn by Roman soldiers. Originally it was used quite sentimentally, and conjured up none of the horrors that it now does. *Caligula* is singular = 'Little Boot', not 'Little Boots'.

31 See below, p. 216 ff.

32 Suetonius, *Gaius* 50.1, tr. Rolfe, J. C., *Suetonius, vol. I with an English*

Not that this is wholly reflected in the surviving official portraits, which are of the standard Julio-Claudian type with a protruding upper lip, high, broad forehead and a thick mop of hair, possibly to disguise the baldness – we are told that it became a capital offence to look down on him, or to mention goats.

Nevertheless, to those who did not know him, this young man with the cute nickname, the son of the popular Germanicus, seemed the perfect antidote to Tiberius – he was the *exoptatissimus Princeps*, the most earnestly desired ruler.[33] On 28 March he was welcomed into Rome by a delighted crowd calling him their 'star', 'chicken', 'baby' and 'nurseling';[34] he received the right to command the armies and the imperial provinces; and soldiers and civilians alike swore an oath of loyalty that is exemplified by an inscription from Aritium on the high road from Olisipo (modern Lisbon) to Emerita (modern Merida) in Lusitania:

> I solemnly swear that I will be an enemy to those who I learn are enemies to Gaius Caesar Germanicus [i.e., Caligula]. If anyone [. . .] shall bring danger to him and his welfare, I will not cease to pursue him with arms and deadly war on land and on sea till he has paid the penalty; I will hold neither myself nor my children dearer than his welfare.[35]

A decree from Assos in the province of Asia indicates the empire-wide enthusiasm at his accession:

> The rule of Gaius Caesar Germanicus Augustus, hoped and prayed for by all men, has been proclaimed and the world has found unbounded joy and every city and every people has

---

Translation by J. C. Rolfe. Introduction by K. R. Bradley, Cambridge, MA and London: Harvard University Press, rev. edn., 1998.
33 Suetonius, *Gaius* 13.
34 Ibid.
35 *CIL*, 2.172 (= *ILS* 190), 11 May 37. Tr. in Lewis, N. and Reinhold, M. (eds.), op. cit., p. 8.

been eager for the sight of the god since the happiest age for mankind has now begun.[36]

For a while it seemed that way. During his honeymoon period Caligula was immensely popular. He afforded the ashes of his mother and brother a proper burial in the Mausoleum of Augustus; he made his uncle Ti. Claudius Nero Germanicus[37] Consul; he adopted Gemellus; he granted his grandmother Antonia Minor the same honours that Livia had enjoyed, even though they didn't get on (when she died on 1 May 37 rumour had it that she had been forced into taking her own life); he banished Tiberius' *spintriae*; abolished treason trials; recalled exiles; repressed informers; publicly destroyed Tiberius' personal papers (which no doubt would have implicated many elite Romans in the destruction of Gaius' immediate family); abolished the sales tax; distributed largesse to the people of Rome; promoted chariot races, beast fights and gladiatorial contests; added an extra day to the Saturnalia festival; paid the Praetorian Guard double the bounty that Tiberius had promised (the first recorded *donativum* to troops that we know of); explored the possibility of cutting a canal through the Isthmus of Corinth; began the construction of the Aqua Claudia and Anio Novus aqueducts; started to improve the harbour at Rhegium to help the grain supply; finished reconstructing the theatre of Pompey; created a circus in the Vatican; and became *Pater Patriae* on 21 September 37.

Caligula the Monster

Unfortunately, first impressions didn't last. Gaius peaked too early. The moment of change seems to have been a serious illness that struck him in the October after his accession. Whether this was mental and/or physical is open to question, but there was 'no

---

36 Dittenberger, no. 797. From the year 37. Tr. Lewis, N. and Reinhold, M. (eds.), op. cit., p. 9.
37 'Ti.' is the abbreviation for Tiberius. Caligula's uncle later became the Emperor Claudius.

more Mr Nice Guy' from now on: Suetonius says the *Princeps* became a *monstrum* (monster) and speaks of *valitudo mentis* ('sickness of the mind');[38] Seneca believed that he just went mad; Josephus says the madness was caused by an aphrodisiac given to him by his wife Milonia Caesonia; Philo attributes it to an illness; Dio blames character defects; Tacitus just sees him as troubled and unpredictable, but not necessarily crazy.

Some modern scholars have attributed his eccentric behaviour to alcoholism, anxiety, epilepsy, hyperthyroidism/thyrotoxicosis, psychopathy, bi-polar disorder and schizophrenia. Others have argued that Gaius was just misunderstood, or noted that his reported behaviour dovetails very neatly with that of the stereotypical Greek tyrant.[39] The only eyewitness account that we possess, Philo's *Legatio ad Gaium*, introduces us to a fidgety egotistical neurotic with an acerbic wit, but not a raving lunatic, despite the fact that Gaius treated Philo with incredible disrespect. Essentially, diagnosis from literature at a distance of almost two millennia is deeply problematical.

It may simply be a case of absolute power corrupting absolutely, or of absolute power *revealing* absolutely, but speculation about whether Gaius was barking mad matters less than the fact that these stories were *told* about him and that people wanted to believe them. Gaius was doing something terribly wrong. The Romans needed to know where they stood with their *Princeps*; if he wasn't consistent, they could never know how to deal with him satisfactorily. When, for instance, Gaius changed his

---

38   Suetonius, *Gaius* 51.1.
39   See, e.g., Jerome, T. S., *Aspects of the Study of Roman History*, New York: Putnam, 1923, pp. 381–421; Andrewes, A., *The Greek Tyrants*, London: Hutchinson, 1956; Morgan, M. G., 'Caligula's Illness Again' *Classical World* 66 (1972–73): pp. 327–9; Massaro, V. and Montgomery, I., 'Gaius: Mad Bad, Ill or All Three?' *Latomus* 37 (1978): pp. 894–909; 'Gaius (Caligula) Doth Murder Sleep' *Latomus* 38 (1979) pp. 699–700; Benediktson, D. T., 'Caligula's Madness: Madness or Interictal Temporal Lobe Epilepsy?' *Classical World* 82 (1988–89) pp. 370–5; Katz, R. S., 'The Illness of Caligula.' *Classical World* 65 (1971–72) pp. 223–5; Barrett, A. A., *Caligula: The Corruption of Power*, New Haven, CT: Yale University Press, 1990, pp. 213–41.

attitude towards Tiberius and made it a treasonable offence to slander his memory, it was all too wrong-footing. And wrong-footed the Romans now were.

Gaius' recovery towards the end of 37 turned the honeymoon period into an acrimonious divorce. Mad or not, Gaius became suspicious of the Senate and looked to base his power more directly on the support of the people. He started to explore the boundaries of his power:

'Remember,' he said, 'that I have the right to do anything to anyone.'[40]

He demanded exceptional respect and responded viciously if he didn't get it: the masses quite liked him, but his courtiers couldn't work out how to respond, the Senators were petrified, and the officers of the Praetorian Guard were humiliated. Yet it also became clear to Caligula that he was not indispensable. He could not afford to let questions about the succession arise, and by the end of May 38 he had permanently eliminated both Macro, who was tricked into giving up his command of the Praetorians and then forced to commit suicide, and Gemellus, whom Gaius suspected of plotting against him.

On 10 June 38 Gaius suffered a heartbreaking tragedy. His favourite sister, Drusilla, died. He ordered her deification, which was relatively uncontroversial, but then he started to assume the trappings of divinity himself. The cult of a living ruler was entirely normal in Rome's Eastern provinces, and Gaius was happy to acknowledge it:

You have offered sacrifice each individually and have held a common festival for my safety, and you have voted me the greatest honours you could. For all these I commend you, and I accept them.[41]

---

40 Suetonius, *Gaius* 29.1, tr. Kershaw, S.
41 *IG*, 7.2711, ll. 21–43 (= Dessau, no. 8792) from Acraephiae, Greece, 19

But doing this at Rome was completely beyond the pale, and Caligula caused outrage by constructing a temple to himself on the Palatine:

> At night he used constantly to invite the full and radiant moon to his embraces and his bed, while in the daytime he would talk confidentially with Jupiter Capitolinus, now whispering and then in turn putting his ear to the mouth of the god, now in louder and even angry language; for he was heard to make the threat: 'Lift me up, or I'll lift you.'[42]

Less frivolous was the command that P. Petronius, the *legatus Augusti pro praetore* of Syria, should erect a cult statue of Caligula in the Holy of Holies of the Temple at Jerusalem. Well-judged delaying tactics by Petronius, and the intervention of Herod Agrippa I, ensured that Caligula was dead before this scheme could be implemented, however.

But if being a god was transgressive, transvestism and behaving like a woman was far worse:

> In his clothing, his shoes, and the rest of his attire he did not follow the usage of his country and his fellow citizens; not always even that of his sex; or in fact that of an ordinary mortal. He often appeared in public in embroidered cloaks covered with precious stones, with a long-sleeved tunic and bracelets; sometimes in silk and in a woman's robe [. . .] and at times in the low shoes which are used by females. But oftentimes he exhibited himself with a golden beard, holding in his hand a thunderbolt, a trident, or a caduceus, emblems of the gods, and even in the garb of Venus.[43]

August 37, tr. in Lewis, N. and Reinhold, M. (eds.), op. cit., p. 526 f.

42   Suetonius, *Gaius* 22.4, tr. Rolfe, J. C., op. cit. The threat is a quotation in Greek from Homer's *Iliad* 23.724, where words are used by Aias against Odysseus after a long and indecisive wrestling match.

43   Suetonius, *Gaius* 52, tr. Rolfe, J. C., op. cit.

Such eccentric behaviour smacked of oriental despotism and effeminacy, despite the fact that his dealings with various women show unreconstructed red-blooded masculinity. Late in 37, at the wedding celebrations of Livia Orestilla and Gaius Calpurnius Piso, the single Caligula reclined opposite the groom, told him, 'Don't have sex with my wife!' and carried the bride off for himself, only to divorce her within a few days in favour of Lollia Paulina, who was likewise swiftly discarded and told never to sleep with another man. Wife number four, Milonia Caesonia, was perfect for him:

> Caesonia [. . .] was of neither outstanding beauty nor youth [. . .] but had abandoned herself to financial and sexual excess [. . .] He would often exhibit her to the troops, dressed up in a military cloak, shield and helmet, and riding beside him, and in fact he even showed her to his friends in the nude.[44]

They married in the late summer of 39, and she bore him a child named Julia Drusilla very close to their wedding day.[45]

All the while Caligula was frittering away the reserves that Tiberius had amassed. One of his most lavish spectacles consisted of constructing a 3.2-kilometre-long bridge of boats from Bauli to Puteoli (modern Pozzuoli) on the Bay of Naples, along which he rode, clad in the breastplate of Alexander the Great, which he had allegedly taken from his sarcophagus. Quite why he did this is baffling: pure eccentricity, blatant megalomania, an attempt to outdo the famous Persian King Xerxes, or the desire to impress a Parthian hostage called Dareios have all been mooted. The staggering opulence of Caligula's ships has been revealed by excavations at Lake Nemi, which uncovered the remains of two 70-metre-long vessels that might have been pleasure barges or ships used in the cult of Isis, which Gaius favoured. A lead pipe stamped *Property of Gaius*

---

44   Ibid. 25.3, tr. Kershaw, S.
45   Just before, says Suetonius (*Gaius* 25); one month later, says Dio (59.23.7).

Caesar Augustus Germanicus, plus tiles bearing their dates of manufacture, tells when the ships were built and for whom. The boats were sheathed in lead, studded with the bronze heads of wolves and lions, and adorned with marble, mosaics, porphyry and precious metals. Piston pumps supplied them with hot and cold running water piped to heated baths and chilled fountains. Sadly, the ships were destroyed in the Second World War.

It was not just the human population of Rome that benefited from Gaius' largesse. He was a huge fan of the Green chariot racing faction, and our sources famously speak of his favourite racehorse Incitatus ('Swift' or 'Flyer') living in absurd luxury. But the development of the story says much about the way Caligula's image is handled by the historians. Suetonius (*c.*70–122) wrote:

> Besides a marble stable, an ivory manger, purple rugs and a collar made of gemstones, he even gave Incitatus a house, a set of slaves and some furniture [. . .] *It is also said that* he marked him out for the consulship.[46]

But by the time of Dio Cassius (*c.*165–235), this rumour was being presented as fact:

> *He even promised* to appoint [Incitatus] Consul, a promise that he would certainly have carried out if he had lived longer.[47]

It is hard to decide whether this is genuine insanity, an example of Caligula's quirky humour, a daft prank against the Senate, or perhaps a form of satire along the lines of, 'Even my horse could do better than you lot. I ought to make him Consul!'

Gaius' lavish expenditure was unsustainable, and when the money ran out, so did his popularity. To balance the books, he resorted to confiscation, extortion and tax rises. Novel

---

46   Suetonius, *Gaius* 55.3, tr. Kershaw, S. (my emphasis).
47   Dio 59.14.7, tr. Cary. E., op. cit. (again, my emphasis).

measures included opening a brothel in his palace in which married women and free-born youths were available, as were loans to the customers at appropriate rates of interest, and the auction of survivors of gladiatorial combats at enormous prices. Suetonius tells 'a well-known story' of Aponius Saturninus, who nodded off at the sale, only for Gaius to tell the auctioneer to take the snoozing Senator's nods for bids, and sell him thirteen gladiators for nine million *sestertii*.

Unsurprisingly, Caligula's relations with the Senate deteriorated. In September 39 he removed both Consuls from office for failing to proclaim a thanksgiving for his birthday. Yet for the Senate to disrespect him was highly risky: he forced fathers to watch their sons' executions; he deliberately prolonged the sufferings of his victims, instructing the executioners to 'Make him *feel* that he is dying';[48] and frequently quoted the line from L. Attius' tragedy *Atreus*: 'Let them hate me, so long as they fear me.'[49]

People did both, but in 37 he was confronted by a truly dangerous conspiracy when Cn. Cornelius Lentulus Gaetulicus, commander of the Upper Rhine army, apparently plotted to set up M. Aemilius Lepidus, a member of the old republican nobility and the ex-husband of Gaius' sister Drusilla, in his place. The executions of Gaetulicus and Lepidus followed, and Caligula's two surviving sisters, Julia Agrippina and Julia Livilla, who were suspected of complicity, were exiled.

Events in the foreign policy arena do not figure very prominently in our sources, although we do have some interesting information concerning Caligula's relationship with the Jews. He appointed his friend Herod Agrippa I, the grandson of Herod the Great (he is called Herod in the *Acts of the Apostles* but Agrippa on his coins), as king of the substantially Jewish area of Galilee and Peraea. Yet Agrippa's zealous Judaism did little to mollify the discord between the Emperor and his Jewish

---

48   Suetonius, *Gaius* 30.1.
49   '*Oderint dum metuant*': Suetonius, *Gaius* 30.1. Cicero, *de Officiis* 1.28; *Tragicorum Romanorum Fragmenta*, no. 203.

subjects. The Prefect of Egypt, A. Avillius Flaccus, became worried about his personal safety under Gaius' regime, and, egged on by a Greek anti-Semitic faction in Alexandria, presided over a pogrom there in 38. The flashpoint occurred when Agrippa tried to transit through Alexandria in secret on his way from Rome to Judaea, but was discovered. Flaccus suspected that Agrippa was there to undermine him, and far from trying to prevent the anti-Jewish mob violence that ensued, he actively encouraged it. Many Jews were rounded up in the theatre where members of the Jewish Council were flogged and some Jewish women were forced to eat pork. Possibly prompted by complaints from Agrippa, Gaius had Flaccus arrested, replaced and executed, but he spurned the delegations sent to Rome by both the Jewish and the Greek factions, and the conflict was still unresolved when he died.

With the Alexandrian controversy still raging, Gaius moved to Gaul in the winter of 39/40. Having installed the future emperor Galba as commander in Germania Superior, probably raised two new legions (XV *Primigenia* and XXII *Primigenia*), and made forays into Germany, Gaius received 'the surrender of Adminius, son of Cunobelinus King of the Britons, who had been expelled by his father and had deserted to the Romans with a tiny force'.[50] This turned his thoughts towards Britain, but what our sources say happened next is unbelievably bizarre:

> He drew up a battle line on the shore of the Ocean, and having deployed ballistas and other artillery, [. . .] suddenly gave the order to his soldiers to gather up sea-shells and fill their helmets and the folds of their clothes, calling them 'spoils from the Ocean, debts to the Capitol and Palatine'.[51]

Dio trots out a similar version:

---

50   Suetonius, *Gaius* 44.2, tr. Kershaw, S.
51   Ibid 46.

He gave the soldiers the signal as for battle [. . .] Then suddenly he ordered them to pick up sea-shells [. . .] He took back the shells to Rome, in order to exhibit his booty there as well.[52]

Yet Tacitus implies that Gaius was serious about invading Britain, and the apparently weird commands on the shore might not be quite as crazy as the sources would have us believe.[53] It is, for example, possible that Suetonius' sea-shells (*conchae*) originate from a military technical term for 'mobile shelters used in siege-assaults' (*musculi*), which is also the word for 'mussels'. Hence, perhaps, the order to 'Pick up the *musculi*!' gets distorted to 'Pick up the *conchae*!' Whatever the reason for aborting the mission, Gaius' spin doctors presented Britain as having been conquered: when Adminius came to render homage, Gaius simply acted 'as if the whole island had surrendered to him'.[54] Back in Rome he was ridiculed for taking the titles Germanicus and Britannicus: because of his well-known adulteries he was jokingly said to have 'subdued/taken in hand' (a sexual double entendre) every/the whole of *Keltike* (= Celtic woman/the Celtic lands) and *Bretannike* (= British woman/ Britain).[55]

Bawdy ridicule was easy enough to handle, but Caligula also managed to alienate the Praetorian Guard so badly that three tribunes (Cassius Chaerea, Cornelius Sabinus and Papinius), the Prefect M. Arrecinus Clemens, the Senators M. Annius Vinicianus, M. Valerius Asiaticus, Cluvius Rufus and L. Nonius

---

52   Dio 59.25.1–3, tr. Cary. E., op. cit.
53   See, e.g., Bicknell, P., 'The Emperor Gaius' Military Activities in AD 40', *Historia* 17 (1968), 496–505; Davies, R. W., 'The Abortive Invasion of Britain by Gaius', *Historia* 15 (1966), pp. 124–28; Philips, E. J., 'The Emperor Gaius' Abortive Invasion of Britain', *Historia* 19 (1970), pp. 369–74; Barrett, A. A., op. cit. pp. 125–39; Woods, D., 'Caligula's Seashells', *Greece and Rome* 47 (2000), 80–87.
54   Suetonius, *Gaius* 44.
55   Dio 59.25.5a. For the sexual overtones of *kheiro* (= 'I take in hand/subdue') see Henderson, J., *The Maculate Muse: Obscene Language in Attic Comedy*, Oxford: Oxford University Press, 1991, p. 27.

Asprenas, and Gaius' powerful freedman Callistus, hatched a plot to murder him. They struck on 24 January 41 at around the seventh or ninth hour. Despite suffering from an upset stomach caused by overindulgence, Caligula had been attending the Palatine Games. Josephus' account, which may include eyewitness testimony from Cluvius Rufus, tells how Caligula was exiting through a narrow passageway when his neck was slashed from behind by Chaerea. Sabinus stabbed him in the chest, and he was finished off by the other conspirators, with Aquila delivering the final blow. Suetonius knew of two accounts, one of which started with him having his jawbone shattered and ended with sword thrusts to his genitals, and Dio talks of the conspirators eating his flesh. But the end result was the same – Caligula was not a god; he had become the sacrificial victim.

The conspirators completed the job with the brutal killings of Gaius' wife Caesonia and daughter Drusilla. But if all this was designed to terminate the dynasty and restore the Republic it failed dismally, since the Praetorian Guard had too great a vested interest in maintaining the continuity of the Principate. Two clear messages had emerged for Emperors and their would-be opponents: (1) any future plot against an Emperor would have to involve the Praetorian Guard, and (2) the only way an Emperor could give up his powers was by giving up his life.

5

The Scholar and the Artist:
Claudius (41–54) and Nero (54–68)

Our bodies grow slowly, but are quickly destroyed [. . .] the sweetness of indolence comes over us, and in the end we love the laziness we once loathed.

Tacitus, *Agricola* 3.1[1]

The Man Behind the Curtains

Gaius' assassination was followed by a brief and bizarre power struggle. His loyal German bodyguards cut down several of the assassins and caused considerable collateral damage; the Senate thought about restoring the Republic, maybe using the urban cohorts; the Roman people, though, gathered in the Forum and chanted that they would not tolerate a return to Senatorial rule; and the Praetorian Guard, who knew that the restoration of the Republic would threaten their lucrative, cushy city-based existence, realized that they needed an alternative to Caligula, and needed him fast. During their rampage through the imperial palace, they stumbled upon Caligula's uncle, Claudius, hiding behind some curtains:

> As he cowered there, a common soldier, who was prowling about at random, saw his feet, and intending to ask him who he was, pulled him out and recognized him; and

---

1   Tr. Kershaw, S.

when Claudius fell at his feet in terror, he hailed him as Emperor.[2]

This account, in which the man with no experience of public life whatsoever was randomly elevated to power entirely against his will, became Claudius' authorized version. Other narratives make the Praetorians much more focused, actively seeking out Claudius, and there is a remote possibility Claudius was actively involved in planning his nephew's demise: the argument goes that if Claudius was involved in the assassination, the absence of evidence is clear proof of it.[3]

The initial few hours after Caligula's murder were vital ones for the survival of both Claudius and the Principate. He was endorsed by the Praetorian Guard on the same day, and the Senate realized they were powerless when the *Praefectus Urbis* defected to the Praetorian Guard with his cohorts, doubtless motivated by Claudius' enormous *donativum*. So the Senate acquiesced, and the following day, 25 January 41, Claudius was invested with all the powers of the *Princeps*, becoming Tiberius Claudius Caesar Augustus Germanicus. Legally speaking, Claudius had no right to be called 'Caesar', but the word was making a transition from a family name to a title that reaches into the modern era as 'Kaiser', 'Tsar' and possibly 'Shah'.

The new Caesar had been born at Lugdunum (modern Lyons) on 1 August 10 BCE, but he had hardly been regarded as the golden boy of the Julio-Claudian dynasty. Apparently his mother, Antonia Minor, frequently referred to him as 'a monster of a man, not finished by Nature, but only begun',[4] and Suetonius described him as

tall but not slender, with an attractive face, becoming white hair, and a full neck. But when he walked, his weak knees

---

2   Suetonius, *Claudius* 10.2, tr. Rolfe, J. C., op. cit.
3   See Levick, B., *Claudius*, New Haven: Yale University Press, 1990, pp. 33–39.
4   Suetonius, *Claudius* 3.2, tr. Kershaw, S.

gave way under him and he had many disagreeable traits [. . .]
he would foam at the mouth and trickle at the nose; he stam-
mered and his head was very shaky at all times.[5]

This may be because he suffered from cerebral palsy, which
his family simply found embarrassing: he remained under
guardianship, like a woman, even after he had come of age, was
kept out of public view, was not given magistracies, and
remained an Equestrian until Caligula finally decided to share
the consulship with him in 37. He was the butt of insults from
relatives who equated his physical disabilities with mental ones,
despite the fact that he became a scholar of considerable talent
and composed numerous learned works in Greek and Latin
(none of which survive) and could read Etruscan. Yet the *tabula
Siarensis* and the *Senatus Consultum de Pisone patre*, which lavish
great acclaim on his brother Germanicus' family, barely
mentioned Claudius, and alongside Tacitus' account of the Piso
affair in Tiberius' reign,[6] this shows just how low his position
in the imperial family was:

> Messalinus [proposed] that Tiberius, Augusta, Antonia, Agrip-
> pina and Drusus ought to be publicly thanked for having
> avenged Germanicus. He omitted all mention of Claudius.
> Thereupon he was pointedly asked by Lucius Asprenas before
> the Senate, whether the omission had been intentional, and it
> was only then that the name of Claudius was added [. . .]
> Clearly, the very last man marked out for empire by public
> opinion, expectation and general respect was he whom fortune
> was holding in reserve as the emperor of the future.[7]

And yet Claudius came unscathed through the first twenty-
four hours of his Principate. However, his not unreasonable

---

5   Ibid 30, tr. Rolfe, J. C., op. cit.
6   See above, p. 75.
7   Tacitus, *Annals* 3.18.4, tr. Church, A. J. and Brodribb, W. J., *The History of
Tacitus Translated into English*, Cambridge and London: Macmillan, 1864.

insecurity made him take a very hard line against any threats, real or imagined, and his first decade in power saw the execution or enforced suicide of more high-ranking Romans than under any other first-century Emperor. First on his list were Caligula's murderer Cassius Chaerea, Julius Lupus, who had killed Caesonia and Drusilla, and Sabinus, who was allowed to go free, but committed suicide anyway.

On the other hand, Claudius tried hard to rectify 'the unjust acts performed by Gaius and by others at his instigation':[8] free practice of Judaism was confirmed; order was restored in Alexandria; treason trials were abolished; there was an amnesty for Senators implicated in Gaius' death; criminal records were burned; and Caligula's stockpile of poisons was destroyed, causing an environmental disaster in the River Tiber. Even so, several attempts were made on his life: Cn. Nonius was discovered with a dagger at a public audience; Claudius was attacked with a hunting knife outside the Temple of Mars; and in 42 L. Arruntius Camillus Scribonianus orchestrated a short-lived and unsuccessful rebellion in Dalmatia. There were still Senators who clung to the old Republican ideals, but Republicanism had little support elsewhere, and anyway, the army backed the Emperor.

Claudius the Conqueror

The perfect way for Claudius to cement his bond with the army was conquest. So despite, or indeed because of, having no military experience, and no clear exit strategy, Claudius invaded Britain. However bizarrely Caligula might have behaved, he had effectively put all the preparations in place, and there was also a ready-made pretext in the fact that the Catuvellauni, under Caratacus and Togodumnus, were threatening Britain's status as a stable and profitable neighbour. They had misjudged how far they could go without provoking Rome. In or before 43,

---

8   Dio, 60.5.1, tr, Cary, E., op.cit.

a certain Berikos [i.e., Verica] who had been driven out from the island as a result of civil war persuaded Claudius to send a force there.[9]

Claudius was up for it:

He sought the honour of a real triumph, and chose Britain as the best field in which to seek this, for no one had attempted an invasion since the time of Julius Caesar and the island at this time was in a turmoil.[10]

The expedition would tick a number of important boxes for Claudius: he needed military kudos to bring him both respect and safety; the economic *pretium victoriae* (= 'reward of victory') was attractive; iron ore and lead (which indicated silver) were known to be present; the Druids had now moved their head-quarters to Mona (modern Anglesey), but could conceivably use their influence to stir up trouble in Gaul; and there was the seductive prospect for a practising historian literally to influence the course of history.

The expeditionary force was formidable, well balanced, and led by highly experienced commanders. Aulus Plautius and *Legio* IX *Hispana* had cut their teeth in the tough frontier territory of the Danube, and his officers T. Flavius Vespasianus ('Vespasian'), Vespasian's elder brother Flavius Sabinus and Cn. Hosidius Geta were first-rate soldiers. The three other legions that are assumed to have made up the invasion force were *Legiones* II *Augusta*, XIIII *Gemina* and XX (later entitled *Valeria Victrix*). But legions frequently operated in '*vexillationes*' (detachments) rather than at full strength, and we know that a centurion of *Legio* VIII *Augusta* also won honours in the campaign, so part of that legion may also have been involved.

9   Dio 60.19.1, tr. in Mann, J. C. and Penman, R. G. (eds.), op. cit. Dio is writing in Greek – the Greek 'b' was coming to be pronounced 'v'.
10   Suetonius, *Claudius* 17.1, tr. in Mann, J. C. and Penman, R. G. (eds.), op. cit.

This makes calculating the numbers difficult, especially since the legionaries were augmented by auxiliaries, who provided the strong cavalry contingent that Caesar had lacked, but a total of 40 000 men is the most quoted figure.

Even so, the invasion was almost aborted. The troops mutinied because they feared campaigning outside the limits of the world they knew, and it took Claudius' imperial freedman Narcissus to bring them into line. However, the delayed departure had unintended benefits:

> [The Romans] were sent over in three divisions [. . .] When they reached the island they found no one to oppose them. On the strength of the reports they received the Britons had concluded that they were not coming and had not assembled to meet them.[11]

The landing places are not known for certain: there are Claudian military features at Richborough (Ruptiae), which has a good enclosed harbour, and Fishbourne Harbour, in the territory of the pro-Roman Atrebates, from where Verica fled, may also have been used (see Map 2).

Once on the island, Plautius forged ahead. Having located and defeated Caratacus and Togodumnus, he won over a section of the Dobunni and continued his advance to 'a river which the barbarians thought the Romans would be unable to cross without a bridge',[12] – either the Medway or the Thames. The Britons were over-optimistic: Plautius had an auxiliary unit of 'Celts' who were specially trained in swimming over rivers, although the fact that the battle lasted two days shows that the Britons resisted stoutly. Dio then describes another river crossing close to what is now central London, where Plautius' 'Celts' again swam across whilst the legionaries crossed by a bridge further upstream. After that the Roman advance ground to a halt in the

---

11   Dio 60.19.4–5, tr. in Mann, J. C. and Penman, R. G. (eds.), op. cit.
12   Ibid. 60.19.5 ff.

wooded territory of the vale of St Albans where they suffered quite severe losses in guerrilla action, although Togodumnus was also killed.

Plautius now withdrew south of the Thames and sent for Claudius:

> He had been instructed to do this if he met any particularly strong opposition, and indeed considerable equipment, including elephants, had already been assembled as reinforcements.[13]

Claudius arrived in Britain in August.

> Taking over the command [. . .] he crossed the river and engaged the barbarians who had assembled to oppose him; he defeated them, and captured Camulodunum [modern Colchester], the capital of Cunobelinus.[14]

When Claudius accepted the surrender of numerous British tribes it was a remarkable moment: after just sixteen days in Britain the person nobody had thought fit to rule Rome had outdone Gaius, Augustus and Caesar. Claudius celebrated a spectacular triumph, presiding over a show in the Campus Martius representing the capture of a town and the surrender of the British kings. He extended Rome's city boundary, as those who had extended the Empire were entitled to do. The Senate voted him the title Britannicus. Coins depicted a triumphal arch inscribed *DE BRITANN(IS)* = '(Commemorating victory) over the Britons', supporting a statue of the Emperor on horseback between two trophies. A real arch in Rome was

> Set up by the Senate and People of Rome because he received the formal submission of eleven Kings of the Britons,

---

13   Ibid. 60.21.1–2.
14   Ibid. 60.21.4.

overcome without any loss, and because he was the first to bring barbarian peoples across the Ocean under the sway of the Roman people.[15]

In the provinces a cult of Victoria Britannica was established in Corinth, and a relief panel on the Sebasteion at Aphrodisias graphically illustrated the conquest: Claudius, heroically nude apart from his helmet, cloak, sword-belt and scabbard, delivers the *coup de grâce* to a slumped woman wearing a tunic with one bare breast, modelled on an Amazon, but personifying Britain.

Claudius never commanded the army in person again, although the Empire was significantly enlarged during his Principate. The client kingdom of Mauretania was organized into two provinces (Mauretania Tingitania and Caesariensis); Lycia, Thrace and Noricum were likewise annexed and provincialized; when Herod Agrippa I died, his kingdom reverted to direct Roman rule; there was fighting along the Rhine and Danube frontiers, in the Crimea and in Armenia; and by the end of his reign, Claudius had been hailed as Imperator a record twenty-seven times.

Messalina and the Freedmen

If love is a battlefield, Claudius was seldom hailed as Imperator there. By his accession he had been unsuccessfully betrothed twice, first to Aemilia Lepida, daughter of the younger Julia, only for the engagement to be broken off when her parents fell into disfavour, then to Livia Medullina, who died on the day of their wedding. When he finally married Plautia Urgulanilla it was not a success. She was divorced for adultery and suspicion of murder, and their son, Claudius Drusus, choked to death on a pear he had thrown into the air and caught in his mouth.

---

15   *CIL* 6. 920 = *ILS* 216 (restored), Capitoline Museum, Rome. Tr. Dudley, D. R., *Urbs Roma. A Sourcebook of Classical Texts on the City and its Monuments*, London: Phaidon, 1967.

Claudius then wed Aelia Paetina, but divorced her in order to marry a woman over thirty years his junior: Valeria Messalina.

Messalina bore Claudius a daughter, Octavia, in 39, and a son, Ti. Claudius Germanicus, later renamed Britannicus, in 41. Messalina's standing is indicated by her appearance on the obverse of coins, where you would expect to see the Emperor, and, confident in her position as mother of the heir apparent, she started eliminating her rivals. Caligula's sister Julia Livilla was an early victim, as was Appius Silanus, who was recalled from Spain to marry Messalina's mother, only to be executed for trying to murder the Emperor. Rumour had it, though, that his real 'crime' was to have spurned Messalina's advances.

Recently, attempts have been made to rehabilitate Messalina as an astute player of court politics who used sex as a weapon, but in the ancient sources she is a shameless nymphomaniac, voraciously seducing everyone from Senators to actors and famously beating a celebrity prostitute in a sex contest, while Claudius either remained ignorant or turned a blind eye:

> [In] her empty reserved cell, naked, with gilded
> nipples, she plied her trade, under the name of 'The Wolf-
> Girl' [. . .]
> She would greet each client sweetly, demand cash payment,
> and absorb all their battering – without ever getting up.
> Too soon the brothel-keeper dismissed his girls:
> *she* stayed right till the end, always the last to go,
> then trailed away sadly, still with burning, rigid vulva,
> exhausted by men, yet a long way from satisfied.[16]

But Messalina pushed things too far. In October 48, while Claudius was at Ostia, for reasons that remain unclear, she and her lover C. Silius went through a wedding ceremony. While

---

16   Juvenal, *Satire* 6.122 ff., tr. Green, P., in *Juvenal: The Sixteen Satires, Translated with an Introduction and Notes by Peter Green*, London: Penguin Classics, 3rd edn., 1998.

Claudius was asking, 'Am I still Emperor?', Narcissus stepped in. The *Princeps* was spirited away to safety; Silius and Messalina were executed.

The Messalina issue highlights the criticism against Claudius that he was dominated by women and ex-slaves. One notable feature of the Principate in general is the pervasive influence of the imperial women, yet at the same time, anyone, female or male, with family or marriage ties to the imperial family was a potential threat to the Emperor, and one common reaction was for him to turn to freed slaves on whose loyalty and expertise he could rely. This, though, alienated Rome's traditional political elite, who detested having to kowtow to people who were their social inferiors. In Claudius' government Narcissus the Chief Secretary, Pallas the Financial Secretary and Callistus the Secretary of Petitions were not only exceptionally powerful and wealthy, but also highly competent, yet our sources, who are often from the Senatorial class, frequently blame them (or Messalina) for negative things that were probably Claudius' fault rather than theirs.

Claudius and the Establishment

Despite Claudius scrupulously observing all its most hallowed protocols, the Senate never warmed to him. The aristocratic tradition excoriated his legal record as meddling, biased, stupid, capricious and just plain vicious, not to mention the fact that he heard sensitive cases behind closed doors. A satirical work attributed to Seneca the Younger, entitled *The Apocolocyntosis ('Pumpkinification') of the Divine Claudius*, purports to describe Claudius' fate after death and ends with a courtroom drama in which Claudius is condemned to rattle dice for ever in a box with no bottom and have to hunt for the dice, which for ever slipped from his fingers (he was a notorious gambler), before being made into a faceless law-clerk. The Establishment also reacted negatively to his generous grants of Roman citizenship, for example the founding of numerous *coloniae* such as Colonia

Agrippina (modern Cologne), the wholesale grant of citizenship to the Alpine Anauni tribe, and the induction of provincials into the Senate. The Princeps' speech, in which he argues for the inclusion of various 'long-haired' Gauls (from Gallia Comata) into the Senate on the basis of Rome's cosmopolitan history and melting-pot culture, is creatively reconstructed by Tacitus and transcribed verbatim on 'the Lyons Tablet', a fine large bronze inscription found in Claudius' birthplace.[17]

The sources are similarly sniffy about Claudius' building projects – 'he carried out large and necessary works, rather than numerous ones'.[18] But they were important. He completed the two aqueducts, the 70-kilometre-long Aqua Claudia and the 87-kilometre-long Anio Novus, which Caligula had begun in 52. A land-reclamation project that involved draining the Fucine Lake using a tunnel through *Monte Salviano* employed 30 000 men for eleven years, and was inaugurated with a mock sea-battle involving 19 000 prisoners, who famously used the phrase, 'Hail Emperor, those about to die salute you!'[19] Perhaps the most important civil engineering project was the construction of a new deep-water harbour, known as Portus, at the mouth of the Tiber, which allowed large grain ships to dock much closer to Rome.

Agrippina the Younger, a Mushroom and a Pumpkin

Back on the domestic front, despite swearing that he would never re-marry after Messalina's execution, Claudius, perhaps persuaded by Pallas, did take a new bride. He was now fifty-eight, and his choice again fell on a younger woman, Caligula's sister Agrippina the Younger, who had allegedly attracted her uncle by behaving in an inappropriate and entirely un-niece-like way. Such a marriage was illegal under Roman law, but the

---

17 *CIL* 13.1668 = *ILS* 212; Tacitus, *Annals* 11.23–25.
18 Suetonius, *Claudius* 20.1, tr. Kershaw, S.
19 *'Have imperator, morituri te salutant!'* Suetonius, *Claudius* 21.6. Gladiators did not shout this before they fought.

persuasive powers of one L. Vitellius convinced the Senate that incest was best for Rome.

Tacitus was outraged:

> From this moment the country was transformed. Complete obedience was accorded to a woman [. . .] this was a rigorous, almost masculine despotism.[20]

Agrippina had the incumbent Praetorian Prefects replaced with the more malleable Sextus Afranius Burrus; she took the title 'Augusta'; she appeared independently from Claudius on coins; she greeted foreign embassies; and she wore a gold-embroidered military cloak at official functions. She was ragingly ambitious, particularly when it came to her son by her previous husband, the noble but brutal Cn. Domitius Aheno-barbus, who had died when the child was three. The boy was called L. Domitius Ahenobarbus. At thirteen he was a crucial three years older than Claudius' son Britannicus, and on 25 February 50, after leverage from Agrippina and Pallas (who were rumoured to be lovers), Claudius adopted him as his son. His contemporaries then knew him as Nero Claudius Drusus Germanicus Caesar; we just call him Nero.

Nero quickly supplanted Germanicus, and in 53 he married Claudius' daughter Claudia Octavia. He didn't really like her, but the union clearly made him the heir apparent. Quite why Claudius preferred Nero to his natural son remains a mystery.

Timing now became everything for Agrippina. If Britannicus reached manhood, as he would in February 55, he could still legally succeed Claudius. So, in October 54, she decided to eliminate her husband. The rather conflicting ancient accounts involve Agrippina, a poisoner called Locusta, the eunuch food-taster Halotus, and a particularly fine mushroom. The outcome was either: (1) Claudius' swift-ish painful death, or (2) an initial

---

20   Tacitus, *Annals* 12.7.5, tr. Grant, M., op. cit.

bout of diarrhoea or vomiting that necessitated a second dose administered through a syringe, or on a feather that Claudius was using to help himself vomit. Some modern authorities think that Claudius died a natural death, although the timing of it is extremely suspicious.

The late Emperor was swiftly deified. Out in the provinces, Claudius the god appears on Aphrodisias' Sebasteion, striding forward in a divine epiphany, drapery billowing around his head, receiving a cornucopia and a ship's steering oar, attributes appropriate to his role as guarantor of the prosperity of land and sea. In Nero's tutor Seneca's *Apocolocyntosis*, though, the divine Augustus rails against the idea of a man with physical disabilities and a speech impediment becoming a god:

> Is this the man you now wish to make a god? Look at his body, born when the gods were in a rage. In short, let him utter three words in quick succession and he can take me as his slave. Who will worship this man as a god? Who will believe in him?[21]

Nero's Five Golden Years

Nero's accession was greeted with delight. Born at Antium on 15 December 37 amid stories of a miraculous childhood, Augustus' great-great-grandson, whose name means 'strong and valiant' in the Sabine language, was sixteen years old. Suetonius says that he was of average height and had a pustular and malodorous body, light blond hair, pretty rather than handsome features, dullish blue eyes, a squat neck, protuberant belly and spindly legs, none of which are prominent on his official portraiture.

He was escorted into the praetorian camp by the *Praefectus Praetorio* Burrus, and the Senate granted him the requisite

---

21 Seneca, *Apocolocyntosis* 11.3, tr. Eden, P. T., in *Seneca: Apocolocyntosis*, Cambridge: Cambridge University Press, 1984.

powers. The ancient tradition presents the first five years of his Principate as a Golden Age, the *Quinquennium Neronis*. Seneca and Burrus joined forces in 'educating' him in philosophy, rhetoric and how to run the Empire. They indulged their student up to a point, while at the same time trying to stymie his pushy mother's attempts to become the power behind the throne. For his part, Nero said he would govern in accordance with Augustan precedent, made the standard ploy of renouncing the abuses of the previous regime, and promised to share the responsibilities of government with the Senate, placing the legend *EX S C* (= 'In Accordance with a Senatorial Decree') on his coins. However, Agrippina's influence also comes through in the official iconography: on coins minted in December 54 her head faces Nero's on the obverse, and at Aphrodisias there is a sculpture that depicts her decked out with a cornucopia – symbol of Fortune and Plenty – crowning a military-looking Nero with a laurel wreath in a reference to her role in his accession. Even so, Agrippina didn't have everything her own way: when she started showing sympathy for Claudius' son Britannicus, he ended up poisoned.

Nero's wife Claudia Octavia turned out to be too much of a shrinking violet. More to his taste was Poppaea Sabina, born in Pompeii in 30 and famous for her charm, beauty, wit and fondness for daily milk baths, but currently involved with, and possibly married to, Nero's fellow party-animal M. Salvius Otho. Our five conflicting accounts of the Nero-Otho-Poppaea love triangle say either that Otho was protecting Poppaea in a bogus marriage until Nero could dump Octavia and marry her instead, or that although Otho and Poppaea were properly married, Nero simply took Poppaea and sent Otho off to govern Lusitania in 58. Poppaea may have used the splendidly opulent Villa Oplontis on the Bay of Naples as a seaside residence.

Regardless of who seduced whom, Poppaea focused on becoming Nero's wife and Empress of Rome. As Nero's desire for self-gratification increased, along with his resentment of anyone who interfered (or might interfere) with it, so did Poppaea's influence with him. Agrippina's desire to maintain her hold over her son led her to have sex with him, but Poppaea was simply more alluring. His mother had to be removed, so Nero tried to engineer an 'accident' by deploying a collapsible ship to drown her in the Bay of Naples. Although the resilient woman survived and swam ashore, she knew the game was up. Nero's response to her message that she was well was to send a detachment of sailors under Anicetus, who commanded the fleet at Misenum, to finish the job. She famously exposed her stomach and said, 'Strike this, Anicetus, strike here, for this bore Nero.' He did.²²

Just after Nero returned to Rome following Agrippina's murder there was a major riot in the amphitheatre at Pompeii between the locals and the inhabitants of Nuceria, which resulted in a ten-year ban on shows in that arena. A fresco depicting the event was found in the house of Actius Anicetius (I.iii.23), and elsewhere graffiti proudly boasts,

Campanians, in our victory you perished with the Nucerians.²³

The Transgressive Emperor

Agrippina's termination also terminated Nero's 'Golden Age'. In 62 a *maiestas* (treason) charge was admitted for the first time, and when Burrus died that year too, he was succeeded as *Praefectus Praetorio* by Ofonius Tigellinus, a latter-day Sejanus who egged Nero on to the perpetration of crime and the gratification of lust. Seneca wisely went into retirement, while Nero divorced Claudia Octavia and then had her banished, murdered and beheaded. Poppaea, who by now was pregnant, got her heart's desire and married Nero. Their daughter, Claudia

---

22   Dio 62.113.5, tr, Kershaw, S.
23   *CIL* IV 1293 = ILS 6443a, tr. in Cooley, A. and M. G. L., *Pompeii: A Sourcebook*, London: Routledge, 2004. Riot: Tacitus, *Annals* 14.17. See also *CIL* IV 3340.143 and 3340.144.

Augusta, was born in January of 41, but sadly, the child died four months later, and Poppaea was pregnant again when Nero allegedly kicked her to death. Nero then married Statilia Messalina.

Criminality and perversion were one thing, but Nero was guilty of far worse in Roman eyes: he was obsessed with music, poetry, acting, chariot racing and Greek athletics. This weighed more heavily in the court of public opinion even than his playing the role of bride in weddings with male partners.[24] Agrippina's death allowed him to indulge his passion for art and literature. Despite some crushing insecurities, he regarded himself as a virtuoso, but unfortunately he simply had delusions of adequacy. He performed at a competent amateur level, with a voice that was described as 'slight and husky', and Suetonius, who had seen his notebooks,[25] is less than complimentary about his poetry, even though Nero won every competition that he entered. Anyone not suitably enthusiastic about one of his performances faced execution, although the future Emperor Vespasian did get away with either leaving the room or falling asleep.

The bottom line was that Nero was totally unsuited to being Emperor of Rome. Whilst Seneca and Burrus had been on the scene everything ran as smoothly as it needed to, Nero devoted himself to his art, and they tried to keep his performances out of the public domain. Yet even so there were tales of him roaming the streets in disguise at night, terrorizing people and then executing those who dared to defend themselves, on the grounds that they had disrespected the Emperor. But now Nero made his public debut in the Greek city of Naples in 64, and followed this up the next year by taking to the stage in Rome, naturally making sure that a hired claque of 5 000 supporters gave him a rousing reception.

24   See, e.g., Tacitus, *Annals* 15.37; Suetonius, *Nero* 29; Dio 62.28.2f., 63.13; Williams, C. A., op. cit., Appendix 2: Marriage between Males, pp. 279 ff.
25   Suetonius, *Nero* 52.

Problems in the West and the East: Boudicca, Armenia and Judaea

In the wider Empire, Nero faced continuous military and diplomatic difficulties, primarily in Britain, Parthia and Armenia, and Judaea. Here the Romans were learning the hard way that administration was more difficult than conquest, and that winning hearts and minds was a much more complex affair than winning battles.

Since Claudius' invasion, Britain had been undergoing a period of both conquest and consolidation: the Fosse Way had been established, forming a crucial SW–NE line of communication (see Map 2); cities like Verulamium (modern St Albans) and Londinium (modern London) were growing; insurgency by Caratacus in Wales had come to an end when Queen Cartimandua of the Brigantes, a formidable confederation that stretched across much of modern Yorkshire and Lancashire and into the Scottish Lowlands, handed him over, and the fifth governor, C. Suetonius Paulinus, was using *Legiones* XIV *Gemina* and XX to eradicate the Druidism on Mona. But then disaster struck.

Prasutagus, king of the Iceni, located chiefly in modern Norfolk, had died without a son and had left half of his kingdom to Nero and half to his daughters. But such an arrangement was not possible under Roman law, and Prasutagus' wishes were not respected:

As if they were war booty his kingdom was devastated by centurions and his household by slaves, [...] To begin with, his wife Boudicca[26] was whipped and his daughters raped. Various Icenian nobles were forcibly deprived of their

---

26   I have opted for the spelling Boudicca. Boadicea probably originates from a misprint. Tacitus most likely spelled her name as it is used here. However, there is evidence that the Britons called her Boudica, pronounced 'BowDEEkah', rhyming 'bow' with 'low'. The Greek sources call her Buduika. See Jackson, K., 'Queen Boudicca?', *Britannia* 10 (1979) p. 255; Williams, C. D., *Boudica and Her Stories: Narrative Transformations of a Warrior Queen,* Newark: University of Delaware Press, 2009, pp. 44 ff.

ancestral estates [. . .] and the king's relatives were treated like slaves.[27]

This maltreatment sparked off a rebellion that spread to the Trinovantes[28] of Essex, similarly treated as 'prisoners and slaves', whose specific grievances centred on the establishment of the imperial cult in the new colony at Camulodunum, which cost them a fortune to administer. To make matters worse, to pay for this kind of thing, the Britons had accepted cash donations from Claudius, and taken on loans from speculators like Seneca, who had lent the islanders forty million *sestertii* at interest. Decianus Catus, the *procurator* of the island, now demanded that the donations be returned and Seneca called in his loan.

In Boudicca the ancient historians found a perfect foil to Nero. They give her all the virtues that Nero lacked, spiced up with a little barbarous eroticism:

> [She] had uncommon intelligence for a woman [. . .] She was very tall and grim; her gaze was penetrating and her voice was harsh; she grew her long auburn hair to the hips and wore a large golden torque and a voluminous patterned cloak with a thick plaid fastened over it.[29]

Her rebel army, about 120 000 strong, attacked, captured and razed Camulodunum, which was practically defenceless. A vexillation of *Legio* IX *Hispana*, commanded by Quintus Petillius Cerialis Caesius Rufus, attempted to relieve the town but was ambushed and routed, perhaps with losses of 2 000 men,[30] although he himself escaped. Suetonius Paulinus responded

---

27 Tacitus, *Annals* 14.31, tr. Kershaw, S.
28 The spelling of the tribal name varies in the ancient sources between Trinobantes and Trinovantes. Philology suggests Trinovantes is closer to the actual form current in Britain.
29 Dio 62.2.2–4, tr. in Mann, J. C. and Penman, R. G. (eds.), op. cit.
30 Tacitus, *Annals* 14.32, says he lost the entire infantry force of his legion.

promptly. *Legiones* XIV *Gemina* and XX started back from Mona, while he went ahead with his cavalry to try to defend Londinium. He also sent for *Legio* II *Augusta* from Isca (modern Exeter), but their *legatus* was in Gaul and Poenius Postumus, the *praefectus castrorum*, refused to march.

Suetonius Paulinus quickly realized that he did not have the resources to defend Londinium, so he decided to sacrifice the city to save the province and headed back north to rejoin his legions. Terrible massacres, which cost tens of thousands of lives, took place at Londinium and Verulamium, where Boudicca's warriors committed some stomach-churning atrocities:

> They hung up naked the noblest and best-looking women.
> They cut off their breasts and stitched them to their mouths,
> so that the women seemed to be eating them, and after this
> they impaled them on sharp stakes run right up the body.[31]

Reunited with his infantry, Suetonius could only deploy around 10 000 men against a vastly superior number of Britons, but even so he knew it was vital to fight early, and he prudently selected a site somewhere between Mancetter and St Albans where the Roman flanks and the rear were protected by woods and hills. Boudicca harangued her warriors, contrasting her hard, manly Britons with the soft, effeminate Romans ruled by Nero: they live in luxury, she said, drink unmixed wine, anoint themselves with oil, take warm baths, and sleep with lads, and ones who are past their prime at that. While Nero may have the name of 'man', she scoffed, 'he is in fact a woman, and the evidence for this is that he sings and plays the lyre'.[32] The Britons were so confident that they brought their wives along to see the victory, installing them in carts at the edge of the battlefield.

But the British optimism was sadly misplaced. The Romans stood their ground, launched their *pila* at the onrushing enemy,

---

31 Dio 62.7.2, tr. in Mann, J. C. and Penman, R. G. (eds.), op. cit.
32 Dio 62.6.3, tr. Williams, C. A., op. cit., 154.

then surged forward and demolished all serious resistance. The Britons were impeded by the ring of wagons, and the Romans spared neither the women nor the baggage animals:

> It was a glorious victory, comparable with bygone triumphs. According to one report almost 80 000 Britons fell [. . .] Boudicca poisoned herself.[33]

Suetonius Paulinus embarked on a policy of reprisals so savage that it caused friction between himself and the new *procurator* Gaius Julius Alpinus Classicianus. This was only defused by the diplomatic efforts of Polyclitus, one of Nero's freedmen. But Suetonius Paulinus' victory was comprehensive: there would be no more rebellions in Britain's lowland zone.

Rome's problems in the East were different. These revolved around the buffer state of Armenia, which separated Rome and Parthia. There had been disagreements and fighting in this area for quite a while, but Nero did succeed in striking an agreement with Parthia, thanks to the expertise of Rome's foremost general Cn. Domitius Corbulo, who had been appointed by Seneca and Burrus. He combined diplomacy and force to achieve a compromise in which the Romans accepted the Parthian nominee Tiridates in Armenia while the Parthians recognized him as a client king of Rome. Tiridates went to Rome and was crowned by Nero in 66, and a relief panel on the Aphrodisias Sebasteion reveals how this was spun: in a composition that likens them to Achilles and the Amazon Queen Penthesilea, Nero supports a slumped personification of Armenia, naked apart from a soft eastern hat, by her upper arms. Nevertheless, the financial strain of Boudicca's revolt and the wars with Parthia was made apparent when Rome's gold and silver coins were reduced in weight and the silver content of the *denarius* was reduced by over 10 per cent.

---

33 Tacitus, *Annals* 14.37, tr. Grant, M., op. cit. In Dio's account Boudicca just gets ill and dies. For the full battle narrative, see Tacitus, *Agricola* 15–16, *Annals* 14.29–39; Dio 62.1–12.

Compromise was harder to achieve in Judaea. An incident that illustrates the tenseness of the situation occurred when St Paul was famously about to be publicly flogged after his arrival in Jerusalem in 58 caused a riot, only to receive an eleventh-hour reprieve:

> And as they bound him with thongs, Paul said unto the centurion that stood by, Is it lawful for you to scourge a man that is Roman, and uncondemned? When the centurion heard that, he went and told the chief captain, saying, Take heed what thou doest; for this man is a Roman. Then the chief captain came, and said unto him. Tell me, art thou a Roman? He said, Yea.[34]

Other Jews were not so fortunate, and in 63, when they gathered in Caesarea to protest about discrimination against them, they clashed with the local Greek citizens. The Roman *procurator*, M. Antonius Felix, sent in the army, and the philhellenic Nero sided with the Greeks. The Jews were livid.

By 66 Judaea had become a time bomb, and in May of that year the Roman *procurator* Gessius Florus detonated it. We have an eyewitness account of what happened from Joseph ben Mattathias, aka Flavius Josephus (his assumed Roman name), who wrote an important account of the Jewish rebellion *(Jewish War)* and a Jewish History *(Jewish Antiquities)*. Now twenty-nine years old, he was an aristocratic Jewish priest and scholar who had been to Rome on a diplomatic mission, but had ended up staying there for two years before returning, with quite pro-Roman sentiments, to Jerusalem. To make up a budget deficit of 400 000 *sestertii*, Florus ordered his soldiers to seize seventeen talents (435 kg) of silver from the Temple treasury in Jerusalem. From the Jewish perspective this was a sacrilegious violation of their most holy place, especially when Florus ordered his Gentile soldiers to force their way in.

The *procurator* responded to the resultant unrest by marching in person from Caesarea to Jerusalem to restore order and get

---

34 *Acts* 22.25–27.

the treasure. When Josephus and the moderate high priest Hanan made conciliatory noises, the uncompromising Florus sent in the cavalry, leading to over 3 000 innocent people being killed and the instigators of the riot being crucified. Further Jewish protests then triggered a second bloodbath, after which Jewish popular opinion swung in favour of nationalism and armed resistance. The nationalist backlash was effective: Florus and most of his cohorts were driven back to Caesarea; the pro-Roman client king, Agrippa, who ruled the adjacent territories, was called in, but he was stoned and driven out; and the Jewish insurgents seized control all over Judaea. Nero turned to C. Cestius Gallus, the newly appointed *legatus Augusti pro praetore* of Syria. In October 66 he marched to Jerusalem with 30 000 troops, but he failed to take the city, and as he retreated he was trapped in a narrow defile near Beth-Horon, where a sizeable army of Jewish rebels slaughtered around 6 000 of his men.

In Jerusalem, meanwhile, the moderates had regained control of the city and of the war strategy. A 'losing draw' would have suited them, but Nero was already smarting from Boudicca's revolt and was fearful that this rebellion might spread to the numerous Jews in Antioch, Alexandria or, worse, Parthia, and so destabilize the whole of the Roman Empire's Eastern flank. The *Princeps* turned to Titus Flavius Vespasianus ('Vespasian'), a veteran of Claudius' invasion of Britain. Vespasian brought in his eldest son, also called Titus Flavius Vespasianus (aka Titus), and made him *legatus* of *Legio* XV *Apollinaris* based in Alexandria, while he himself assumed command of *Legiones* X *Fretensis* and V *Macedonica* based in Syria (although he decided against deploying XII *Fulminata*, defeated at Beth-Horon). Vespasian gathered his army, augmented by auxiliaries and allies, in Syria during the winter of 66–7, after which he and Titus pacified Galilee and laid siege to Jerusalem: their mission would be accomplished in due course, but not in Nero's reign, and not without terrible bloodshed.[35]

---

35   See below, pp. 145.

The Fire at Rome and the Christians

In the early hours of 19 June 64 a catastrophe occurred at Rome. A fire broke out in the Circus Maximus area, raged through the valley between the Palatine and the Esquiline Hills, burned for several days, and then erupted again to leave three out of Rome's fourteen regions in smoking ruins, and only four of them unscathed. Tacitus says that Nero was at Antium when the disaster struck, and that he made some concerted relief efforts and imposed new health and safety regulations; Suetonius and Dio Cassius say that he sang the *Sack of Troy* in full stage gear while the city burned; and conspiracy theorists believed that he started the blaze on purpose, although Tacitus dismissed this speculation as rumour. Neither did he 'fiddle' while Rome burned: the Romans did not use violin-type instruments and none of the sources says he played the lyre-like instrument called the *fidicula* – the *kithara* was his instrument of choice. Dio has him wearing a *kithara*-player's garb, but no source explicitly makes him play during the fire, whereas they all make him sing or declaim. The origin of the saying 'Nero fiddled while Rome burned' is uncertain, and in fact no written evidence has been discovered for the phrase, despite its fame.[36]

Nero didn't have to search very far for scapegoats. Tacitus' narrative seems to imply that Christians were not responsible for the fire, but nevertheless many Romans suspected that they were. There was all sorts of speculation about secret rituals and criminal activities – the Eucharist was interpreted as literal cannibalism – which were punishable by death under Roman law. Furthermore, the early Christians were not especially neighbourly, mainly because their neighbours were their fellow Christians, as opposed to their kinsfolk, compatriots, or people who lived around them, and their insular lifestyle raised suspicions in a world where, as Galen said, everyone knew each other, whose son was whose, what education they had received,

---

36 Gyles, M. F., 'Nero Fiddled While Rome Burned', *The Classical Journal*, vol. 42, no. 4 (Jan. 1947), 211–217.

how much property people owned, and how everybody conducted themselves.[37] So, because everyone automatically thought that the Christians really were guilty, there was relatively little popular opposition to their executions, which took place under *cognitio extra ordinem*, a process that was all legal and above board. However, when Nero deviated from the norm by inventing incredibly perverse and sadistic methods of execution, even the Romans' high tolerance for violence was tested:

> In spite of a guilt which had earned the most exemplary punishment, there arose a sentiment of pity, due to the impression that they were being sacrificed not for the welfare of the state but to the ferocity of a single man.[38]

Christians were exposed to wild animals (not unusual: *damnatio ad bestias* was a pretty standard sentence) and were set ablaze, smeared with pitch, to illuminate the night (grotesquely unusual). The Christian writers Tertullian, Lactantius and Sulpicius Severus all regarded Nero as the first persecutor of Christians; other texts equate him with the Antichrist; some modern thinkers maintain that the number 666 in the *Book of Revelation* is a code for Nero; and by the fourth century Christian writers were stating that Nero killed the Apostles Peter (crucified upside down on the Vatican hill) and Paul (beheaded along the Via Ostiensis).

Damnatio Memoriae

Nero's attempt to deflect the blame onto others was an abject failure, and his public image was irrevocably damaged when he

---

37   Galen, *De Praetotatione* 4 (ed. G. Kuhne, Leipzig 1827), XIV, 624.
38   Tacitus, *Annals* 15.44, tr. Jackson, J., *Tacitus: The Annals with an English Translation by John Jackson, Books XIII – XVI*, Cambridge, MA, and London: Harvard University Press, 1937. Suetonius, *Nero* 16, also mentions persecutions of Christians (of which he seems to approve), but not in the context of the fire.

exploited the devastation to construct his own ultra-palatial *Domus Aurea* ('Golden House'), featuring a lake and a colossal statue of himself, in the centre of Rome. 'Now, at last, I can begin to live like a human being,' he said.[39] But soon he would die like an outlaw.

In 65 the *Princeps* had to face a major conspiracy that aimed to replace him with C. Calpurnius Piso. The plot was betrayed, but Subrius Flavus, a tribune of the Praetorian Guard who took part in it, told the young Emperor why he had done what he had:

> I hated you, yet not a soldier was more loyal to you while you deserved to be loved. I began to hate you when you became the murderer of your mother and your wife, a charioteer, an actor, and an incendiary.[40]

Piso and various big names, including Lucan, Seneca, C. Petronius (possibly the author of the *Satyricon*) and Thrasea Paetus (a Stoic philosopher and long-time critic of Nero), were either executed or took their own lives. But the writing was on the wall for Nero.

Nevertheless, in September of 66 Nero left Rome to tour Greece. He had the date of the Olympic Games shifted to 67, so that he could compete in them, and despite being thrown from his ten-horse chariot, helped to remount and failing to stay the course, he was still proclaimed the victor. At the Isthmian Games at Corinth on 28 November 67 he released Greece from Roman administration and taxation. Another grand scheme to cut a canal through the Isthmus of Corinth came to nothing, however.

All the while, the tide was turning against him, particularly since his self-indulgence led him to fail to indulge the army and its commanders. Prompted by the warnings of his freedman

---

39 Suetonius, *Nero* 31.2.
40 Tacitus, *Annals* 15.67, tr. Church, A.J. and Brodribb, W. J., op. cit.

Helius, Nero returned to Italy. Unfortunately for him, however, the governor of Gallia Lugdunensis, C. Iulius Vindex, rebelled in March of 68. Vindex was an Aquitanian Gaul, but also a Roman Senator, and seems to have had some private difficulties, but the combination of his and the Gauls' hatred of their obligations to Rome was a very powerful one. He was able to put an army of 20 000 into the field. Whether this was a 'nationalistic' movement is disputed: unlike the Jews, the Gauls (and the Germans, for that matter) tended to think in tribal terms rather than in overarching national ones, even though they all spoke the same language group. In any case, Vindex was defeated and killed by the Rhine legions under L. Verginius Rufus, at Vesontio (modern Besançon) in Gallia Lugdunensis. However, even though Vindex failed, he had initiated an unstoppable process: in Hispania Tarraconensis the elderly Servius Sulpicius Galba declared himself 'Legate of the Senate and Roman People' and minted coins with legends like *ROM RENASC* ('Rome Reborn'), *LIBERTAS RESTITUTA* ('Liberty Restored') and *SALUS GENERIS HUMANI* ('Salvation of Mankind'); in Africa L. Clodius Macer, *legatus* of the *Legio* III *Augusta*, cut off the grain supply to Rome; Galba's agents won over C. Nymphidius Sabinus, the *Praefectus Praetorio*, who got the Praetorian Guard to defect; and the Senate declared Nero a public enemy. In the face of this, the *Princeps* simply lost his nerve. He took refuge in his freedman Phaon's villa, and there committed suicide in June 68. His famous last words were, reputedly, 'Dead. And so great an artist!'[41] The Julio-Claudian dynasty died with him.

Nero became the first Emperor to suffer *damnatio memoriae* – his reign was officially expunged from the record by order of the Senate. At the Sebasteion at Aphrodisias there is a relief on which a heroically nude Claudius, wearing the *corona civica* ('citizen crown') that was awarded to Roman leaders for saving citizens' lives, joins hands with Agrippina, who is holding ears

---

41 Suetonius, *Nero* 491.

of wheat like a fertility goddess. Claudius is being crowned by the personified Roman People or Senate, yet somewhat bizarrely, the Greek inscription on the base reads: *[Neron] Klaudios Drousos Kaisar Sebastos.* The builders had made a mistake and placed a relief showing Claudius onto a base made for Nero, but they were able to get away with it by erasing Nero's name, *Neron,* after his *damnatio memoriae.* Yet the late Emperor still had supporters who placed flowers on his grave every year, and there are some modern scholars who think Nero's memory should be rehabilitated rather than damned.

6

The Long Year 69
(aka The Year of the Four Emperors)

*The secret of the Empire has been made public: an Emperor
could be created elsewhere than in Rome.*

Tacitus, Histories 1.4.2.

Emperor 1: Galba

The fallout from Nero's suicide was a devastating crisis that
raised the spectre of the Republican Civil Wars, whose memory
was still very raw even at about one hundred years' distance.
We now enter the 'Year of the Four Emperors' or the 'Long
Year 69'.

Given that Nero had eliminated most of his male relatives,
left no heirs, and made no provisions for a successor, there
was great uncertainty as to who would become the next *Princeps*. Rome's armies were split as to where their allegiance
should lie, so only civil war could settle the issue. There was no
realistic possibility of Rome reverting to being a Republic: the
price of peace and stability was rule by one man. The only
question was, 'Who?'

After the army of Germania Superior had crushed Vindex
in 68, their commander L. Verginius Rufus offered his allegiance to the Senate, while his troops offered him the
Principate. His rather smug self-written epitaph tells us that he
refused the offer:

Here lies Rufus, who once routed Vindex
and freed the Empire not for himself, but for his Fatherland.[1]

Rufus focused his loyalty on the septuagenarian Servius Sulpicius Galba, the leader of the Spanish rebellion,[2] who is said to have intercepted orders from Nero for his own execution and to have thought about suicide. In his youth Galba had been adopted by Livia and went on to outlive his wife and two sons. During his rise to becoming a highly esteemed Senator he had impressed the people in exciting new ways:

As Praetor in charge of the games of the Floralia he gave a new type of show: tightrope-walking elephants.[3]

Since 61 he had been the governor of Hispania Tarraconensis. He was the antithesis of Nero, a hard-boiled, old-school Roman aristocrat, devoted to *disciplina* and *severitas*, which led to accusations of cruelty and stinginess. Suetonius also says that

in terms of his sexual preferences he was more attracted to males, particularly ones who were hard bodied and past the prime of their youth (*exoleti*).[4]

However, since he maintained the dominant, insertive role, and restricted his relationships to prostitutes and slaves, this caused no scandal at Rome. On the contrary, his prospects were good. The *Praefectus Praetorio* Nymphidius Sabinus had promised the Praetorian Guard a donative of 30 000 *sestertii* per man in Galba's name, and when the Senate recognized him as the replacement Emperor, he headed for Rome and assumed the title of Caesar.

---

1   Quoted by Pliny the Younger, *Letters* 9.19.1, tr. Kershaw, S.
2   See above, p. 120.
3   Suetonius, *Galba* 6.1, tr. Kershaw, S. Cf. Suetonius, *Nero* 11.1.
4   Suetonius, *Galba* 22, tr. Kershaw, S. For *exoleti* see p. 79 and n. 22 above. See also Richlin, A., *The Garden of Priapus. Sexuality and Aggression in Roman Humor*, New Haven and London: Yale University Press, 1983.

Galba aready commanded *Legio* VI *Victrix*, and he used money raised by the confiscation and sale of Nero's property in Spain to assemble his own legion, referred to by Tacitus as *Legio* VII *Galbiana* and VII *Hispana*, and subsequently known as VII *Gemina*. He was sluggish about getting to Rome, though, and his policies seem bizarrely contradictory. He rewarded the Gallic tribes that had supported Vindex's revolt, and punished the ones that had helped suppress it. The Rhine legions only swore allegiance to Galba on Verginius Rufus' say-so, and yet Galba replaced Rufus with the old, lame, incompetent Hordeonius Flaccus, much to the displeasure of his troops.

At Rome, meanwhile, Nymphidius Sabinus was pursuing his own agenda to become either the sole *Praefectus Praetorio* for life, and hence the power behind the throne, or the actual power on the throne. But to his disappointment, Galba installed a former financial official called Cornelius Laco to succeed him in the post. Laco was totally unsuited for this command, and Nymphidius, who had expected a better reward for bringing the Praetorian Guard over to Galba, planned a coup. Sadly for him, his plan backfired when he was killed by the Praetorians. Galba then became tangled up in other people's promises. First, he refused to pay the Praetorian Guard the *donativum* that Nymphidius had originally pledged to them on his behalf, and then, when some sailors from the Misenum fleet whom Nero had enrolled, or promised to enrol, in a legion asked Galba to keep his promise, he sent in the cavalry and decimated the survivors.

Galba finally arrived in Rome in October 68, accompanied by Nero's old drinking buddy and ex-husband of Poppaea Sabina, M. Salvius Otho, the governor of Lusitania, who had joined his cause. Because of his age, Galba didn't have time on his side, and he proceeded to commit one gaffe after another. His advisory circle comprised three corrupt, inept and mutually hostile men who were commonly known as his 'pedagogues': Laco, 'intolerably arrogant and indolent';[5] Titus Vinius, ex-commander of *Legio*

---

5   Suetonius, *Galba* 14.2.

VI *Victrix*; and Icelus, his freedman. Galba imposed some stringent economic austerity measures that were certainly necessary but still seem to have caused hardship and resentment among the masses, who by now were starting to miss Nero. The military became unhappy when he disbanded the imperial corps of German bodyguards and refused to pay any *donativum* to either the Praetorian Guard or the German legions, on the idealistic but utterly naive principle that

I choose my soldiers. I don't buy them.[6]

The money would have been well spent, because on 1 January 69 the troops in Germania Superior refused to renew their oath of allegiance. The next day, at the instigation of the legionary *legatus* Fabius Valens, the legions of Germania Inferior proclaimed their overall commander, Aulus Vitellius, Emperor. The day after that the legions of Germania Superior followed their lead. These seven powerful legions were swiftly joined by those of Britain, Gaul and Spain. Galba responded by adopting the thirty-year-old Lucius Calpurnius Piso Frugi Licinianus as his son and heir. This man was a descendant of Pompey the Great, but he had no experience, and the army really didn't care who he was. One man who did care, though, was Otho: having been the first provincial governor to join Galba's cause, he had hoped to succeed him. So he organized a conspiracy among the Praetorian Guard.

At dawn on 15 January 69, Galba went to perform a sacrifice on the Palatine Hill. Otho went down to the Forum, where twenty-three soldiers hailed him as Emperor. This was not exactly the turnout that he had been hoping for, but he was carried to the Praetorian camp, and his rebellion gained impetus. Rumours reached Galba, initially that Otho had been elevated to the purple, and then that he had been murdered. So he went down to the Forum to assert his control. There, though,

---

6 Tacitus, *Histories* 1.5, tr. Kershaw, S.

he was surrounded by a mob, deserted by his men, tipped out of his litter, and publicly assassinated. Piso was dragged out of the temple of Vesta and butchered as well. That evening the Senate granted Otho all the requisite imperial honours. Rome now had two new Emperors: Otho in Rome and Vitellius on the Rhine. The Year of the Four Emperors was well under way.

Historians have been tough on Galba, and none more so than Tacitus:

> By universal consent capable of ruling the Empire, if he had not been Emperor.[7]

Yet the ramifications of his few months in power were enormous. His adoption of Piso – on the premise that 'the principle of choice will stand in the place of liberty'[8] – represented a decisive break from the old hereditary system. But in January 69 'choice' really meant 'the most successful general'.

Emperor 2: Otho

The official incumbent was a prime example of an Emperor being created elsewhere than at Rome, having been governor of Lusitania in Spain for around a decade. Born on 28 April 32, M. Salvius Otho was from a recently ennobled patrician family, and had built on a misspent youth in which he roamed the streets at night and snared drunkards in a blanket, to become a louche playboy who even accused Nero of stinginess. Plutarch described the 'softness and effeminacy' of his body, and Juvenal called him a 'faggot' (*pathicus*) who even outdid Cleopatra in his primping and preening,[9] but his tenure in Spain after 'Poppaea-gate' was effective and honourable,[10] and the legions

---

7   Ibid. 1.49.
8   Ibid. 1.16. See Haynes, H., *Tacitus on Imperial Rome: The History of Make-Believe*, Berkeley and Los Angeles: University of California Press, 2003, pp. 50 ff.
9   Plutarch, *Galba* 25.1 (cf. *Otho* 4.3, 9.3); Juvenal, *Satires* 2.99 ff.
10   See above, p. 108.

of the Danube, the East, Egypt and Africa all gave him their backing.

Once installed as *Princeps*, he seems to have tried to please all of the people all of the time. He brought the Praetorian Guard on board with a *donativum*, became quite popular with the plebs by reversing Nero's *damnatio memoriae*, curried favour with the Senate by following a strict constitutionalist line and seems to have been quite generous in his grants of citizenship in the provinces. Yet despite this, Otho failed to win political confidence at Rome or to overcome military anarchy abroad. The volatility of the situation at Rome was highlighted when Otho decided to replace some of Rome's garrison with a cohort of Roman citizens from Ostia. He ordered weapons to be taken from the Praetorian camp to Ostia by night, so that the replacement troops would be adequately armed, but the Praetorian Guard thought this was a Senatorial counter-coup against Otho. When they stormed the imperial palace to confirm the emperor's safety, all they did was scare Otho and his Senatorial dinner guests half to death.

Outside Rome, Otho had to contend with Vitellius, who stood at the head of the mighty Rhineland army, augmented by contingents from Spain, Gaul, Britain and Raetia, with whom he began a Hannibalesque assault over the Alps into Italy in February. Against this army Otho could deploy the four legions of Pannonia and Dalmatia, the three legions of Moesia, plus the Praetorian Guard and a force of gladiators. Although still heavily outnumbered, Otho made a rapid diversionary strike that initially allowed him to hold a position on the River Po, where he hoped to unite all his forces.

On or around 10 April, Otho himself arrived at Bedriacum, near Cremona in northern Italy. By this time the Vitellian forces were building a bridge over the Po, so Otho ordered a large contingent to establish a forward base from where they could interdict the completion of the bridge. However, these troops got themselves strung out along the via Postumia, and, encumbered by their baggage train and with their retreat cut off by the river, they were assaulted and cut to pieces by the Batavian auxiliaries of Vitellius' commanders Aulus Caecina Alienus and Fabius Valens at the First Battle of Bedriacum on 14 April.

Otho was not present at the battle, having led a large force to Brixellum (modern Brescello) to deal with any Vitellian units that might have already crossed the Po. When the horseman who brought word of the disaster to Otho was received with incredulity, he responded:

> 'Would that this news were false, Caesar; for most gladly would I have died hadst thou been victor. As it is, I shall perish in any case, that no one may think that I fled hither to secure my own safety.' [. . .] With these words, he slew himself.[11]

Despite the messenger's dramatic gesture, Otho knew that prolonging the conflict would only precipitate another bloody round of civil war. Enough was enough:

> I hate civil war, even though I conquer; and I love all Romans, even though they do not side with me. Let Vitellius be victor.[12]

On 16 April 69, in an act that was true to Roman ideals, but baffling to his critics in the context of his debauched reputation, Otho committed suicide. As Plutarch put it,

> when he was gone, those who applauded his death were no fewer or less illustrious than those who blamed his life.[13]

---

11   Dio 64.11.1, tr. Cary. E., op. cit.
12   Ibid. 64.13.1.
13   Plutarch, *Otho* 18.2, tr. Perrin, B., *Plutarch's Lives with an English Translation by Bernadotte Perrin, in Eleven Volumes, vol. XI,* Cambridge, MA.: Harvard University Press, 1926. Otho's death receives detailed treatment in all our sources. See: Plutarch, *Otho* 15–18; Tacitus, *Histories* 2.46–50; Suetonius, *Otho* 9.3–12.2; Dio 64.11–15.

Emperor 3:Vitellius

It is hard to establish the truth about the man who succeeded Otho. The sources present Aulus Vitellius as a cruel, corrupt, gluttonous, gambling shoe-fetishist who carried Messalina's shoe about with him and kissed it, but much of the history was written under the regime that ousted him. We hear of his marriage to Petroniana, who bore him a son, blind in one eye, whom Vitellius killed just prior to their divorce, and of a more settled second marriage to Galeria Fundana, who bore him another son and a daughter. He had ascended the *Cursus Honorum* and been rather surprisingly appointed governor of Germania Inferior by Galba late in 68.

He was in the vicinity of Lugdunum when news about Otho's suicide broke. By 19 April, the Senate had recognized him as Aulus Vitellius Germanicus Imperator Augustus, although he was quite circumspect about assuming the *Princeps'* traditional titles (he only became 'Caesar' in November). He moved southwards through Italy, looting, pillaging and allegedly squandering fortunes on lavish drunken banquets. He inspected the corpse-strewn battlefield of Bedriacum with joy, remaining unmoved that so many citizens were denied a proper burial, and finally reached Rome in late June or early July.

Once installed in the capital, however, Vitellius appears to have acted with restraint: the survivors from Otho's forces, and the Danubian legions that had arrived too late to fight, were sent back to their old postings or redeployed at a safe distance (even though some leading centurions were put to death); Otho's brother Salvius Titianus was pardoned; Vitellius took part in meetings of the Senate; Equites were awarded posts customarily held by freedmen; and entertainment was provided for the plebs. To emphasize his loyalty to the troops who had made him what he was, Vitellius replaced Otho's Praetorian Guard and urban cohorts with sixteen Praetorian cohorts and four urban units drawn from the army of Germany. Unfortunately, the influx of tens of thousands of soldiers into

Rome sparked off some violent clashes. Vitellius didn't have the money to pay his troops the bonus they had been promised, and indiscipline, unsanitary conditions and brawls with civilians ensued, while Vitellius installed himself in the Golden House of Nero and offloaded responsibility for public order to Caecina and Valens.

Unfortunately, mutual animosity between Caecina and Valens didn't help the situation, and to make matters worse, by mid-July news had filtered through that the legions under the Prefect of Egypt, an Alexandrian Jew called Ti. Julius Alexander, had sworn allegiance to the fourth potential Emperor of the year: Vespasian. Despite having had reasonable success in the vicious war against the Jewish rebels that had broken out in 66, Vespasian and his son Titus had put this on hold since Nero's death, and had been monitoring the situation in the Empire with a keen eye.

A shrewd, plain-speaking man with a nice line in self-deprecating down-to-earth humour, Vespasian had been born in an opulent villa that has quite recently been excavated, to parents of Equestrian status at Falacrinum (modern Falacrine) near the Sabine town of Reate in 9, and he had the regional accent to prove it. Suetonius describes him as a strong, well-proportioned man with the expression of someone straining to empty his bowels.[14] As Aedile under Caligula, he preformed his duties so badly the Emperor ordered his soldiers to heap the mud left uncleaned on the streets into his toga. With Flavia Domitilla he had a daughter, also called Flavia Domitilla, and two sons, the above-mentioned Titus and Titus Flavius Domitianus, aka Domitian (see Genealogy Table 2). His wife didn't live to see him become Emperor, but in any case his political career seems to have benefited more from a liaison with Antonia Minor's freedwoman Antonia Caenis, a recommendation from Claudius' freedman Narcissus, and the patronage of the family of the Vitellii. Vespasian made a name for himself during

---

14   Suetonius, *Vespasian* 20.1.

Claudius' invasion of Britain by capturing Vectis (the Isle of Wight), and he received the *ornamenta triumphalia* for his efforts. Josephus overdoes the praise somewhat:

> With his troops he had added Britain, till then almost unknown, to the Empire, and thus provided Claudius, the father of Nero, with a triumph which cost him no personal exertion.[15]

Vespasian went on to govern Africa in the early 60s, where he was once pelted with turnips in a riot at Hadrumetum (Sousse), and then to tour Greece with Nero in 66, before being selected to take on the Judaean revolt in 67. He was regarded as

> an energetic commander, who could be trusted not to abuse his plenary powers [...] nothing, it seemed, need be feared from a man of such modest antecedents.[16]

Conveniently, but coincidentally, his brother Titus Flavius Sabinus, another British veteran, was *Praefectus Urbis* in Rome.

Vespasian played the whole situation very cannily. He had been keeping open the option to carry on campaigning in Judaea, or to get involved in the power struggles, and now he made his move. The six legions in the Danubian provinces had close links with those of the East, which comprised three in Syria under C. Licinius Mucianus, the three in Judaea, and the two commanded by Ti. Julius Alexander who, *ex officio*, had control of much of Rome's grain supply. The 'official' declaration of Vespasian as *Princeps* came on 1 July 69 on Ti. Alexander's initiative, and Vespasian subsequently dated his reign from this point. The legions of Egypt, Judaea, Syria and the Danube 'spontaneously' rallied to him, followed by the other Eastern provinces and several client kings.

---

15 Josephus, *de Bello Judaico* 3.1.2, tr. in Mann, J. C. and Penman, R. G. (eds.), op. cit.
16 Suetonius, *Vespasian* 4.5, tr. Graves, R., op. cit.

Vespasian's strategy was to secure control of Rome's grain supplies at Alexandria, and maybe advance into Africa to complete the stranglehold, while Mucianus set off for Italy through Asia Minor and the Balkans, annihilating a group of invading tribes from over the Danube en route. But events acquired a momentum of their own. M. Antonius Primus, who was *legatus* of *Legio* VII *Galbiana*, currently stationed in Pannonia, and Cornelius Fuscus the *procurator* of Illyricum, jumped the gun and invaded Italy with the legions of Moesia, Pannonia and Dalmatia before Mucianus had arrived.

Primus was probably outnumbered two to one, but he decided to strike before Vitellius could gather reinforcements from Germany. He was helped by the fact that, of Vitellius' two main lieutenants, Valens was sick and Caecina had become a Flavian collaborator ('Flavian' after Vespasian's middle name Flavius). However, Caecina's soldiers stayed loyal to Vitellius, arrested Caecina, and joined up with the other Vitellian forces who were trying to hold the River Po. Vitellius was still at Rome, though, leaving his troops, who were already ill-disciplined, poorly trained and unaccustomed to the local heat, practically leaderless. The rival armies engaged on a night in late October or early November at the Second Battle of Bedriacum. When dawn broke, Primus' *Legio* III *Gallica*, which had served in Syria, turned to salute the rising sun in accordance with local custom. The Vitellian forces thought they were hailing Eastern reinforcements, lost heart and then their camp, and the Flavian forces won the day.

Forty thousand armed men now burst into Cremona, settling old scores and perpetrating four days of sickening war crimes. When a decree was finally issued that citizens of Cremona should not be kept as slaves, the captives became financially worthless, and so they were massacred, unless they were fortunate enough to be ransomed. Valens had started feeling better, but he was captured while raising an army in Gaul and Germany, and executed; Caecina subsequently had a reasonable career under Vespasian.

Primus now pressed on to Rome, while the three legions of Spain, followed by those of Gaul and Britain, went over to the winning side. When Vitellius tried to block the Apennine passes, his troops surrendered without a fight at Narnia (modern Narni in Umbria), but at Rome the people and the praetorians were made of sterner stuff. Vespasian's brother Sabinus managed to persuade Vitellius to abdicate, but an angry mob would not allow this to happen. On 18 December they drove Sabinus onto the Capitol and took it by storm. The Temple of Jupiter Optimus Maximus was set on fire (though whose fault this was is unclear):

> And so the Capitol, with its gates closed, undefended and unpillaged, was utterly destroyed by fire.[17]

Sabinus was killed in the fighting, but Vespasian's younger son Domitian was able to get away by disguising himself as a devotee of Isis.

Two days later the armies of the Danube fought their way into the city. Butchery followed. Vitellius tried to evade capture by disguising himself and barricading himself into a doorkeeper's cell, but he was discovered and dragged off to the Gemonian steps. His mutilated corpse was hurled into the Tiber – a satisfyingly humiliating end for Flavian propagandists and hostile biographers. Yet even so, as Tacitus wrote, 'with the death of Vitellius the war ended rather than the peace began'.[18]

Emperor 4: Vespasian

Rome's fears of becoming a second Cremona were alleviated when Mucianus arrived and neutralized any potential opposition, notably by 'eliminating' Vitellius' son, and stripping Primus of his authority, leaving him to slope off to complain fruitlessly to Vespasian, who was still in Egypt. The Senate acknowledged Vespasian as the fourth Emperor of the Long Year 69, and made him and Titus the Consuls for 70. The nineteen-year-old

---

17   Tacitus, *Histories* 3.71, tr. Kershaw, S.
18   Ibid. 4.1.

Domitian was appointed Praetor with the powers of a Consul, but behaved like he was far more powerful than that, taking up residence in the imperial palace, representing the Flavian family in the Senate and seducing any female he could get his hands on. However, for now the real power lay with Mucianus, a man of alluring charm but with an image tainted by public failings and private scandal. Tacitus describes him as a mixture of dissipation and energy, politeness and arrogance, good and evil, and comments that although his public image appeared praiseworthy, there were 'nasty secrets' concerning his private life.[19] It has been argued that this was Tacitus' elliptical way of saying 'he was gay', but it is more nuanced than that. Suetonius says that Mucianus was 'of well-known *impudicitia*'[20] (i.e., he had a predilection for the receptive role in sex), and the point of that remark is that he was the *receiver* in homosexual sex (*pathicus, cinaedus* and, as here, *impudicus* are the Latin words used for this) and thus not a 'real man'; you had to be the active, penetrating partner; passive, penetrated partners were, by definition, women, slaves or the young: 'in Roman terms a man is fully a *vir* ("man") when he penetrates, regardless of the sex of his penetrated partner.'[21] For a freeborn adult male to assume a passive role meant instant excoriation, but Vespasian had two genuine sons, and this may have ultimately induced Mucianus, 'a man who would find it easier to transfer the imperial power to another, than to hold it for himself',[22] to give way to his claims.

Vespasian, meanwhile, finally left Alexandria having added to his 'divine majesty and authority' by performing some rather Jesus-esque 'miracles' – healing a poor man who was blind, and another who was lame.[23] He arrived in Rome in around the

---

19 Ibid 1.10.
20 Suetonius, *Vespasian* 13.
21 Williams, C. A., op. cit., 184. Cf. Morgan, G., *69 AD: The Year of the Four Emperors*, Oxford: Oxford University Press, 2006, p. 174. Vespasian criticized Mucianus privately by saying, 'Yes, but *I* am a man.' Suetonius, *Vespasian* 13.
22 Tacitus, *Histories* 1.10, tr. Church, A.J. and Brodribb, W. J., op. cit.
23 Suetonius, *Vespasian* 7.2. Much has been made of the similarities.

early autumn of 70, having somehow managed to keep his nose clean amidst all the violence. Nevertheless, the task awaiting him in rebuilding Rome physically, politically, economically and possibly morally was extremely challenging.

Tacitus put it in a nutshell. 'At Rome the Senate voted Vespasian everything customary for Emperors.'[24] Vespasian's imperial position was legally defined under the *lex de imperio Vespasiani* ('Law Regulating Vespasian's authority'), which still survives in fragmentary form. This grants him the right to conclude treaties, convene and put proposals to the Senate, and nominate people for office. Whatever the Julio-Claudian emperors had done through *auctoritas*, he could now do by right:

> Vespasian [is authorized] to transact and do whatever things divine, public and private he deems to serve the advantage and the overriding interests of the state.[25]

It also puts an official stamp of approval on his rise to power.

> Whatever was done, executed, decreed or ordered before the enactment of this law by the Imperator Caesar Vespasianus Augustus, or by anyone at his order or command, shall be as fully binding and valid as if they had been done by order of the people or plebs.[26]

His power was absolute and the Senate had legitimized it. Once upon a time, Suetonius tells us, a stray dog picked up a human hand (*manus* in Latin) at a crossroads, brought it to where Vespasian was breakfasting and dropped it under the table.[27] It had been a good omen: *manus* in Latin means both 'hand' and 'power': the question was now, how would he use that power?

---

24 Tacitus, *Histories* 4.3, tr. Kershaw, S.
25 *CIL* 6.930 = *ILS* 244, ll. 17 ff., tr. in Lewis, N. and Reinhold, M. (eds.), op. cit. p. 12.
26 Ibid., 11.29 ff.
27 Suetonius, *Vespasian* 5.4.

7

The Flavian Dynasty (69–96): Vespasian, Titus and Domitian

[To help mortal men] is the road that Roman leaders have taken, and it is this road that the greatest ruler of all time is treading, at a pace favoured by heaven, along with his offspring, as he brings relief to an exhausted world.
                    Pliny the Elder, *Natural History* 2.5(7)[1]

Vespasian: The Challenges of Ruling Rome

Any analysis of Vespasian's reign is hampered by a tailing-off of the ancient source material. Especially frustrating is the fact that the later books of Tacitus' *Histories* are lost, breaking off early in 70. Nevertheless, it is obvious that Imperator Caesar Vespasianus Augustus found himself in a challenging situation: Rome's Capitol was in ruins; the Judaean revolt was far from over; there was unrest in other provinces; client kingdoms were rebelling or cutting deals with barbarians who were threatening the frontiers; the victorious armies were undisciplined; renegade soldiers were running amok in the countryside; the Empire's administration was a shambles, and money was scarce. The situation resembled that which had faced Augustus around one hundred years before, and some kind of post-civil-war restoration of peace and stability was once more paramount.

---

1 Tr. Rackham, H. A., *Pliny: Natural History in Ten Volumes, I, Praefatio, Libri I, II*, Cambridge, MA: Harvard University Press, rev. edn., 1949.

Factions in the Senate squabbled over precisely who, according to protocol, should deliver their congratulations to Vespasian. Valerius Asiaticus proposed that the delegates be chosen by lot as usual; the 'stiff-necked republican'[2] Stoic philosopher C. Helvidius Priscus, son-in-law of Nero's victim Thrasea Paetus, wanted the members chosen by magistrates under oath, in the hope that they could exert a pro-Republican/anti-Principate influence. But the majority realized that everything now depended on amicable relations between the Senate and the *Princeps*, and Priscus was voted down. He made his point by being the only man to greet the Emperor by his private name of Vespasianus.

On his arrival in Rome, Vespasian shored up his position by paying donatives to the troops, installing Titus as *Praefectus Praetorio* in 72, and securing the title of *Princeps Iuventutis* ('Leader of the Youth') for him and Domitian. Titus dropped the title quite quickly, but Domitian held it throughout Vespasian's reign in what was a clear dynastic statement: the Flavians were here to stay.

Priscus also clashed with Valerius Asiaticus over whether the Emperor should control the State finances, and again Priscus lost the argument. Vespasian's challenge was to stimulate growth and to reduce the deficit, which amounted to some four billion *sestertii*, equivalent to around 500 per cent of the empire's annual tax receipts.[3] Yet despite seeming to have adopted a moderate and commonsensical approach to this, he still received criticism. Suetonius says that the emptiness of both the Treasury (*aerarium*) and the Privy Purse (*fiscus*) forced Vespasian into heavy taxation and unethical business dealings, but he does acknowledge that he spent his income effectively, however questionable its sources might have been.[4] Vespasian imposed a new tax in Egypt, which led to the Alexandrian mob calling

---

2 Wellesley, K., *The Year of the Four Emperors*, London and New York: Routledge, 2000, 3rd edn., p. 209.

3 The original manuscript of Suetonius put the figure at forty billion: Suetonius, *Vespasian* 16.3.

4 Suetonius, *Vespasian* 16.1.

him Cybiosactes after one of their outrageously stingy kings whose name means 'Dealer-in-square-pieces-of-salt-fish'; his tax on urine (used by fullers) from public latrines, which lead to the receptacles being called *vespasiani* (they still are in Italy and France), was notorious; and after the destruction of the Temple of Jerusalem in 70 he also levied the *fiscus Iudaicus*, a new empire-wide tax on all Jews – women, children, the elderly and slaves included – that effectively diverted the half-shekel that they contributed to the Temple of Jerusalem to that of Jupiter Capitolinus in Rome.

Other revenue streams included taking over 'free' states such as the cities of Achaea liberated by Nero, which allowed Vespasian to acquire the tax receipts that now become due; reducing client kingdoms such as Commagene, which Antiochus IV had held since Caligula's reign, to provincial status; and assessing the cost-benefit outcome of military conquest and acting accordingly, as was the case in Germany and Britain. There was also a peace dividend as people returned to farming, trading and the like, and new coins advertised the fact with the legend *ROMA RESURGE(N)S*: 'Rome rising again'.

Vespasian's expenditure included subsidizing Senators who lacked the necessary property qualifications, restoring numerous cities throughout the empire, and giving state salaries for teachers of Latin and Greek rhetoric. He also built a new stage for the Theatre of Marcellus, hosted opulent state banquets to the benefit of the food industry, and embarked on various large-scale building projects in Rome that provided much-needed employment for what he dubbed 'my little plebs'.[5]

The first priority was to restore the Capitol. To Helvidius Priscus' proposal that the work be undertaken at public expense, but that Vespasian should help, the Emperor's response was to carry the first load of debris away 'on his own neck'.[6] Work also commenced on a Temple to the Deified Claudius, a temple of

---

5 *'Plebiculam'* – Suetonius, *Vespasian* 18.
6 Suetonius, *Vespasian* 8.5.

Pax (Peace), and the iconic (Flavian) Amphitheatre or 'Hunting Theatre', known since medieval times as the Colosseum (or Coliseum). In a wonderful stroke of populism on Vespasian's part, this was constructed on the site of the artificial lake of Nero's Golden House. According to a specialist in reconstructing 'ghost' inscriptions from the pin holes that once held bronze letters, the original building inscription of the amphitheatre read:

> Imperator Caesar Vespasianus Augustus ordered this new amphitheatre erected from the spoils of war.[7]

The war in question was the Jewish war, whose successful conclusion yielded immense amounts of booty.[8]

If the fabric of Rome needed some tender loving care, so did its ruling elite. So Vespasian

> reformed the Senatorial and Equestrian orders, now weakened by frequent murders and continuous neglect, replacing undesirable members with the most eligible Italian and provincial candidates available.[9]

This moved the 'provincialization' of Rome's elite orders on at quite a pace, and at the same time the Equites assumed a much more significant role in the administration of the Empire at the expense of freedmen. Vespasian still needed the Senate's administrative skills, but it came to exercise less and less initiative.

The Senate had its champions, of course, notably Helvidius Priscus. But he lost pretty well every confrontation he sought, and was ultimately exiled, possibly because he was advocating Senatorial input into the decision-making about the succession. Vespasian is said once to have rushed tearfully out of the Senate

---

7 Alföldy, G., 'Eine Bauinschrift aus dem Colosseum', *ZPE* 109, 1995, 195–226. Not all scholars accept Alföldy's hypothesis, but the funding undoubtedly came from the spoils of war.

8 See below, pp. 145 ff.

9 Suetonius, *Vespasian* 9.2, tr. Graves, R., op. cit.

shouting, 'Either my son will succeed me or nobody else will!'[10] Clearly the issue was non-negotiable, and in the end Priscus was killed, albeit possibly contrary to Vespasian's wishes. The prime suspect was Marcellus Eprius, the prosecutor of Thrasea Paetus and a bitter enemy of Priscus, although in 79 he himself was condemned for treason by Titus and committed suicide by cutting his throat with a razor. Another victim of this alleged conspiracy was Vitellius' treacherous ex-general Caecina, killed as he left a banquet attended by Titus, who discovered 'proof' of the plot in the form of a speech in Caecina's handwriting, supposedly to be delivered to the Praetorian Guard. Most likely Titus regarded these men as old, expendable and in the way.

The Challenges of Ruling the Empire

It was not just at Rome that Vespasian faced opposition. From the outset he had to cope with trouble caused by Julius Civilis, a Batavian chieftain who had served in the *auxilia* and now had Roman citizenship:

> He was unusually intelligent for a native, and passed himself off as a second Sertorius or Hannibal, whose facial disfigurement he shared.[11]

During the Year of the Four Emperors, Civilis had engaged in some vigorous trouble-making, ostensibly on Vespasian's behalf, using eight Batavian cohorts that had once fought for Vitellius, plus fighters from his own tribe and from others on both banks of the lower Rhine. When the Flavian forces won the Second Battle of Bedriacum, the legionaries who were left in Germany swore allegiance to Vespasian, but Civilis just carried on fighting, but against Roman authority rather than for

---

10 Dio 66.12.1, tr. Kershaw, S.
11 Tacitus, *Histories* 4.13, tr. Wellesley, K., *Tacitus: The Histories*, London: Penguin, rev. edn., 1975. The disfigurement was the loss of one eye; Sertorius had rebelled against Sulla's dictatorship in 80–72 BCE.

Vespasian. Some other tribes, notably the Treveri and Lingones, joined his *Imperium Galliarum* (Empire of the Gauls), and the native auxiliary regiments deserted en masse. Together these insurgents overran all but two of the legionary camps along the Rhine, but that was as far as it went. Gaul was not a nation, and intertribal rivalries were strong: the Sequani defeated the Lingones; the Mediomatrici, on the borders of the Treveri, stayed loyal; the Remi condemned the rebels; and once Vespasian was confident of his position at Rome, the Roman army surged into the Rhineland. Vespasian's close relative Petillius Cerialis put a stop to the rebellion, and Tacitus' *Histories* break off in mid-sentence with Civilis suing for peace. We do not know what happened to him.

Civilis' revolt undoubtedly revealed weaknesses along the Rhine frontier. Between the Rhine, Upper Danube and Main Rivers there is a re-entrant angle that made the provinces vulnerable to attack, so Vespasian entrusted the task of annexing this area, called the *Agri Decumates* (broadly the Black Forest area – see Map 4), to Cn. Pinarius Clemens, who did so in two years of efficient campaigning. The town of Aquae Flaviae (modern Wiesbaden) was founded to function as an administrative centre. All the unrest of the Long Year 69 had also denuded the Danube frontier of troops, and this was exploited by Sarmatian raiders. Their attacks were repelled relatively easily, but Vespasian still moved to consolidate his hold on the region by building roads and reinforcing Rome's military presence in the Danube provinces.

On Rome's Eastern frontier, reorganization rather than expansion was the order of the day. Vespasian amalgamated Cappadocia, Lesser Armenia and Galatia into one 'super-province'; the whole area was provided with a network of military roads; Judaea was converted into an 'armed' province by the posting of legionary troops once the bloody war there had been brought to an end;[12] and the client kingdoms of Commagene

---

12 See p. 145 below.

and Transjordan were annexed and assimilated into the province of Syria. Tacitus implies that some of these clients' only real worth was monetary, but the wealth of the deposed Tiberius Claudius Antiochus Epiphanes Philopappus of Commagene was deployed in an effective way: he is honoured on his grandson's funerary monument, which is still a famous feature of the Athenian skyline. Legionary bases were established at the principal crossings of the River Euphrates in a display of military might that kept the peace between Rome and Parthia for quite a while.

On the empire's southern border, C. Calpetanus Rantius Quirinalis Valerius Festus, *legatus* of *Legio* III *Augusta*, had L. Calpurnius Piso, the Proconsul of Africa, murdered in 70, allegedly to prove his loyalty to Vespasian (he was himself connected by marriage to Vitellius). He then found himself obliged to put down a local conflict in his province between Oea (modern Tripoli), which had called in the Garamantes from the Sahara desert, and Lepcis Magna. Festus expelled the Garamantes and was duly awarded the *ornamenta triumphalia*. *Legio* III *Augusta* moved forward to a base at Theveste (modern Tebessa, just west of the modern Tunisian–Algerian border).

Agricola in Britain

In Britain, Vespasian set out to expand Roman-held territory. Since he had campaigned there under Claudius, Roman control had advanced to a line running north-east from Isca (Exeter) to Lindum (Lincoln), along the Fosse Way (see Map 2), and by 67 Nero had felt that the province was secure enough to withdraw *Legio* XIV *Gemina*. South of the Fosse Way, Tiberius Claudius Cogidubnus (or Togidubnus), a dependent ruler who seems to have supported Roman rule from the very beginning and who was possibly in residence at Fishbourne, evidently worked on Vespasian's behalf. In 69 Vitellius had appointed Vettius Bolanus as governor, replacing M. Trebellius Maximus. The latter had achieved some much-needed post-Boudiccan consolidation, but had become embroiled in mutinies among the troops and was conducting a running feud with M. Roscius Coelius, commander of *Legio* XX *Valeria Victrix*. Anti-Roman elements among the Brigantes took advantage of this:

> The leader in this was Venutius, a man of barbarous spirit who hated the Roman power. In addition he had motives of personal hostility against Queen Cartimandua [. . .] Her power had grown when she captured king Caratacus by treachery and handed him over to embellish the triumph of the Emperor Claudius [. . .] Venutius had been her husband. Spurning him, she made his armour-bearer Vellocatus her husband, and her partner in government [. . .] The people of the tribe declared for Venutius [who] summoned his support-ers. The Brigantes rallied to him, reducing Cartimandua to the last extremity. She besought Roman protection. Our alae and cohorts fought indecisive battles, but at length rescued the queen from danger. The kingdom went to Venutius; we were left with a war to fight.[13]

When Vespasian acceded to the purple, he decided to rectify the situation by reducing the whole of Roman Britain to regular Roman rule.

The swashbuckling Petillius Cerialis, the conqueror of Civilis and *legatus* of *Legio* IX *Hispana* during Boudicca's revolt, was made the new governor of Britain in 71. Bringing *Legio* II *Adiu-trix* with him, and supported by Tacitus' father-in-law Gnaeus Julius Agricola, who replaced Coelius as commander of XX *Valeria Victrix*, he advanced northwards, established IX *Hispana* at Eboracum (York), smashed the power of the Brigantes and was rewarded with a consulship in 74. His capable successor, Sextus Julius Frontinus, turned his attention to Wales, overrun-ning the south and preparing for the invasion of the north by establishing a legionary base at Deva (Chester). Towards the

---

13 Tacitus, *Histories* 3.45, tr. in Mann, J. C. and Penman, R. G. (eds.), op. cit.

end of Vespasian's reign, Agricola subdued north Wales and completed the conquest of the island of Mona, before pushing beyond the Brigantes into Scotland. As Tacitus put it:

> But when Vespasian [. . .] restored stable government to Britain, there came a succession of great generals and splendid armies, and the hopes of our enemies dwindled.[14]

Vespasian's Death and Deification

Vespasian appears to have stayed in Rome from July 70 onwards, and to have died rather unexpectedly on the night of 23–4 June 79 at the age of sixty-nine. He started to suffer some intestinal problems, and in the spa of Aquae Cutiliae near to Reate he suffered a particularly virulent bout of diarrhoea. With the famous last words, 'An emperor ought to die standing', he did so as he struggled to his feet.[15] His other near-death quip, 'Oh no! I think I'm becoming a god,'[16] had an element of truth to it, since he was indeed hailed as *divus*. Titus may have delayed this a little, but as Pliny the Younger remarked,[17] it was the interests of the heir that motivated the deification: the Flavians were plebeian, and so needed prestige from whatever source they could get it. In fact, numerous parties benefited from ruler cult: the Emperor who was offered the tribute; the initiator(s) of the cult, who could advertise their homage; the individual who proposed and perhaps paid for the buildings, ceremonies and games that made up the cult; and the people who benefited from new facilities. To that end, construction began of a Corinthian temple in Vespasian's honour, which still stands ruined in the Roman Forum.

---

14   Tacitus, *Agricola* 17, tr. Mattingley, H., *Tacitus: The Agricola and the Germania, Translated with an Introduction by H. Mattingley, Translation Revised by S. A. Handford*, Harmondsworth: Penguin, 1970.

15   Suetonius, *Vespasian* 24.

16   Ibid. 23.4, tr. Kershaw, S.

17   *Panegyricus.* 11.1.

Vespasian himself was interred in the Mausoleum of Augustus, with whom he can be justifiably compared: he had ended the civil wars that had brought him to power; he had ruled moderately and conscientiously; he was sensitive to the soldiers' interests; he had surrounded himself with (mostly) able advisers; and had ultimately brought peace to a rebuilt Empire. Everything was back to normal:

> Think, by way of illustration, on the times of Vespasian, and thou shalt see all these things: mankind marrying, rearing children, sickening, dying, warring, making holiday, trafficking, tilling, flattering others, vaunting themselves, scheming, praying for the death of others, murmuring at their own lot, hoarding, coveting a consulate, coveting a kingdom.[18]

Titus' Back-Story: The First Jewish Revolt ('The Great Revolt')

There was never any doubt that Titus' transition to power would be seamless. Rather like Tiberius had been towards the end of Augustus' life, Titus was Vespasian's 'partner in the Empire', and he was acknowledged as *Princeps* by the Senate, assuming the titles of Augustus, and, by September, *Pater Patriae*. On his accession he was in his late thirties, highly experienced in military and administrative matters, and had two ex-wives. Arrecina Tertulla had died soon after their wedding, and his union with Marcia Furnilla had been dissolved when her family got on the wrong side of Nero. Titus had a daughter named Flavia Julia, but from which marriage it is not clear.

From 66 to 70 Titus had been at the sharp end of the revolt in Judaea, where the whole situation had exposed a number of problems with Rome's imperialism for both rulers and subjects. The Jews accommodated the divine Roman Emperor by sacrificing twice a day to both him and the Roman people, and back

---

18 Marcus Aurelius, *Meditations* IV.32, tr. in Brown, P., *The Making of Late Antiquity*, Cambridge, MA, and London: Harvard University Press, 1978, p. 6.

in Tiberius' reign Jesus had advocated consensus by telling the Pharisees to 'Render therefore unto Caesar the things which are Caesar's; and unto God the things that are God's',[19] effectively acknowledging that taxes paid both to Rome and to the Jewish Temple could exist side by side. On the other side, John the Baptist told Roman soldiers, 'Do violence to no man, neither accuse any falsely; and be content with your wages.' [20] However, it was not simply a case of Romans versus Jews: many tax-gatherers in Judaea came from a Jewish elite that did very well out of the Roman Empire, making taxation a real bone of contention within Jewish society.

When Roman forces moved into Judaea in 67, they laid siege to Jotapata (Yodfat) in Galilee. It was brutal. Vespasian himself was wounded, and horrendous injuries were inflicted on the defenders by the Roman catapults. One man's

> head was knocked clean off by a stone, and his skull was thrown for over half a kilometre. In the day time as well, a pregnant woman who had just come out of her house had her stomach struck so violently that the foetus was ripped out to about a hundred metres away. Such was the power of the stone-thrower.[21]

As Titus led the final assault, the Jewish commander, Joseph ben Mattathias, hid in a cave with forty other rebels. They made a suicide pact. On Joseph's suggestion they drew lots for each man to kill the one next to him. Joseph made it through to the final two, persuaded his companion to surrender and prophesied Vespasian's elevation to the purple. Having been spared, he defected to Rome and was henceforth known as Flavius Josephus.[22]

Titus was bearing down on Jerusalem when the news broke

---

19   *Matthew* 22.21; *Mark* 12.17; *Luke* 20.25.
20   *Luke* 3.14.
21   Josephus, *de Bello Judaico* 3.7.23, tr. Kershaw, S.
22   See above, p 115.

that Nero had committed suicide. Military activity in Judaea was suspended, and Vespasian sent Titus to greet the new Emperor Galba. Events conspired to prevent him making it to Rome, though, and while the Year of the Four Emperors took its course, Titus returned to Judaea to assume the supreme command there and in Syria. Jerusalem became the focus of operations once again.

The siege of Jerusalem began in the spring of 70 and took 140 days. With two pro-Roman Jews, Vespasian's early backer Ti. Julius Alexander, and Flavius Josephus on Titus' staff, the Romans followed their best military practice and deployed *Legiones* V *Macedonica*, XII *Fulminata*, XV *Apollinaris* and X *Fretensis* to make terraces, ramps, towers and battering rams and smash through the city's fortifications. Titus breached the walls of the New City, completed the circumvallation of the Inner City, inflicted starvation on the defenders, and stormed the outer Temple court. Amidst utter carnage, the Temple was burned to the ground – something that friendly sources like Josephus assert that Titus tried to avoid, and more hostile ones see as a deliberate policy decision.[23]

Overall, it had been 'job done' with typical Roman efficiency. Coinage celebrated *IUDAEA CAPTA* and the Temple's treasures were displayed in the triumph that Titus and Vespasian celebrated in 71. The golden menorah, silver trumpets and the table for the showbread are still visible carved in relief on the Arch of Titus at Rome. The last remnants of the resistance were mopped up in spring of 74 when the new governor of Judaea, L. Flavius Silva, with *Legio* X *Fretensis* and assorted auxiliaries, took the seemingly impregnable fortress of Masada, held by Eleazar ben Yair and a group of extremists often called Zealots but better termed *Sicarii* after their characteristic curved flick-knives. Silva enclosed Masada's steep-sided rocky hill with a line of circumvallation and constructed a quite astonishing siege

---

23 The only substantial surviving account of the siege is Josephus, *de Bello Judaico* 5–6.

ramp up which a tower with a massive battering ram was deployed. Josephus records that the *Sicarii* killed their families and then themselves rather than surrender. Of the 960 defenders the only survivors were two women and five children.

Following the war in Judaea, Titus enjoyed an illicit romantic interlude in the already complex love life of the Jewish princess Berenice of Cilicia, the sister and, some said, lover of M. Julius Agrippa II, great-grandson of Herod the Great and client king of Chalcis, north-east of Judaea. In Juvenal's *Satires*, a lady called Bibula goes on a shopping spree that includes

> a famous diamond ring – once flaunted
> by Berenice, which adds to its price: a gift from her brother,
> that barbarous prince Agrippa, a token of their incest,
> in the land where monarchs observe the Sabbath barefoot,
> and tradition leaves pigs to attain ripe old age.[24]

But to the Romans Berenice looked rather too much like another Cleopatra VII, and although she went to Rome in 75, her relationship with Titus had to end (with mutual sorrow) when he became Emperor.

Titus' love life, along with the supposed servile origin of his mother, his alleged heavy-handedness as *Praefectus Praetorio*, lurid rumours of late-night revels, male prostitutes and eunuchs, and even a story mentioned by the Emperor Hadrian that he poisoned his father, made people fear that Titus might turn out to be Nero II. But he seems to have been sensitive to these worries, and he managed to transform himself into 'the delight and darling of the human race',[25] the man who once bemoaned the fact that he had not done anyone a favour since the previous evening with the words, 'My friends, I have wasted a day.'[26]

---

24   Juvenal, *Satire* 6.156 ff., tr. Green, P, op. cit.
25   Suetonius, *Titus* 1.
26   Suetonius, *Titus* 8.1, tr. Kershaw, S.

Vesuvius Erupts

Titus' new persona was put to the test by a huge humanitarian disaster that struck only months into his reign:

> Mount Vesuvius burst open at its summit, and so much fire spurted forth that it consumed the surrounding countryside together with the towns.[27]

The towns in question were Pompeii and Herculaneum, along with a number of other settlements and some seaside villas owned by affluent Romans. The circumstances of their destruction and subsequent preservation now provide us with invaluable information about Roman social, economic, religious and political life: bakeries still contain loaves of bread in their ovens; fulleries (processing and cleaning plants for wool) shed light on one of the area's key industries; factories for *garum* (fish sauce – which even has a kosher variety) were equally pungent and lucrative; wine and take-away food shops sustained the workforce; we hear of bankers and bath attendants, chicken-keepers and cloak-sellers, felt-workers and furnace stokers; cesspits and their contents allow us to get 'up close and personal' with the Roman world; a brothel displays explicitly adventurous erotic frescoes; the enormous virtuoso 'Alexander mosaic' shows Alexander the Great charging into the fray to defeat Darius III;[28] on the frieze from the Villa of the Mysteries a series of stupendously rendered life-size figures (*megalographia* is the technical term for this) perform enigmatic rituals that involve a 'female Pan' suckling a goat, a kneeling woman unveiling a phallus, and a half-naked winged female demon in high boots flagellating a young woman while a naked woman dances on

---

27   Eusebius, *Chronicle* 79 CE, tr. in Cooley, A. and M. G. L., op. cit.
28   It is conventionally said to depict the Battle of Issus in 333 BCE, but there are also persuasive arguments in favour of Granicus (334 BCE) or Gaugamela (331 BCE). See Cohen, A., *The Alexander Mosaic: Stories of Victory and Defeat*, Cambridge: Cambridge University Press, 1997.

tiptoes with castanets;[29] the opulent Villa of the Papyri at Herculaneum had an extraordinary collection of over 1 000 rolls of carbonized papyrus, which, with great ingenuity, are currently being deciphered, edited and translated; and a recent TV programme claims that 'the skeletons of a pair of twins show what were *almost certainly*[30] the signs of congenital syphilis', supposedly putting paid to the idea that the disease was brought to Europe from the New World by Christopher Columbus, although we might object that there is no peer-reviewed publication to explain how related bacteria were ruled out, and that it's extremely difficult to differentiate between syphilis and closely related non-venereal diseases like yaws, which is found all around the Mediterranean and is common in children.

The archaeology of the cities of Vesuvius is noisy. Inscriptions harangue us from public buildings:

> Gaius Quinctius Valgus, son of Gaius, and Marcus Porcius, son of Marcus, quinquennial *duumviri*, for the honour of the colony, saw to the construction of the amphitheatre at their own expense and gave the area to the colonists in perpetuity.[31]

Programmata, 'posters' painted on walls, tell you whom to vote for and why:

> I beg you to elect Gaius Julius Polybius *aedilis*. He brings good bread.[32]

---

29   'Ultimately, its purpose remains a mystery', Berry, J., *The Complete Pompeii,* London: Thames & Hudson, 2007, p. 202; 'To be honest, this is all completely baffling', Beard, M., *Pompeii: The Life of a Roman Town,* London: Profile Books, 2008, p. 131.
30   My emphasis.
31   *CIL* X 852 = *ILS* 5627, tr. in Cooley, A. and M. G. L., op. cit. Quinquennial *duumviri* were local magistrates.
32   *CIL* IV 429 = *ILS* 6412e, tr. Kershaw, S.

All the after-hours drinkers ask you to elect Marcus Cerrinius Vatia *aedilis*. Florus and Fructus wrote this.[33]

There is scurrilous filth above the beds in the brothel:

Scordopordonicus (= 'Mr. Garlic-farter') fucked whoever he wanted here in good style.[34]
I came, I fucked, I went home.[35]

A witty fuller parodies Virgil:

Fullones ululamque cano, non arma virumque
I sing of fullers and an owl, not of arms and the man.[36]

There are announcements for shows:

At the dedication ᐞPoly(bius?)ᐞ of the games of Gnaeus Alleius Nigidius Maius [. . .] There will be a hunt, athletes, sprinklings, awnings. Good fortune to Maius, leader of the colony.[37]

'Stats' from gladiatorial combats show us who won, when, how often, and what happened to the losers:

Games [. . .] on the 12, 13, 14, 15 May
Thracian versus *murmillo*:

---

33 *CIL* IV 581 = *ILS* 6418d, tr. Kershaw, S.
34 *CIL* IV 2188, tr. Kershaw, S. He mis-spells the Latin for 'fuck' as 'was', and uses *quem*, the masculine for 'whoever', when (presumably) he means *quam* (feminine).
35 *CIL* IV 2246, tr. Kershaw, S.
36 *CIL* IV 9131, tr. Kershaw, S. The line is written on the wall of a house belonging to a fuller called M. Fabius Ululitremulus and is in the same metre as Virgil's *Aeneid*, whose opening words are *arma virumque cano* (= 'I sing of arms and the man'). The owl (*ulula*) is a symbol of fullers, because of its link to their patroness, Minerva, and the parody also puns on the fuller's name.
37 *CIL* IV 1177 = *ILS* 5144, tr. in Cooley, A. and M. G. L., op. cit. Polybius is the name of the sign-writer.

Won.Pugnax, Neronian, fought 3.
Killed.Murranus, Neronian, fought 3.

Heavily armed fighter versus Thracian:
Won.Cycnus, Julian, fought 9.
Reprieved. Atticus, Julian, fought 14.[38]

A celebrity Thracian gladiator called Celadus boasts of his big female fan-base:

He makes the girls sigh.[39]
Glory of the girls.[40]

Teachers give their 'learning outcomes':

Whoever has paid me the fee for teaching, let him have what he seeks from the gods.[41]

People insult one another:

Equitias' slave Cosimus is a big queer and a cocksucker with his legs wide open.[42]

Market days are listed:

In the consulship of Nero Caesar Augustus and Cossus Lentulus, son of Cossus [i.e., 60], 8 days before the *Ides* of February [i.e., 6 February], Sunday, 16 (day of the new) moon, market at Cumae, 5 (days before the *Ides* of February), market at Pompeii.[43]

---

38   *CIL* IV 2508, tr. in Cooley, A. and M. G. L., op. cit.
39   *CIL* IV 4342, 4397, tr. Kershaw, S.
40   *CIL* IV 4345, tr. Kershaw, S.
41   *CIL* IV 8562, tr. in Cooley, A. and M. G. L., op. cit.
42   *ILS* 648, tr. Richlin, A., op. cit.
43   *CIL* IV 4182, tr. in Cooley, A. and M. G. L., op. cit.

Traders advertise themselves:

> Marcus Vecilius Verecundus, draper.[44]

Amorous invitations are made:

> My life, my delight, let us play this game for a while: this bed
> be a field and I your steed.[45]

Some verses urge a drunken mule driver to

> Take me to Pompeii, where my sweet love lives.[46]

And Gaius Pumpidius Dipilus woz 'ere:

> Gaius Pumpidius Dipilus was here, five days before the *nones*
> of October when Marcus Lepidus and Quintus Catulus were
> consuls [i.e., 2 October 72 BCE].[47]

In fact, all human life was there. But then, seemingly out of
nowhere, it was wiped out.

We have an incredibly vivid eyewitness account from two
letters written to Tacitus by the Younger Pliny, a Roman admin-
istrator and poet whose uncle, Pliny the Elder, was the
commander of the naval base at Misenum on the Bay of Naples.
Most conventional accounts date the eruption to IX *Kal. Septem-
bris*, i.e., 24 August 79, although there is now some doubt about
this. Pliny's text may have been corrupted, and could possibly
read III *Kal. Novembris, Kal. Novembris* or IX *Kal. Decembris*

---

44 *CIL* IV 3130, tr. Kershaw, S.
45 *CIL* IV 1781, tr. Varone, A., in 'Voices of the Ancients. A stroll Through Public
and Private Pompcii, in Ministetio per i Bene Culturale e Ambientali Soprintendenza
Archeologica di Pompcii, *Rediscovering Pompeii*, Rome: L'Erma di Bretscheider,
1992, p. 39.
46 *CIL* IV 5092, tr. Kershaw, S.
47 *CIL* IV 1842, tr. in Cooley, A. and M. G. L., op. cit.

(30 October, 1 November or 23 November respectively); the victims were largely wearing heavy woollen garments; quantities of autumnal fruits have been found; and a coin of Titus discovered in the House of Gold Bracelet bears the legend *TR P VIIII IMP XV COS VII PP* = 'with Tribunician power for the ninth time [conferred on 1 July], acclaimed Imperator for the fifteenth time [epigraphic sources suggest that this honour could not have been granted before 8 September], Consul for the seventh time [securely dating the coin to 79], Father of his Country'.

Yet if the date remains unclear, the unfolding of the tragedy is not. It started with a minor explosion of steam (the 'phreatomagmatic opening phase'). Then around noon a huge column of hot gas and pumice erupted from the volcano, rising to a height of 15 to 30 kilometres. This phase of explosive volcanic eruptions is now called the 'Plinian phase' after the way Pliny described it:

> Its general appearance can best be expressed as being like [an umbrella] pine, for it rose to a great height on a sort of trunk and then split off into branches.[48]

He tells of hot, thick ash falling, followed by bits of pumice and blackened stones, charred and cracked by the flames. This material fell on Pompeii at the rate of 15 cm per hour for around the next eighteen hours. There was a threat that people would get trapped in their houses by falling debris, and outdoors people tied pillows over their heads to protect themselves. During the night, broad sheets of fire and leaping flames blazed on Mount Vesuvius, made all the more frightening by severe earth tremors.

By around dawn, Pompeii was covered to a depth of more than 3 metres. Three hundred and ninety-four bodies have been

---

48 Pliny *Letters* 6.16.5, tr. Radice, B., in *Pliny: Letters, Books I–VII, Panegyricus, with an English Translation by Betty Radice*, Cambridge, MA and London: Harvard University Press, 1969.

recovered from the pumice layers, 88 per cent of them in buildings, where walls and roofs had collapsed.[49] Herculaneum,
which was not downwind of the eruption, received less pumice
(20 cm or so) at this stage. Pliny says that there was darkness,
blacker and denser than any ordinary night, which they relieved
by lighting torches and lamps. Tsunamis struck the coast:

> We also saw the sea sucked away and apparently forced back
> by the earthquake: at any rate it receded from the shore so
> that quantities of sea creatures were left stranded on dry
> sand.[50]

There was panic, but despite the falling material those who
fled into the open air had the greater chance of survival at this
stage. However, this changed around daybreak as the eruption
column began to collapse, and the first of six pyroclastic density
currents ('PDCs', also known as *nuées ardentes*), avalanches of
hot ash, pumice, rock fragments and volcanic gas, hurtled down
the sides of the volcano at speeds of 100 kilometres per hour or
more:

> The cloud sank down to earth and covered the sea; it had
> already blotted out Capri and hidden the promontory of
> Misenum from sight [. . .] I looked round: a dense black cloud
> was coming up behind us, spreading over the earth like a
> flood [. . .] Darkness fell, not the dark of a moonless or cloudy
> night, but as if the lamp had been put out in a closed room.[51]

---

49 There will undoubtedly be many more. A detailed breakdown of the precise
locations and dates of the finds (correct as of 2003) is given in Luongo, G., Perrotta,
A., Scarpati, C., De Carolis, E., Patricelli, G. and Ciarallo, A., 'Impact of the AD 79
explosive eruption on Pompeii, II. Causes of death of the inhabitants inferred by
stratigraphic analysis and areal distribution of the human casualties', *Journal of
Volcanology and Geothermal Research* 126 (2003) 169–200.

50 Pliny *Letters* 6.20.9, tr. Radice, B., op. cit.

51 Ibid. 6.20.11–14.

No one in their path stood a chance. At Herculaneum, which was overwhelmed to a depth of 3 metres by searing hot ash, more than 300 victims sheltering in the arcades by the sea met a swift but agonizing end: a woman swept off a terrace 20 metres above; a soldier knocked face down by the force of the blast, his fingers scrabbling at the sand; a small horse; a lady wearing jewel-encrusted gold rings, golden bracelets and earrings; a seven-month-old baby in the arms of a fourteen-year-old girl; and a 10-metre-long Roman boat thrown keel-up on the beach, with its helmsman nearby, clutching an oar. An hour or so later, a second PDC hit Herculaneum, depositing another 1.5 metres of ash, tearing down walls, columns and statues. In the end, Herculaneum was buried to depth of 15 to 18 metres in what used to be thought was boiling mud, but which is in fact ignimbrite: the gas trapped in the deposit of pyroclastic flows escapes and the ash gets welded together because of the heat, forming a solid, hard rock.

The third PDC reached the nearest gate of Pompeii at about 6.30 a.m. At around 7.30 a.m. a fourth surge overwhelmed the interior of the town, killing many of the surviving residents, 650 of whose remains have been discovered, mainly by asphyxiation, but also by thermal shock or physical trauma caused by the force of the eruption. About half the people were indoors at the time, and the majority of them were in groups rather than on their own. In the *Giornale di Napoli* for 12 February 1863, Giuseppe Fiorelli, then director of the excavations at Pompeii, wrote:

On the third of this month [. . .] at the height of five meters above the soil[52] [. . .] we came to a place where the earth gave way under the trowel, revealing a hollow cavity deep enough to reach in at arm's length and remove some bones. I realized immediately that this was the impression of a human body,

---

52   The victims had evidently emerged from shelter and been overcome by the fourth PDC while heading down one of the streets on top of the material that had been deposited during the earlier phase of the eruption.

and I thought that by quickly pouring in scagliola, the cast of an entire person would be obtained. The result surpassed my every expectation.[53]

Fiorelli talked of the 'very bodies of the ancients, stolen from death [*rapiti alla morte*], after eighteen centuries of oblivion', and another letter by Luigi Settembrini, entitled 'The Pompeians', published in the same newspaper five days later, put it perfectly:

But now you, my friend Fiorelli, have discovered human pain, and whoever is human can feel it.[54]

Guidebooks glibly tell you that Pompeii is a 'city frozen in time', which gives us 'a complete snapshot of Roman everyday life'. It does nothing of the sort. It gives you an enlarged picture of pure, unmitigated horror. There is a group with the family silver; a slave hampered by the iron bands around his ankles; a pregnant late-teenage girl with her unborn child still in her womb, and her arthritic elderly relatives; a guard-dog chained to the entrance of its owner's house; eighteen adults and boys in the lavatory of the great gymnasium; and a rich lady taking refuge in the gladiatorial barracks. It is often (wrongly) said that this lady was conducting a sordid affair with a hunky gladiator, but if she was it was probably even more interesting than that interpretation implies: her body was found with seventeen other people and a dog. All these casualties shared a similar fate to Pliny's asthmatic uncle, who collapsed amid the flames and smell of sulphur, choked by the dense fumes as he rushed from Misenum to help the stricken population and to get a view of the volcanic phenomena.

Two more surges hit Pompeii in quick succession, killing anyone who may have survived thus far, and adding another 60

---

53   *Giornale di Napoli*, 12 February 1863.
54   Ibid.

to180 cm of debris. The volcanic activity probably lasted for several more days, or indeed weeks, leaving the town buried to a depth of 6 to 7 metres. Precisely what proportion of the inhabitants died is hard to tell, although recent estimates lean towards approximately 2 000 at Pompeii. Young males are under-represented among the dead, so it may be that they simply ran for it as soon as the eruption started. Specific named victims include Agrippa, the son of a Jewish princess called Drusilla who was the daughter of Agrippa I, and Antonius Felix, Claudius' *procurator* of Judaea. Another incredibly moving set of documents is the Epigraphic Alba from Herculaneum. These marble slabs, dateable to the last decade of the city's life, contain lists of 450 legible names of residents of Herculaneum, many of whom must have perished.[55]

Titus, however, made disaster relief a priority:

> He conveyed not only [. . .] a series of comforting edicts but [helped] the victims to the utmost extent of his purse. He set up a board of ex-Consuls, chosen by lot, to relieve distress in Campania, and devoted the property of those who had died in the eruption and left no heirs to a fund for rebuilding the stricken cities.[56]

But, although the region as a whole recovered reasonably quickly, the cities were not rebuilt.

Further problems occurred the next year, in the form of a bad fire in Rome, which destroyed temples, public buildings and thousands of dwellings, and a virulent outbreak of plague. But Titus' humanitarian efforts bolstered his popularity, and he acquired a reputation for generosity, notwithstanding Dio's less than gushing assessment that, 'in financial matters, Titus was frugal and made no unnecessary expenditure'.[57]

---

55   *CIL* 10.1403; *AE* 119.
56   Suetonius, *Titus* 8.3–4, tr. Graves, R., op. cit.
57   Dio 66.19.3, tr. Kershaw, S.

The 'Sacred Pornography of Cruelty': The Colosseum/Coliseum

Whether or not the completion of a 50 000-capacity gladiatorial arena can be classified under 'frugality' and/or 'necessary expenditure', the Colosseum project was finally inaugurated in 80, a decade after Vespasian had started the process. Its name comes partly from its size, but also perhaps from a statue of Nero (the 'Colossus') that stood close by. The cost was immense, but so was the booty from the Jewish War, and even though it was still not quite finished, Titus staged a hundred-day festival at venues across the entire city of Rome.

The poet Martial's *Book of the Shows*, written to commemorate the Amphitheatre's inauguration, begins with a gruesomely pornographic re-enactment of the mythological tale of Pasiphae and the Cretan bull:[58]

> Believe that Pasiphae was mated to the Dictean bull; we have seen it, the old legend has won credence. And let not hoary antiquity plume itself, Caesar: whatever Fame sings of, the arena affords you.[59]

There were gladiators, although only one contest is described – the only one, in fact, to be described in any surviving ancient source:

> As Priscus ['Ancient'] and Verus ['True'] each drew out the contest and the struggle between the pair long stood equal, shouts loud and often sought discharge for the combatants. But Caesar obeyed his own law (the law was that the bout go on without shield until a finger be raised [as a sign of submission]) [. . .] But an end to the even strife was found: equal

---

58   For the myth, which leads to the birth of the Minotaur, see Kershaw, S., op. cit., pp. 275–7.

59   Martial, *De Spectaculis Liber* 5(6), tr. Shackleton Bailey, D. R., in *Martial: Epigrams edited and translated by D. R. Shackleton Bailey, Volume 1*, Cambridge MA, and London: Harvard University Press, 1993.

they fought, equal they yielded. To both Caesar sent wooden swords [symbolizing discharge from the obligation to fight again] and to both palms. Thus valour and skill had their reward.[60]

There were fights featuring elephants, a rhino, bulls, lions and tigresses, and women, albeit not ones 'of social distinction', were involved in wild beast hunts. Suetonius says that 5 000 animals were killed on the first day alone, and Dio puts the grand total at 9 000.[61] There is controversy over whether the arena was flooded as part of the shows. Dio states that

> Titus [. . .] filled this same theatre with water and brought in horses and bulls and some other domesticated animals that had been taught to behave in the liquid element just as on land. He also brought in people on ships, who engaged in a sea-fight there, impersonating the Corcyreans and Corinthians.[62]

Suetonius implies otherwise:

> Titus staged a sea-fight on the old artificial lake, and when the water had been let out, used the basin for further gladiatorial contests and wild beast hunts.[63]

The substructures that now comprise the basement area of the Colosseum would not have allowed flooding to take place, but the first versions of these are thought to be of post-Titan date, and the pro-/anti-flooding debate, which covers the

---

60   Ibid., 31(27; 29).
61   Suetonius, *Titus* 7.3; Dio 66.25.1.
62   Dio 66.25.2 f., tr. Cary. E., op. cit. The Corcyreans and Corinthians had famously fought one another in the fifth century BCE, triggering the Peloponnesian War between Athens and Sparta.
63   Suetonius, *Titus* 7.3, tr. Graves, R., op. cit. Martial's *De Spectaculis Liber* 27(24) also mentions sea-battles, but in an unspecified venue.

questions of venue, sight lines, water supply, drainage, etc., has been vitriolic since the nineteenth century.

Mark Twain regarded the Colosseum as 'the monarch of all European ruins'.[64] Its elliptical outer ring is almost 50 metres high; the long axis is 188 metres and the shorter one 156 metres. The travertine outer facade is divided into four tiers and embellished with 'applied' (i.e., purely decorative) Tuscan columns on the lower level, Ionic on the second, and Corinthian on the third. The fourth tier is divided by Corinthian pilasters into sections where square windows are positioned at regular intervals. Above the windows is a set of corbels used to hold the masts which supported a great awning (*velarium*) that provided shade for the spectators, who took their seats via the seventy-six numbered arches on the ground floor. The four arches on the main axes were not numbered, and it is usually assumed (on practically zero evidence) that these were allocated to the gladiators, authorities and the imperial entourage, although the 'royal box' on the south side, which can also be accessed from outside the building via an underground passageway, could have been reserved for the Emperor.

Admission was probably free, but the seats were carefully segregated on the basis of civic status – seeing and being seen were a crucial part of the experience – and every amphiteatregoer doubtless had a 'ticket' specifying the entrance archway, *maenianum* (block/level) and row of the seat. The 'ringside' area (the *ima cavea*), which had good-quality stone seats, was allocated to various VIP groups of magistrates, colleges of priests and foreign diplomats, with a special seating area, the *subsellia*, set aside for Senators and their families. 'Health and Safety' considerations meant that they were well protected from activities in the arena below. The second sector (*maenianum primum*) had marble seats reserved for Equestrians. The plebs took up the third (*maenianum secundum imum*) and the fourth sectors

---

64 Twain, M., *The Innocents Abroad, or, the New Pilgrims' Progress*, Hartford: American Publishing Company, 1869, p. 276.

(*maenianum secundum summum*), whilst the fifth (*maenianum summum in ligneis*), which comprised a series of wooden steps crowned with a colonnaded portico, was set aside for slaves, non-citizens and women, effectively ensuring that no woman with any social pretensions would go there.

The performers are usually said to have entered the arena through gates on the long axis, called in modern guidebooks, but not by ancient Romans, the Porta Triumphalis (west, for the living) and the Porta Libitinaria (east, for the verifiably dead). As its name suggests, the arena (Latin *harena* = 'sand') was a sandy surface, and it stood on wooden staging above a complex of underground rooms and passages called the *hypogeum*, which was completed by Domitian. The *hypogeum* contained rooms for storing scenery and props, dressing rooms, and alternative ways into the arena for the gladiators, wild beasts and auxiliary staff, such as lifts that could bring the performers up into the arena to good dramatic effect. Tunnels led into the *hypogeum* from outside the amphitheatre: the passage on the central axis went to the barracks of the gladiators (the Ludus Magnus). Various ancillary facilities in the neighbourhood included the *Sanitarium* where wounded gladiators were treated, the *Spoliarium*, where dead gladiators were taken, the *Armamentarium* (armoury), and the *Summum Choragium* where props and staging equipment were stored.

These days a large cross, erected originally by Mussolini's Fascist regime, stands on the north side; outside, on the east wall, is a Latin inscription installed by Pope Benedict XIV in 1750:

> The Flavian amphitheatre, famous for its triumphs and spectacles, dedicated to the gods of the pagans in their impious cult, redeemed by the blood of the martyrs from foul superstition.

Yet, despite various Christian accounts dating from the fifth century or later that may indicate otherwise, there is no watertight evidence for any Christian ever being martyred for their faith in the Colosseum. They *may* have been (many were martyred 'in Rome'), but it was in the interests of later Christians to assert that they were: '"Martyr Acts" [...] acted as a kind of sacred pornography of cruelty, tying the Christian message to gruesome and gory deaths at the hand of the Roman authorities.'[65]

Domitian Comes to Power

Titus remained popular during his short reign, but in the summer of 81 he fell ill, and on 3 September he died in the same villa as Vespasian had done. He was forty-two. The mourning was deep and the conspiracy theories plentiful: had Domitian ordered him to be left for dead when he was ill? Had Domitian placed him in a chest packed with snow in order to bring on a chill? Had Domitian poisoned him? Or had Titus just rashly used the baths when he was poorly?[66] We don't know. But fratricide or not, Domitian delivered the funeral eulogy, had Titus deified, and completed the Temple of Vespasian and Titus. Apparently, Titus had one last unspecified regret: Dio wonders whether this was to do with not taking his brother's wife, or his life.[67] He also suggests that, like certain rock stars of today, Titus' reputation benefited from an early death.

The twenty-nine-year-old person who now emerged from his elder brother's shadow was tall, cultivated a self-consciously modest expression and had large, dimly sighted eyes. He was good-looking in his younger years, although he rather went to seed later on and wrote a book, *On Haircare*, in response to going bald. He was reputedly idle and lustful: his 'sexercise' consisted of what he called 'bed-wrestling'; he personally depilated his concubines; and he swam with the most vulgar whores.

---

65 Hopkins, K. and Beard, M., *The Colosseum*, London: Profile Books, 2005, p. 105.
66 Suetonius, *Domitian* 2.3 (left for dead); Dio 66.26.2–3 (snow); Aurelius Victor, *De Caesaribus* 10.11, Philostratus, *De Apoll.* 6.32 (poison); Plutarch, *De Sanitate Tuenda* 3 (bathing).
67 Suetonius, *Titus* 10.1; Dio 66.26.2–3.

Or so says Suetonius.[68] Domitian was also a solitary individual, spending an hour a day catching flies and stabbing them with a sharp stylus. His would not be an easy Principate.

Domitian's conjugal choices are illuminating (see Genealogy Table 2). Titus' daughter (Domitian's niece) Flavia Julia had been offered to him as a bride, but he had spurned her in favour of Domitia Longina, daughter of Nero's star general Corbulo. This was not a bad choice, and it gave Domitian some military credibility by association, but it was also a stormy relationship: their only child died in infancy and Domitian exiled her around 83–4 for adultery with a pantomime actor called Paris. He revisited the idea of marrying Flavia Julia, but recalled Domitia Longina to Rome, where she lived with him until his death, in which she possibly had a hand.[69] Flavia Julia is said to have died when Domitian forced her to have an abortion in the late 80s.

Once he had been hailed as Emperor by the Praetorian Guard, and the Senate had formally ratified their choice, Domitian had all that he needed to rule: *imperium*, the title Augustus, tribunician power, the office of *Pontifex Maximus* and the designation *Pater Patriae*. The first item on his 'to do list' was to acquire military credentials.

Domitian's Military Campaigns

Ultimately, Domitian would be acclaimed Imperator twenty-two times, and one man who would contribute to that tally was on his third tour of duty in Britain, of which he was the governor: Cn. Julius Agricola. Agricola's daughter was married to Tacitus, said to be probably a better biographer than Agricola was a general, and whose *Agricola* gives us excellent, if rather panegyrical, insights into the campaigns. Vespasian had appointed Agricola in 77 or 78, and after quashing a rebellion by the Ordovices in

---

68   Suetonius, *Domitian* 22.1.
69   Interestingly, even after Domitian's *damnation memoriae,* she continued to refer to herself as the Emperor's wife (as, for instance, on brick stamps datable to 123: *CIL* 15.548a–9d).

Wales, sending his auxiliary cavalry swimming across the Menai Straits to capture Mona, mopping up pockets of resistance among the Brigantes left over from Cerialis' governorship,[70] and advancing to the River Tay, he consolidated the Forth–Clyde line, which Titus (then Emperor) may have envisaged as the limit of Roman expansion (see Map 2). Under Domitian, Agricola became uneasy about a possible uprising by the northern tribes, so he moved beyond the Forth–Clyde line into the territory of the Caledones, whereupon they retaliated by attacking Roman installations 'without provocation',[71] and thus gave him his *casus belli*.

The first campaign saw *Legio* IX *Hispana*'s camp attacked by night, and only narrowly saved by XX *Valeria Victrix*, but the following year Agricola confronted the Caledones at the battle of Mons Graupius in 83 or 84. Despite being urged on by Calgacus' immortal denunciation of Roman imperialism, 'where they make a desert they call it peace',[72] the natives were easily beaten. Agricola's legions didn't even have to engage, as his auxiliaries inflicted 10 000 casualties.

The Battle of Mons Graupius marked the end of Roman expansion in Britain for a while. Agricola was recalled, and although Tacitus states that 'Britain was totally subdued and immediately abandoned',[73] because of Domitian's jealousy of Agricola's success, the reality was that troops were urgently needed in central Europe: a vexillation of *Legio* II *Adiutrix* was transferred to the Danube front in 85, and the rest of the legion followed shortly afterwards; all the territory beyond the Forth was given up; and the British garrison was permanently reduced to three legions, II *Augusta*, IX *Hispana* and XX *Valeria Victrix*.

One of Domitian's military problems was a war against the Chatti that had broken out along the middle sector of the Rhine frontier in 82 or 83. He took the field against them personally,

---

70   See above, p. 143.
71   Tacitus, *Agricola* 25.
72   Ibid. 30. See above, p. 60.
73   Tacitus, *Histories* 1.2, tr. Kershaw, S.

smashed their power, expanded the area of Roman control in the Wetterau and established a permanent boundary there as well as along the eastern edge of the *Decumates Agri*, and celebrated a triumph in the summer of 83 (even though the war dragged on for a few more years).

Domitian was generally popular with his soldiers, not least because he increased their pay by one-third (the first rise since Augustus), and he would need their loyalty to deal with a serious threat on the Danube (see Map 4). Led by Decebalus, the Dacians, who occupied modern Romania, had invaded Roman territory in 85 and killed Oppius Sabinus, the governor of Moesia. Domitian's punitive response, led by the *Praefectus Praetorio* Cornelius Fuscus, was successful enough for Domitian to celebrate a triumph in 86. But Fuscus then got himself killed in further fighting and Domitian had to return to the region, where Tettius Julianus, the new governor of Upper Moesia, defeated the Dacians in (probably) 88.

Domitian's problems just wouldn't go away. In January 89, L. Antonius Saturninus, who commanded the legions of Germania Superior, mutinied. Fortunately for the Emperor, the Rhine thawed just in time to prevent Saturninus' barbarian allies from crossing the ice to join him. Saturninus was killed in battle, the *putsch* was duly suppressed, and to discover any conspirators who were in hiding Domitian tortured his captives by applying fire to their private parts, although two men avoided death by claiming that they were *impudici* (played the receptive role in sex), and therefore too effeminate to be guilty.

With the region now more stable, he converted the military districts of Germania Superior and Inferior into regular provinces and redeployed some of the Rhine troops to the Danube. He also made a deal with Decebalus whereby the Dacian would become a nominal client king and protect the lower Danube in return for subsidies. This allowed the Romans to attack the Marcomanni ('Border Men') and Quadi. The source material is poor for this, but it seems that Domitian was back on the Danube in 92 to take on the Suevi (also spelled Suebi) and the

Sarmatians in a campaign that took about eight months, and saw the destruction of a Roman legion. By January 93, Domitian had returned to Rome, but only to celebrate an *ovatio* rather than a triumph. The Danube had clearly become the Empire's crucial frontier area, needing nine legions as opposed to the Rhine's six.

Domitian's Domestic Policies

On the home front Domitian was one of Rome's greatest builders. The fire in Titus' reign had left the city in need of a facelift, and Domitian stepped up to the plate by building, restoring or finishing around fifty projects, including: the fourth incarnation of the Temple of Jupiter Capitolinus, which used at least 12 000 talents of gold to gild the bronze roof tiles; the finishing touches to the Colosseum; the *Ludus Magnus*, Rome's largest gladiator barracks, complete with its own mini-amphitheatre; and the 'awesome and vast'[74] *Domus Flavia* (the official part of the imperial palace) and *Domus Augustana* (Domitian's opulent private residence) on the Palatine. He also had a massive Villa at Alba, his 'Alban fortress',[75] just outside Rome, and he initiated infrastructure and defence projects on an Empire-wide basis.

From 86 onwards he celebrated the lavish Capitoline Games, with contestants coming from all over the Empire to compete in chariot racing, athletics, gymnastics, music, oratory and poetry. He also presented elaborate and often bizarre spectacles: night-time gladiatorial contests; dwarves versus women; food showered on the public from ropes stretched across the top of the Amphitheatre; all-night banquets for the people.

All this was expensive, but Domitian handled the economy firmly and deftly. Soon after he became *Princeps*, he raised the silver content of the *denarius* by about 12 per cent, and, although he had to devalue it in 85 as military and public expenses caught

---

74   Statius, *Silvae* 4.2.
75   Juvenal, *Satire* 4.145. Cf. Tacitus, *Agricola* 45.

up with him, he was still able to keep the currency standard at a higher level than in Vespasian's day. He tried to promote grain production by banning the planting of new vines in Italy and ordering the destruction of all or some vineyards in the provinces, but backed down in the face of strong opposition. In the end, though, he left the treasury in surplus.

Domitian was also rigorous in administering justice, and tough on corruption:

> He took such care to exercise restraint over the city officials and the governors of the provinces that at no time were they more honest or just.[76]

He was also big on public order and morality. Three Vestal Virgins were executed for unchastity in 83, and in 91 Cornelia, the chief Vestal, suffered the archaic punishment of being buried alive.

Overall his policies seem to have had a positive effect on the welfare of the Empire, and while he was alive writers like Statius and Martial had nothing but praise for him. But anyone who liked to style himself 'Our Lord and God', allowed only gold or silver statues of himself above a certain weight to be erected on the Capitol, and renamed September 'Germanicus' and October 'Domitianus' after himself and his triumphs was inevitably going to clash with the Senate. Late in 85 he conferred on himself the unprecedented office of *Censor Perpetuus*, Censor for life.[77] This not only allowed him the supervision of public morality, but also empowered him overtly to determine who might, or might not, be a Senator. This was utterly odious to the nobility, as was the fact that he used Equites more than any previous Emperor and often favoured non-Italians, especially Easterners, for senior appointments.

Further disrespecting the Senate's dignity, he relied heavily upon his *amici* ('friends') in the *Consilium Principis* (Privy

---

76   Suetonius, *Domitian* 8.1, tr. Rolfe, J. C.., op. cit.
77   Eighteen months was the normal duration.

Council) for policy making, a system ridiculed by Juvenal in a satirical poem about how to cook an enormous turbot:

> But alas, no big enough dish could be found for the fish. A summons went out to the Privy Council, each of whom quailed beneath the Emperor's hatred, whose drawn, white faces reflected that great and perilous 'friendship'.[78]

They were probably right to be afraid: Domitian executed at least eleven Senators of Consular rank and exiled many others. This was not as bad a record as Claudius', but Domitian's *attitude* counted for much, and the Senate gained some measure of revenge via the literary tradition that subsequently excoriated him.

There is vilification of Domitian from another quarter too. On the basis of scant and ambivalent evidence, Domitian is often portrayed as a persecutor of Christians on a par with Nero. Jews certainly felt the impact of his extension of the *fiscus Iudaicus*, which came to include not only those who were born Jewish or had converted to Judaism, but also people who kept the fact that they were Jews a secret, or lived as Jews without professing Judaism. Suetonius was an eyewitness to this process in action:

> I recall being present in my youth when the person of a man ninety years old was examined before the *procurator* and a very crowded court, to see whether he was circumcised.[79]

Domitian's cousin, the Consul T. Flavius Clemens, was put to death in 95 on a charge of 'atheism', and a number of others who had 'drifted away into Jewish customs' were similarly condemned.[80] Romans at this date generally regarded Christians as a Jewish sect, and it may be that those who 'lived as Jews

---

78 Juvenal, *Satires* 4.72 ff., tr. Green, P., in *Juvenal: The Sixteen Satires, Translated with an Introduction and Notes by Peter Green*, London: Penguin Classics, 3rd edn, 1998.
79 Suetonius, *Domitian* 12.2, tr. Rolfe, J. C., op. cit.
80 Suetonius, *Domitian* 15.1; Dio 67.14.1 f.

without professing Judaism' were in fact Christians. In Rome there was an early Christian cemetery called 'the Cemetery of Domitilla' after Clemens' wife, on ground that she owned, and another man charged with 'atheism' was Acilius Glabrio, whose family had a crypt in the Christian Cemetery of Priscilla. Spurning Rome's state religion if you weren't a Jew counted as atheism, which became a common accusation against Christians. So it could be that Clemens, Domitilla and Glabrio were Christians, although to extrapolate from there, as some have done, and talk of Empire-wide persecutions, and to associate Domitian with the Beast of *Revelation* and Rome with Babylon 'the mother of the fornications [. . .] drunk with the blood of the saints and with the blood of the martyrs of Jesus'[81] is perhaps stretching the evidence somewhat.

Domitian's Reign of Terror and Death

The execution of Clemens showed just how suspicious the Emperor had become. Saturninus' rebellion of 89 had not helped the overall atmosphere, and prior to that, probably in 82–3, Clemens' brother T. Flavius Sabinus was executed on the grounds that the herald had declared him elected Emperor, not Consul. Domitian supposedly said that no one believed in conspiracies against Emperors unless they had been killed, and his last years degenerated into a paranoid reign of terror. Two of the highest-profile victims were Stoics: Arulenus Rusticus, author of a panegyric on Thrasea Paetus, and Herennius Senecio, author of the *Life* of Helvidius Priscus, both of whose books were publicly burned.

On 18 September 96 it was time to believe in conspiracies. Two groups of people decided to get their retaliation in first: various members of Domitian's domestic staff, who had access to the private quarters, were fearful for their jobs and lives; and certain Senators, who had overlapping concerns with the

---

81 *Revelation* 17:5, 6; Cf. 2:10, 13; 6:11; 13:15; 20:4.

domestics, but were also driven by ideological and/or practical considerations. His wife Domitia Longina may have been in the plot, and the two Praetorian Prefects, T. Petronius Secundus and Norbanus, certainly knew about it. The Senate as a whole could be guaranteed to approve, and someone had already been selected to fill the dead man's shoes – the elderly and respectable M. Cocceius Nerva, even though he was also one of Domitian's *amici*. The man who dealt the first blow was a steward called Stephanus, and though the Emperor put up a decent fight (Nerva heard a rumour that Domitian had survived and almost fainted), he was overcome by further stabs from other assassins.

There were mixed reactions to Domitian's death: the legions generally liked him, but there was no one to lead them in an act of vengeance; the general public were ambivalent; and the Senate were ecstatic. While they ordered all inscriptions referring to him to be effaced and all records of his reign obliterated, authors such as Tacitus and Pliny set to work to damn him for eternity. The hitherto pro-Domitian Martial now changed his tune:

> Flavian race, how much the third inheritor took away from you! It would almost have been worthwhile not to have had the other two.[82]

The Flavian dynasty had come to its end. Rome now entered a new era under the first of what Machiavelli called Rome's 'Five Good Emperors'.[83]

---

82 Martial, *De Spectaculis Liber* 37(33), tr. Shackleton Bailey, D. R., op. cit.
83 Machiavelli, N., *Discourses on the First Decade of Titus Livy*, 1517, Book I, chapter 10.

8

A Hat-Trick of 'Good' Emperors:
Nerva, Trajan and Hadrian (96–138)

If a man were called to fix the period in the history of the world during which the condition of the human race was most happy and prosperous, he would, without hesitation, name that which elapsed from the death of Domitian to the accession of Commodus.

E. Gibbon[1]

Nerva (96–98)

With the end of the Flavian dynasty there is a dramatic drop-off in the quantity and quality of our written source material, but one document that does provide some hard facts is the *Fasti Ostienses*, a marble calendar from Ostia. This tells us:

> 14th day before the Kalends of October [18 September 96]: Domitian killed. On the same day, Marcus Cocceius N[erva] proclaimed Emperor.[2]

If the accession looked odd in that the Empire now fell under the control of a sickly sexagenarian who was a long-time Flavian supporter with close ties to Domitian and a tendency to puke

---

1 Gibbon, E., *The History of the Decline and Fall of the Roman Empire*, London: Strahan & Cadell, 1776–1788, vol. I, chapter 3.31.

2 *I. Ital.* XIII 1, p. 195 under 96 CE, tr. Kershaw, S.

up his food, he was nevertheless of proven competence and, crucially for Rome, he had no children.

Nerva Caesar Augustus as he was now known declared Domitian's *Domus Flavia* 'open house', and took up a more modest abode in the *Horti Sallustiani*. He publicly renounced terrorism, recalled exiles and restored property confiscated by the previous incumbent. But if people complained that under Domitian no one had been allowed to do anything, the Consul T. Catius Caesius Fronto said that under Nerva anyone could do whatever they liked. Everyone

> acted for himself, brought his personal enemies to trial (if they were not too powerful), and had them condemned amid the general confusion and chaos.[3]

Nevertheless, most sources depict Nerva as a man who at least tried to do the right thing: 'I have done nothing that would prevent my laying down the imperial office and returning to private life in safety,' he said.[4] He was certainly keen to balance the budget, and he abolished many sacrifices and spectacles and forbade the erection of gold or silver statues to himself on the Capitol. Yet he still found funds to grant sixty million *sestertii*'s worth of land allotments to Italy's urban poor, and cut inheritance tax. Under his *alimenta* ('nourishments') scheme, Italian landowners were offered low-interest loans, whose proceeds were put into trusts for the maintenance of poor children in Italy.[5] Nerva also dedicated the Forum built by Domitian, which now became known as the Forum of Nerva, or the Forum Transitorium, as well as building granaries, making repairs to the Colosseum, building roads,

---

3 Pliny, *Letters* 9.13.4, tr. Radice, B., in *Pliny: Letters, Books VIII–X, Panegyricus, with an English Translation by Betty Radice,* Cambridge, MA, and London: Harvard University Press, 1969.

4 Dio 68.3.1 tr. Cary, op. cit.

5 This may have been the work of Trajan, who certainly extended the programme, as did Antoninus Pius, and Marcus Aurelius.

establishing veteran colonies in Africa, and reinstating pantomime performances.

Nerva also brought several elder statesmen out of retirement
to help him govern, notably Sextus Julius Frontinus, an
ex-governor of Britain whom he appointed as curator of the
water supply, on which Frontinus published an important book,
de Aquis Urbis Romae. Nerva preferred to consult his own *amici*
and *consilium* rather than the Senate, which inevitably caused ill
feeling, and in 97 he detected a conspiracy led by L. (or C.)
Calpurnius Crassus. However, he merely dropped hints that he
knew about it, and banished Crassus. Such leniency was unwise,
especially since Nerva's regime was vulnerable because Domitian had been a military man, whereas he had been appointed
without the involvement of either the provincial armies or the
Praetorian Guard. The latter mutinied under Casperius Aeli-
anus in 97. Nerva was taken hostage; the Praetorians demanded
the surrender of Domitian's murderers; Nerva resisted their
demands and bared his throat to the soldiers; the conspirators
were seized and killed anyway; but although Nerva survived, he
was still forced into a public expression of thanks to Casperius.

To lose the support of the Praetorians was as good as a death
sentence, but in October 97 Nerva's experienced and popular
governor in Germania Superior, M. Ulpius Traianus ('Trajan'),
won a victory in Pannonia. Trajan commanded both legions and
respect, and Nerva adopted him as his son and heir, buying himself
enough time to die of natural causes. By inaugurating this practice
of adopting a competent army officer as his successor on the basis
of ability rather than family, or indeed nationality, Nerva had
created an important precedent that introduced one of the Roman
Empire's greatest periods of strength and stability.

Trajan (98–117)

Born in Italica in the province of Hispania Baetica on (probably) 18 September 53, Imperator Caesar Nerva Traianus
Augustus, alias Trajan, was the first non-Italian to be Emperor

of Rome, although there is a deafening silence about this in Pliny's monumental speech known as the *Panegyricus*, delivered to the Senate on 1 September 100. The new *Princeps* had served as military tribune in Syria under his father, married Pompeia Plotina from Nemausus (modern Nîmes), become a guardian of P. Aelius Hadrianus (the future Emperor Hadrian), and had ascended the politico-military ladder of success, largely under Domitian, to become governor of Germania Inferior, which is where he was when Hadrian delivered him a handwritten note from Nerva notifying him of his adoption.

What Trajan didn't know about the business of government wasn't worth knowing, and by the end of January 98 he was Emperor of Rome. He ticked all the right Roman boxes too: respected by the troops, noble, well connected, popular and not too old:

> His association with the people was marked by affability and his intercourse with the Senate by dignity, so that he was loved by all and dreaded by none save the enemy.[6]

Apparently, Trajan liked a drink, and kept male slaves as his '*delicati*' ('darlings'), but Dio says that he indulged his taste for boys with a moderation that never 'bothered' any of them.[7] And so he ultimately earned the title *optimus princeps*, 'best emperor'.

Trajan didn't go to Rome immediately. Domitian had mobilized a force in Pannonia and Moesia on the Danube frontier totalling some 70 000 men just before his death, so Trajan probably had one eye on forestalling any potential trouble, be this with his own troops or with their barbarian opponents. There was some conflict, although we know nothing about the result (the Romans declared neither victory nor peace), but by October 99 Trajan was back in Rome and receiving a very enthusiastic welcome.

---

6   Dio 68.7.3, tr. Cary, E., op. cit.
7   Ibid. 68.7.4. Cf. Dio 68.21.2; *Historia Augusta, Hadrian* 2.7, 4.5.

A new Golden Age, which Tacitus called *beatissimum saeculum*, was often said to be dawning, and Trajan worked hard to instil a sense of the 'spirit of his age' in his staff – the phrase appears several times in letters that he exchanged with Pliny the Younger. He preferred to exercise *auctoritas* rather than *imperium*, treated the Senate with great respect, used Equestrians rather than imperial freedmen, rewarded his associates with high office and promotions, and must have been at ease with multiculturalism, since his Consuls included Greeks from Asia Minor, a Moorish chieftain, the last known descendant of Herod the Great, and Gaius Julius Epiphanes Philopappus, grandson of the last king of Commagene. Nerva's *alimenta* scheme continued to function, and he sent officials called *curatores* to Italian municipalities having financial difficulties to help rehabilitate them.

On a more private level the Emperor had to juggle the interests of senior officers with those of his family, which were dictated by Pompeia Plotina. She is often seen as the power behind the throne, but, on entering the palace for the first time, she is supposed to have turned to face the populace and said that she hoped she would leave it the same person she was when she entered. Pliny's *Panegyricus* praised her modest attire, moderate number of attendants and her unassuming manner. It looked like everyone's heart was in the right place.

Trajan the Warrior, Part 1

Trajan's heart was also in something he was very good at: warfare. Pliny celebrates his popularity with the troops, and his willingness to share hardships and dangers with them, although Dio is more apologetic:

> And even if he did delight in war, nevertheless he was satisfied when success had been achieved, a most bitter foe overthrown and his countrymen exalted.[8]

---

8   Dio 68.7.5, tr. Cary, E., op. cit.

By 101 he was in action on the Danube frontier against the Dacian king, Decebalus. Trajan brought in legions and auxiliaries from Germany, Britain and elsewhere, and formed two new ones, XX *Ulpia* and (probably later) II *Traiana*. He then struck hard into Decebalus' territory. The Dacian warriors wielded a formidable two-handed scythe known as a *falx*, but they were no match for Trajan's men: their army was defeated towards the end of 101; Decebalus' counter-attack was repulsed; Trajan's forces advanced to the Dacian capital of Sarmizegethusa (modern Varhély); and in autumn 102 Decebalus sought peace. He was allowed to retain his throne as a client king, but Roman garrisons were installed in his territory. An amazing bridge, 1 135 metres long with twenty stone piers connected by arches, was then constructed over the Danube by Trajan's master engineer and architect Apollodorus of Damascus. The Emperor returned to Rome, celebrated a triumph, and the Senate awarded him the title *Dacicus*.

Decebalus had got off lightly, but unfortunately for his people he broke the treaty in 105. This time Trajan's response was practically genocidal. He marched into Dacia in the early summer of 106, crossing via Apollodorus' bridge. Decebalus decided to avoid a pitched battle and instead tried to assassinate Trajan in his camp and to achieve a settlement by capturing and ransoming his senior officers. All to no avail. Trajan's troops bore down on Sarmizegethusa, which was swiftly captured. Decebalus committed suicide rather than be paraded in a Roman triumph, and so the Romans had to make do with exhibiting his severed head on the steps of the Capitol.

The *Fasti Ostienses* confirm that the war was over by the autumn of 106. Dacia became the first Roman province north of the Danube, a colony ultimately called Colonia Ulpia Traiana Augusta Dacica Sarmizegethusa was founded close to Sarmizegethusa, Dacia's gold mines were exploited, and the war booty was enormous – reputedly (although no doubt exaggeratedly) more than 2.25 million kg of gold, twice as much silver and over 500 000 prisoners. Trajan ploughed these funds back into infrastructure, social projects and donatives to the people. He could afford to be generous, and his coins said as much by featuring the image of *Abundantia* (Abundance personified). Ten thousand gladiators fought and 11 000 animals were killed in a victory celebration that lasted 123 days. As the contemporary satirist Juvenal was later famously to complain, this too suited the spirit of the age:

> The public has long since cast off its cares; the people that once bestowed commands, consulships, legions and all else, now meddles no more and longs eagerly for just two things: bread and circuses.[9]

A monument to Trajan's Dacian campaigns still stands in Rome: Trajan's Column. Designed by Apollodorus of Damascus, and dedicated on 2 May 113, it is 100 Roman feet (about 30 metres) high, and features a 200-metre-long continuous spiral of relief sculpture that wraps itself twenty-three times around the column's exterior and portrays 2 600 figures taking part in 155 distinct scenes. It shows Trajan himself planning, sacrificing, supervising, consulting and haranguing, before it culminates in Decebalus' suicide, the pursuit of the Dacian leaders, and mass deportations. This extraordinary monument to regime change and ethnic cleansing also became Trajan's mausoleum; Dacia is now called Romania.

Trajan and Peace

In 107, Trajan returned to Rome, whose cityscape changed radically under his Principate. Marble seating was installed in the Circus Maximus; Rome's largest set of public baths opened on 22 June 109; a new aqueduct brought water over 60 kilometres to the Janiculum Hill; and Apollodorus of Damascus was the brains behind an enormous Forum complex that was so

---

9 Juvenal, *Satire* 10.80 f., tr. Bell, A., in Köhne, E., 'Bread and Circuses: The Politics of Entertainment', in Köhne, E., Ewiglebe, C. and Jackson, R. (eds), *The Power of Spectacle in Ancient Rome: Gladiators and Caesars*, London: British Museum, 2000, p. 8.

large that all the other imperial Fora would have fitted into it. An ancillary market complex served as both a shopping centre and the headquarters of Rome's *annona* (Grain Supply Agency), and a vast hexagonal harbour that could accommodate over one hundred vessels was constructed at Portus at the Tiber mouth. Juvenal described it as 'a man-made breakwater that no natural harbour could equal'.[10] Centum Cellae (modern Civitavecchia, which is still the port of Rome) also benefited from a new harbour, while other ports received upgrades and enhanced road links. Outside Italy the wonderful Alcántara Bridge in Spain still spans the Tagus River, proudly bearing its original inscription, 'I have built a bridge which will last forever'.

Building religious bridges with some of the Empire's inhabitants was not so easy, though. In 109 or 110 Trajan sent Pliny the Younger to Bithynia-Pontus on the southern shore of the Black Sea. Their correspondence forms a priceless insight into the challenges faced by those who administered Rome's Empire on the ground, and one issue that landed on Pliny's desk concerned what to do about the ever-increasing number of people accused of being Christians. Pliny was at his wits' end about how to deal with what he regarded as a degenerate extremist cult (*superstitio*):

> I have never been present at an examination (*cognitio* – a formal trial) of Christians. Consequently, I do not know the nature or the extent of the punishments usually meted out to them, nor the grounds for starting an investigation and how far it should be pressed. Nor am I at all sure whether [. . .] a pardon ought to be granted to anyone retracting his beliefs, or if he has once professed Christianity, he shall gain nothing by renouncing it; and whether it is the mere name of Christian which is punishable, even if innocent of crime, or rather the crimes associated with the name.[11]

---

10   Juvenal, *Satire* 12.78 f., tr. Green, P., op.cit.
11   Pliny, *Letters* 10.96.1–2, tr. Radice, B., op. cit.

He goes on to tell Trajan that he asks them if they are Christians, warns them three times of the punishments this entails, sends them to Rome for trial if they are Roman citizens and executes them if they are not. Revering Trajan's statue and the images of the gods, and reviling the name of Christ is sufficient to gain a reprieve. Trajan reassures him that he is doing the right thing, and advises him not to hunt Christians out, but to deal with everything on a case-by-case basis: *paenitentia* ('repentance') brings pardon, guilt brings punishment, and anonymous denunciations are not to be entertained.

Trajan the Warrior, Part 2

When the king of Nabataea (roughly the area of modern Jordan) died, Trajan annexed this long-standing Roman client state as a province called Arabia (105–6), and coins celebrated *ARABIA ADQUISITA*. At the other end of the Empire, in Britannia, a new frontier was established along the line of Agricola's strategic east–west road across the Tyne–Solway isthmus, usually known by its medieval name of the Stanegate (see Map 2 and 3A). The forts at Corbridge and Carlisle were supplemented by five others, including Vindolanda, with small fortlets and watchtowers in between. A wonderful find from the Vindolanda fort, dated to 97–102/3, seems to be a military memorandum about the fighting techniques of the British cavalry:

> The Britons don't wear armour (?). There are too many cavalry. The cavalry do not use swords nor do the bloody Brits (*Brittunculi*) mount in order to throw javelins.[12]

The very first tablet discovered at Vindolanda speaks of creature comforts for the men:

> I have sent (?) you [. . .] pairs of socks from Sattua, two pairs

---

12   *Tab. Vindol.* II 164, tr. Kershaw, S. The word *Brittunculi* is new and deeply patronizing.

of sandals and two pairs of underpants, two pairs of sandals
[. . .] Greet [. . .] Elpis [. . .] Tetricus and all your messmates
with whom I pray that you live in the greatest good fortune.[13]

A letter from the cavalry commander Masc(u)lus to Flavius
Cerialis, prefect of *cohors* VIIII *Batavorum*, shows that the auxiliaries had specific needs:

> Masclus to Cerialis his king, greeting. [. . .] My fellow-soldiers
> has [*sic*] no Celtic beer (*cervesam*). Please order some to be sent.[14]

Enigmatically, *Legio* IX *Hispana* is last heard of in Britain
doing building work on its fortress at Eboracum in around 108,
leading to some fanciful stories of its destruction by Scottish
tribesmen at this time. These are no longer credible: most likely
it was redeployed to the Rhine, where a tile stamp with its name
has been found at Noviomagus (modern Nijmegen), and one of
its officers, Aninius Sextus Florentinus, who is buried at Petra
in Jordan, was *legatus* of the legion in 121.

If shoring up Britain's frontiers was all about security, the
same can not really be said for Trajan's massive invasion of
Parthia. The flashpoint came when King Osroes I of Parthia
installed first his nephew Axidares and later his brother Partha-
masiris on the throne of Armenia without Roman approval.
Rome would not allow rogue states to threaten the precarious
balance of power in the region, and Trajan's response was
uncompromising: only the conquest and provincialization of
Parthia would rectify the situation.

Both the chronology and the topography of the ensuing
events are confused, but it looks like Trajan arrived in Antioch
in January 114. He put together an army of possibly 80 000

---

13 *Tab. Vindol.* II 346, tr. Bowman, A. K. *Life and letters on the Roman Frontier:
Vindolanda and its People*, London: British Museum Press, 1994.
14 *Tab. Vindol.* III 628, tr. Kershaw, S. Masc(u)lus spells 'have' *habunt* rather
than *habent*. See Bowman, A. K. and Thomas, J. D., 'New writing tablets from
Vindolanda', *Britannia* 27 (1996), 299–328.

men, rejected Parthian diplomatic initiatives, and provincialized Armenia. From Armenia he headed down into Mesopotamia in 115, capturing Ctesiphon and Babylon, before reaching the Persian Gulf in the area of modern Basra. He is said to have lamented that he was too old to follow further in Alexander the Great's footsteps, but at least Rome now had two new provinces: Mesopotamia and Assyria. *PARTHIA CAPTA*, effectively 'Mission Accomplished', said the coinage.

So far so spectacularly good. This was the largest area that Rome's Empire would ever encompass (see Map 4). But in reality Mesopotamia had only been overrun, not consolidated. As Trajan's forces advanced, insurgency broke out behind them and the Parthians made incursions from the territory they still held. The Jewish population in Cyrenaica also rebelled, and before the end of 116 the unrest had spread to Egypt, Palestine, Cyprus and Anatolia. Trajan brought most of the rebels to heel – some 220 000 non-Jews perished in Cyrenaica alone – but nevertheless started a managed withdrawal. He ceded some parts of Armenia and handed Mesopotamia over to the Parthian prince Parthamaspates as a client ruler, but although his coins claimed that he had 'given the Parthians a king' (*REX PARTHIS DATUS*), the Parthians never acknowledged him.

Trajan tried unsuccessfully to take the strategically situated desert city of Hatra in the *Al Jazirah* region of present-day Iraq, which guarded the caravan routes connecting Mesopotamia with Syria and Asia Minor, but inhospitable climatic conditions started to affect his troops, and he had to withdraw. Dio writes that Trajan's own health now started to deteriorate, and that he withdrew to Antioch, before setting out for Rome, leaving Hadrian in command of Syria. He never made it home:

Trajan himself suspected that his sickness was due to poison [. . .] but some state that it was because the blood, which descends every year into the lower parts of the body, was in his case checked in its flow. He had also suffered a stroke, so that a portion of his body was paralysed, and he was dropsical all over. On coming to Selinus in Cilicia, which we also call Traianopolis, he suddenly expired.[15]

It was 9 August 117. Rome's first non-Italian Emperor was also the first to die outside Italy. His ashes were placed in a golden urn in the base of his Column and his deification went through on the nod. If his reign was indeed the 'well-managed confidence trick' that one scholar suggests,[16] that is surely the point: that was the best way to rule Rome. Trajan had raised the bar for future incumbents of the Principate very high. In the fourth century, the Senate would pray for new Emperors to be 'More fortunate than Augustus, better than Trajan',[17] and in his *Divine Comedy*, Dante gave him a place in Paradise – never an easy thing for a pagan to achieve.

Hadrian Becomes Emperor (117–138)

It was Trajan's governor of Syria and first cousin once removed, Hadrian, who now acceded to the throne as Imperator Caesar Traianus Hadrianus Augustus. He had been born into a family of prosperous aspirational provincials on 24 January 76, either in Italica, where Trajan also hailed from, or in Rome. When his father, P. Aelius Afer, died in 86, the childless Trajan and P. Acilius Attianus, also from Italica, became Hadrian's guardians. In 100, following some leverage by Trajan's wife Pompeia Plotina, Hadrian made a dynastically important marriage of convenience to Trajan's great-niece Vibia Sabina (see Genealogy Table 3). This turned out to be a childless and unhappy relationship – Hadrian later said that if he'd been a private citizen

15 Dio 68.33.2 f., tr. Cary, E., op. cit.
16 Bennett, J., *Trajan Optimus Princeps. A Life and Times*, London and New York: Routledge, 1997, p. 208.
17 Eutropius, *Breviarium* 8.5.3, tr. Bird, H. W., *The Breviarium ab Urbe Condita of Eutropius, The Right Honourable Secretary of State for General Petitions, Dedicated to Lord Valens Gothicus Maximus & Perpetual Emperor, translated with an Introduction and Commentary by H. W. Bird*, Liverpool: Liverpool University Press, 1993.

he would have divorced her, whilst she supposedly had an abortion so as not to produce 'another monster'[18] – but even so the marriage lasted for over thirty-six years.

Hadrian himself was tall and elegant, and he quite literally changed the face of the Roman world by sporting a beard. Whether he did this to conceal blemishes on his face or to channel the Greek philosophers he admired is unclear, but no high-ranking Roman would be on trend any longer if he was clean-shaven. His portraits also show a highly distinctive diagonal kink in both his lower earlobes, which may have been a symptom of coronary artery disease.[19] There were stories of a misspent youth, but once Hadrian toed the line he worked his way rapidly through the *Cursus Honorum*, seeing a good deal of military action on Rome's northern frontier along the way. In 112, rather unusually, he became both a citizen and the chief archon (magistrate) of Athens, from where Trajan picked him up in 113 en route to his Parthian campaign, before installing him as governor of Syria in 117.

Hadrian was the only viable successor to Trajan from inside the imperial household, and he commanded the Empire's largest military forces, but Trajan may only have adopted him as his son (if at all) on his deathbed. Dio says that Hadrian's accession was engineered by Pompeia Plotina, who concealed Trajan's death for several days so that she could forge the necessary official documents; another conspiracy theory makes Plotina get a servant to impersonate Trajan and make the adoption announcement after the real Trajan had died. Regardless of the truth, when news of Trajan's death reached Antioch on 11 August, the armies of Syria acclaimed Hadrian as Emperor.

As ever we are hampered by inadequate source material. This includes a complete biography that forms part of a complex work known as the *Historia Augusta*. It comprises a series of

---

18   *Epitome de Caesaribus* 14.8.
19   See Petrakis, N. L., 'Diagonal Earlobe Creases, Type A Behavior and the Death of Emperor Hadrian', *Western Journal of Medicine* 132.1 (Jan. 1980).

lives of Roman rulers written by (probably) a single anonymous author sometime in the fourth or fifth centuries. It provides some pretty accurate material, but it has a tabloid newspaper ethos and is prone to shaky chronology and blatant invention: 'propaganda directed to a popular audience'.[20] It is hard for us to work out what kind of person Hadrian was, or what drove him.

Imperial Policies

Hadrian's first significant policy decision was to pull the troops back across the Euphrates out of what is now Iraq, and revert to a policy of supporting local rulers such as Vologaeses[21] II, who became the client king of Armenia, and served as a counterbalance to Osroes I in Parthia. The Jewish insurgency in Mesopotamia and elsewhere was brought to heel, but the revolt had caused considerable damage, and reconstruction was now necessary:

> The Emperor Caesar Traianus Hadrianus Augustus [. . .] ordered the restoration for the city of Cyrene of the baths together with the porticoes and ball courts and other appurtenances, which had been torn down and burned in the Jewish revolt.[22]

There were also worries in Dacia and the Danubian regions. About a month after his acclamation, Hadrian abandoned Trajan's gains across the lower Danube, and by 118 he had stabilized the situation along that frontier. But now there were challenges to face in Rome.

---

20 Baynes, N. H., *The Historia Augusta: Its Date and Purpose*, Oxford: Clarendon Press, 1925, p. 57.
21 Also spelled Vologaesus, Vologases and, on coins, Ologases.
22 AE 1928, 2, tr. in Lewis, N. and Reinhold, M., op. cit., p. 332. Another inscription, AE 1928, 1, mentions the restoration of a road that had been 'ripped up and ruined in the Jewish revolt'.

In June or July 118 the *Fratres Arvales* sacrificed because of Hadrian's arrival in Rome. His donatives to the troops and largesse to the people were double the usual amounts, but when he scrutinized the Empire's finances he discovered an eye-watering 900 million *sestertii* in outstanding uncollectable debts. So, in order to start his reign with a clean slate, he publicly burned the tax records, an act depicted in relief on the *plutei Traiani*, now housed in the Senate house in the Forum Romanum.

His dealings with the Senate were fractious. Even before he had arrived in Rome four ex-Consuls, who may have hated his 'unheroic' abandonment of Trajan's Eastern conquests, were implicated in a plot to assassinate him. They were tried by the Senate *in absentia* (and in Hadrian's absence too), condemned and executed. Hadrian disclaimed responsibility, but it still soured his relationship with the Senate. Another source of tension was his willingness to promote outsiders to the imperial ruling class: unity through diversity was not the kind of slogan that appealed to the Roman Senate. But Hadrian would tolerate no dissent, and when the historian Suetonius, then Hadrian's chief secretary for correspondence in Latin (*ab epistulis*), got rather too 'informal' with Vibia Sabina in 122, he was fired.

Like a number of his predecessors, Hadrian made extensive use of the Equites in the imperial civil service. They supplanted freedmen in the imperial household and even sat on Hadrian's imperial council, and a bureaucratic career structure started to develop, with formal titles defining their status: a *procurator* was *vir egregius* ('outstanding man'), an ordinary Prefect *vir perfectissimus* ('most perfect'), and a *Praefectus Praetorio* was *vir eminentissimus* ('most eminent').

One of Rome's most enduring legacies is her legal system. Hadrian engaged the expert jurist Salvius Julianus from Pupput (in modern Tunisia) to codify the Praetors' *Edictum Perpetuum* (the set of rules compiled over the centuries by the Praetors for the interpretation of the law). This became the basis of subsequent Roman legal procedure and Salvius Julianus also served as a judge alongside the Emperor and the other great jurists, P. Juventius Celsus and L. Neratius Priscus.

Another area where Hadrian had a strong personal interest was the army. He was very keen on discipline and training, and is said to have had all the attributes of a conventional 'good general' – mucking in with the soldiers' meals and labours, but also weeding out 'banqueting-rooms, porticoes, covered arcades and ornamental gardens' from the camps, and exerting strict control over military purchases.[23] An inscription at Lambaesis (modern Tazoult-Lambese in Algeria) preserves his speech to *Legio* III *Augusta*, whose exercises he had overseen,[24] revealing a strong personal involvement with military discipline and training, as does the tombstone of one of his bodyguards:

> I am the man once well known on the Pannonian shore, brave and foremost among a thousand Batavian men: with Hadrian as my judge I was able to swim the vast waters of the deep Danube in full armour [. . .] While an arrow from my bow was hanging and descending in the air [. . .] I shot another [. . .] and split it in two. No Roman or barbarian could ever best me [. . .] It remains to be seen whether anyone else will rival my deeds.[25]

Hadrian on Tour

Many of these military inspections took place on the extensive tours that Hadrian made of the Empire:

> Hadrian travelled through one province after another, visiting the various regions and cities and inspecting all the

---

23 *Historia Augusta, Hadrian* 11.1.
24 *ILS* 2487. See Speidel, M. P., *Emperor Hadrian's Speeches to the African Army: A New Text*, Mainz: Verlag des Römischen-Germanischen Zentralmuseums, 2006.
25 *CIL* 3.3676 = *ILS* 2558, tr. Boatwright, M. T., in Barrett, A. A. (ed.), *Lives of the Caesars*, Oxford: Blackwell, 2008, p. 164; see also Dio 69.9.6.

garrisons and forts [. . .] He personally viewed and investigated absolutely everything.[26]

The trips began in 121 (see Map 4), and their precise itineraries and aims are a little elusive, but it seems that he headed into Gallia Narbonensis and Gallia Lugdunensis, Germania Superior and Inferior, Raetia, Noricum and, in 122, Britannia. From there he moved south into Gallia Narbonensis and wintered in Tarraco (modern Tarragona in Spain). In 123 he crossed the Mediterranean to Syria, moving as far as the Euphrates before turning north to the Black Sea, to Trapezus (modern Trabzon) in Cappadocia. By that winter he had gone back to Bithynia et Pontus. Spring 124 saw him in Ilion/Troy (modern Hisarlık) and moving on to Smyrna (Izmir) and Ephesus prior to ending up in Athens, via Rhodes. From Athens he visited Greek sites such as Delphi in 124, before he returned to Rome via Sicily. By late 125 he was in residence at his newly built villa at Tivoli, close to Rome.[27]

In 128 this great seeker-out of curiosities gave in to his wanderlust once more. Again, details are hazy, but his tour seems to have encompassed Africa and Mauretania, a brief return to Rome, and Athens again, where he was hailed as Olympios. Having wintered in Athens in 128–9, with at least one excursion to Sparta, he headed into Asia, taking in Ephesus and Miletus, turning inland down the Meander River valley, then heading into Pisidia and Cilicia and ending up in Antioch in autumn 129. In 130 he took in Palmyra, Trajan's newly acquired province of Arabia, plus Judaea and Egypt.[28] In 131 he took the coastal route along Judaea, Syria, Cilicia, Pamphylia and Lycia, tramped through Thrace, Moesia, Dacia and Macedonia, and wintered yet again in Athens (131–2), where he was acclaimed Panhellenios and Panionios. His final return to Rome was probably in 132.

---

26   Dio 69.9.1, tr. Cary, E., op. cit.
27   See below, p. 198 f.
28   For events in Egypt, see below, p. 195 f.

These effects of Hadrian's visits can still be seen at archaeological sites all along his routes. For instance, there were new city foundations like Antinoopolis in Egypt and Mursa (modern Osijek) in Upper Pannonia, reconstructions of devastated cities like Cyrene, and temples, baths, theatres, amphitheatres, harbour works, roads, aqueducts and cisterns were built all over the Empire, many of them in his honour.

Hadrian's Wall

Securing the Empire's borders was paramount, and consolidation rather than expansion became the order of the day. Hadrian seems to have envisaged the Empire as a mighty fortress, and to that end there is still a lasting monument to his name in Britannia: Hadrian's Wall (see Map 3A). The find in 2003 of the Staffordshire Moorlands Pan, a beautiful metal *trulla* (a high-quality 'mess tin') inscribed with the names of various forts on the Wall (Maia, Cogabatta, Uxelodunum and Cammoglanna), bears the legend *rigore vali aeli draconis*, which is tricky to translate but could indicate that it was known as *Vallum Aeli* – the 'Wall/Ditch of Aelius'.[29]

There was clearly trouble in Britannia at the start of Hadrian's reign: the *Historia Augusta* says that 'the Britons could not be kept under Roman sway'.[30] Hadrian himself arrived in 122 as part of his first tour, bringing with him, we think, *Legio* VI *Victrix* commanded by Aulus Platorius Nepos, with its accompanying auxiliaries. Coins bearing the legend *Adventui Aug Britanniae* (= 'For the Arrival of the Emperor in Britain') on the reverse, along with a very un-military-looking *Britannia* who personifies the prosperous central and southern zones of the province, commemorated the visit, but the only mention of Hadrian's responsibility for the Wall is in the *Historia Augusta*:

---

29 British Museum, PE 2005, 1204.1.
30 *Historia Augusta, Hadrian* 5.2, tr. Magie, D., *The Scriptores Historiae Augustae with an English Translation by David Magie, Volume I,* Cambridge, MA, and London: Harvard University Press, 1921.

[Hadrian] set out for Britain, and there he corrected many abuses and was the first to construct a wall, eighty miles in length, which was to separate the barbarians from the Romans.[31]

There is nothing like this anywhere else on Rome's frontiers. Construction probably commenced in 122, and work was still going on after 130, over which time there were numerous changes to the original plan. This envisaged a 3-metre-wide stone wall running 72 kilometres from the Tyne to the River Irthing, which would then be extended westwards by a 45-kilo-metre-long, 6-metre-wide turf rampart to Bowness-on-Solway. Every Roman mile (*c.*1.6 kilometres) there was a fortified gate-way with a tower ('milecastle'), whose style corresponds to the three legions that built the wall (II *Augusta*, VI *Victrix* and XX *Valeria Victrix*), and in between the milecastles there were two further small towers. The milecastle-plus-tower system was extended south-westwards down the Cumbrian coast for another 32 kilometres. The main forts were initially on the Stanegate, although three new forts – Birrens (Blatobulgium), Netherby (Castra Exploratorum) and Bewcastle (Fanum Coci-dii) – were also constructed further to the north. However, as the complex took shape, the forts, sixteen in total,[32] were inte-grated into the fabric of the wall, the unfinished sections of the stone wall were reduced to 2.4 metres, and parts of the turf rampart were replaced with stone (the entire turf section was ultimately replaced with stone after Hadrian's time). To the east, the wall was extended from Newcastle, where a bridge bearing

---

31 Ibid. 11.2.
32 The sixteen forts, from west to east, were: Bowness (Maia); Drumburgh (Congavata); Burgh-by-Sands (Aballava); Stanwix (Uxelodunum, probably the HQ, with a signalling system reaching back to the legionary fortress at York); Castlesteads (Camboglanna); Birdoswald (Banna); Carvoran (Magnis); Great Chesters (Aesica); Housesteads (Vercovicium); Carrawburgh (Brocolitia); Chesters (Cilurnum); Halton Chesters (Onnum); Rudchester (Vindovala); Benwell (Condercum); Newcastle (Pons Aelius); Wallsend (Segedunum).

Hadrian's family name, the Pons Aelius, crossed the Tyne, to Wallsend.

There was more to all this than just turf, bricks and mortar: the complex also included a large V-shaped ditch on the north side of the wall; a communication road to the south; and the *vallum* – a 6-metre-wide, flat-bottomed ditch flanked by mounds and crossed by causeways opposite each fort and milecastle, which defined the southern side of the complex.

The true purpose of the wall is hard to ascertain. Walls keep people in as well as out, control as well as exclude, and serve political and psychological as well as military functions. The Romans certainly made a clear distinction between their territory and *barbaria* or *barbaricum* ('the lands of the barbarians'), but the glib assertion that it was there to keep out hordes of Braveheart-style woad-painted Picts and Scots[33] from pillaging 'England' is anachronistic and wrong. The Roman army didn't fight behind fixed defences; the stone sections were not designed as a fighting platform like a city wall; the turf bank would not have been much of a hindrance to a determined force of terrorists/freedom-fighters; the *vallum* effectively allowed the Romans to control any traffic through the wall-zone, levy taxes on goods, and monitor barbarian toing and froing; the whole system divided the still unsettled Brigantes to the south from the Novantae, Selgovae and Votadini to the north; it brought changes in traditional pasture lands; on the east–west axis it provided a fortified roadway across the province; the towers provided elevated observation points; and the forts were excellent bases from which to sally northwards in force. The heavy provision of cavalry is significant, since although the wall was constructed by legionaries it was manned by some 9 500 auxiliaries, around 4 000 of whom were cavalry. And of course, the fact that Hadrian had set the province's borders in stone and turf did not inhibit

---

33 Picti ('Painted Men') is a much later blanket term for the entire spectrum of tribes living north of the Wall. See below, p. 343. The tribes of the Scotti in Ireland were not a threat at this time either.

the Roman army's readiness for renewed expansion at any moment – the poet Virgil had long ago made Jupiter prophesy that the Empire would have no limits of time or space.

Hadrian the 'Greekling'

Hadrian was not just renowned for military structures: his reign brought an Empire-wide building boom in which he was very hands-on. In his beloved Athens the massive Temple of Olympian Zeus, an unfinished project dating back to the time of Peisistratos in the sixth century BCE, was completed in spectacular style, and the city was endowed with a superb new library. At Rome Hadrian rounded off Trajan's Forum with the Temple of the deified Trajan and Plotina, but by far the largest project there was the massive Temple of Venus and Roma on the Velian Hill, sited on an artificial platform 145 x 100 metres where the vestibule of Nero's Golden House had once stood. It was begun on 21 April 121, a festival day that Hadrian now converted into a celebration of the foundation of Rome, while the coinage proclaimed a new Golden Age. The design was the subject of a notorious spat between the Emperor and Trajan's master-architect Apollodorus of Damascus, who had the temerity to critique the temple, only to end up dead.[34]

More important in terms of the legacy of Rome's architectural achievement was the Pantheon. The sheer technology and logistics of assembling the materials are astonishing enough: massive monolithic Corinthian columns, 5 Roman feet wide and 40 high, made originally from grey Egyptian granite from Mons Claudianus, with white Pentelic marble bases and Luni marble capitals; other columns of rose granite from quarries at Aswan; a enormous bronze entrance door on a threshold of Africano marble; the floor paved with squares, and circles within

---

34   Dio 69.4.1–5. There is much in the story that doesn't add up, and many scholars dismiss it as fiction. See, e.g., Ridley, A. T., 'The Fate of an Architect: Apollodorus of Damascus', *Athenaeum* 77 (1989), 551–65.

squares, of coloured granite, marble and porphyry; and the tour de force – a staggering hemispherical concrete dome that still makes every person who enters the building stop in their tracks and gawp skywards in open-mouthed awe when they first walk in. The *oculus* (central circular hole), about 8.8 metres across, lined with a ring of bronze, provides a wondrous, uncanny light that tracks imperceptibly across the interior. The symbolism of the building is still a bone of contention, but the date is clear enough: the architrave bears an inscription that reads:

Marcus Agrippa, son of Lucius, three times consul, made this.

This references Agrippa's dedication of a sanctuary on the site in *c.*25 BCE, but brick stamps from the rotunda allow us to date Hadrian's new Pantheon to between 118 and 128.

The Pantheon is very much Hadrian's building, and marks him out as a man of deep-seated cultural interests:

Aelius Hadrianus was more suited to eloquence and the stud-ies of peacetime, and after peace had been restored in the east he returned to Rome. There he began to devote his attention to religious rituals, to laws, to the gymnasia, and to teachers, so much so that he established an institute of liberal arts which was called the Athenaeum.[35]

The *Historia Augusta* describes him as being greatly inter-ested in poetry, expert in arithmetic, geometry and painting, not to mention being proud of his musicianship and the author of an autobiography (published under someone else's name) and some love poetry. He had a prodigious memory, a great head for figures, loved dogs and horses, and was so devoted to Greek culture that he acquired the nickname *Graeculus*,

---

35 Aurelius Victor, *De Caesaribus* 14, tr. Scarre, *Chronicle of the Roman Emperors: The Reign by Reign Record of the Rulers of Rome*. London: Thames & Hudson, 1995, p. 98.

'Greekling'. But being talented, driven, competitive and extremely powerful also meant he could hold quirky (or down-right awful) tastes: he liked Antimachus of Colphon better than Homer, Ennius more than Virgil, and a short poem that he wrote shortly before his death oozes with twee diminutives:

> Little soul, little wanderer, little charmer,
> Body's guest and companion,
> To what places will you set out for now?
> To darkling, cold and gloomy ones –
> And you won't make your usual jokes.[36]

The *Historia Augusta* comments that this was as good as his poetry got.

Yet he was not insensitive, and not without wit. One anecdote tells of him visiting the public baths (and so mixing with the hoi polloi) and noticing a veteran soldier who had served under him (he knew all their names, apparently) rubbing himself against the wall. On asking why the marble was doing the rubbing, he was told that the old man couldn't afford a slave to do it, and so he gave him some slaves and the money for their maintenance. But on his next visit, when there was an entire wall full of old men rubbing their backs, he simply made them rub one another down in turn.

Antinous

'Hadrian was gay';[37] Hadrian was bisexual; Hadrian was a paedophile. There is probably truth in all those statements, but that is to judge him by twenty-first-century words and concepts that were pretty well meaningless to his contemporaries. There was no Latin word for 'homosexuality': what mattered was the role that a man assumed in sex, and this was viewed entirely in

---

36 *Historia Augusta, Hadrian* 25.9, tr. Opper, T., *Hadrian: Empire and Conflict*, London: The British Museum Press, 2008, p.221.
37 Opper, T., op. cit., p.168.

phallocentric terms.[38] Other emperors might have indulged themselves in oral sex, played the receptive role in intercourse, exhibited a scandalous desire for well-hung men, formally married males either as bride or as groom, married their nieces, or had incestuous relations with their sister or mother,[39] but Hadrian was never accused of anything like this: he took the active role in his sexual encounters, and that was manly. It was Roman.

The person who has caused all the modern interest and controversy was a youth from Bithynia called Antinous. Hadrian probably met him in 123 or 124, when Antinous would have been thirteen or fourteen, and was inseparable from him ever after. A poem by the Greek poet Pankrates describes them going lion-hunting together. Hadrian wounded the beast . . .

> But slew him not, for of purpose he missed the mark,
> Wishing to test to the full the sureness of aim
> Of his beauteous Antinous.
> [The wounded lion then makes a ferocious attack . . .]
> In such wise he came against the glorious god, upon Antinous
> Like Typhoeus of old against Zeus, slayer of giants.[40]

Other sources preferred to see Antinous as the Ganymede to Hadrian's Zeus/Jupiter.[41]

Antinous was exquisitely beautiful, and Hadrian's relationship with him was intense. One predictably outraged later Christian writer dubs Antinous a 'shameless and scandalous boy',[42] but there seems to have been no scandal at the time. What did attract criticism

---

38 See above, p. 134.
39 See, e.g., Suetonius, *Julius Caesar* 2, 49–52; *Augustus* 68; *Tiberius* 45. *Historia Augusta, Commodus* 10 f.; *Elagabalus* 8–12. Nero, Elagabalus, Claudius and Agrippina, Domitian and Julia and Caligula all commit at least one of these transgressions.
40 P.Oxy. VIII, 1085, tr. Opper, T., op. cit. For the mythical fight between Zeus and Typhoeus, see Kershaw, S., op. cit, pp. 38 ff.
41 Zeus/Jupiter abducted the beautiful youth Ganymede to be his cup-bearer on Mount Olympus. See Kershaw, S., op. cit., pp. 237 ff.
42 St Athanasius, *Apologia Contra Arianos*, Part III, 5.230.

was Hadrian's reaction to Antinous' sudden death by drowning in the Nile in 130. He wept 'like a woman',[43] founded a new city close to where he had died and named it Antinoopolis, and had images of him disseminated right across the Empire (only Augustus and Hadrian himself have more surviving statues). Sometimes Antinous is depicted as a beautiful, languorous, pouting, sexy young man; at other times he appears in the guise of gods such as Dionysus, Vertumnus, Silvanus or Osiris; and a dedication by Q. Siculus compares him to the eternally youthful foreign god Belenus:

> If Antinous and Belenus are equal in age and beauty, why shouldn't Antinous also be what Belenus is?[44]

Hadrian did indeed have Antinous deified, and there may have been a cult centre to him in his posthumous incarnation of Antinous-Osiris at Hadrian's villa at Tibur (modern Tivoli). But there was all sorts of gossip about his death: Hadrian himself said Antinous fell out of a boat, yet there was talk that the Emperor had persuaded or forced Antinous to take his own life as a sacrifice to prolong his own. This version appealed to the conspiracy theorists because Antinous died on the same day that the Egyptians celebrated the death of Osiris, who drowned in the river and was subsequently reborn.

The Bar Kokhba Revolt

If the foundation of Antinoopolis attracted adverse comment, Hadrian's attempt to refound Jerusalem provoked a horrendously bloody rebellion. The city had not been officially rebuilt after the ravages of the Great Jewish revolt, but if Hadrian expected the Jews to applaud his decision to turn Jerusalem into a Roman city by the name of Colonia Aelia Capitolina, he was woefully mistaken. Jewish unhappiness was made worse by Hadrian's

---

43   *Historia Augusta, Hadrian* 14.6; cf. Dio 69.11.4.
44   *CIL* 14 3535 = *CLE* 879, tr. Kershaw, S.

earlier decision to outlaw circumcision ('they were forbidden to mutilate their genitals' is how the *Historia Augusta* puts it),[45] not to mention the fact that one of the city gates carried *Legio* X *Fretensis'* insignia of a boar, or the plan to build a temple to Jupiter Optimus Maximus on the site of the old Temple of Solomon.

Hadrian's insensitivity towards the Jews is difficult to fathom, especially since the contemporary writer Pausanias describes him as the Emperor

> who has gone furthest to honour religion, and among all sovereigns done most for the happiness of each of his subjects [and who] has never willingly gone to war.[46]

But go to war he did. In 132 there was a massive uprising centred on Judaea led by Shimon bar Kosba. He took on the name Bar Kokhba, or 'Son of the Star', which indicates his messianic convictions; his detractors dubbed him Bar Koziba, 'Son of the Lie', and St Jerome later claimed that he fanned a lighted straw in his mouth with puffs of breath so that he appeared to be breathing fire.[47] But Bar Kokhba had charisma: he took the title *nsy' Ysr'l* (Prince of Israel); his rebels declared the 'Redemption/freedom of Israel'; Rabbi Akiba, the premier Jewish religious authority, was on his side; and his highly effective guerrilla tactics inflicted such havoc on the Roman forces that Judaea quickly fell into his grasp.

The situation was so serious that Hadrian drafted in his finest general, Sextus Julius Severus, all the way from Britain. Severus turned the conflict into a process of ethnic cleansing and extermination. Bar Kokhba made his last stand at Bethar near Jerusalem in 135. His death ended a war that had seen, according to Dio, fifty fortresses and 985 villages razed to the ground, 585 000

---

45   *Historia Augusta, Hadrian* 14.2.
46   Pausanias 1.5.5, tr. Levi, P., in *Pausanias: Guide to Greece, Volume 1, Central Greece, Translated with an Introduction by Peter Levi*, London: Penguin Classics, rev. edn,1979.
47   Jerome, *Against Rufinus* 3.31.

killed in the various engagements, many Jews sold into slavery, and 'as for the numbers who perished from starvation, disease or fire, that was impossible to establish'.[48] The so-called 'Cave of Letters', found in a wadi west of the Dead Sea, contained signed letters from Bar Kokhba, along with mirrors, a glass plate, bronze jugs and house keys, hidden there during the fighting. But no one came back for them. At Rome Hadrian was hailed as Imperator, although he did not accept the usual greeting 'I and the legions are in health' because the attrition rates of the Roman troops had been so enormous. Judaea was literally wiped off the map by being renamed Syria-Palestina, and the Jewish population were forbidden even to set foot on the land around Jerusalem.[49]

Hadrian's Last Years

Towards the end of his reign, Hadrian ceased travelling and stayed in Italy. Throughout his Principate, work had been going on at Tibur, some 28 kilometres to the east of Rome, on what since the Renaissance has been called 'Hadrian's Villa', although it was by no means his only one. It is stupendously opulent. Considerably larger than Pompeii, its known structures alone, many of which feature audaciously innovative designs, comprise some 900 rooms and corridors defining subtly nuanced public, semi-public and private spaces, and there are 4.8 kilometres of underground passageways for the thousands of staff who included bookkeepers, archivists, accountants, landscape gardeners, stewards, gamekeepers, and 'security men' from the Praetorian Guard. In many ways it was 'a living microcosm of the empire'[50] and a memento of his travels, referencing all manner of famous landmarks:

> He actually gave to part of it the names of provinces and places of the greatest renown, calling them, for instance, the Lyceum,

---

48   Dio 69.14.1, tr. Cary, E., op. cit. How he arrives at these figures we do not know.
49   Eusebius, *Church History* 4.6.
50   Opper, T., op. cit., p. 133.

Academia, Prytaneum, Canopus, Poecile and Tempe. And in order not to omit anything, he even made a Hades.[51]

There was a theatre, baths, accommodation of various status levels, kitchens, sanitation, courtyards, viewing platforms, hydraulic jets, fountains, cascades, pools, canals, grottoes, dining areas (Hadrian adored banquets), and sculpture that was carefully integrated into the architectural ensemble, such as a copy of Praxiteles' notorious Aphrodite of Cnidus, exhibited in a replica of the temple where the original statue stood.

Yet Hadrian's pleasure in his villa was somewhat spoiled by personal difficulties in his final years, especially as his health deteriorated – bad nosebleeds, says Dio – and the issue of the succession raised its ugly head. It was obvious that Hadrian was not going to have a son, and the person in provisional pole position was his only male blood-relation, his eighteen-year-old great-nephew Cn. Pedianus Fuscus Salinator. But in obscure circumstances that harked back to the affair of the four ex-Consuls,[52] Pedianus Fuscus and his nonagenarian grandfather Lucius Julius Ursus Servianus, who was also Hadrian's brother-in-law, both ended up dead. Then, late in 136, Hadrian announced his successor, to widespread astonishment: the Senator L. Ceionius Commodus. He was good-looking and well connected politically, but he was also frivolous, extravagant, completely lacking in military experience, and he had tuberculosis and regularly coughed up blood. Still, he was renamed L. Aelius Caesar and sent off to govern Pannonia.

Late in 137 the Empress Sabina died and was deified, and on the night of 31 December L. Aelius Caesar also died. Hadrian now chose a distinguished and wealthy but sonless and probably rather soulless fifty-one-year-old by the name of T. Aurelius Fulvius Antoninus Boionius Arrius (see Genealogy Table 3). But Hadrian was also looking further ahead, and he made Antoninus

---

51 *Historia Augusta, Hadrian* 26.5, tr. Magie, D., op. cit.
52 See above, p. 186.

in his turn adopt a teenager (the nephew of Antoninus' wife) called Marcus Annius Verus (now to be known as Marcus Aelius Aurelius Verus – Hadrian nicknamed him Verissimus (= 'Truest') in a play on his *cognomen* Verus, 'True') – and the seven-year-old son of the late L. Aelius Caesar, now named Lucius Aelius Aurelius Commodus. History knows them as the Emperors Marcus Aurelius and Lucius Verus respectively.

Meanwhile Hadrian's heart condition caused him considerable distress. A papyrus fragment from Egypt preserves some lines of text that might be the only surviving scraps of Hadrian's autobiography, written just before he died, and couched as a series of letters to Antoninus:

> I want you to know that I am being released from my life neither before my time, nor unreasonably, nor piteously, nor unexpectedly, nor with faculties impaired.[53]

Yet at the age of sixty-two he seems to have contemplated suicide, but nature took its course on 10 July 138 at an imperial villa at Baiae.

The Senate immediately sought his *damnatio memoriae*, and the *Historia Augusta* says Hadrian died *invisus omnibus*, 'hated/ unseen by all'.[54] He was provisionally buried at Puteoli, in the grounds of a villa once owned by Cicero, before his remains were transferred to the Gardens of Domitia in Rome, and then finally laid to rest alongside Sabina and Aelius Caesar in his mausoleum, which was dedicated by Antoninus in 139. The dedicatory inscription refers to Sabina as *Diva*, but not to Hadrian as *Divus*: clearly Antoninus had to continue to fight with the Senate to clear his adoptive father's name and secure his deification. For that act of filial piety, many thought, he acquired the *cognomen* Pius, 'the Dutiful'.

---

53   Grenfell, B. P., Hunt, A. S. and Hogarth, D. G., *Fayûm Towns and their Papyri*, London: Offices of the Egypt Exploration Fund, 1900, no. 19, = PFayum 19, tr. in Opper, T., op. cit., p. 219.
54   *Historia Augusta, Hadrian* 25.7.

9

Peace, Power and Prosperity: The Antonines

> *There is a Chinese curse which says 'May he live in interesting*
> *times.' Like it or not, we live in interesting times. They are*
> *times of danger and uncertainty; but they are also the most*
> *creative of any time in the history of mankind.*
>
> Robert F. Kennedy, *The Day of Affirmation speech*,
> 6 June 1966

Antoninus Pius (138–161): 'Keep Calm and Carry On'

Antoninus Pius did not live in interesting times. He was a boring
Emperor who lived in boring times, and he worked night and
day to keep things boring. His reign was not one of danger or
uncertainty, nor was it a hotbed of creativity. On the contrary:
'this age of indolence passed away without having produced a
single writer of original genius or who excelled in the arts of
elegant composition',[1] and one might say that the Antonines
'did nothing in particular and did it very well'.[2] Yet Rome was,
at least superficially, now at the height of its security and
prosperity.

His uneventful reign was presented as a Golden Age in Aelius
Aristides' speech *To Rome*, delivered in Pius' reign:

---

1 Gibbon, E., op. cit., chapter II, part IV.
2 Gilbert, W. S., No. 16: SONG (Lord Mountararat and Chorus), 'When Britain
really ruled the waves', from *Iolanthe*, 1882.

In your Empire – and with this word I have indicated the entire civilized world – [. . .] no one worthy of rule or trust remains an alien, but a civil community of the World has been established as a free Republic under one, the best, ruler and teacher of order.[3]

To be *pius* in Roman eyes was to have a finely tuned sense of duty towards your family, state and gods. It was not a sexy quality, but it enabled Antoninus to rule the Empire effectively and with a light touch. He appears affable, conscientious, polite to his underlings, very considered in his decision-making and keen to make the good of the community his prime concern. Not much occurred in the way of scandal (that we know of) and he was happy to delegate the day-to-day process of government to experienced governors and administrators.

Antoninus had been born at Lanuvium (modern Lanuvio), 32 kilometres south-east of Rome, into a family with Gallic roots on 19 September 86. He had ascended to the top of the *Cursus Honorum*, married M. Annius Verus' daughter Annia Galeria Faustina some time between 110 and 115, and governed Asia from 130 to 135. Following his very smooth accession to the purple on 10 July 138, he assumed the name Imperator Caesar Tiberius Aelius Hadrianus Antoninus Augustus, adding Pius and *Pater Patriae* shortly afterwards. Faustina was honoured with the title of *Augusta*.

Unlike his predecessor, Antoninus was not a great traveller. He stayed in Italy for his entire reign:

It is easy for him to abide in his place and manage the world through letters; these arrive almost as soon as written, as if borne on wings.[4]

---

3   Aelius Aristides, *To Rome* 60, tr. in Nicolet, C., *The World of the Citizen in Republican Rome*, Berkeley and Los Angeles: University of California Press, 1980, p. 18.
4   Ibid. 33, tr. in Hadas, M. (ed.), *A History of Rome, from its Origins to 529 AD, as told by the Roman Historians*, New York: Doubleday, 1956.

Pius focused on hearing petitions, issuing new laws and rescripts (replies to petitions), and dealing with religious issues. His building work was primarily concerned with completion and restoration, but there were new projects like the impressive Temple of Antoninus and Faustina, which still stands in the Forum at Rome as the Church of San Lorenzo in Miranda, complete with a rather odd baroque facade. He distributed cash to the plebs on nine occasions, paid a *donativum* to the soldiers when his daughter got married, founded an order of destitute girls, and promoted games featuring huge numbers of exotic animals. But all this was relatively conservative, and he purportedly left the public treasury with a robust credit balance of 675 million *denarii*. There were anecdotes about his personal parsimony, but he used his own money to distribute wine, oil and wheat in a time of famine, and he also oversaw humanitarian relief at Rome following a bad fire, flooding and a collapse of grandstands in the Circus Maximus in which over 1 000 people died. Epigraphic evidence also shows a genuine concern for the welfare of the provinces, where his procurators were under strict instructions to levy reasonable amounts of tribute and were held accountable it they exceeded proper limits. So, on the whole, the Empire prospered:

> With such care did he govern all peoples under him that he looked after all things and all men as if they were his own.[5]

Rome also celebrated the nine-hundredth anniversary of her foundation in 148.[6] This was the perfect opportunity for a *pius* ruler to reaffirm Rome's core values, and it chimed in well with Pius' personal role model, Rome's second king Numa Pompilius,[7] whom Aeneas (another paragon of *pietas*) sees on his visit to the Underworld:

5   *Historia Augusta, Pius* 7.1 tr. Magie, D. op. cit.
6   The traditional date of Rome's foundation was 753 BCE: 753 + 148 − 1 (there is no 'Year Zero') = 900.
7   Conventionally ruled 715–673 BCE.

Who is that in the distance, bearing the hallows, crowned
with
A wreath of olive? I recognize – grey hair and hoary chin –
That Roman king who, called to high power from humble
Cures,
A town in a poor area, shall found our system of law.[8]

For the author of the *Historia Augusta* the comparison was
not a bad one:

He was justly compared to Numa, whose good fortune and
pietas and tranquillity and religious rites he ever maintained.[9]

Coins were minted with the legends *TRANQVILLITAS* and
CONCORDIA on them, as well as others that trumpeted
FELICITAS TEMPORVM (= 'the happiness of the times').
'Keep calm and carry on' was very much the order of the day,
as was well expressed by his adoptive son Marcus Aurelius in
his *Meditations*:

Do all things as a disciple of Antoninus. Think of his
constancy in every act rationally undertaken, his invariable
equability, his piety, his serenity of countenance, his sweetness of disposition, his contempt for the bubble of fame, and
his zeal for getting a true grasp of affairs.[10]

Yet there were still two men who conspired against him. The
first was Titus Atilius Rufus Titianus, whose name we find
erased from the *Fasti Ostienses*, where the entry for 15 September
145 also says that Judgment was passed on Cornelius Priscianus
in open session in the Senate, because he disturbed the province
of Spain in hostile fashion.

---

8   Virgil, *Aeneid* 6.808 ff, tr. Day Lewis, C., op. cit.
9   *Historia Augusta, Pius* 13.4, tr. Magie, D., op. cit.
10   Marcus Aurelius, *Meditations* 6.30, tr. Haines, C. R., *Marcus Aurelius, Edited
and Translated by C. R. Haines*, Cambridge, MA.: Harvard University Press, 1930.

The *Historia Augusta* adds that Priscianus died by his own hand, and that Pius didn't allow any investigation into his conspiracy.

The Antonine Wall

Despite all the 'tranquillity-propaganda', there was a reasonable amount of military activity during Antoninus' reign:

> He conquered the Britons, through his legate Lollius Urbicus (another wall, of turf, being set up when the barbarians had been driven back), and compelled the Moors to sue for peace [in the first half of the 140s]; and he crushed the Germans and Dacians [in the late 150s] and many peoples, including the Jews, who were rebelling, through governors and legates. In Achaea too, and Egypt, he put down rebellions and frequently curbed the Alani when they began disturbances.[11]

However, Aelius Aristides says that most people in the Empire heard of these distant operations 'as if they were myths/ faraway bad dreams'.

The fighting in Britain was about as far away from Rome as one could get, and the motives and objectives are not known. Pausanias says

> [Antoninus Pius] annexed the greater part of the territory of the Brigantes in Britain, because the Brigantes started an invasion of Genounia, which is subject to Rome.[12]

---

11 *Historia Augusta, Pius* 5.4 f., tr. Birley, A., *Lives of the Later Caesars: The First Part of the Augustan History, with Newly Compiled Lives of Nerva & Trajan,* London: Penguin, 1976.
12 Pausanias 8.43.4, tr. Levi, P., in *Pausanias: Guide to Greece, Volume 2, Southern Greece, Translated with an Introduction by Peter Levi,* rev. edn., London: Penguin Classics, 1979.

Quite where Genounia is only Pausanias knows (= the land of the Votadini?), and he may be using 'Brigantes' rather loosely (= the Selgovae?). It may also be that Antoninus simply needed some cheap military glory, and it was the only conflict for which he was hailed as Imperator (in 142). It started in 139 and was overseen by Quintus Lollius Urbicus, who operated well north of the Forth–Clyde isthmus, across which he then constructed a new wall on the successful conclusion of the campaign.

This so-called Antonine Wall (see Map 3B) was built of turf by the same legions that made Hadrian's Wall. It featured a large ditch on the northern side, six primary forts and several other fortlets integrated into it, an east-west military way, plus various outpost forts to the north and protecting the western coast. It has been suggested that although Hadrian's Wall had been 'a tactical success [it was] a strategic failure because it was built in the wrong position',[13] and so Antoninus simply shifted the entire frontier system north to where Agricola had earlier found 'a good place for halting the advance'.[14] The garrisons of Hadrian's Wall were moved forward, and lowland Scotland was reoccupied.

Then around 155 there *was* a serious rebellion among the Brigantes. This prompted a managed withdrawal from the Antonine Wall, and preparations were made to recommission Hadrian's Wall. The situation was stabilized under a new governor, Cn. Julius Verus, and an inscription found in 1751 (now lost) records rebuilding activity on Hadrian's Wall:

Legio VI *Victrix Pia Fidelis* rebuilt this when [Sextus Sulpicius] Ter[tullus] and [Quintus Tineius] Sac[erdos Clemens] were consuls [i.e., in 158].[15]

However, the Antonine Wall was reoccupied shortly before Antoninus' death in 161, as the Romans moved north for a

---

13   Breeze, D. J., *The Northern Frontiers of Roman Britain*, London: Batsford, 1982, p. 97.
14   Tacitus, *Agricola* 23.
15   *RIB* 1389, from Heddon-on-the-Wall, tr. Kershaw, S.

second time, staying (in the currently dominant, but by no means unanimous, scholarly view) until about 163, when a methodical, strategic abandonment to the Hadrianic frontier then ensued.

By the time his wall was abandoned, Antoninus Pius was already dead. Predictably he had made careful plans for the succession: his daughter Faustina had married his adoptive son Marcus Aelius Aurelius Verus in 145 and now had several children by him; Marcus himself had been granted tribunician power and greater proconsular power; and he and Lucius Aelius Aurelius Commodus had held multiple consulships. These two men would accede to the purple as Marcus Aurelius and Lucius Verus.

Even Pius' death was boring. Having eaten rather too much Alpine cheese he became delirious, gave the watchword 'Equanimity', and gave up the ghost at his estate at Lorium near Rome on 7 March 161. He was deified by the Senate, and his adopted sons erected a red granite column in the Campus Martius, whose base depicted Eternity taking Antoninus and Faustina up to heaven. His successor spoke glowingly of his positive qualities:

Constancy, equability, piety, serenity of expression, sweet nature, contempt for empty fame, determination to understand issues and never to dismiss a question until he had scrutinized it thoroughly. He never found fault with his critics, was never in a hurry, refused to listen to slander [. . .] He was always loyal to his friends, he revered the gods but was not superstitious.[16]

Marcus Aurelius and Lucius Verus: Concordia Augustorum[17] (161–169)

Had Hadrian still been alive in 161, he would doubtless have approved of the outcome of the accession process. He had insisted that Antoninus Pius adopt both Marcus Annius Verus

16 Marcus Aurelius, *Meditations* 6.30.2, tr. Haines, C. R., op. cit.
17 Coins of 161 and 162 show Marcus and Lucius standing with clasped hands and bear the legend *Concord[ia] Avgvstor[um]*.

(thereafter known as Marcus Aelius Aurelius Verus) and Lucius Ceionius Commodus (currently Lucius Aelius Aurelius Commodus). Marcus was the front runner, but he refused to become Emperor unless the same powers and titles (apart from *Pontifex Maximus*, which could not be shared) were conferred on Lucius too. They both became Augustus, but other name changes ensued: Marcus dropped the name Verus in favour of Antoninus, to honour his adoptive father; Lucius took the discarded name of Verus instead of Commodus; and they then reigned jointly as Marcus Aurelius Antoninus and Lucius Aurelius Verus. Unsurprisingly this has caused quite a bit of confusion among our sources.

Marcus' wife Faustina had already borne nine children, of which just four girls had survived (see Genealogy Table 3). The *Fasti Ostienses* show that their first child, Domitia Faustina, had been born on 30 November 147, and on 31 August 161 Faustina gave birth again, this time to twin boys, who were named Titus Aurelius Fulvus Antoninus, after Pius, and Lucius Aurelius Commodus, after Lucius. Lucius Verus, who seems to have still been unmarried, was now betrothed to Marcus' eldest daughter, the eleven-year-old Lucilla.

Marcus regarded Lucius as better than himself when it came to military activities, but there was no doubt that Marcus was still the senior partner. Lucius was a colourful character, reputedly one of Rome's best-looking Emperors, sporting a fine beard and given to highlighting his blond hair with gold dust. He was well educated, too, having studied with the celebrated rhetorician M. Cornelius Fronto and the Stoics Apollonius of Chalcedon and Plutarch's nephew Sextus of Chaeronea, and he had a taste for the Good Life, but not in the philosophical sense that Marcus did, even if the latter did use opium.[18]

Marcus Aurelius was sometimes called 'the Philosopher', and we are told that

---

18   See Africa, T. W., 'The Opium Addiction of Marcus Aurelius,' *JHI* 22 (1961), 97–102.

Ever on his lips was a saying of Plato's, that states prospered where philosophers were kings or the kings philosophers.[19]

Marcus had also studied with Fronto, as well as with the Athenian sophist and 'billionaire' Herodes Atticus and various influential Stoics through whom he became acquainted with the works of Epictetus. At the heart of Stoic teaching was the idea that 'nothing is of ultimate value to a man except his moral integrity',[20] and Marcus tried hard to take this on board. Later in his life he would outline his thoughts, in Greek, in his own 'self-help' book, the *Meditations*.

Fighting

Rome's new Emperors treated the plebs like fellow citizens, and were prepared to tolerate freedom of speech, but if they were intending to spend their reign philosophizing and partying, they had an instant wake-up call from the Parthians. Vologaeses III invaded Armenia, installed his own nominee, Pacorus, as king, and destroyed the Roman legion that was sent in to restore order.[21] The Parthians then moved into Syria, and to make matters worse a British war was on the cards and there were problems with the Chatti beyond the Upper German frontier.

In the summer of 162 Marcus dispatched Lucius Verus to Syria with a massive army and several top-flight generals. Out in the East Statius Priscus managed to seize the Armenian capital Artaxata in 163, found a new one, and garrison it. He was a formidable commander: Lucian says that he merely shouted out and twenty-seven of the enemy fighters dropped dead.[22]

---

19   *Historia Augusta, Marcus Aurelius Antoninus* 27.7, tr. Magie, D., op. cit.
20   Long, A. A., 'Epictetus and Marcus Aurelius', in Luce, T. J. ed., *Ancient Writers: Greece and Rome: Vol. II*, New York: Charles Scribner & Sons, 1982, p. 987.
21   It might have been *Legio* IX *Hispana*, last attested at York under Trajan and in the early second century at Nijmegen, but perhaps then transferred to the East by Hadrian.
22   Lucian, *How to Write History* 20.

Lucius' commander M. Pontius Laelianus did much to restore discipline in the Syrian army by rigorous kit inspections and a clampdown on drinking and gambling, and Fronto writes that Lucius himself acted as a role model, marching

> on foot at the head of his men as often as he rode on horseback, putting up with the blazing sun and choking dust, his head exposed to sun and shower, hail and snow – and to missiles. He sweated unconcernedly as if engaged in sport [...] He took a belated bath after his work was done and ate simple camp-food, drank local wine. He often slept on leaves of turf. Through so many provinces, so many open dangers of sieges, battles, citadels, posts and forts stormed, he lavished his care and advice. [23]

Other sources see it rather differently, however, and make him party his way along the warpath and spend a lot of time at the resort of Daphne near Antioch, where he struck up an affair with the gorgeous and gifted Panthea from Smyrna. Marcus responded by sending out Lucilla, Lucius' intended bride, to Ephesus, where the marriage took place in 164. The fourteen-year-old was given the title *Augusta*, and she ultimately gave Lucius three children.

Lucius was certainly a good delegator, and this allowed the professionalism of the Roman army to see the campaign through: they installed the pro-Roman Mannus to the throne of Osrhoene; followed up by capturing the city of Nisibis (modern Nusaybin in Turkey, right on the Syrian border), where the Parthian general narrowly escaped by swimming the Tigris; and they advanced down the Euphrates, scored a victory at Dura-Europos, destroyed Seleuceia on the Tigris, and sacked Ctesiphon. Lucius took the title *Parthicus Maximus*. The next year C. Avidius Cassius took Rome's legions over the Tigris into

---

23   Fronto *Principia Historiae* 13–15, tr. in Birley, A. R., 'The Wars and Revolts', in van Ackeren, M. ed., *A Companion to Marcus Aurelius*, Chichester: Wiley-Blackwell, 2012, p. 219.

Medea (modern Iran), further east than any Roman army had gone before, whereupon Lucius started calling himself *Medicus*, 'of Medea' (as did Marcus, who had had another son named Annius Verus in 162, although in 165 one of the twins – T. Aurelius Fulvus Antoninus – died). Vologaeses III fled, while the Romans consolidated their grip on the border regions and finally withdrew in 166. Avidius Cassius now became governor of Syria, and Lucius returned to Rome where he and Marcus celebrated a joint triumph. The *Historia Augusta* jokes that, because of Lucius' behaviour on campaign, the Parthian War was described as the 'Histrionic/Theatrical' War.

Then disaster struck. The troops who returned home had contracted what is often called the Antonine Plague, an illness incurable at the time whose symptoms were described by the contemporary Greek physician Galen as diarrhoea, high fever and the appearance of pustules on the skin after nine days. It was possibly smallpox. Galen left Rome for his home city Pergamum (modern Bergama), where there was an important healing sanctuary. It was a wise move. Mortality estimates vary, but the death toll may have run into millions.

Lucius kept up his self-indulgent lifestyle, though. He was obsessed with chariot racing – he carried a gold statue of his favourite horse, Volucer, around with him, and the animal was given a tomb on the Vatican Hill – and had a pub built in his house where he spent a lot of time gambling, feasting and drinking. Sometimes, for a change of scene, he would dress in ordinary clothes and get drunk and fight in taverns and brothels.

There was, however, fighting of a very different order to be done. While the Parthian War had been under way, the so-called Marcomannic War[24] broke out in the Danube frontier zone and escalated into something extremely threatening to the Roman Empire: population movements in what is now Poland and the

---

24 *Historia Augusta, Marcus Aurelius Antoninus* 12.13. It comes to be referred to as the German War, the Northern War or the War of Many Nations as more tribes enter the picture.

Ukraine started to impact on tribes bordering Rome's Empire, who now sought sanctuary within the Empire and threatened war unless they were taken in (see Map 4). The Danube frontier had also been weakened by the deployment of many of its troops to the east, and now the Germanic Marcomanni and Quadi and the Sarmatian Iazyges moved into Roman territory. The Germans moved across Raetia, Noricum and Pannonia, raided northern Italy and laid siege to Aquileia (the ancient ancestor of Venice). Marcus and Lucius had to delay their response because of the virulence of the plague, but they took to the field in 168.

The arrival of Rome's two Emperors at Aquileia caused 'several kings to retreat, together with their peoples'.[25] Lucius was keen to return to Rome, but Marcus insisted on pressing on to address the problems on the Danube, and so they crossed the Alps, 'pressed further on and settled everything that pertained to the defence of Italy and Illyricum'.[26] With the situation back under control, and new measures taken to strengthen the defences of northern Italy, the two Emperors wintered at Aquileia. A spring offensive may have been scheduled but when plague struck their camp they took Galen's medical advice and set off back to Rome in January or February 169.

Just two days into the trip Lucius suffered a stroke in his carriage. Three days later, at the age of thirty-eight, he died at Altinum (modern Altino). There were rumours of a plot by his mother-in-law, Faustina, along with suspicion of an illicit relationship, and also talk of his having been poisoned by Marcus. All of this seems implausible, and becoming sole Emperor was definitely not the easy option for Marcus. He also suffered a bereavement before campaigning resumed when his son Annius Verus Caesar died, leaving him with four daughters and the eight-year-old Commodus. Funds for the war were raised by auctioning property from the palaces, and a recruitment crisis necessitated the conscription of slaves, gladiators and common criminals, as well

---

25   *Historia Augusta, Marcus Aurelius Antoninus* 14.2, tr. Kershaw, S.
26   Ibid. 14.6.

as two new legions, II *Italica* and III *Italica*. An inscription from the Roman Forum that was probably erected early in Marcus' reign gives the dispositions of the legions throughout the Empire, and has the two new ones added at a later date:[27]

Province	Legions
Germania Superior	VIII *Augusta*, XXI *Primigenia*
Germania Inferior	I *Minervia*, XXX *Ulpia*
Spain	VII *Gemina*
Africa	III *Augusta*
Egypt	II *Traiana*
Cappadocia	XII *Fulminata*, XV *Apollinaris*
Syria	III *Gallica*, IIII *Scythica*, XVI *Flavia*
Arabia	III *Cyrenaica*
Judaea	VI *Ferrata*, X *Fretensis*
Mesopotamia	I Parthica*, III *Parthica**
Upper Pannonia	I *Adiutrix*, X *Gemina*, XIV *Gemina*
Lower Pannonia	II *Adiutrix*
Upper Moesia	IIII *Flavia*, VII *Claudia*
Lower Moesia	I *Italica*, V *Macedonica*, XI *Claudia*
Noricum	II *Italica*
Raetia	III *Italica*
Dacia	XIII *Gemina*
Italy	II *Parthica**
Britain	II *Augusta*, VI *Victrix*, XX *Victrix*

* = these legions were also added later

Marcus Aurelius, Sole Emperor (169–180)

Marcus eventually arrived back at the northern frontier in the autumn of 169, but although the literary sources concerning the ensuing campaigns are sketchy, we do still possess the Column of Marcus Aurelius in Rome, now in the Piazza Colonna. Standing 100 Roman feet high, it has a spiral relief that

27   *CIL* 4 3492 = *ILS* 2288.

celebrates Marcus' campaigns versus the Marcomanni and the Iazyges. Having wintered at Sirmium (modern Sremska Mitrovica in Serbia), Marcus resumed the offensive in 170, but it appears that the Romans suffered a reverse that cost them 20 000 casualties. Acting on the advice of a dodgy prophet called Alexander, Marcus had thrown two lions into the Danube as offerings to make sure that 'victory would be won'. The lions swam the river in one direction and barbarians poured across in the other, whereupon the prophet claimed that he had never specified *which* side would win.

The Marcomanni and Quadi crossed over the Alps, besieged Aquileia and destroyed the city of Opitergium (modern Oderzo). In 171 the lower Danube frontier was violated as other tribes made their way through the provinces of Moesia, Macedonia and Achaea before their attack fizzled out in the vicinity of Athens. Moments of divine intervention supposedly helped the Romans, such as the 'Rain Miracle', depicted on the Column of Marcus Aurelius, which rescued some struggling Roman troops in enemy territory. The date and location of that event are uncertain, but the Romans now started to regain the upper hand. When the Marcomanni attempted to return home laden with booty, Marcus intercepted and destroyed them at the Danube, before returning the plunder to the provincials from whom it had been taken. The Marcomanni accepted a peace settlement, coins proclaimed *GERMANIA SUBACTA* ('Germany subjugated'), and Marcus took the name Germanicus.

Having established new headquarters at Carnuntum in Pannonia Superior (between modern Vienna and Bratislava on the Archäologischer Park Carnuntum), Marcus took the offensive against the Quadi and the Iazyges, with the intention of establishing new provinces of Marcomannia and Sarmatia. However, his plans came to naught. In 175 his hitherto trusted friend C. Avidius Cassius, who was now in charge of all the Eastern provinces, proclaimed himself Emperor. There were also whispers that Marcus' wife Faustina was implicated, but Avidius received no significant backing. Marcus made peace with the Iazyges, taking the title Sarmaticus, and headed east, only to discover that Avidius had been murdered by one of his own centurions.

Marcus still felt it prudent to tour the Eastern provinces as far as Alexandria, and Faustina, who had been given the title of *Mater Castrorum* ('Mother of the Camp'), accompanied him. However, she died suddenly in the foothills of the Taurus Mountains. There are two traditions concerning her death. One, supported by Marcus' correspondence with Fronto, was that it was caused by gout; the other makes her commit suicide after learning of the failure of Avidius' conspiracy. There were also insinuations that she was an adulteress who had given birth to Commodus by a gladiator, but these look rather like clichéd 'sinister narrative templates'[28] of the Livia or Agrippina the Younger type, and Marcus was grief-stricken at her death.

On their way back to Rome, both Marcus and Commodus were initiated into the Eleusinian mysteries. They arrived at the end of 176, and Commodus, who was still only fifteen years old, was granted *imperium* and nominated as Consul for 177, in which year he was also given proconsular and tribunician powers, the name Augustus, and the title *Pater Patriae*. Imperator Caesar Lucius Aurelius Commodus Augustus had effectively become joint Emperor of Rome.

Marcus spent less than two years in the capital before warfare dragged him back to the Danube, taking Commodus with him. The Roman armies were gaining the ascendancy, but Marcus fell ill and died at either Vindobona (Vienna) or Sirmium on 17 March 180. His ashes were laid to rest in Hadrian's mausoleum and Commodus made a stress-free transition to power. Against his late father's wishes, he struck peace deals with the tribes in the frontier zone and pulled the trans-Danubian garrisons back across the river.

Some modern writers find it hard to like Marcus Aurelius,

---

28 Freisenbruch, A., *The First Ladies of Rome: The Women Behind the Caesars*, London: Jonathan Cape, 2010, p. 214.

seeing him as 'cold, self-sufficient and joyless, the fine flower of paganism running to seed',[29] but the Romans tended to view him as practically perfect. Many felt that it was downhill all the way from now on: as Dio put it, 'our history now descends from an Empire of gold to one of iron and rust',[30] and Edward Gibbon famously took it upon himself 'from the death of Marcus Antoninus [i.e., Aurelius], to deduce the most important circumstances of [Rome's] decline and fall, a revolution which will ever be remembered and is still felt by the nations of the earth'.[31]

Commodus (180–192): Debauchery and Conspiracy

> Commodus was guilty of many unseemly deeds, and killed a
> great many people.[32]

With Commodus, the Roman Empire re-enters 'interesting times'. He shared his birthday, and a good many personal qualities, with Caligula, and like Nero he was still in his teens when he acceded to the purple. Dio, who knew him personally, says that he was not naturally wicked, but guileless, simple, cowardly and ignorant. Herodian, another eyewitness, talks of his

> well-developed body and a face that was handsome without
> being pretty. His commanding eyes flashed like lightning; his
> hair, naturally blond and curly, gleamed in the sunlight as if it
> were on fire; some thought that he sprinkled his hair with
> gold dust before appearing in public, while others saw in it
> something divine, saying that a heavenly light shone round
> his head. To add to his beauty, the first down was just begin-
> ning to appear on his cheeks.[33]

---

29   Wells, C., *The Roman Empire*, London: Fontana Press, 2nd edn., 1992, p. 218.
30   Dio 72.36.3, tr. Cary. E., op. cit.
31   Gibbon, E., op. cit, vol. 1, part 1, chapter 1.
32   Dio 72.4.1.
33   Herodian 1.7.5, tr. Echols, E. C., *Herodian of Antioch's History of the Roman Empire*, Berkeley and Los Angeles: University of California Press, 1961.

The youthful down duly became a fully-fledged beard. The *Historia Augusta* refers to him being vigorous enough for debauchery, but otherwise as weak and sickly, and having 'such a conspicuous growth on the groin that the people of Rome could see the swelling through his silken robes', which became the source of scurrilous verses.[34] He was also left-handed.

Rather like with Nero, there were high hopes for his Principate, yet when he returned in triumphal procession to a hero's welcome at Rome in October 180, Saoterus, his 'partner in depravity', sat in his chariot and was publicly showered with kisses by him. This Bithynian Greek freedman was Commodus' *a cubiculo* ('chamberlain'), and once again the delegation of serious government business to favourites, especially ones of servile status, led to intrigue, conspiracy and reprisals. Saoterus was murdered just before the first plot against Commodus was hatched by his older sister, Lucius Verus' widow Lucilla, in 181 or 182. The ostensible reason was her jealousy of Bruttia Crispina, whom Commodus had married in 175. Claudius Pompeianus Quintianus, who may have been Lucilla's husband's nephew, ambushed Commodus in an underground passage in the Colosseum, but instead of thrusting his sword into the unsuspecting Emperor he shouted, 'The Senate sends this dagger to you!', lost the element of surprise, and was ushered away to his death. The backlash was predictable: amidst a welter of other killings, Lucilla and Quadratus were executed, and so was Tarrutienus Paternus, co-commander of the Praetorian Guard, who may have ordered Saoterus' death. Paternus' colleague Tigidius Perennis now assumed control of the Praetorians, while deteriorating relations with the Senate meant that government by favourites became Commodus' system of choice.

This arrangement suited both parties:

> Perennis indulged the emperor's youthful appetites, permitting him to spend his time in drinking and debauchery, [. . .]

---

34 *Historia Augusta*, *Commodus* 13.1 f., tr. Magie, D., op. cit.

relieved him of imperial cares and responsibilities [and] assumed full personal charge of the Empire, driven by his insatiable lust for money.[35]

Commodus' 'appetites' allegedly centred on Dionysiac revelry with an assembly of 300 concubines and 300 male prostitutes past the age of adolescence (*exoleti*), chosen on the basis of their good looks. The *Historia Augusta* also notes that he was 'not free from the disgrace of intimacy with young men, defiling every part of his body, including his mouth, in dealings with persons of either sex', and that 'he kept among his minions certain men named after the genitals of both sexes, whom he delighted to kiss'. To a Roman, fellatio and cunnilingus form two aspects of one repellent phenomenon that has nothing to do with homo- or heterosexuality, but is all to do with befouling the mouth by oral-genital contact: *fellatores* are not exclusively 'homosexual' any more than '*cunnilingi*' are 'heterosexual', but both are disgusting to conventional Roman sensibilities. Commodus was also very fond of a staggeringly well-hung man whom he lovingly called Onos ('Donkey').[36]

Eventually Perennis' hubris caught up with him. There had been an outbreak of warfare in Britain, which had seen northern tribesmen cross 'the wall that separated them from the Roman legions'[37] – which one is not specified, though Hadrian's is more likely – before the governor Ulpius Marcellus took punitive measures. Although there was no more warfare on the frontier in Commodus' reign, there was certainly unrest among the troops, who tended to blame Perennis whenever they didn't get what

---

35   Herodian 1.8.1 f., tr. Echols, E. C., op. cit.

36   See *Historia Augusta, Commodus* 5.4 (concubines and *exoleti*); 5.11 (oral defilement, though Magie's Loeb translation prudishly omits 'including his mouth'); 10.8 (minions); 10.9 ('Donkey'). Cf. the stories told about Elagabalus, p. 256 below.

37   Dio 73.8.2. See Breeze, D. J., *The Northern Frontiers of Roman Britain*, London: Batsford, 1982, p. 126 f.

they wanted. In 185, having failed to persuade a certain Priscus to declare himself Emperor, they sent a delegation of 1500 men to Rome, who told Commodus that Perennis was plotting against him. Commodus took the accusation at face value, and the inevitable executions were insisted upon by the man who took Perennis' place of power, his bitter rival Cleander.

Cleander, who hailed from Phrygia, was of servile origin. Able, avaricious, corrupt and unscrupulous, he had become Commodus' *cubicularius* (head of bedroom servants), married the Emperor's concubine Damostratia, eliminated his rivals and amassed a huge personal fortune. Combining corruption and terror he conferred and/or sold Senatorial rank, military commands, procuratorships and governorships. Unsurprisingly this prompted a second coup against the Emperor in March 187. Maternus, a military deserter-turned-desperado who had been ravaging Spain and Gaul, infiltrated Italy with his brigands and planned to assassinate Commodus at the festival of Cybele, using men disguised as Praetorian Guards. But the scheme was betrayed, Maternus was beheaded and Commodus retreated into security-conscious isolation.

Cleander's supremacy lasted until a serious famine struck Rome in 190, which was possibly exacerbated by the grain commissioner Papirius Dionysius in order to bring him down. An angry mob sought out Commodus at his estate near the city to demand Cleander's execution. Cleander sent in the cavalry, who pursued the crowd back to Rome, but in the urban environment the horsemen were pelted with stones and roof tiles, and the rioters were joined by some of Rome's garrison. Commodus had been kept in the dark about these events, but once his sister Fadilla told him what was going on he responded with alacrity. Cleander's head ended up impaled on a long spear and thrown to the mob, while his two sons were put to death and all his known friends were killed. The bodies were dragged through the streets, mutilated and thrown into a sewer.

Gladiator and 'Roman Hercules'

Commodus would never again trust anyone else with the running of the Empire, but the problem for Rome was that he had no interest in doing it himself:

> He no longer had any regard for the 'good life'; night and day, without interruption, licentious pleasures of the flesh made him a slave, body and soul.[38]

Symptomatic of this was the treatment of Iulius Iulianus, who was now sole *Praefectus Praetorio*: he was humiliated by being pushed into a swimming pool in front of his staff, made to dance naked for the Emperor's concubines, and then murdered. Commodus styled himself The Emperor Caesar Lucius Aelius Aurelius Commodus Augustus Pius Felix Sarmaticus Germanicus Maximus Britannicus, Pacifier of the Whole Earth, Invincible, the Roman Hercules, *Pontifex Maximus*, etc., etc. He also insisted on being called not 'Commodus, son of Marcus', but 'Hercules, son of Zeus': Herodian says that he started wearing a lion skin and carrying a club, and Dio that vast numbers of statues were erected representing him in the garb of Hercules.[39] He seems to have come to believe that he *was* Hercules.

Commodus was nothing if not egotistical. In 190 he renamed the months of the year to reflect his names and titles. Starting with January they were now *Lucius*, *Aelius*, *Aurelius*, *Commodus*, *Augustus*, *Herculeus*, *Romanus*, *Exsuperatorius* ('the Supreme'), *Amazonius* (linking him to Hercules' Labour of acquiring the girdle of the Amazon Queen), *Invictus* (Invincible), *Felix* (Fortunate) and *Pius* (Dutiful).[40] Similarly, he is said to have given the name Commodianus (or Commodiana, depending on grammatical gender) to the

---

38   Herodian 1.13.7, tr. Echols, E. C., op. cit.
39   Ibid. 1.14.8; Dio 72.15.6.
40   Dio 73.15.3. See Kershaw, S., op. cit., 2007, pp. 150 ff.

Roman legions, the African grain fleet, the city of Carthage (absurdly termed *Alexandria Commodiana Togata*,)[41] his mansion on the Palatine, the Roman people and the 'Fortunate' Senate. The Senate were not so fortunate when the designation *Senatus Populusque Romanus* (SPQR) was switched to *Populus Senatusque Romanus*, but in general the army and the lower classes liked him. His coins proclaimed a new Golden Age and he took the opportunity to play the 'New Romulus' and 'refound' Rome as *Colonia Lucia Aelia Commodiana*.

It is perhaps Commodus' exploits as a gladiator that have most determined his image for posterity, notably in the Hollywood blockbuster *Gladiator*:[42]

> Commodus: 'The general who became a slave. The slave who became a gladiator. The gladiator who defied an emperor. Striking story!'

Promoting gladiatorial games was a 'Good Thing', but appearing in them was something entirely different. At (probably) the *Ludi Plebeii* of November 192 an audience from all over the Empire witnessed their Emperor, in the guise of Hercules the Hunter, shoot deer, roebuck, lions – a hundred with a hundred javelins – and leopards, a tiger, an elephant and a hippopotamus, as well as decapitating ostriches with crescent-headed arrows. Dio, who saw it happen, was terrified:

> Having killed an ostrich and cut off its head, he came up to where we were sitting, holding the head in his left hand and raising his bloody sword in his right. He said nothing, but

---

41   See Corey Brennan, T., 'Tertullian's *De Pallio* and Roman dress in North Africa', in Edmonson, J. and Keith, A., *Roman Dress and the Fabrics of Roman Culture*, Phoenix Supplementary Volume XLVI, Toronto, Buffalo and London: Toronto University Press, 2008, pp. 258–270.

42   Directed by Ridley Scott, DreamWorks SKG, Universal Pictures, Scott Free Productions, 2000.

wagged his head with a grin, showing that he would treat us likewise.[43]

That was just in the morning. In the afternoon, Commodus fought as a gladiator, scoring a record number of victories for a left-hander. Senators and Equites had no option but to watch horror-struck, and to join in the acclamations:

You conquer, you will conquer; from the dawn of time, Amazonian, you conquer![44]

Such outrageous behaviour could only end badly. It seems that Commodus planned to kill the incoming Consuls on New Year's Day 193, and then emerge as sole Consul wearing the equipment of a *secutor*-style gladiator – a brimless helmet with two small eye holes; a short- to medium- length sword; a tall, oblong, curved shield (*scutum*) with a boss; an armband (*manica*) of heavily quilted linen on his right arm; a gaiter and short greave on his left leg, and a gaiter on his right; plus a loin-cloth (*subligaculum*) and a wide metal belt (*balteus*). Neither his *cubicularius* Eclectus, the *Praefectus Praetorio* Q. Aemilius Laetus, nor his favourite concubine Marcia were able to talk him out of this. They then discovered a wax tablet in the Emperor's handwriting with a list of people scheduled for death that night, and they themselves were at the top of it. So they decided to make a pre-emptive strike. Marcia administered poison in either wine or beef, but when Commodus puked it back up they sent in an athlete called Narcissus to strangle him, thereby ensuring that by not 'taking the iron' like a true gladiator, the Emperor died like a *noxius* (condemned criminal).

The *Historia Augusta* quotes the Senate's acclamations on Commodus' death, and their decree pertaining to the abuse of his corpse and his *damnatio memoriae*:

---

43   Dio 73.21.1–2, tr. Cary, E., op. cit.
44   Ibid. 73.20.2, tr. Kershaw, S.

Let the memory of the murderer and the gladiator be utterly wiped away [. . .] Let the slayer of the Senate be dragged with the hook [. . .] More savage than Domitian, more foul than Nero. As he did unto others, let it be done unto him.[45]

They also wanted the informers punished in a rather Herculean manner, by either lions or the club. In fact, Commodus' remains ended up in the Mausoleum of Hadrian, and he was deified four years later by Septimius Severus.

The Muse of History never repeats herself. She is like a jazz musician endlessly and creatively improvising around an underlying structure, but nevertheless the Roman Empire must at least have wondered whether a familiar refrain would break out: would it be like the death of Nero all over again, with savage civil war, or like the aftermath of Domitian, with an elderly ruler inaugurating a time of prosperity, or maybe some new narrative?

45   *Historia Augusta, Commodus* 19.1—2, tr. Magie, D., op. cit. See also Kyle, D. G., *Spectacles of Death in Ancient Rome,* London and New York: Routledge, 1998, pp. 224 ff.

10

The 'Year of the Five Emperors' and Rome's First African Ruler (193–211)

On his first day as Emperor, when the tribune asked for the watchword, he gave 'let us make war'.

Historia Augusta, Pertinax 5.7[46]

Pertinax

Before daybreak on New Year's Day 193 Commodus' *cubicularius* Eclectus and the *Praefectus Praetorio* Laetus smuggled the dead Emperor's corpse out of the Vectilian Villa where the murder had taken place, and headed for the house of the *Praefectus Urbis* Publius Helvius Pertinax. A knock on the door in the middle of the night was normally an indicator of impending violence or death, but Laetus and Eclectus assured Pertinax that the tyrant was dead, and offered to install him in his place. Neither Dio nor Herodian implies that Pertinax knew anything about this scheme, and his ignorance of the plot certainly remained the official line, but both the *Historia Augusta* and Julian assume that he was the designated replacement from the outset, and in any case, someone had clearly informed an elderly man called Claudius Pompeianus of these events. Pompeianus was a Syrian who had married Marcus Aurelius' daughter Lucilla after Lucius Verus died. He had once been Commodus' mentor, but was currently living in disgusted retirement on his country estates.

Pertinax accepted an invitation to go to the Praetorian camp. There he promised the Guard a *donativum* of 12 000 *sestertii* per man in return for their support. This was quite a bit less than they had received from Marcus Aurelius, but they took the money anyway and proclaimed Pertinax Emperor. Pertinax then headed for the Senate, who were vigorously damning Commodus' memory, where he was approached by Pompeianus. Pertinax offered Pompeianus the throne, but his offer was refused, which in turn allowed Pertinax to make the obligatory pretence of reluctance – his propaganda would claim that although he had been chosen by the soldiers he didn't really want to be Emperor – whereupon the Senate unanimously fell into line and confirmed him as Imperator Caesar Publius Helvius Pertinax Augustus, the first in what is sometimes, and slightly erroneously, dubbed the Year of the Five Emperors.

The mere fact of Pertinax becoming Emperor tells an incredible tale of social mobility. Now aged sixty-six, he had been born in Alba Pompeia (modern Alba) in north-west Italy. His father, Helvius Successus, was a freedman, and had called his son Pertinax to reflect the 'pertinacious' way he conducted his own business dealings. Helvius had also invested wisely in his son's education, sending him to Rome to study with the grammarian Sulpicius Apollinaris. Pertinax had then become a teacher in his own right, before embarking on a meteorically successful military career in Syria, Britain and the Danube, and then moving into high-level administrative posts. He became a Senator, *Consul Suffectus*, and held governorships in the two Moesias, Dacia, Syria and Africa, before being appointed *Praefectus Urbis* at Rome by Commodus. On the way he had received helpful patronage from the aforementioned Claudius Pompeianus, and also made a politically judicious but 'open' marriage to the ex-Consul Flavius Sulpicianus' daughter Flavia Titiana: both partners indulged in unsuitable affairs.

On the whole, Pertinax seems to have been well respected by the Senate, possibly because he was very deferential and unthreatening:

> He was a venerable old man, with a long beard and swept back hair. The appearance of his body was on the fat side [. . .] but his stature was imperial. His speaking ability was average, and he was smooth rather than affable.[47]

Dio, whose political career benefited from Pertinax' accession, says that 'he also conducted himself in a very democratic manner toward us Senators; for he was easy of access, listened readily to anyone's requests, and in answer gave his own opinion in a kindly way'.[48] But if his attitude towards the Senate struck the right tone, as did both his refusal to pander to the lewdness of imperial freedmen and his prudent management of the economy, his relationship with the Praetorian Guard proved his undoing. It only took until 3 January for them to try to invest the distinguished Senator Triarius Maternus Lascivius in his place, although he fled naked (we are not told why) to Pertinax and subsequently left Rome.

Dio tells us that

> Laetus [who was now *Praefectus Praetorio*], however, did not remain permanently loyal to Pertinax, or, I might better say, he was never faithful even for a moment; for when he did not get what he wanted, he proceeded to incite the soldiers against him.[49]

This initially resulted in an unsuccessful attempt to install the Consul Q. Pompeius Sosius Falco as Emperor. Pertinax, who was at Ostia checking up on the corn supply, rushed back to

---

47   *Historia Augusta, Pertinax* 12.1, tr. Kershaw, S.
48   Dio 74.3, tr. Cary, E., op. cit.
49   Ibid. 74.6.

Rome, blamed corrupt freedmen for his financial difficulties, lied about giving as much to the soldiers as Marcus Aurelius had done, and spared Falco's life, although numerous Praetorians were subsequently put to death. Pertinax had sworn never to execute a Senator, but the perceived inconsistency in the treatment of the soldiers, whether this was on Pertinax's orders or on Laetus', pretending it was on Pertinax's, proved fatal to the Emperor. On 28 March, 200 or 300 soldiers stormed unopposed into his residence. Either through bravery or through stupidity Pertinax tried to reason with them. The precise details vary, but one soldier took the offensive, and Pertinax was hacked down in a welter of sword-blows.

Dio's verdict is that Pertinax

> failed to comprehend, though a man of wide practical experience, that one cannot with safety reform everything at once, and that the restoration of a state, in particular, requires both time and wisdom.[50]

He should have said that one cannot with safety alienate the Praetorian Guard.

Sold to the Highest Bidder! Didius Julianus Buys the Empire

If the citizens of Rome had been hoping that Pertinax would be Nerva II, with a Golden Age to follow, they were to be bitterly disappointed. What they got was civil war, a series of short-lived would-be Emperors, and perhaps the most bizarre accession to date.

The soldiers who had murdered Pertinax carried his head on a pole back to the Praetorian camp, where an extraordinary series of events now played itself out. Pertinax's father-in-law, the *Praefectus Urbis* T. Flavius Sulpicianus, was already at the

---

50 Ibid. 74.10.

camp, trying to find out what was going on. He wanted the Praetorians to proclaim him Emperor. But so did another senior Senator, M. Didius Severus Julianus. Essentially the two of them embarked on an auction for Roman Empire. Back in 111 BCE the African prince Jugurtha had said of Rome:

> It is a city for sale, and it will meet a premature death if it finds a buyer.[51]

Three centuries later it did find one: in a bare-faced bidding-war, Flavius Sulpicianus offered 20 000 *sestertii* per soldier, but Didius Julianus used his outstretched fingers to indicate an extra 5 000. The Roman Empire was sold. Didius Julianus went to the Senate House, where the abject, terrified Senators, Dio Cassius included, conferred on him tribunician power, the title of Imperator, and the rights of a Proconsul.

Rome's new owner was not a complete nobody. Born of mixed Italian and African origin in 137, he had been brought up at the home of Marcus Aurelius' mother Domitia Lucilla, commanded *Legio* XXII *Primigenia* in Germany in the early 170s, served as Consul with Pertinax, who allegedly 'always called him his colleague and successor',[52] and had held five provincial governorships. The question was, could he govern what he had just bought? According to Dio, the signs were not good:

> Finding the dinner that had been prepared for Pertinax, he made great fun of it, and sending out to every place where by any means whatever something expensive could be procured at that time of night, he proceeded to gorge himself, while the corpse was still lying in the building, and then to play at dice.[53]

---

51 Sallust, *Bellum Iugurthinum* 35.10, tr. Kershaw, S.
52 *Historia Augusta, Julianus* 2.3.
53 Dio 74.13.1, tr. Cary, E., op. cit.

Herodian is similarly dismissive, speaking of his drinking, debauchery, luxurious living and profligate practices to the detriment of his duties to the state.[54]

Imperator Caesar Marcus Didius Severus Julianus Augustus' support was precarious in the extreme: there was no guarantee that the provincial armies would accept him just because the Praetorian Guard has sold him the world; the Senate were deeply unhappy; and the people of Rome rioted and started to agitate on behalf of C. Pescennius Niger, the governor of Syria. That might have been a manageable situation for Julianus, but two other powerful provincial governors, both from African families, now put forward their claims as well: D. Clodius Albinus in Britain, and L. Septimius Severus in Pannonia Superior.

Pescennius Niger made the first move. His four Syrian legions proclaimed him Emperor in April, but he made the mistake of trying to consolidate support at Antioch, and lost the initiative. Clodius Albinus, who like Didius Julianus' mother came from Sousse, also declared himself in April. He could call on three legions and plenty of auxiliaries, but it was Septimius Severus, the man from Lepcis Magna in modern Libya, who was the most focused and ruthless player. He could count on the backing of some sixteen legions from the armies of the Rhine and Danube, and he was also the nearest to Rome.

Having been proclaimed Emperor by *Legio* XIV *Gemina* stationed at Carnuntum on 9 April, Septimius also made a pact with Clodius Albinus, offering him the title 'Caesar' (effectively from now on, 'heir apparent'), which Albinus accepted. So with one potential rival sitting on his hands on the other side of the English Channel, Septimius could concentrate on taking Rome.

As Septimius homed in on the capital, Aquileia and Ravenna fell without resistance. Didius Julianus' responses included threats, negotiation, magic rituals, assassination attempts and

---

54 Herodian 2.7.1. *Historia Augusta, Didius* 3.8 dismisses much of this as vicious rumour, however.

building fortifications, all of which came to nothing, since his envoys kept defecting and the Praetorian Guard, 'demoralized by the fleshpots of the city and intensely averse to active service',[55] degenerated into a useless laughing stock:

> the Praetorians did nothing worthy of their name and of their promise, for they had learned to live delicately; the sailors summoned from the fleet stationed at Misenum did not even know how to drill; and the elephants found their towers burdensome and would not even carry their drivers any longer, but threw them off, too.[56]

For his part, Septimius worked assiduously to undermine his rival, whose supporters melted away. Julianus realized that the game was up. Dio was present on 1 June when he summoned the Senate and asked them to appoint Septimius as joint ruler. But the compromise came far too late: Septimius had no interest in a power-sharing agreement; the Praetorian Guard changed sides; and the Consul Silius Messalla convened another meeting of the Senate, where Dio and the others voted on three motions:

> We thereupon sentenced Julianus to death, named Septimius Emperor, and bestowed divine honours on Pertinax.[57]

Julianus was a solitary gibbering wreck in the imperial palace when he met his fate.

> A [military] tribune was sent to kill Julianus, that cowardly and wretched old man who had in this way purchased with his own money his miserable death.[58]

---

55   *Historia Augusta, Julianus* 5.9, tr. Magie, D., op. cit.
56   Dio 74.16.3, tr. Cary, E., op. cit.
57   Ibid. 74.17.4. Cf. Herodian 2.12.6–7.
58   Herodian 2.12.7, tr. Echols, E. C., op. cit.

Apparently his last words were rather pathetic: 'But what terrible thing have I done? Whom have I killed?'[59]

Septimius Severus, the African Emperor (193–211)

When Julianus was killed on 1 June 193, Septimius Severus was still some 80 kilometres from Rome. Nine days later his army flooded into the city in triumph having put the Senate and the Praetorians firmly in their place. A hundred-strong delegation of Senators had met him at Interamna (modern Terni), where he had them searched for concealed weapons, before receiving them, armed himself and accompanied by many armed men. The Praetorian Guard were also summoned (or tricked) to meet him 'in their undergarments'[60] outside the city, where they were 'netted like fish in his circle of weapons'.[61] They were stripped of their clothing and their employment, and forbidden to come within 100 Roman miles of Rome on pain of death; anyone directly involved in the murder of Pertinax was executed. A new Praetorian Guard was recruited from Septimius' loyal Danubian legions, but he retained Julianus' *Praefectus* Flavius Juvenalis, who had conveniently changed sides when offered the chance. Septimius did install a new co-commander of the Guard though, D. Veturius Macrinus, and more significantly a fellow-African and distant relative called C. Fulvius Plautianus became the new Prefect of the *Vigiles* and proceeded to seize Pescennius Niger's adult children. These changes effectively put an end to Italians dominating the Praetorian Guard and were symptomatic of changes in the balance of power right across the Empire.

Dio Cassius witnessed Septimius' entry into Rome at first hand:

> The whole city had been decked out with garlands of flowers and laurel and adorned with richly coloured stuffs, and it was

---

59   Dio 74.17.5, tr. Kershaw, S.
60   *Historia Augusta, Severus* 6.11.
61   Herodian 2.13.5.

ablaze with torches and burning incense; the citizens wearing white robes and with radiant countenances, uttered many shouts of good omen; the soldiers, too, stood out conspicuous in their armour as they moved about like participants in some holiday procession; and finally we [Senators] were walking about in state.[62]

Septimius posed as the avenger of Pertinax, whose name he included in his grandiose new title: Imperator Caesar Lucius Septimius Severus Pertinax Augustus. He provided the late ruler with magnificent obsequies in the Campus Martius: a pyre was constructed in the form of a three-storey tower adorned with ivory, gold and statues, on top of which was a gilded chariot. When the consuls set light to the pyre an eagle flew from it, symbolizing Pertinax's deification.

Rome's first 100 per cent African Emperor was

small of stature but powerful, though he eventually grew very weak from gout; mentally he was very keen and very vigorous. As for education, he was eager for more than he obtained, and for this reason was a man of few words, though of many ideas. Towards friends not forgetful, to enemies most oppressive, he was careful of everything that he desired to accomplish, but careless of what was said about him.[63]

His family were upwardly mobile wealthy denizens of Lepcis Magna, and his future had seemed particularly rosy when, early in his career, he consulted an astrologer who gave him a reading predicting *ingentia,* 'great things'. He married a woman named Paccia Marciana, moved to Rome, became a Senator, and pursued a career of governorships and military commands under Marcus Aurelius and then Commodus,

---

62   Dio 75.1.4, tr. Cary, E., op. cit.
63   Ibid. 77.16.

which culminated in his governorship of Pannonia Superior in 191. His success was partly due to Rome's 'African mafia', especially Q. Aemilius Laetus,[64] and although he was totally Romanized, he never lost his local accent: in all probability he pronounced his name Sheptimiush Sheverush.[65]

His marriage to Paccia Marciana was childless, but his second marriage, to Julia Domna, produced two sons in quick succession: L. Septimius Bassianus (better known by his nickname Caracalla) in 188, and P. Septimius Geta the year after (see Genealogy Table 4). He had, allegedly, chosen Julia Domna because it was written in the stars that she would marry a king, but she was a colourful character in her own right: the daughter of the high priest of the sun god Elagabal at Emesa (modern Homs) in Syria, striking to look at, adept at political machinations, a patroness of writers and philosophers, and well known for her scandalous love affairs:

> [Septimius] kept his wife Julia even though she was notorious for her adulteries and even guilty of conspiracy.[66]

There is a certain amount of irony in this. Septimius prided himself on his old-school Roman qualities of *rigor*, *disciplina*, *severitas*, etc., and felt that Rome's population was not living up to the morals and values of their ancestors, but when he tried to enact the old *lex Julia de adulteriis*[67] he created a backlog of literally thousands of indictments and he had to give up the process. Even the barbarians were disgusted, if we can believe Dio's story of a conversation between a Caledonian woman and Julia Domna. The empress was teasing her about 'free love' in

---

64 See pp. 222 ff.

65 See Birley, A. R., *Septimius Severus: The African Emperor*, rev. edn., New Haven, Con: Yale University Press, 1988, p. 35.

66 *Historia Augusta, Severus* 18.8, tr. Kershaw, S. Dio, however, has nothing to say about this, and there is a strongly hostile historical tradition that seeks to discredit her.

67 See p. 51 above.

Britain, only to get the reply: 'We fulfil the demands of nature in a much better way than do you Roman women; for we consort openly with the best men, whereas you let yourselves be debauched in secret by the vilest'.[68]

Septimius did not stay in Rome for long. He still had the problem of the wannabe Emperor Pescennius Niger to deal with, but first he underwent an image change where rather than working a soldierly look he took on a heavily bearded style. Then he announced that he was embarking on a Parthian War, but headed for his real target – Byzantium, where Niger was based.

It was a classic East v West clash, with Pescennius Niger's six legions from Egypt and Syria confronting Septimius' sixteen mighty Danubian ones. The result was a foregone conclusion: Septimius' battle group drove Niger's men back towards the end of 193, scoring victories near Cyzicus and at Nicaea (modern Iznik), while his fleet brought troops to lay siege to Byzantium; the provinces of Asia and Bithynia fell into Septimius' hands; Egypt recognized his authority; and in Spring 194, in a toughly contested battle at Issus (where Alexander the Great had famously defeated Darius III of Persia), his troops deployed *testudo* tactics and destroyed Niger's army. Niger himself fled but was apprehended and beheaded. However, not even the display of his severed head could induce the defenders of Byzantium to capitulate: it took more than a year to bring them to submission, after which the city's imposing walls were torn down.

Septimius tinkered with the provincial arrangements in the East: the province of Syria was now divided into two: Syria Coele ('Hollow Syria'), which had quite a Hellenistic cultural flavour, and Syria Phoenice, 'Phoenician Syria', with a more strongly Semitic one. A vicious backlash also took place against the individuals and cities that had supported Niger. Such was the extent of the reprisals that a great many people fled to

---

68   Dio 77.16.4 f., tr. Cary, E., op. cit. Dio found 3 000 adultery indictments when he was consul.

Parthia rather than face Septimius' severity. This duly provided him with a pretext to invade Parthia, and in the first half of 195 he crossed the Euphrates into northern Mesopotamia. Dio says he did this out of a 'desire for glory',[69] but it would do him no harm to bring his and Niger's legions together against Rome's traditional enemy, and the Parthians could not be allowed to support his rival and the fugitives with impunity. In fact, Septimius encountered little meaningful resistance. The kingdom of Osrhoene was made into the Roman province of Osrhoena, a chunk of Mesopotamia was organized as a Roman province of the same name with two legions stationed in it, and Septimius received three salutations as *Imperator* as well as taking the titles *Arabicus* and *Adiabenicus*.

The elimination of Niger and the annexation of new territory was really just a prelude to more important events at Rome and in the West. Septimius sought to link himself to the Antonine dynasty by (falsely) claiming that he was the son of Marcus Aurelius; Julia Domna received the title *Mater Castrorum* ('Mother of the Camp') like Marcus' wife Faustina; and Septimius' elder son Septimius Bassianus, aka Caracalla, was renamed Marcus Aurelius Antoninus. When the seven-year-old boy was given the title 'Caesar', Septimius' dynastic plans were made crystal clear: Clodius Albinus had been granted this title to buy him off in the struggle with Niger, so replacing him with Caracalla was an open invitation to a fight.

Clodius Albinus had a certain amount of support in the Senate, and we hear that Septimius dispatched agents to assassinate him and put about allegations that he had been behind Pertinax's murder. For his part, Albinus proclaimed himself Augustus (i.e., Emperor), but was declared a public enemy on 15 December. Popular unease about the situation manifested itself in a demonstration against civil war in the Circus Maximus, but events now had their own momentum. Albinus commanded the three legions of Britain, *Legio* VII *Gemina* in Spain, and

---

69   Ibid. 76.1.1.

forces from the Rhineland, but he was still outnumbered by an adversary who was better prepared. In February 197 the armies converged outside Lugdunum, where Septimius prevailed after some bloody fighting in which he was thrown from his horse and only escaped by throwing off his imperial cloak.[70] The defeated Albinus committed suicide and Septimius rode his horse over his naked body before having it thrown into the Rhône, and his severed head was sent back to Rome.

Whereas Albinus had minted coins at Lyons professing his *CLEMENTIA* ('clemency') and *AEQUITAS* ('fairness'), Septimius is said to have lauded the severity and cruelty of notorious Republican hard-men like Sulla and Marius, and deprecated the mildness of Pompey and Caesar. He argued that it was totally hypocritical for the Senators to criticize his 'brother' Commodus, when 'only the other day one of your number [. . .] was publicly sporting with a prostitute who imitated a leopard'.[71] The reprisals of 'the Punic Sulla' were savage: Albinus' wife and children were killed, as were many of his supporters and their wives; twenty-nine Senators were put to death; and Commodus was deified. Herodian summarizes the situation very well:

> But here is one man who overthrew three Emperors after they were already ruling, and got the upper hand over the Praetorians by a trick: he succeeded in killing Julianus, the man in the imperial palace; Niger, who had previously governed the people of the East and was saluted as Emperor by the Roman people; and Albinus, who had already been awarded the honour and authority of *Caesar*.[72]

---

70 Herodian 3.7.2. Dio 76.6 tells it differently, though: Severus loses, sees his men in flight, rips off his riding cloak, draws his sword, and rushes into the fugitives in the hope that he might stop the rout or die in the attempt.

71 Dio 76.8.2. If Severus was now 'son of Marcus Aurelius', that made him Commodus' 'brother'.

72 Herodian 3.7.8 tr. Echols, E. C., op.cit.

In an acknowledgement of where his true power-base was, Septimius curried favour with the people of Rome by staging extravagant and exotic shows in the arena, and with the army, notably by improving the legionaries' basic pay from 1 200 to 2 000 *sestertii* and ending Augustus' restrictions on their right to marry. Then it was time to head for the East once more. Parthia must be destroyed . . .

There was a slightly unsettled atmosphere on the Eastern frontier. The Parthian king, Vologaeses IV, had retaliated against the Roman incursion of 195 by attacking the frontier outpost of Nisibis, which had been taken during that campaign. Now, however, the Roman intentions were much more serious. The Emperor raised three new legions, I, II and III *Parthica*, all commanded by Equestrian prefects rather than Senatorial legates. Dio tells us that I and III were quartered in Mesopotamia but II *Parthica* was stationed in Italy, where it could both control Rome and function as a strategic reserve. By late summer 197 Septimius had established his headquarters at Nisibis. His invasion force sailed along the Euphrates before marching against Ctesiphon on the Tigris, which they took relatively easily. In a fate not uncommon in antiquity, the adult males were killed and the women and children enslaved, while the Parthian royal treasury was looted. Northern Mesopotamia became a Roman province once again, and on the centenary of Trajan's accession, 28 January 198, Septimius took the title of Parthicus Maximus, named the nine-year-old Caracalla 'Augustus' (co-Emperor), and made his younger son Geta 'Caesar': essentially he now had an heir and a spare.

Septimius Severus had become the greatest expander of the Empire since Trajan, but he doesn't seem to have intended to annex all the territory he had just conquered. As the loot-laden army withdrew, he made two costly and unsuccessful assaults on the fortress city of Hatra. From there he moved to Palestine and then to Egypt, where he combined administration with sightseeing, taking in the embalmed corpse of Alexander the Great, a Nile cruise, and visits to the pyramids and Thebes

(Luxor). From there he headed back to Syria, where in 202 he took the consulship with the thirteen-year-old Caracalla as his colleague: never before had two co-Emperors been Consul at the same time.

Having returned to Rome via the Danubian provinces and taken the opportunity to put on shows and make generous donations to the Praetorian Guard and the plebs, Septimius revisited the land of his birth. Lepcis Magna, which is now one of the most spectacular of all the ancient archaeological sites, benefited immeasurably. An unusual four-way triumphal arch straddles a major crossroads in celebration of Septimius' victory over Parthia, and when M. Iunius Punicus erected statues to the Emperor, Julia Domna, Caracalla and Geta,[73] Septimius reciprocated as only an Emperor can. He conferred *ius Italicum* (exemption from tribute) on the city, which came to be embellished with some outstanding architecture: one of the most impressive Forums in the Empire, a stunning space some 300 by 200 metres surrounded by colonnades and incorporating a temple to the Genius of Septimius; an imposing basilica at least 30 metres high with columns of exotic red granite and green marble, plus white marble pilasters depicting the mythology of Hercules and Bacchus; an improved aqueduct; a first-rate port with a lighthouse; a colonnaded street that ran from the harbour to the main Hadrianic Baths, which were repaired; a new entrance to the Macellum (Market Place); and state-of-the-art athletic facilities. Dio thought this was a monumental waste of money:

> He [. . .] spent a great deal uselessly in repairing other buildings and in constructing new ones; for instance, he built a temple of huge size to Bacchus and Hercules.[74]

---

73   *IRT* 392, 403, 422, 434. Geta's name was erased following his assassination in 211 by Caracalla.
74   Dio 77.16.3, tr. Cary, E., op. cit.

This may refer to the enormous temple at Lepcis: Bacchus and Hercules are not only the patron deities of the Severan family, but are commonly identified with Lepcis' patron deities Shadrapa and Melquart, illustrating an important blending of African and Roman traditions.

By 203 Septimius and his entourage were back in Rome, and again there was lavish spending: the impressive Arch of Septimius Severus was dedicated in the Forum in 203; the Septizodium (or Septizonium) became a kind of ancient Roman Trevi Fountain on the south-east corner of the Palatine; and there were the Baths of Severus. The following year saw the celebration for the seventh, and ultimately the final time, of the *Ludi Saeculares* ('Secular Games'), last held six years prematurely (they ran on a 110-year cycle) by Domitian in 88.

The End of Septimius Severus' Reign

All Septimius' building and festivities could not obscure the fact that tensions were breaking out. Before the Eastern campaign he had promoted C. Fulvius Plautianus to *Praefectus Praetorio*. Plautianus, also from Lepcis, had not only engineered the murder of his Praetorian colleague Q. Aemilius Saturninus and wheedled his way into becoming the Emperor's closest confidant, but also had his eyes on the throne himself:

> He wanted everything, asked everything from everybody, and would take everything. He left no province and no city unplundered, but snatched and gathered in everything from all sides [. . .] He castrated a hundred Roman citizens of noble birth [so that Publia Fulvia] Plautilla, his daughter, whom Caracalla afterwards married, should have only eunuchs as her attendants in general, and especially as her teachers in music and other branches of art.[75]

---

75 Ibid. 76.14.1.

Plautilla apparently had a dowry that would have sufficed for fifty women of royal rank, but her marriage to Caracalla was a disaster: he detested her and his father-in-law, not to mention his younger brother, all of whom seemed to stand in the way of *him* becoming sole ruler of Rome. For his part, Plautianus also treated Julia Domna so outrageously, conducting investigations into her conduct that involved torturing women of the nobility, that she was driven to study philosophy.

The denouement came in 205 when both Caracalla and Geta were Consuls. Plautianus was executed on the evening of 22 January. What really happened is not entirely clear: in Dio's version Caracalla fabricated a supposed plot against himself and Septimius by Plautianus, and when Plautianus tried to defend himself against the accusation, Caracalla had him killed; in Herodian's version, which reads like official propaganda, the plot was genuine, but Plautianus was betrayed by his own henchman. Caracalla now divorced Plautilla, who was banished to the island of Lipari. He never remarried.

One of the two new Praetorian Prefects who replaced Plautianus was the eminent jurist Aemilius Papinianus ('Papinian'). This was a sign of Septimius trying to offset some of his legal workload: he was conscientious about administering the law, but needed expert guidance, and his reign is often said to have inaugurated a Golden Age of jurisprudence, notably through the talents of Papinian and two other great Roman lawyers, Julius Paulus ('Paul') and Domitius Ulpianus ('Ulpian'). The influence of these men on the modern world cannot be overestimated: their view of Roman law still underlies the modern legal systems of much of Europe and America.

By this time, however, Septimius was in his 60s, his health was on the wane, and his teenaged sons were going off the rails in an orgy of sibling rivalry. He was under no illusion about what Caracalla was like, and Dio alleges that he considered putting him to death, like Septimius felt Marcus Aurelius should have done with Commodus. But he didn't. So when the governor of Britain, another African by the name of Lucius Alfenus Senecio, sent dispatches saying that the barbarians there were in revolt and overrunning the country, Septimius was delighted: here was an opportunity both for glory and to instil some much-needed military discipline into his offspring. He and Caracalla shared the front-line command, while Geta was elevated to joint Emperor and entrusted with the logistics. Campaigns in around 208, 209 and 210 used Eboracum as the military headquarters, and saw successful salients well to the north of the Antonine Wall. Ethnic cleansing was on the cards:

> Let nobody escape utter destruction at our hands, not even any child in its mother's womb if it is male; let nobody escape utter destruction.[76]

But events intervened.

Septimius was obsessed with astrology, and Dio says that he knew he would not return from Britain:

> He knew this chiefly from the stars under which he had been born, for he had caused them to be painted on the ceilings of the rooms in the palace where he was wont to hold court, so that they were visible to all, with the exception of that portion of the sky which, as astrologers express it, 'observed the hour' when he first saw the light.[77]

As Septimius' health worsened Caracalla curried favour with the army, besmirched Geta, and attempted to persuade the doctors to hasten the old man's end by their treatments.[78] Dio carries a story of Caracalla trying to stab his father in the back, and only desisting when the shouts of some nearby riders warned Septimius about what was happening. But he

---

76   Ibid. 77.15.1, tr. Kershaw, S.
77   Ibid. 77.11.1, tr. Cary, E., op. cit.
78   Herodian 3.15.2

could have waited: Septimius Severus died of natural causes at Eboracum on 4 February 211, aged sixty-five.

The British campaign was called off. Caracalla and Geta returned to Rome, where their father's ashes were deposited in Hadrian's mausoleum just prior to his official deification. He had left the Empire in rude financial health, but Edward Gibbon described him as the 'principal author of the decline and fall of the Roman empire'.[79] For the moment, though, the most pressing question was how well his two sons might, or might not, cooperate in ruling, and how they would react to his last words, quoted 'exactly and without embellishment' by Dio: 'Agree amongst yourselves, enrich the soldiers and despise all the others.'[80]

79   Gibbon, E., op. cit., vol. I, part 1, chapter 5.
80   Dio 77.15.2, tr. Kershaw, S.

11

The Severan Dynasty:
Odd Emperors and Interesting Women
(211–235)

> *Caracalla was a bad lot, Elagabalus worse, and Severus
> Alexander remains a vague figure for want of evidence. The
> women, after Septimius' death, were the backbone of the
> dynasty. It would be interesting to see what Tacitus would
> have made of them . . .*
>
> Colin Wells[1]

Divided and Ruling: Caracalla (211–217) and Geta (211)

When Septimius Severus died, Caracalla was twenty-two
years old and Geta twenty-one. The tradition paints the
younger brother in quite idealized terms as kind, courteous
and popular, although the *Historia Augusta* refers to him
overdoing the food, wine and sex; Caracalla appears as a
distorted caricature: an angry young man prone to cruelty,
violence, debauchery and megalomania. He was never officially called Caracalla. That was a nickname that referred to
his dress sense:

> [He] invented a costume of his own, which was made in a
> rather foreign fashion out of small pieces of cloth sewed
> together in a kind of cloak [*caracalla/caracallis*]; and he [. . .]

---

1 Op. cit. p. 268.

wore this most of the time himself, in consequence of which he was given the nickname Caracallus.[2]

The name stuck, and by the fourth century Caracallus had become Caracalla.

The two brothers seethed with mutual hostility and pointedly refused to cooperate on any significant policy areas. Amicable co-existence as joint Emperors being completely out of the question, they split the imperial palace down the middle, and even considered doing the same with the Roman Empire. They abandoned that idea after some heavy emotional blackmail from their mother Julia Domna, and concentrated on plotting one another's downfall instead. In December 211, after initially intending to perpetrate the act at the Saturnalia festival but being too obvious about it, Caracalla talked Geta into attending a meeting with himself and their mother to talk about a possible reconciliation, but had him struck down by his soldiers (or struck him down himself):

> When Geta saw them, he fled for safety to his mother, hung upon her neck, clung on to her bosom and breasts, moaned and howled: 'Mother who gave me birth! Mother who gave me birth! Help me! I am being slaughtered!'.[3]

Damnatio memoriae followed as Caracalla tried to erase all record of Geta's existence from inscriptions, coins, sculptures and paintings. Every possible epigraphic and visual reference to him has been eradicated from the Arch of Septimius Severus in the Roman Forum and from the four-faced arch at Lepcis Magna, and especially striking is a painted tondo found in the Fayum that depicts Septimius Severus, Julia Domna, Caracalla and Geta, except that Geta's face has not only been erased, but smeared with excrement.[4]

---

2   Dio 79.3.3, tr. Cary, E., op. cit. Cf. *Historia Augusta, Caracalla* 9.4.
3   Dio 78.2.3, tr. Kershaw, S.
4   Berlin, Staatliche Museen, *inv.* 31.329. See Varner, E. R., *Mutilation and Transformation:* Damnatio Memoriae *and Imperial Roman Portraiture,* Leiden: Brill,

Caracalla: The Brutal Populist

Sources hostile to Caracalla took a very nostalgic and idealized view of this victim of fratricide, but it was not until Elagabalus came to the throne in 219 that Geta's reputation was officially restored and his mortal remains finally laid to rest in the Mausoleum of Hadrian. Caracalla paid a generous *donativum* to the troops, and then went in for a purge of Geta's supporters: friends and associates; anyone who had lived in his half of the imperial palace; all his attendants; anyone who had the slightest acquaintance with him, be they athletes, charioteers, singers or dancers; distinguished Senators including on the flimsiest charges by anonymous accusers; both Praetorian Prefects, Papinianus and Patruinus; governors and procurators friendly to Geta; numerous members of the imperial family; and, as he had threatened long ago, his own wife Plautilla. The Praetorian Guard ran amok among the population of Rome in an orgy of pillage and bloodshed that lasted over a fortnight and caused 20 000 deaths.

Caracalla seems to have had a secure grasp of the pressure points of Roman politics, since the soldiers immediately received a 50 per cent pay rise. This of course increased the pressure on the treasury. Given that Ulpian defined *tributum* (tribute, taxes) as what is 'paid to the soldiers',[5] a military pay rise would entail a concomitant tax hike. And there were plenty of soldiers to pay. Dio Cassius gives us a valuable list of the legions and their dispositions in his day (he was working on his history during Caracalla's reign, and a comparison with the inscription from Marcus Aurelius' time[6] illustrates the way the legions were sometimes relocated in response to changing military needs):

2004, pp. 173 ff.

5   *Digest* 55.126.27.

6   *CIL* 4 3492 = *ILS* 2288. See above, p. 213.

Province	Legions
Germania Superior	VIII *Augusta*, XXII *Primigenia*
Germania Inferior	I *Minervia*, XXX *Ulpia* (omitted by Dio)
Spain	VII *Gemina*
Africa	III *Augusta*
Egypt	II *Traiana*
Cappadocia	XII *Fulminata*, XV *Apollinaris*
Syria	III *Gallica*, IIII *Scythica*, XVI *Flavia*
Arabia	III *Cyrenaica*
Judaea	VI *Ferrata*, X *Fretensis*
Mesopotamia	I *Parthica*, III *Parthica*
Upper Pannonia	X *Gemina*, XIV *Gemina*
Lower Pannonia	I *Adiutrix*, II *Adiutrix*
Upper Moesia	IIII *Flavia*, VII *Claudia*
Lower Moesia	I *Italica*, XI *Claudia*
Noricum	II *Italica*
Raetia	III *Italica*
Dacia	V *Macedonica*, XIII *Gemina*
Italy	II *Parthica*
Upper Britain	II *Augusta*, XX *Valeria Victrix*
Lower Britain	VI *Victrix*

In 212, Caracalla issued an edict known as the *Constitutio Antoniniana*, which granted Roman citizenship to virtually all free inhabitants – male *and* female – of the Empire.[7] Rather strangely, it was not mentioned on the coinage, and Dio is cynical about it, arguing that it was intended to increase revenues by vastly increasing the number of people liable to tax. Yet it was a deeply significant moment in the extension of 'Romanness' across the Empire's ethnically diverse population. From now on any free man or woman born in Britain, Spain, Greece, Egypt, Syria or wherever could say those famous words, 'I am a Roman citizen', even though by this time the most important privileges of citizenship only applied to the higher of the two citizen classes, the *honestiores*

---

7   Ulpian, *Digest* 1.5.17; Dio 78.9.5.

(Senators, Equites, army officers, etc.), as opposed to the *humiliores* (everyone else). In law the *honestiores* were subject to less severe punishments – rarely death, and never forced labour in the mines, crucifixion or being thrown to the beasts.

Other revenue-raising policies included requiring the Senators to pay heavy contributions, doubling inheritance and emancipation taxes, and frequently levying the *aurum coronarium* (a contribution in gold to the Emperor that was originally collected on the occasion of triumphs, imperial accessions, anniversaries and adoptions, but which metamorphosed into a general ad hoc tax), which hit the more prosperous urban classes particularly hard. To counter the effects of a general upward trend in inflation, Caracalla created a new silver coin, the *antoninianus*, which was intended to replace the *denarius* at double its value, even though it only contained about one and a half times its worth in precious metal.

Another major part of Caracalla's expenditure was the construction of the vast, state-of-the-art *Thermae Antoninianae* (Baths of Caracalla), a complex that impresses visitors to Rome even now:

> Among the public works which he left at Rome was the notable Bath named after himself, the *cella soliaris* of which, so the architects declare, cannot be reproduced in the way in which it was built by him. For it is said that the whole vaulting rested on gratings of bronze or copper, placed underneath it, but such is its size, that those who are versed in mechanics declare that it could not have been built in this way.[8]

In 213 Caracalla embarked on a tour of the provinces, moving to Gaul, campaigning in Raetia against the Alemanni (also spelled

---

8   *Historia Augusta, Caracalla* 9.4, tr. Magie, D., *The Scriptores Historiae Augustae with an English Translation by David Magie, Volume II*, Cambridge, MA, and London: Harvard University Press, 1924. The *cella soliaris* (the precise meaning of this is obscure) is probably the massive *frigidarium* (cold room) of the bath complex, which also contained a swimming pool.

Alamanni or Alamani = 'All Men'), and taking on the Cenni, a Germanic tribe whose warriors were said to have used their teeth to pull out the missiles that had wounded them so that they could keep their hands free for unimpeded fighting. Caracalla assumed the *cognomen* Germanicus Maximus, but also became quite fond of the local tribesmen. He chose some of the strongest and most handsome for his personal bodyguard, but also liked to dress up as a German in a short, silver-embroidered cloak and blond wig. At one point he visited the shrine of the Celtic healing-god Grannus, and having then moved down via Thrace into Asia Minor he also visited the healing sanctuary of Asclepius at Pergamum, where his treatments included dream therapy. He also started channelling Alexander the Great in an overt way. His portraits show an interesting combination of a tough grumpy old soldier crossed with a hint of Alexander, and Herodian says that he filled all Rome with statues and paintings designed to suggest that he was a second Alexander. He started wearing Macedonian-style clothing, and visited the site of Ilium (Troy) where he performed rituals at the supposed Tomb of Achilles.

By 215 Caracalla had made his way to Antioch in Syria, after which he set off for Alexandria, ostensibly to visit the city that Alexander had founded and to pay his respects to the god Serapis, whom his father had also venerated. Unfortunately he was also bearing a grudge. The Alexandrians had given him a glittering welcome, but they were also fond of joking at his expense. Whatever the real cause, he assembled the young men of the city on false pretences, and surrounded them with his troops.

> While slaughtering the Alexandrians and living in the sacred precincts, [Caracalla] sent word to the Senate that he was performing rites of purification on those very days when he was in reality sacrificing human beings to himself at the same time that he sacrificed animals to the god.[9]

---

9   Dio 78.23.2, tr. Cary, E., op. cit.

The massacre left the mouths of the Nile and the entire shore around the city stained red with blood.

Caracalla's real ambition, however, was to ape Alexander and Trajan by conquering the East. He relocated to Antioch and sought to exploit the internal tension in Parthia between two rival claimants to its throne: Vologaeses V and Artabanus V. Caracalla backed the latter and agreed to marry his daughter. The Romans crossed the Euphrates and Tigris rivers and moved deep into Parthian territory, where they were welcomed with flowers, wild dancing, pounding drums and copious amounts of alcohol. But when the Parthians abandoned their horses and put their quivers and bows away, Caracalla gave the order to attack. The Romans slaughtered a great number of the Parthians, took large amounts of booty and prisoners, and marched away unopposed. En route they burned towns and villages, and Caracalla gave free rein to his soldiers to carry off as much of anything they wanted as they could.

The Roman army wintered at Edessa (modern Şanlıurfa in Turkey). Doubtless Caracalla was very pleased with himself at the time, but a retrospective analysis of the situation a decade into the future might have made him alter his opinion. He had made a significant contribution to the demise of the Parthian Empire, but with its takeover by the Sasanian dynasty in Persia under Ardashir I (*c.*223–*c.*240), and especially his successor Shapur I (*c.*240–*c.*270), Rome was out of the frying pan and into the fire.

Like his hero Alexander the Great, Caracalla was fated to die in the East. His trusted friend Flavius Maternianus (or Materianus) either uncovered or fabricated a plot against him involving the *Praefectus Praetorio* M. Opellius Macrinus. Unfortunately for the Emperor, the letter recommending Macrinus' elimination accidentally found its way into the possession of its intended victim, who therefore got his retaliation in first. On 8 April 217 Caracalla was heading for Carrhae in order to honour the god Lunus (the Semitic male moon-deity Sîn), but as he was taking a toilet break Macrinus' accomplices took his life. Responsibility for the actual assassination devolved onto a disaffected ex-soldier called Martialis, although the story had it that he was in turn cut down by Caracalla's German or Scythian bodyguard(s).

The *Historia Augusta* describes the late ruler as 'the most unfeeling of human beings, in a word a fratricidal, incestuous enemy of his father, mother, and brother',[10] but the army were upset by his death. His ashes were sent to Julia Domna at Antioch, from where they were transported to the Mausoleum of Hadrian at Rome. Caracalla was deified at Macrinus' request.

Macrinus versus the Imperial Women: 217–218

Macrinus, born *c.*165 in Caesarea in Mauretania (modern Cherchell in Algeria), has the distinction of being the first Roman Emperor to come from a non-Senatorial background. The armies in the East seem to have been unaware of his possible involvement in Caracalla's assassination, and they saluted him as Emperor on 11 April 217. But the women of the imperial family would ensure that his reign was brief.

The new Emperor hoped to make some sort of accommodation with Artabanus V, but the Parthian smelled Roman vulnerability and took the offensive. The upshot was a hard-fought battle in the vicinity of Nisibis, followed by a rather inglorious peace treaty under which Rome retained Mesopotamia by buying off the Parthians at an extortionate price. Other settlements were reached with the Armenians and the Dacians, who had also taken the change of Emperor as an opportunity to attack the Romans. None of this was doing Macrinus' public image a great deal of good, and neither did he endear himself to the populace when he stayed on in Antioch, despite Rome suffering a particularly violent electrical storm that caused a fire which damaged the Colosseum and caused flooding in the Forum. He also had difficulties in matching Caracalla's free-spending relationship with the army, whose allegiance started to waver.

In terms of his dynastic arrangements, Macrinus got his

---

10   *Historia Augusta, Caracalla* 11.5, tr. Kershaw, S.

eight-year-old son Diadumenianus made Caesar, but he seems not to have reckoned with some incredibly feisty, formidable and politically active imperial women who were not going to allow the Severan dynasty to go down without a fight. When Caracalla's mother Julia Domna had heard of her son's death, despite her hatred for him ever since the murder of Geta,

> she was so affected that she dealt herself a violent blow and tried to starve herself to death.[11]

Dio relates that she flirted with the idea of seizing power herself before going back to Plan A and starving herself – she was already terminally ill with breast cancer – although Herodian hints that her suicide was forced onto her by Macrinus.[12] She was, nevertheless, deified, leaving her recently widowed sister Julia Maesa to preside over a family that included her two daughters, Julia Soaemias and Julia Mamaea, and their respective sons, Varius Avitus Baddianus and Alexianus Bassianus (see Genealogy Table 4).

Whether it was Julia Maesa who came up with the scheme herself (she certainly had the wherewithal to buy the allegiance of the legions), or whether it was Eutychianus and Gannys, some family 'friends' from Emesa, is unclear. But someone certainly decided to have Avitus, who looked a lot like his cousin Caracalla, proclaimed Emperor. He, Julia Soaemias and Julia Maesa were smuggled into the camp of *Legio* III *Gallica* near Emesa, and on 15 May 218 the fourteen-year-old boy was duly acknowledged as Caracalla's illegitimate son but legitimate successor, under the name Marcus Aurelius Antoninus.

Macrinus responded to the uprising of the 'False Antoninus' (a slur that Dio continually makes) by declaring war on Avitus, Alexianus, their mothers and their grandmother, and unofficially associating his own son Diadumenianus with the throne. When battle was joined, the pro-Severan army

---

11   Dio 79.23.1, tr. Cary, E., op. cit.
12   Dio 79.23–4; Herodian 4.13.8.

made a very weak fight, and the men would never have stood their ground, had not Maesa and Soaemias [. . .] leaped down from their chariots and rushing among the fleeing men restrained them from further flight by their lamentations.[13]

This turned the battle in their favour. Macrinus was defeated, and although he escaped from the battle, he was duly captured and executed, as was Diadumenianus. Their severed heads were stuck on pikes, their names erased from inscriptions and papyri, and Diadumenianus suffered the further indignity of having one of his honorific inscriptions thrown into a latrine at Ostia. The Severan dynasty was back with a vengeance.

Religious Fanaticism and Weird Sex: Elagabalus, 218–222

Although Rome's new fourteen-year-old Emperor was acclaimed by the name Marcus Aurelius Antoninus, he is usually known as Elagabalus (occasionally Heliogabalus), after the sun god Elagabal of Emesa, whose high priest he was. Rome seldom did well under teenage Emperors, and Elagabalus' reign was no exception, although many of the tales of his bizarre sexual practices sound like the typical uncorroborated stories that crystallized around many 'bad' Emperors. We might note that whatever he allegedly got up to, the day-to-day running of the Empire seems to have carried on perfectly competently.

After Macrinus had been done away with, the Roman armies in the East sided with Elagabalus, who spent the last half of 218 at Antioch and then at Nicomedia eliminating Macrinus' supporters. One prominent victim was Gannys, even though he had assisted Elagabalus' rise to power. The pretext was that he was forcing the boy to live in a respectable manner, but Gannys was also said to be the lover of the Emperor-mother Julia Soaemias, and may well have been turning into something

---

13   Dio 79.38.4, tr. Cary, E., op. cit.

of a threat. In any case, regardless of their relationship, the real beneficiaries of Gannys' death were Julia Soaemias herself, and Elagabalus' grandmother Julia Maesa.

Having wintered in Nicomedia, the Emperor and his family set off for Rome in the spring of 219 with a weird companion: a conical black stone. Apparently the stone was worshipped as though it had been sent from heaven, and it had various small projecting pieces and markings that people liked to believe formed a rough picture of the sun. As a manifestation of the Emperor's eponymous god Elagabal, the stone was installed on the north-east corner of the Palatine Hill where an enormous new temple called the Elagabalium was erected to accommodate it. Rome's traditional religious sentiments were shocked by the cult practices:

> I will not describe the barbaric chants which Sardanapalus [i.e., Elagabalus], together with his mother and grandmother, chanted to Elagabal, or the secret sacrifices that he offered to him, slaying boys and using charms, in fact actually shutting up alive in the god's temple a lion, a monkey and a snake, and throwing in among them human genitals, and practising other unholy rites, while he invariably wore innumerable amulets.[14]

The Sardanapalus reference is a smear by Dio. He was a stereotypical 'Oriental' mythical Assyrian king, noted for his effeminacy.

A second temple was erected on the edge of Rome, and at midsummer the black stone was transferred there from the temple on the Palatine along a route paved with gold dust in a chariot drawn by six white horses, while the Emperor ran backwards in front of it holding the reins, looking up into the 'face' of his god. If this wasn't bad enough, Elagabalus intended to make Elagabal Rome's principal deity over and above Jupiter,

---

14   Ibid. 80.11.

and declared that the religions of the Jews and the Samaritans, and the rites of the Christians had to be transferred to the temple.

Of course, the sun god needed a wife, and Elagabalus opted for Vesta, whose sacred fire was transferred to the Elagabalium along with the sacred objects held in her shrine, notably the Palladium, the sacred statue of Athena which Aeneas had reputedly rescued from Troy and was tended by the Vestal Virgins. This was all too much for Roman public opinion, though, and an alternative spouse was eventually selected: the Carthaginian moon goddess Caelestis, aka Tanit, who also had a large stone that was the focus of her worship.

Elagabalus was also involved in a number of earthly marriages – up to five in some sources. Almost as soon as he had arrived in Rome in 219 he had married the noble Julia Cornelia Paula, who was proclaimed *Augusta*, only to be divorced when no child was immediately forthcoming. In 220, to universal opprobrium, he married Julia Aquilia Severa. She was a Vestal Virgin, and this was a horrendous violation of Roman law. Elagabalus' justification for his actions sounds incredibly lame:

> He sent a letter to the Senate asking to be forgiven his impious and adolescent transgression, telling them that he was afflicted with a masculine failing – an overwhelming passion for the maiden. He also informed them that the marriage of a priest and a priestess was both proper and sanctioned.[15]

But Severa was unable to produce an instantaneous heir, and she too found herself divorced, this time in favour of Annia Aurelia Faustina, a great-granddaughter of Marcus Aurelius. The marriage took place in July 221, but by the end of the year Elagabalus was back with his true love, the Vestal ex-Virgin Severa.

Although each of his wives held the title of *Augusta*, the real power lay with their mother-in-law and her mother. Soaemias

---

15   Herodian 5.6.2, tr. Echols, E. C., op. cit.

and Maesa, both also called *Augusta*, seem to have managed affairs of state pretty adeptly, and they were so powerful that they were invited to meetings of the Senate – the only two women we know of to have been offered this privilege. Maesa was honoured as *Augusta, Mater Castrorum et Senatus* ('Mother of the Army Camp and the Senate'), and Soaemias as *Mater Castrorum et Senatus et Totius Domus Divinae* (adding, 'and the Whole Divine House'). They even set up a *Senaculum* ('Women's Senate') chaired by Soaemias, although rather than functioning as a feminist think-tank it became a forum for discussing female protocol and fashion – who could wear gold or jewels on her shoes, who should make the first move in kisses of social greeting, and so on – and later satirists and moralists, like Erasmus in his *Senatulus* of 1529, used it as a vehicle to attack what they saw as female vanity and the ludicrousness of a female parliament. In essence, the tradition uses these women to reflect on Elagabalus. The author of the *Historia Augusta* wrote that he was totally under Soaemias' control,

> so much so that he didn't carry out any public business without her permission, although she lived like a complete whore and practised every type of disgusting activity in the palace.[16]

Lewdness was the order of the day. Elagabalus' supposed extreme sexual proclivities became notorious.

He may have had several wives, but he also had lots of illicit extra-marital intercourse, delighted in harnessing teams of naked women to a wheelbarrow and making them drive him around on their hands and knees, and is himself depicted nude and ithyphallic on a cameo that shows him brandishing a whip over two fashionably coiffured naked women who are pulling his chariot.[17] However, it was his feminization, and the way he conducted his

---

16 *Historia Augusta, Elagabalus* 2.1, tr. Kershaw, S.
17 Wheelbarrow (*pabillum*): *Historia Augusta, Elagabalus* 29.2; cameo: Paris, Bibliothèque Nationale, Cabinet des Médailles, 304.

man-to-man relationships, that caused the real disgust. This started with his fashion sense. Julia Maesa advised him that wearing his purple and gold priest's outfit – complete with necklaces, bracelets and a tiara – would look not only foreign and barbaric but effeminate too. But to no avail – he enjoyed his transvestism:

> He had the whole of his body depilated, deeming it the chief enjoyment of life to appear fit and worthy to arouse the lusts of the greatest number [. . .] By night he would go to the taverns dressed in a wig, and work as a landlady. He often went to the best known brothels, drove out the working girls, and became a prostitute himself.[18]

Some things got him particularly aroused:

> Men who were hung like donkeys (*onobeli*) were avidly sought out from the whole city and from the sailors.[19]

The *onebeli* received high-ranking posts on the basis of the size of their manhood, while his charioteer, a Carian slave called Hierocles, became his 'husband' and the partner in some S&M-style role play:

> [This 'woman' Elagabalus] wished to have the reputation of committing adultery, so that in this respect, too, he might imitate the most lewd women; and he would often allow himself to be caught in the very act, in consequence of which he used to be violently upbraided by his 'husband' and beaten, so that he had black eyes.[20]

However, transsexual games were not enough. He wanted the real thing:

18   *Historia Augusta, Elagabalus* 5.5, tr. Magie, D., op. cit; Dio 80.13.2 f., tr. Kershaw, S.
19   *Historia Augusta, Elagabalus* 8.7, tr. Kershaw, S.
20   Dio 80.15.3, tr. Carey, E., op. cit.

He asked the doctors to engineer a woman's vagina in his body by means of an incision, offering huge fees for doing this.[21]

Hand in hand with this went some astonishing feasting. On the menu were camel-heels, peacock and nightingale tongues, flamingo brains, heads of parrots, fish cooked in blue sauce to make them look like they were in the sea, peas with gold pieces and rice with pearls. Even his dogs were fed on goose livers, and his lions on pheasants. Yet this did not necessarily mean glorious over-indulgence for the party-goers: some were seated on air-pillows, which deflated during dinner; others were offered desserts made from wax, wood, ivory or stone; and we hear of parasites being bound to a turning water wheel and being called 'Water-Ixions' after the mythological transgressor of the divine order.[22]

Another thing that upset the aristocracy was Elagabalus' appointment of men of lowly origin to lofty government positions, such as P. Valerius Comazon, who ascended from a family of professional entertainers to become *Praefectus Praetorio* in 218, the charioteer Cordus who became prefect of the *Vigiles*, and Claudius, a barber who took over the grain supply. Rome's Establishment would not tolerate a situation like this for long, and neither would the army. Inevitably, Elagabalus was faced by constant challenges to his position: *Legio* III *Gallica* soon turned against him and tried to make their commander Verus Emperor, although he was executed; an officer of *Legio* IIII *Scythica* based in Syria named Gellius Maximus also declared himself Emperor, but suffered the same fate; and Seleucus, a figure of uncertain identity, also failed.[23]

Julia Soaemias stuck by her son, but his grandmother now started to look at other possibilities. The rift between the *Augustae* became apparent when, in an attempt to diffuse the tensions, Elagabalus agreed to adopt his younger cousin called Alexianus

---

21 Ibid. 80.16.7, tr. Kershaw, S.
22 See Kershaw, S., op. cit., 2007, p. 286.
23 The fifth-century historian Polemius Silvius adds Uranius, Sallustius and Taurinus to the list of usurpers.

Bassianus, who assumed the name Marcus Aurelius Alexander, and the title of Caesar, on 26 June 221. The family was now split between Elagabalus, backed by his ambitious mother Soaemias, and Alexander, supported by his politically wily mother Julia Mamaea (Soaemias' sister) and his grandmother Julia Maesa.

Towards the end of 221 Elagabalus tried to have Alexander murdered, but the attempt backfired. Nobody would do the deed. By March the following year Elagabalus was well and truly sick of Alexander's popularity, but the Praetorians, who had been carefully cultivated by Mamaea, had had enough of him:

> [Elagabalus] made an attempt to flee, and would have got away somewhere by being placed in a chest, had he not been discovered and slain, at the age of eighteen. His mother, who embraced him and clung tightly to him, perished with him; their heads were cut off and their bodies, after being stripped naked, were first dragged all over the city, and then the mother's body was cast aside somewhere or other, while his was thrown into the river.[24]

The *Historia Augusta* relates that Elagabalus was slain whilst taking refuge in a latrine, and that his corpse was shoved into a sewer before being hurled into the Tiber. He acquired the derogatory nickname Tiberinus as a result of this, to go with his unsurpassed collection of others: False Antoninus; the Assyrian; Sardanapalus; Gynnis (= 'Womanish Man'); and Tractitius (derived from the Latin for 'to drag'). Needless to say, he suffered *damnatio memoriae*, although Gilbert and Sullivan have made sure he never quite faded into obscurity: the song 'I Am the Very Model of a Modern Major-General' from *The Pirates of Penzance* (1879) contains the classic line: 'I quote in elegiacs all the crimes of Heliogabalus.'

---

24   Dio 80.20, tr. Cary, E., op. cit.

The 'Miserly Woman and the Timid, Mother-dominated Youth': Alexander Severus, 222–235

Rome immediately acquired another teenaged Emperor. Indeed, if it is correct that Alexander had been born in Arca Caesarea (Arqa in modern Lebanon) in Phoenicia on 1 October 208, he had just become the youngest Emperor that Rome had ever had. He is generally known as Alexander Severus (or Severus Alexander). The historian Dio was Consul in 229, but only a tiny scrap of this particular part of his history survives, which is all the more frustrating given that Alexander advised him to spend his consulship away from Rome, because he could not guarantee his safety. It would be wonderful to know why that was.

Officially Alexander Severus' father was Gessius Marcianus, but although there were rumours about him being an illegitimate child of Caracalla it was really his mother Mamaea who mattered most:

> Completely dominated by his mother, he did exactly as he was told. This was the one thing for which he can be faulted; that he obeyed his mother in matters of which he disapproved because he was over-mild and showed greater respect to her than he should have done.[25]

Alexander's grandmother Julia Maesa also wielded a great deal of power, so much so that, in reality if not in theory, Rome was being governed by women. After Maesa's death in 223 or 224, Mamaea became not merely *Mater Augusti et Castrorum et Senatus et Patriae* ('Mother of the Emperor, the Army Camp, the Senate and the Fatherland'), but even *Mater Universi Generis Humani* ('Mother of the Whole Human Race').

Mamaea used the expertise of the jurists Ulpian and Paulus, who were Prefects of the Praetorian Guard and members of Alexander's *consilium*, but still found the Praetorians

---

25 Herodian 6.1.10, tr. Echols, E. C., op. cit.

problematical. There had already been violence between them and the city populace when Ulpian fell foul of them one night in 223 or early 224. He had eliminated their previous commanders, Julius Flavianus and Geminius Chrestus, but the soldiers exacted their revenge by murdering him, even though he took refuge with Alexander and Mamaea in the palace.

Further difficulties arose in relation to Alexander's marriage to the blue-blooded Sallustia Barbia Orbiana. When she took the title of *Augusta* it put Mamaea's nose severely out of joint:

> Although [Alexander] loved the girl and lived with her, she was afterward banished from the palace by his mother, who, in her egotistic desire to be sole empress, envied the girl her title.[26]

Orbiana's father L. Seius Sallustius may also have been raised to the rank of Caesar, but in 227, when Mamaea's insults became too much for them to endure, he took refuge in the Praetorian camp. This was interpreted as an act of treason, and Mamaea had him executed, while Orbiana was banished to Libya. This was not what Alexander wanted, but he was totally dominated by his mother.

Yet compared to the predecessor's reign, Alexander's was relatively calm, and Mamaea tried to put the politics of consensus at the heart of her regime: relations with the Senate were cordial; religious equilibrium was restored when the black stone was sent back to Syria and the Elagabalium on the Palatine Hill was converted to the Temple of Jupiter Ultor; Apollonius of Tyana, Christ, Abraham and Orpheus are all said to have received due respect; building projects improved the face and facilities of Rome; jurists held high office; literary figures like Dio Cassius held consulships; and the Greek cultural movement known as the Second Sophistic continued to flourish, especially in the great cities of Athens, Pergamum,

26   Ibid. 6.1.9.

Smyrna and Ephesus. Philostratus, who published his *Lives of the Sophists* under Alexander Severus, had coined this phrase to describe the activities of celebrity itinerant orators from *c.*60 to 230.[27] They would improvise virtuoso declamations on moral or Greek historical dilemmas: *Leonidas Inspires his Men to Fight to the Death*; *Which Side of a Woman is the Most Pleasing, Front or Back?*; *Is Water or Fire More Useful?*; or more frivolous themes like *In Praise of Baldness*. Synesius argued that

> Just as man is the most intelligent, and at the same time the least hairy of earthly creatures, conversely it is admitted that of all domestic animals the sheep is the stupidest, and that this is why he puts forth his hair with no discrimination, but thickly bundled together. It would seem that there is a strife going on between hair and brains, for in no one body do they exist at the same time.[28]

Synesius also observed that none of the hairy Spartans survived the defeat by the Persians at Thermopylae in 480 BCE,[29] and now after some three centuries of domination by the Parthians, the Persians were resurgent. A new and highly ambitious ruling dynasty called the Sasanids, under the capable and ruthless Ardashir I (*c.*223–*c.*240), had come to power in their old Iranian heartland. Ardashir was originally a Parthian vassal, but he had overthrown the last Parthian king, Artabanus V, and once he was officially installed as *Shahanshah* ('King of Kings') he aimed at restoring the Persian Empire to its former majesty. This would inevitably entail the conquest of practically

---

27 The First Sophistic designates the art of rhetoric in the fifth and fourth centuries BCE.

28 Synesius, *In Praise of Baldness*, 5, tr. Fitzgerald, A., *The Essays and Hymns of Synesius of Cyrene: Including the Address to the Emperor Arcadius and the Political Speeches*, Oxford: Oxford University Press, 1930.

29 See Kershaw, S., *A Brief Guide to Classical Civilization*, London: Robinson, 2010, p. 93 and p. 138.

all of Rome's Eastern possessions. Rome had a new enemy in the East.

In 230 Ardashir's army made an incursion into the Roman province of Mesopotamia, took Nisibis and Carrhae, and menaced Syria. Alexander Severus responded by heading east, accompanied by his mother and advisers, and picking up troops from the Danube frontier en route. Before he could launch a counter-offensive, his administration had to face down a mutiny by *Legio* II *Traiana* in Egypt, but once this was dealt with he led one of three salients back against the Persians. The Roman assault met with mixed results and both sides suffered heavy losses, but at least a settlement of sorts was reached in 233 that allowed Alexander to return to Rome and celebrate a somewhat spurious triumph. For his part, Ardashir refrained from attacking Roman territory for the remainder of Alexander's reign: there would be plenty of opportunity for his son Shapur I (*Sapor* in Latin) in the years to come.

There was no respite for Alexander Severus in Rome:

The governors in Illyria reported that the Germans had crossed the Rhine and the Danube Rivers, were plundering the Roman Empire, and with a huge force were overrunning the garrison camps on the banks of these rivers, as well as the cities and villages there.[30]

Alexander and his mother based themselves at Moguntiacum (Mainz) in Germania Superior in 234, and with the Roman forces bolstered by the return of soldiers from the East, preparations were put in place for a major offensive. A pontoon bridge was constructed over the Rhine, but early in 235 Alexander made what was literally a fatal mistake. He tried to buy the Germans off. This may have been sensible – Herodian tells us that, 'the avaricious Germans are susceptible to bribes and are

---

30   Herodian 6.7.2., tr. Echols, E. C., op. cit.

always ready to sell peace to the Romans for gold'[31] – but the army, who already had issues about their pay and conditions and didn't like the fact that the Empire was being run by a mummy's boy (or by his mummy), looked on it as a shameful exhibition of weakness:

> Alexander was doing nothing courageous or energetic about the war; on the contrary, when it was essential that he march out and punish the Germans for their insults, he spent the time in chariot racing and luxurious living.[32]

They turned to a semi barbarian ex-shepherd from Thrace called Gaius Julius Verus Maximinus. This gritty character had risen rapidly through the ranks, and although he was prone to rioting 'in a barbarian way' and could 'hardly speak Latin',[33] Alexander had put him in charge of training new recruits. In February or March 235, as the soldiers were mustered for their normal drill they decked out Maximinus in the imperial purple and proclaimed him Emperor. He accepted after the normal show of reluctance, and then moved to catch Alexander unawares.

The Emperor was in camp at Vicus Britannicus (modern Bretzenheim) fairly close by, and he was made aware of the situation before the rebels got to him, but instead of using this to his advantage he threw a teenage tantrum (even though he was twenty-six years old):

> Bursting from the imperial headquarters as if possessed, weeping and trembling, he denounced Maximinus for his disloyalty and ingratitude, and listed all the favours he had done the man.[34]

---

31 Ibid. 6.7.9.
32 Ibid. 6.7.10.
33 *Historia Augusta, The Two Maximini*, 3.1; 2.5
34 Herodian 6.9.1, tr. Echols, E. C., op. cit.

His soldiers' loyalty lasted just as long as it took Maximinus' men to arrive:

> Clinging to his mother and, as they say, complaining and lamenting that she was to blame for his death, he awaited his executioner. After being saluted as Emperor by the entire army, Maximinus sent a tribune and several centurions to kill Alexander and his mother.[35]

The killings brought the Severan dynasty to an end. Maximinus ordered the usual *damnatio memoriae* of Alexander and Mamaea, who had their names and titles expunged from inscriptions and their portraits mutilated. However, three years later, Alexander Severus was deified by the Senate and his name was re-inscribed on many of the damaged inscriptions. It was an indication of the confusion that was about to engulf the Roman world.

---

35   Ibid. 6.9.6.

12

The Omnishambles (235–285)

*The Roman Empire degenerated to a species of barbarity, and
fell to decay.*

Zosimus, *New History* 1.29[1]

The Emperors of the 'Time of Chaos'

Maximinus Thrax 235–238
Gordian I 238
Gordian II 238
Pupienus and Balbinus 238
Gordian III 238–244
Philip the Arab 244–249
Decius 249–251
Trebonianus Gallus 251–253
Aemilius Aemilianus 253

Gallienus 253–268   Valerian 253–260

The Gallic Empire
Postumus 260–269
Claudius II Gothicus 268–270   Laelianus 269
Marius 269
Quintillius 270   Victorinus 269–271
Aurelian 270–275   Tetricus 271–274

Tacitus 275–276
Florianus 276
Probus 276–282
Carus 282–283

Numerian 283–284   Carinus 283–285

---

1 Tr, Vossius, G. J., *History of Count Zosimus, Sometime Advocate and Chancellor
of the Roman Empire*, London: Green and Chaplin, 1814.

With the accession of Maximinus the Thracian ('Maximinus Thrax'), Rome embarked on five decades of what some historians see as 'transition', but most refer to as crisis, chaos, implosion, anarchy, or something similar. Amidst a seemingly endless list of Emperors, usurpers, rebels and outlaws, nearly all of whom were assassinated, the Empire faced dangerous challenges from barbarians outside its borders (see Map 5) and economic meltdown within them. In a sense, there was nothing new about these problems, and Rome was no stranger to dynastic infighting, civil wars, usurpations, rebellions, barbarian invasions, religious conflicts, military disasters, inflation, disruption of commerce, harsh and unfair tax-collection, plagues and an excessive influence by the army over politics: so far Rome had coped with them and had survived. Now, though, many of these problems happened at the same time, and everything fed into everything else in a deafening howl of feedback: the external, internal, military, political, social and economic problems all reinforced each other in unprecedented and very frightening ways.

Maximinus Thrax and the Year of the Six Emperors

If the Roman Empire thought it had had enough of a dynasty that gave them effete, under-age, religious fundamentalists who were dominated by their mothers, it now got what it wanted. Maximinus Thrax (ruled 235–238) was an absolute beast of a man:[2] 2.6 metres tall, naturally barbaric, brutal, handsome in a manly way, but very sweaty:

> He would often collect his sweat and put it in wine cups [. . .] and in this way he could show off one or two litres of it.[3]

---

2   *Historia Augusta, The Two Maximini* 9.2 uses the Latin word *animal*; see also, e.g., 2.2, 6.9, 28.8; cf. Herodian 6.8.1, 7.1.2.

3   *Historia Augusta, The Two Maximini* 4.3, tr. Kershaw, S.

Some called him Hercules, others Cyclops.

But perhaps Rome should have been careful what she wished for. The new Emperor installed his son, also named Maximinus, as Caesar, and thereby laid bare his dynastic intentions. Rather than trying to negotiate with the German tribes, he launched a vigorous offensive against the Alemanni, and took up a position at Sirmium, from where he could keep an eye on the Dacians and Sarmatians. Yet this caused his undoing. The campaigns were expensive, particularly since he increased army pay, and he insisted on a draconian tax collection policy to pay for them.

One flashpoint came in Africa, where some wealthy young landowners from Thysdrus (modern El-Djem) murdered one of Maximinus' procurators and proclaimed M. Antonius Gordianus Sempronianus Romanus Africanus (Gordian I), the octogenarian Proconsul of Africa, as Emperor. He then named his son, known as Gordian II, as co-Emperor. Gordian II had a taste for exotically flavoured wine and an eye for the ladies:

> It is said that he had twenty-two concubines [. . .] from each of whom he left three or four children. He was nicknamed the Priam (*Priamus* in Latin) of his times, but often the crowd jokingly called him not Priamus but Priapus.[4]

For about three weeks the two Gordians became the focus for the insurgency against Maximinus, but at the instigation of Capelianus, the governor of Numidia who had a personal grudge against Gordian I, *Legio* III *Augusta* and their supporting Numidian cavalry turned against them and put an end to their ill-equipped and disorganized rebellion in a one-sided battle outside Carthage:

---

4 *Historia Augusta, The Three Gordians* 19.3–4, tr. Magie, D., op. cit. The joke works nicely in Latin: in Greek mythology Priam had fifty sons (see Kershaw, S., op. cit., 2007, pp. 240–3); Priapus was a rustic god who looked after the produce of your vegetable garden, and was depicted with a huge penis, symbolizing both fertility and his power to ward off trespassers by sexually violating them. See Richlin, A., op. cit.

Shoving and trampling one another, more were killed by their own mass than by the enemy.[5]

Gordian II was killed in action and his grief-stricken father hanged himself.

Italy also turned against Maximinus. Unable to tolerate his barbarian origins, the Senate deposed him by proclaiming him an enemy of the state, mobilizing all the forces in Italy that they could muster, and devolving the government onto the distinguished seventy-four-year-old soldier M. Clodius Pupienus Maximus and the pleasure-loving patrician D. Caelius Calvinus Balbinus as joint Emperors. However, neither the plebs nor the Praetorians liked Balbinus, and the new rulers were forced to make M. Antonius Gordianus (Gordian III), the nephew of Gordian II, Caesar.[6]

Maximinus marched on Rome, but, in the face of some tough opposition, his soldiers turned against him. In some traditions Maximinus took his own life after witnessing his son murdered by mutineers at Aquileia, whose citizens had reputedly resisted his siege operations to the extent of using their women's hair for bow-strings. Other versions have both father and son butchered by disaffected soldiers, and their heads displayed on poles. In Rome Pupienus and Balbinus fell to quarrelling, presenting the Praetorians with an opportunity to kidnap and kill them, which was gleefully accepted.

Rome was now ruled by a thirteen-year-old. The exact course of events around this time is notoriously difficult to establish, but even though Gordian III (ruled 238–244) had been elevated to the purple by the military, he still seems to have commanded reasonable cross-constituency support: the Senate approved because he was one of them; the troops were happy because he was a young man and very much under the control of C. Furius

---

5   Herodian, 7.9.7, tr. Echols, E. C., op. cit.
6   In some sources (e.g., Aurelius Victor and Eutropius) there are only two Gordians, with II and III being combined, although the author of *Historia Augusta, The Three Gordians* regards these authorities as 'uninformed'.

Sabinus Aquila Timesitheus, the *Praefectus Praetorio*, whose daughter Tranquilliana he married; and the people called him their 'darling'. Nevertheless, there were some serious challenges to be met. Pupienus and Balbinus had been on the point of confronting the Carpi from Dacia and the Goths, who were attempting to cross the Danube and attacking some Greek towns on the Black Sea.

The Goths, according to Jordanes' *Getica*, were a Germanic people coming from what is now Sweden, although archaeologically the Gothic confederacy is associated with the Sîntana de Mureş-Černjachov culture, which spreads from Romania to the Ukraine. They spoke an east-Germanic language, used Germanic personal names, and were physically tall, sporting beards and long blond or red hair. They wore skins and furs, were adept horsemen, capable agriculturalists and stock raisers, and fought very effectively by forming their wagons into a defensive laager that protected their formidable cavalry strike force.

The Goths were driven back by Timesitheus in 238, and repulsed again in 242, the same year in which Gordian III set out with Timesitheus to fight the Persians. The Romans had some successes on the battlefield, but Timesitheus died of an illness. He was replaced as *Praefectus Praetorio* by M. Julius Philippus, aka Philip the Arab, who could well have connived in the assassination of Gordian III in the spring of 244 while he was at Dura-Europus on the Syrian front.

Dark Times for the Empire: 244–268

'Philippus Arabs', who came from an Equestrian family of Arab descent, was duly proclaimed Emperor and held the throne from 244 to 249. Ecclesiastical authors of the fourth and fifth centuries speak of him as the first Christian Emperor,[7] but if

---

7 See Shahid, I., *Rome and the Arabs: A Prolegomenon to the Study of Byzantium and the Arabs*, Dumbarton Oaks: Harvard University Press, 1984, pp. 65 ff.

he was he never professed his faith in public. Philip certainly seems to have been keen to establish a dynasty, though, and he associated his six-year-old son with himself, as well as delegating responsibility for Eastern affairs to his brother Priscus under the title *Rector Orientis* (Governor of the East). He also made the most of the PR possibilities of Rome's millennium celebrations, which took place on 21 April 248.

In dealing with the problems on the Empire's periphery, Philip tried to buy off the Persians with half a million *denarii*, in order to focus on other enemies, notably the Alemanni, who had made an incursion across the upper Rhine, and the Carpi and Goths, who were still making life difficult on the lower Danube. Unfortunately for Philip, his response was inhibited by having to deal with a series of usurpers: M. Silbannacus (Rhine region – known only from a unique coin in the British Museum); possibly Sponsianus (Danube – although he is known only from gold coins found in 1713, which could be forgeries); Ti. Claudius Marinus Pacatianus (Upper Moesia); M. Fulvius Rufus Iotapianus (Cappadocia and Syria, claiming descent from Alexander the Great); L. Julius Aurelius Sulpicius Uranius Antoninus (Syria); and the ex-Consul C. Messius Quintus Decius Valerinus, whom Philip had put in charge of the Danube forces facing the Goths. We are told that Decius was

> clothed in purple and forced to undertake the government, despite his reluctance and unwillingness.[8]

But that didn't stop him marching towards Rome and killing Philip in battle near Verona in September 249.

It would be entirely understandable if Decius really had been reluctant to become Emperor of Rome: recent history would suggest that if he survived more than two years he would have had a good innings. Initially he appears to have struggled with his image: he had already used three different

---

8   Zosimus, *New History* 1.22, tr. Vossius, G. J., op. cit.

permutations of his name, and now he opted for C. Messius Quintus Traianus Decius. The introduction of 'Traianus' allowed him to make use of the *Thirteenth Sibylline Oracle*, which spoke of a king who

> will rule mighty Rome, skilled in war, emerging from the Dacians, of the number 300.[9]

Three hundred is the numerical value of the Greek letter *tau*, the initial letter of Traianus; the Dacian reference is a little off-beam (Decius was born in Pannonia), although the Emperor Trajan had conquered Dacia at the beginning of the previous century.

In the belief that neglect of Rome's traditional gods was having a deleterious effect, he sought to bolster their cults. At the beginning of 250 he issued a decree that all his subjects should perform a sacrifice to the 'ancestral gods', and do so in front of officials. In Egypt, Aurelia Belias and her daughter Kapinis complied:

> In your presence, in accordance with the regulations, I have poured libations and sacrificed and tasted the offerings, and I ask you to certify this for us below. May you continue to prosper. [Then in a 2nd hand] We, Aurelius Serenus and Aurelius Hermas saw you sacrificing. [In a 3rd hand] I Aurelius Hermas certify. [1st hand again] The first year of the Emperor Caesar Gaius Messius Quintus Traianus Decius Pius Felix Augustus, 21 June 250.[10]

However, significant numbers of Christians refused to do this, and a persecution ensued. *The Golden Legend (Aurea Legenda)*,

---

9 *Orac. Sib.* 13.81–83, tr. Potter, D. S., *Prophecy and History in the Crisis of the Roman Empire: A Historical Commentary on the Thirteenth Sibylline Oracle*, Oxford: Clarendon Press, 1990.

10 *P. Mich. inv.* 263, tr. Special Collections, the University of Michigan Library. See Potter, D. S., *The Roman Empire at Bay, AD 180–395*, London and New York: Routledge, 2004, pp. 241 ff.

compiled by Jacobus de Voragine in 1275, has it that St Agatha was tortured and had her breasts cut off (a defining feature of her later iconography – she is also the patron saint of breast cancer sufferers) and says that she 'gave up the ghost, and rendered her soul, the year of our Lord two hundred and fifty-three in the time of Decius, the Emperor of Rome'. St Fabian, the Pope from 236 to 250, was another victim, and the Roman martyrology also puts the death of St Christopher ('Christ-Bearer' in Greek) during Decius' reign, while some important escapees from the persecutions were a group of Christian soldiers known as the Seven Sleepers of Ephesus (their names vary between the Eastern and Western traditions), who hid in a cave where they fell into a miraculous slumber, only awakening during the very Christian reign of Theodosius II.[11] Nevertheless, it seems that the Christians remained extremely resilient, and Decius terminated the persecutions after just over a year.

Decius' less spiritual problems centred on a plague that was sweeping across the Empire, the Goths who were flooding into it, and the plebs at Rome who were making an abortive attempt to replace him with a Senator called Julius Valens Licinianus. No rival could possibly hope to take the throne unless backed by an army, which Licinianus didn't have, but Decius found that even possession of the army itself was no guarantee of safety. In 250 the Goths under King Cniva crossed into Moesia Inferior, overran Macedonia and Thrace, including Philippopolis (Modern Plovdiv in Bulgaria), and in the following July they inflicted a disastrous defeat on the Roman army at the Battle of Abritus (or Abrittus, and also known as the Battle of Forum Terebronii/Trebonii, close to Razgrad in modern Romania). The fourth-century Christian apologist Lactantius vividly described the death of the persecutor:

He was suddenly surrounded by the barbarians, and slain, together with great part of his army; nor could he be honoured

---

11   See below, p. 397.

with the rites of sepulture, but, stripped and naked, he lay to be devoured by wild beasts and birds, a fit end for the enemy of God.[12]

Decius had ruled for about the average length of time for this era. It seems that before he died Decius had selected the ex-Consul P. Licinius Valerianus, the future Emperor Valerian, to oversee the Empire's administration, but it was his loyal, aristocratic legate of Moesia, C. Vibius Trebonianus Gallus, who was proclaimed as his successor. Gallus concluded a treaty with the Goths and adopted Decius' younger surviving son Hostilianus (his other son Herennius died in or just before the battle of Abritus) as his co-ruler with the title Augustus, only for him to die of the plague soon afterwards. Gallus' own son Volusianus partnered him for the rest of his reign, and again the Christians became scapegoats for many of the Empire's difficulties. There was certainly much to be concerned about, since in 253 some Franks ('Fierce People') and Alemanni managed to cross the Rhine and pillage Gaul and Spain before they went home, while the Goths refocused their attacks on Greece and Asia Minor. To make things even worse, M. Aemilius Aemilianus was proclaimed Emperor by his troops. He was a Moorish ex-Consul who had been successfully beating off the Goths as commander of the 'Pannonian units' or the 'army in Moesia',[13] but in the summer of 253 he invaded Italy. Gallus ordered Valerian, who had command of the armies of the Upper Rhine, to come to his help, but his own soldiers murdered him before Valerian showed up.

Valerian's forces decided that they now wanted their commander to be Emperor, but even before the armies could engage, Aemilianus found himself assassinated by his own troops near Spoletium (modern Spoleto):

---

12 Lactantius, *On the Deaths of the Persecutors* 4.3, tr. Fletcher, A., in Roberts, A and Donaldson, J. (eds.), *The Ante-Nicene Fathers, Vol. VII, Fathers of the Third and Fourth Centuries: Lactantius, Venantius, Asterius, Victorinus, Dionysius, Apostolic Teaching and Constitutions, Homily, and Liturgies*, Edinburgh: T & T Clark, 1886.
13 Zosimus, *New History* 1.28; Zonaras 12.21.

Aemilius came from an extremely insignificant family, his reign was even more insignificant, and he was slain in the third month.[14]

If becoming Roman Emperor was now effectively a death sentence, Valerian's stay on death row lasted from 253 to 260.[15] His background made him acceptable to the Senate, who also ratified the installation of Valerian's forty-year-old son, P. Licinius Egnatius Gallienus, as Augustus, rather than merely Caesar. The two men effectively divided the Empire between them, Valerian overseeing the Eastern half and placing Gallienus in charge of Rome and the West.

Gallienus' assignment was to drive back assaults from the Goths who were constantly attacking Greece and Asia, the Franks and Alemanni who were pillaging Gaul again, the Saxons who were raiding the North Sea coastline, and see off a revolt by the Berber tribes of North Africa. There was also the small matter of Ingenuus, the governor of Pannonia Inferior, who had himself proclaimed Emperor. The Alemanni took the *Agri Decumates,* but otherwise Gallienus met these challenges very successfully, and he cemented the stability of the Danube area by making an alliance with King Attalus of the Marcomanni and taking his daughter Pipa as his concubine, despite being married to Cornelia Salonina.

Gallienus and his father didn't sing from the same hymn sheet when it came to the Christians. Valerian reinstated Decius' persecutions, which resulted in the martyrdom of Bishop Cyprian of Carthage, who had controversially evaded Decius' persecution by going into hiding, but now changed tack and practised what he preached in his *De Exhortatione Martyrii* by refusing to sacrifice to the pagan deities. He was beheaded on 14 September 258. However, Eusebius says that Gallienus

---

14   Eutropius, *Breviarium* 9.6, tr. Bird, H. W., op. cit
15   See, e.g., Meijer, F., *Emperors Don't Die in Bed*, London and New York: Routledge, 2004.

reversed Valerian's policies and allowed the Christians freedom of worship.

In the East, Valerian was confronted by even greater problems. These are illustrated by the *Res Gestae Divi Saporis*, a trilingual inscription from the walls of the Cube of Zoroaster (Ka'ba-ye Zartosht) at Naqsh-e Rustam in Iran. It tells, in his own words, how King Shapur I of Persia raided the province of Syria:

> We attacked the Roman Empire and we destroyed an army of 60 000 men at Barbalissus. Syria and its surrounding areas we burned, devastated and plundered. In this one campaign we captured of the Roman Empire 37 cities.[16]

One of these was Antioch. When Valerian tried to rescue the city of Edessa, which was besieged by the Persian army:

> [Valerian] had with him [troops from] Germania, Raetia [plus the names of some 29 Roman provinces], a force of 70 000 men. Beyond Carrhae and Edessa there was a great battle between the Emperor Valerian and us. We made the Emperor Valerian prisoner with our own hands; and the commanders of that army, the *Praefectus Praetorio*, Senators and officers, we made them all prisoner, and we transported them to Persia. We burned, devastated and plundered Cilicia and Cappadocia [the names of 36 cities follow].[17]

Gallienus probably heard about his father's capture in 260, but rather than asking for his return, he claimed the whole Empire as his own, even though the invasions and usurpations he faced were escalating at an alarming rate. Roman tradition speaks of pretenders dubbed the 'Thirty Tyrants' who sought

---

16   *The Inscription Of Shapur I At Naqsh-E Rustam In Fars*, 4–5., tr. Maricq, A., 'Res Gestae Divi Saporis', *Syria* 35, 1958, pp. 295–360.
17   Ibid, 9 ff., tr. Maricq, A., op. cit., pp. 295–360.

power around this time (even though the *Historia Augusta* actually lists thirty-two, thirty of them from Gallienus' reign, of whom only nine are authentic). Gallienus' son, Valerian the Younger, was assassinated, while on the periphery of the Empire the Roxolani and Sarmatians attacked Pannonia, and an incursion by the Alemanni was only checked after it had reached northern Italy.

And it got worse. Later Christian writers could not conceal their *Schadenfreude* at the fate of their oppressor, which they saw as a lesson for future 'adversaries of Heaven':

> [Valerian] wasted the remainder of his days in the vilest condition of slavery: for Shapur, the king of the Persians, who had made him prisoner, whenever he chose to get into his carriage or to mount on horseback, commanded the Roman to stoop and present his back [. . .] Afterward, when he had finished this shameful life under so great dishonour, he was flayed, and his skin, stripped from the flesh, was dyed with vermilion, and placed in the temple of the gods of the barbarians [. . .] as an admonition to the Romans.[18]

Shapur I commemorated his victories over Rome on various rock-reliefs: one at Bišâpur in Eastern Iran shows Gordian III prostrate and Shapur I holding Valerian by the wrist; another at Naqsh-e Rustam depicts Philip the Arab kneeling and Valerian standing; and the largest, also at Bišâpur, shows Shapur I with all three of the aforementioned Emperors, although Valerian is shown unfettered and in full Imperial regalia, and shows no sign of maltreatment.

Things were undoubtedly looking really grim for Rome. Hindsight suggests that this could have been the moment when Rome's Empire imploded, but Gallienus clearly had other intentions. The *Historia Augusta* is not kind about him:

---

18   Lactantius, *On the Deaths of the Persecutors* 5.2 ff., tr. Fletcher, W., op. cit.

Gallienus, continuing in luxury and debauchery, gave himself up to amusements and revelling and administered the commonwealth like boys who play at holding power.[19]

This is unfair: he was a cultured and philhellenic individual, and his reign witnessed an end to the persecution of the Christians alongside some vibrant intellectual and artistic achievements, notably the activities of the Neo-Platonist philosopher Plotinus. Gallienus also spent more time personally leading campaigns than he did at Rome, and he scored some significant victories.

These successes doubtless owed something to his reorganization of the army. This involved establishing a highly mobile independent cavalry force with its headquarters at Mediolanum (modern Milan), which was equidistant from the Rhine and the Danube, whose first leader was probably one Aureolus. This strategic rethink was as much to do with internal factors as external ones: providing logistical support to the armies became more efficient; potentially dangerous groups of soldiers came under more direct imperial control; banditry and brigandage could be more easily pre-empted; and mobile reserves could also confront any barbarian incursions on Roman territory from beyond Rhine and Danube frontiers. Gallienus also excluded practically all Senators from military posts, thereby clearing the way for the Equites to receive the majority of commands and provincial governorships. In terms of finance, he was aware that the needs of the army trumped everyone else's, and, recognizing the need for more money, he embarked on a policy of quantitative easing by minting more coins and debasing the currency, which inevitably led to inflation.

Another set of problems for Gallienus was the formation of the 'Gallic Empire' under the governor of Germania Inferior, M. Cassianius Latinius Postumus, and events in Odenathus' Palmyrene kingdom. Postumus declared his *Imperium*

19　*Historia Augusta, The Two Gallieni* 4.3, tr. Magic, D., op. cit.

Galliarum (Gallic Empire) in 260. This comprised the three Gauls plus the two Germanies, and by 261 Britain and Spain were with him too. Postumus had no desire to be Emperor of Rome, though, and his breakaway was really an attempt to secure a level of local security that Gallienus couldn't guarantee. Happy to be Emperor of his new realm, he established his own Senate, Consuls and coinage, and located the capital at Colonia Agrippina. Postumus lasted until he was murdered by his own troops in the summer of 269, but his breakaway empire would keep going until Aurelian brought it back into the fold in 274.[20]

In the East, Odenathus (also spelled Odenaethus or Odenatus or Odainath), the ruler of the great Syrian oasis caravan city of Palmyra, had been exploiting the weaknesses of Rome and Persia to make himself a major player in the region. Gallienus awarded him the title of *dux* and *corrector totius Orientis* ('General and Regulator of the Whole East') for his services against Shapur I and a usurper called Quietus. Odenathus led successful incursions into Persian territory, and was careful to acknowledge Rome's supremacy, but he was murdered in suspicious circumstances in 267. His widow, Zenobia (*Bath Zabbai* in Aramaic), took control in the name of their young son, Vaballathus. She was one of the great female figures of antiquity:

> Her face was dusky and of a swarthy colour, her eyes were black and unusually powerful, her spirit was divine, and she was unbelievably attractive.[21]

Morally unimpeachable, cultured, fond of hunting and drinking, and falsely claiming descent from Cleopatra VII, she had big ideas for the Palmyrene state, but for the moment, provided that she kept the East secure, Gallienus was prepared to tolerate her regime.

---

20   See p. 283.
21   *Historia Augusta, The Thirty Tyrants* 30.15, tr. Kershaw, S.

Internal threats were probably more to the forefront of Gallienus' mind than exotic queens anyway. Aureolus, the commander of the cavalry force at Mediolanum, proclaimed himself Emperor while Gallienus was fighting off a massive invasion by Goths and a Germanic people called the Heruli in 268. They had sacked Athens, but although the official Emperor Gallienus defeated them in a significant engagement at Naïssus (modern Niš in Serbia), he had to turn back in order to defeat Aureolus and then besiege him at Mediolanum. And there Gallienus fell victim to a conspiracy, assassinated by the commander of the Dalmatian cavalry. Aureolus declared himself Augustus, but ultimately gave himself up to M. Aurelius Claudius (later Claudius II Gothicus), who had maintained the siege. Aureolus was executed; Gallienus was pilloried by later historians; and Rome acquired the first of its so-called Illyrian emperors.

The Fightback Begins: 268–275

Gallienus had been acutely aware of just how precarious the Roman Empire's situation was, but had not been given the time to get to grips with it: at this stage in its history, with the constant menace of foreign invaders, the deep internal divisions, the lack of any principle of succession other than violence, and the army's all-too-powerful role in politics, the Empire was still at risk of disintegrating. Yet in fact it still had a minimum of 200 years to go, and one of the reasons that it survived the immediate crisis was the responses of a series of very competent, highly energetic and extremely aggressive soldier-emperors.

The first of these was Claudius II Gothicus, born in Illyria, who reigned from 268 to 270. The ancient tradition about him is one of unadulterated hero-worship. The *Historia Augusta* describes him as a man of gravitas, purity and abstemiousness who was so strong that he could knock a horse's teeth out with his bare fists, and concludes:

Both the Senate and people adored him so much both before, during and after his rule that it is universally agreed that neither Trajan, nor the Antonines, nor any other Emperor was so loved.[22]

On the credit side he smashed an invasion by the Alemanni near Lake Benacus (Garda) in 268 and liberated Illyria from the Goths in an engagement near to Naïssus, after which he took the nickname 'Gothicus Maximus'. On the negative side the Goths won a victory in Thrace in 270, and Claudius failed to exploit a change of ruler in the Gallic Empire, despite the fact that Spain returned to its allegiance to Rome. He was also powerless to stop Zenobia moving into Asia Minor and Egypt, where she defeated the Roman garrison and threatened Rome's grain supply. Fortunately for Claudius II, the Goths were smitten by plague; but unfortunately he contracted it as well and died at Sirmium in August 270. A tale grew up that his death was actually a voluntary scapegoat sacrifice on behalf of the Empire, prompted by a consultation of the Sibylline Books.

Claudius II Gothicus was deified and his brother Quintillus became Emperor, maybe for as little as seventeen days.[23] The SPQR liked him, and a milestone in Mauretania proclaims his official titles as 'Imperator Caesar Marcus Aurelius Claudius Quintilus [*sic*], Unconquered, Pious, Happy, Augustus, *Pontifex Maximus*, [Holder of] Tribunician Power, Father of his Country',[24] but the Danube legions had other ideas and threw their weight behind the cavalry commander L. Domitius Aurelianus ('Aurelian'). As Aurelian bore down on Italy, Quintillus committed suicide by opening his veins.[25]

---

22 *Historia Augusta, Claudius* 18.4, tr. Kershaw, S.
23 E.g. *Historia Augusta, Claudius* 12.5; Eutropius 9.12; Zonaras 12.26. Other sources give seventy-seven days or 'a few months (or days)', and there was at least time for most mints to strike coins.
24 *ILS* 573.
25 *Historia Augusta, Aurelian* 37.5–6; Zonaras 12.26. John of Antioch, *fr.* 154 *FHG* IV, p. 599, says that Quintillus had a physician open his veins. At *Historia*

Having been recognized as Emperor in around September 270, Aurelian's first job was to deal with a series of barbarian invasions, principally by some new Germanic intruders, the Vandali ('Vandals'), who were beaten back after they had entered the Danube valley in concert with the Sarmatians, and the Alemanni and Iuthungi, who got as far as Placentia (modern Piacenza) before being repulsed in 271. He then went to Rome, saw off his political opponents, and was hailed as Germanicus Maximus. The image that he presented of himself was of a no-nonsense, bullet-headed soldier with a crew cut and designer stubble.

Aurelian left his mark on Rome by constructing the Aurelian Wall, which is still an impressive feature of Rome's cityscape. The capital was enclosed by a wall of brick-faced concrete 4 metres thick, 6.5 metres high and 18.8 kilometres long. There were 381 projecting towers placed at intervals of 100 Roman feet (29.6 metres) except along the Tiber, and eighteen major stone gates, flanked by semicircular towers, plus at least half a dozen postern gates. It is symptomatic of Rome's nervousness and shows signs of being built in haste, but because the goal of the potential invaders was not really total conquest it was designed to repel marauders rather than to withstand a siege. It was finally completed in the reign of Probus (276–282).

There were still enemies within – we hear of usurpers named Domitianus, Septimius and Urbanus – although these were quickly dealt with, and Queen Zenobia was becoming a serious menace in the East. On his way to sort her out, Aurelian smashed a Gothic force, but also came to the decision that the occupation of Dacia was more trouble than it was worth. So he ordered an orderly evacuation, before pressing on towards Palmyra.

By 272 Aurelian was in Syria with a force that included some new units raised specifically for or during this campaign, such as *Legio* I *Illyricorum*. Zenobia's main military threat was her *clibanarii* (heavily armoured horsemen who get their name from

---

Augusta, Aurelian 16.1 we get contradictory information, namely that Quintillus was murdered.

the word for an iron bread oven), but when the two sides engaged at Immae near Antioch, the lighter Roman cavalry lured them into a chase before rounding on them when they had exhausted themselves and their steeds in the viciously hot sun. Zenobia evacuated Antioch, but pretended that she had won, and even claimed that Aurelian had been captured. So the populace was quite surprised when he turned up in person shortly afterwards. He then captured the fort at Daphne by adept use of the *testudo* formation, consolidated his position, and received reinforcements who included some Palestinians who fought with clubs.

Zenobia's forces regrouped at Emesa, where Aurelian accepted the offer of battle. In the end, the issue was largely decided by his Palestinian clubmen, and Zenobia's forces ended up besieged in Palmyra. When the queen, now calling herself Augusta, then left the city on a fast camel she was intercepted and captured by Aurelian's men at the Euphrates. There are two accounts of what happened to her: a mundane one in which she perished en route to captivity in Rome, and a much sexier one in which she was paraded in Aurelian's triumph:

> She was decked out with gems that were so enormous that she struggled under the burden of her ornaments [. . .] Furthermore, her feet were bound with gold, her hands with golden chains, and not even her neck was without a chain of gold, the weight of which was supported by a Persian jester.[26]

While Zenobia was subsequently accommodated close to Hadrian's villa at Tivoli, her subjects rebelled again. They clothed Septimius Antiochus, who may or may not have been a son of Zenobia, in purple, but Aurelian responded instantly, and Palmyra was so savagely sacked and looted that it never really recovered. A revolt in Egypt by partisans of Zenobia was

---

26   *Historia Augusta, Thirty Tyrants* 30.24 ff., tr. Kershaw, S. Cf. *Historia Augusta, Aurelian* 34.3.

given similarly short shrift, and Aurelian took the title *Restitutor Orientis* (Restorer of the East).

Aurelian now had the opportunity to bring the breakaway Gallic Empire back under Roman control. C. Pius Esuvius Tetricus (Tetricus I) was on the throne, having been put there through the influence and bribery of Victoria, the mother of his precursor Victorinus. The rival commanders converged in February or March 274 near Châlons-sur-Marne. It was an odd battle: Tetricus I and his son Tetricus II surrendered, but their soldiers didn't, which caused severe casualties on both sides. Some sources say that Tetricus I had made a deal with Aurelian to betray his army, making a nice quotation from Virgil in the process:

Redeem me from this doom, unconquered one![27]

Aurelian did indeed spare Tetricus I and his son, although they were displayed along with Zenobia in his triumph.

Aurelian now sought to upgrade himself to *Restitutor Orbis* ('Restorer of the World'), but his efforts didn't meet with universal approval, as when he tried to improve economic confidence and curb inflation by reforming the silver coinage, only to provoke violent rioting by workers in the mints of Rome. He also sought to foster religious unity in a way that had echoes of Elagabalus, albeit in a more restrained manner. This centred around the cult of Sol Invictus (the Unconquered Sun), who was now officially recognized as the chief deity of the Roman state and received a magnificent temple on the Campus Agrippae. Further, Aurelian was the first Roman Emperor to assume the official title of *Deus* (God) in his lifetime: inscriptions refer to *Deus Aurelianus* (the god Aurelian), and coins struck to commemorate the re-unification of the Empire carry the legend *DEO ET DOMINO NATO AURE-LIANO AVG* on one side and *RESTITUT ORBIS* on the other. In other words, Aurelian is not just restorer of the world but *born*

---

27 Virgil, *Aenid* 6.365, where the words are spoken by the ghost of Palinurus to Aeneas. Tr. Day Lewis, C., op. cit.

(*nato*) god (*deo*) and master (*domino*). He was turning the 'Principate' into the 'Dominate'.

Rome's living god was not immortal, though, and in 275 he was heading for Persia when he was killed in a plot instigated by his private secretary Eros that was carried through by the Praetorians. It may be that the conspirators feared that their lives were in danger, but the main consequence of their action was to put Rome itself into danger.

Into Danger Once Again: 275–285

Aurelian was quite a hard act to follow, and in any case he had no appointed successor. So the army asked the Senate to choose. They selected one of their own, the seventy-five-year-old M. Claudius Tacitus (no relation to the historian) who was in Campania at the time. It looks like he had to cope with threats from the Franks and the Alemanni in the north, and a major incursion by the Heruli from the region of the Sea of Azov, who overran Pontus, Galatia, Cappadocia and Cilicia before Tacitus and his half-brother M. Annius Florianus routed them in the spring of 276. Tacitus gloried briefly in the title of *Gothicus Maximus* before he was slain at Tyana or Tarsus on his way back to Europe by disgruntled Syrian nobles.

Next up was Florianus:

Florianus, who had succeeded Tacitus, was in power for two months and twenty days and did nothing worth remembering.[28]

The reason for this was that M. Aurelius Probus had been put forward by the rival armies of Syria, Phoenicia and Egypt. Florianus' soldiers, who were unaccustomed to the Eastern climatic conditions, became demoralized, instigated a coup, imprisoned him, and either killed him or strongly hinted that he

---

28   Eutropius, *Breviarium* 9.16, tr. Bird, H. W., op. cit.

should kill himself, once it was clear that Probus would be the new ruler.

Probus in Latin means 'excellent in a moral sense', and this is how the tradition presents him to us: 'equal to, or better than, any [of Rome's great leaders], if mad envy does not disagree'.[29] He was also an adept warrior-Emperor out of the same mould as Aurelian, and he would need all of these skills, as the punning (and possibly fictitious) epitaph erected by his soldiers indicates:

> Here lies the Emperor Probus, and indeed a man of probity, the victor over all barbarian tribes and also the victor over pretenders.[30]

The phrase 'all barbarian tribes' conjures up a rather misleading image of hundreds of thousands of them overwhelming Rome's borders, but although they were very frightening and often destructive, their actual numbers were probably relatively small. The barbarians now needing Probus' attention were the Franks and the Alemanni, who were devastating Gaul and the Rhineland, the Burgundiones (a Germanic people) and the Vandals, who were terrorizing Raetia, and the Goths, who needed to be expelled from the Danubian provinces. Probus rose manfully to the task and by 279 he could focus on Asia Minor, where a brigand called Lydius the Isaurian was pillaging Pamphylia and Lycia. Lydius was shot by a turncoat artillery expert, after which the final item on Probus' agenda was a rebellion in Upper Egypt by the Blemmyae. By the end of 279 he seemed to have a secure grasp of both the Eastern and the Western provinces.

One interesting decision that Probus took was to allow large numbers of Bastarnae from Scythia (roughly modern Moldova), Goths, Vandals, Alemanni and Franks to settle in Gaul and in

---

29 *Historia Augusta, Probus* 22.1, tr. Kershaw, S.
30 Ibid. 21.4.

the Danubian provinces, perhaps to rectify depopulation caused by warfare and plague. For their part, the barbarians probably felt that they would be better off inside the Roman frontiers: essentially they were looking for lands to farm, not to destroy Rome, and many of them served as recruits in the Roman army. Probus' policy would cause difficulties later on, but for now he seemed pleased enough with himself to assume the title 'Persicus Maximus', although precisely why is not specified. The pleasure of the barbarians at being allowed to settle within the Empire is perhaps reflected in the name that some of them were given: *laeti*, 'the Happy Ones' in Latin (although the term may also be a Germanic one denoting serfs).

Securing the Empire was no guarantee of internal peace, though. The pretenders that Probus' epitaph speaks of appeared in the persons of Proculus and Bonosus, who proclaimed themselves joint Emperors at Colonia Agrippina. Proculus hoped to bring the Franks onside, but instead they turned him in to Probus, while Bonosus hanged himself when his military situation became desperate. Another rebellion by 'some other fellow in Britain'[31] was swiftly quashed, but a more dangerous challenge came in the East, where the Moorish-born Iulius Saturninus, a one-time friend of Probus, started calling himself Imperator Caesar Iulius Saturninus Augustus. However, Probus was spared the need to take action when Saturninus was killed by his own soldiers.

Probus could now relax in true Roman style, and towards the end of 281 he celebrated a triumph: the Circus Maximus was turned into a temporary forest for a beast hunt where the people were allowed to take thousands of ostriches, stags, wild boars and other animals; 100 lions, 100 lionesses, 200 leopards and 300 bears made a spectacle 'bigger than it was enjoyable'[32] in the Colosseum; and many captive Blemmyae, Germans, Sarmatians and Isurian brigands were made to fight as gladiators

---

31   Zonaras 12.29, cf. *Historia Augusta, Probus* 18.5.
32   *Historia Augusta, Probus* 19.7, tr. Kershaw, S.

after being displayed in the triumph. However, by focusing on more peaceable measures, Probus would cause his own demise. As he turned to economic restoration he deployed his soldiers in drainage projects on the Nile and the Danube, constructing temples and bridges in Egypt, finishing off Rome's Aurelian Walls and planting new vineyards in Gaul and the Danube area. But his peacetime boast that Rome would soon have no need of armies was not a message the soldiers wanted to hear.

Nevertheless, the following spring Probus was on the warpath again, intending to campaign against the Persians. He had reached the vicinity of his birthplace, Sirmium, when M. Aurelius Carus, the *Praefectus Praetorio*, proclaimed himself Emperor with the backing (or insistence) of the armies of Raetia and Noricum. Probus dispatched some men to suppress the uprising, but they simply joined up with Carus, and when news of this prompted further defections, Probus' days were numbered. The *Historia Augusta* relates that the soldiers rebelled as a result of being made to work on civilian projects, and that they killed Probus as he took refuge in an iron-clad watchtower, after which they built him a 'massive tomb on a high mound' adorned with the epitaph quoted above.[33]

Carus now set a new precedent: he was Rome's first Emperor not to seek the Senate's endorsement for his accession. The *Historia Augusta* describes him as 'a mediocre man',[34] but he had a good deal of military experience, and clearly harboured dynastic aspirations, giving the status of Caesar to his two sons, M. Aurelius Carinus and M. Aurelius Numerianus. Having subsequently promoted Carinus to Augustus, Carus detailed him to oversee the Western provinces and set off with Numerianus to complete his predecessor's unfinished business with Persia. This can only have been a vanity project, since Persia under Vahram II was by now a shadow of what it had been under Shapur I. Having successfully engaged with Sarmatians

---

33 Ibid. 21.3.
34 *Historia Augusta, Carus, Carinus and Numerian* 3.8.

and Quadi on the Danube as they marched east, the Roman battle group advanced through Mesopotamia and took Ctesiphon, and Carus assumed the title Persicus Maximus. But there, in July or August 283, both the vanity and the expedition stopped. Most of the ancient sources say that Carus was hit by a thunderbolt, although disease and assassination cannot be ruled out (or definitively ruled in).

Numerianus was a good orator and a decent poet, but whether he would have made a successful Emperor is hard to tell. He was swiftly made co-Augustus with Carus, but as he was overseeing an orderly withdrawal of the Roman troops from Persia it was said that he contracted a serious eye infection, which meant that he had to travel in a closed litter. No one thought any more about this until a hideous stench started to emanate from the litter and his rotting corpse was discovered. Whatever the cause of his death, and of the concealment of his body, suspicion fell onto his father-in-law, the *Praefectus Praetorio* Aper. On 20 November 284 a military assembly was convened at which the troops acclaimed the Dalmatian-born commander of the *domestici* (Imperial Guard), C. Aurelius Valerius Diocles, as Augustus. Diocles publicly eliminated his immediate opposition in a highly dramatic (and possibly very carefully choreographed) way:

> When someone asked how Numerian had been slain, he drew his sword and pointing to Aper, the *Praefectus Praetorio*, he drove it through him, saying as he did so, 'It is he who contrived Numerian's death.'[35]

There is also a tale that Diocles followed this up with a well-chosen quotation from Virgil:

> Well might you boast, Aper, 'You die by the right hand of great Aeneas.'[36]

---

35   *Historia Augusta, Carus, Carinus and Numerian* 13.2, tr. Magie, D., op. cit.
36   Virgil, *Aeneid* 10.830, tr. Kershaw, S., where the words are spoken by Aeneas

Diocles now took the name Diocletianus ('Diocletian'), and if he was channelling Rome's great hero Aeneas, his first job would be to get his followers back to Italy. But Carinus still controlled the Western provinces and was giving various recalcitrant barbarians a good kicking: the Germans on the Rhine, and the Quadi on the Danube succumbed to his military prowess, and he celebrated a triumph in 284. He also campaigned in Britain and took the title Britannicus Maximus, and it was there that he heard news of his brother's death.

Carinus is absolutely slated by the author of the *Historia Augusta*, which might well be an indication of the effectiveness of Diocletian's propaganda:

> When he found out that his father had been killed by lightning, that his brother had been done away with by his own father-in-law and that Diocletian had been hailed as Augustus, Carinus perpetrated even greater acts of vice and wickedness.[37]

We are presented with a staggering catalogue of this: tales of adultery, paedophilia, and the 'evil use of the enjoyment of his own sex'; 'unwonted vices and inordinate depravity'; murder; 'debaucheries and lusts'; arrogance towards the Senate; the marriage and divorce of nine wives, some discarded while they were pregnant; and a palace full of 'actors and harlots, pantomimists, singers and pimps'. He wore jewels on his shoes, hosted ridiculously opulent banquets, swam among apples and melons, and strewed his banqueting-halls and bedrooms with roses. His plunge-baths were always cooled with snow, and having once bathed in a naturally tepid pool he screamed at the bath-attendants, "This is water for a woman that you have given me' (his most famous saying).[38]

If Carinus really was busy doing all this, it seems extraordinary that he found the time to see off a pretender who

---

to Lausus as he kills him.

37 *Historia Augusta, Carus, Carinus and Numerian* 18.1, tr. Kershaw, S.

38 Ibid. 16–17.

dubbed himself Imperator Caesar Marcus Aurelius Sabinus Iulianus Pius Felix Augustus early in 285. However, the real danger was the imminent arrival of Diocletian and his powerful Eastern army. They met halfway at the River Margus (Morava, close to modern Belgrade). It would be winner takes all, including control of the historical tradition, and *damnatio memoriae* for the loser. The 'authorized version' that therefore comes down to us is that Carinus managed to snatch defeat from the jaws of victory. He looked likely to win the battle, but was thwarted at the crucial moment, either by the desertion of his army or as a consequence of his alleged depravity:

> He put to death very many innocent men on false charges, seduced the wives of nobles, and even ruined those of his school fellows who had taunted him at school, even with trivial banter.[39]

One of his commanders was the husband of one of those unfortunate women, and he slew Carinus at his moment of triumph. Carinus' own wife, Magnia Urbica, died at roughly the same time, and her memory, along with those of her husband, Carus and Numerianus, received the inevitable official condemnation. When their inscriptions were erased, Rome symbolically acquired a clean sheet on which to write its future history. A new era had just dawned.

---

39   Eutropius, *Breviarium* 9.19, tr. Bird, H. W., op. cit.

13

The Empire Strikes Back: Diocletian and the Dominate (284–312)

> *[Diocletian] was a very industrious and capable Emperor, and the one who was the first to introduce in the Roman Empire a practice more in keeping with royal usage than with Roman liberty, since he gave orders that he should be revered with prostration, although before him all (Emperors) were simply greeted. He had his clothing and shoes decorated with gems, whereas previously the Emperor's insignia comprised only the purple robe.*
>
> Eutropius *Breviarium* 9.26[1]

Diocletian and Maximianus

As it emerged from its age of anarchy, Rome's 'broken society' craved a strong, energetic government that could deliver stability, confidence, and law and order, mend the material and financial damage of the last fifty years, and fight corruption. In Diocletian it now had the hard case it needed, a 'man with a plan' who would grab it by the balls and drag it into a new era. Diocletian seldom minced his words, and some scholars have felt that his head-on approach to problem-solving came at the price of totalitarianism:

---

1 Tr. Bird, H. W., op. cit. Aurelius Victor writes that Diocletian was intelligent, sensible and experienced, but a bit uncivilized; the *Historia Augusta, Carus, Carinus and Numerian* says he was shrewd, focused, prudent and loyal; the Christian Lactantius calls him a perpetrator of mischief and criminality.

In this view the Empire was oppressive, drab, uniform and regimented, governed by puritanical autocrats and self-seeking officials. Its resemblance to Stalin's USSR or Hitler's Third Reich was not surprising.[2]

One reason for this viewpoint is that Diocletian seems to have finalized the Roman Empire's transformation from the Principate (*Princeps* = 'First Among Equals') to the Dominate (*Dominus* = 'Lord and Master').[3] The Roman Emperor started to resemble the Hellenistic kings who succeeded Alexander the Great or the Great Kings of Persia rather than Augustus, demanding prostration and working a gorgeous, bejewelled Oriental look. As Peter Brown puts it, we 'pass from one dominant lifestyle, and its forms of expression, to another; [. . .] from an age of equipoise to an age of ambition'.[4]

Diocletian realized that to remain at Rome would effectively make him a sitting duck. Threats to his power were more likely to materialize in the frontier regions, and for him not to be there in person to deal with them might prove an open invitation to potential usurpers. So his staff (*comitatus*) and court (*sacrum cubiculum*) became peripatetic, and he only went to Rome once in his entire reign. He also decided that any aspirations he had towards world domination would need both mortal and divine assistance. So in 285 he named his Illyrian brother-in-arms M. Aurelius Valerius Maximianus as Caesar, adopted him as his son, and split up the responsibilities of government: Maximianus was to oversee Italy, Africa, Spain, Gaul and Britain, while Domitian took the Danube and the East. On the divine level,

---

2   Halsall, G., *Barbarian Migrations and the Roman West, 376–568,* Cambridge: Cambridge University Press, reprinted with corrections, 2009, p. 65. Halsall is mainly discussing the influential view of A. H. M. Jones in his important work *The Later Roman Empire. A Social, Administrative and Economic Survey,* Oxford: Basil Blackwell, 1964.

3   Aurelian had already taken steps in this direction (see above, p. 283 f.), but Diocletian's reign represents the culmination of the process.

4   Brown, P., *The Making of Late Antiquity,* Cambridge, MA, and London: Harvard University Press, 1978, p. 34.

Jupiter and Hercules were integrated into the system. In a speech known as the *Second Panegyric for Maximianus*, delivered on 21 April 291, an anonymous orator asked:

> Shall I rehearse the divine origin of your family, which you attest to not only by your immortal deeds but even by your succession to the name?[5]

This is an open reference to the fact that Maximianus had taken the name Herculius and Diocletian that of Iovius – they were assimilating the roles of Jupiter (Jove) and Hercules (also father and son) in ruling the universe. The porticos of Pompey's theatre at Rome were renamed the *porticus Iovia* and the *porticus Herculia* in their honour, and some see a parallel here with the Christian belief in God the Father and God the Son.

Diocletian's role involved touring the Danube and the East: he campaigned in Raetia; installed Tiridates III as King of Armenia; reorganized the Syrian frontier; and fought with the Sarmatians and the Saracens. Maximianus was the junior partner, but he was promoted to Augustus in 286, partly as a reward for crushing some Bagaudae (or Bacaudae: 'the Warriors' in Celtic) in Gaul. Some scholars regard the Bagaudae as bands of insurgent peasant-farmers-cum-dispossessed-outlaws driven to brigandage by Roman oppression, although more recent work suggests that they were characters who took over local leadership without Roman authorization, making them bandits or rebels only in the eyes of the Empire. Over the next few years Maximianus beat off the Alemanni and Burgundiones on the upper Rhine, and got a Frankish chief to make peace in return for being acknowledged as 'King of the Franks'. Saxon and Frankish pirates in the English Channel posed more of a challenge, and M. Aurelius Mausaeus Carausius may have installed

---

5   *Panegyrici Latini* XI [3], 2.3, tr. Mynors, R.A.B., in Nixon, C.E.V. and Rodgers, B. S., *In Praise of Later Roman Emperors: The Panegyrici Latini. Introduction, Translation and Historical Commentary. Transformation of the Classical Heritage vol. 21*, Berkeley: University of California Press, 1994. Cf. VII [6], 8.2; IX [5], 8.1.

the first elements of a new fortification system in Britain stretching from the Wash to the Solent to guard against them. The forts are still known by the title given them in a document produced in 400 (give or take twenty-five years each way) and preserved in medieval manuscripts known as the *Notitia Dignitatum*: the Forts of the Saxon Shore.

However, it was Carausius himself who was more of a menace to Diocletian. He was the admiral of the Channel Fleet based at Gesoriacum (modern Boulogne), but he moved across to Britain, proclaimed himself Augustus, and set up a breakaway *Imperium Britanniarum* rather like Postumus' *Imperium Galliarum*. His coinage, which was of a much higher quality than that of the rest of the Empire, tells a fascinating tale: Carausius, Diocletian and Maximianus (in the place of honour), along with the legend *CARAVSIVS ET FRATRES SVI* ('Carausius and his Brother Emperors'), appear on the obverse, while Victory as *COMES AVGGG* ('the Helper of the 3 Augusti') is on the reverse. He also issued medallions that bore the letters *I.N.P.C.D.A.* This is a coded (but obvious to a Roman) reference to a line in Virgil's 4th *Eclogue*:

Iam nova progenies caelo demittitur alto
Now a new generation is let down from high heaven.[6]

This is reinforced by the words *VICTORIA CARAVSI AVG* ('the Victory of the Emperor Carausius'). It is brilliant PR, and Carausius successfully defied Maximianus until he was assassinated by his right-hand man, Allectus, in 293.

Men United: The Tetrarchy

The year 293 saw a far more significant event, however: the creation of the Tetrarchy ('Rule of Four'). Diocletian remained the main man and made all the key decisions, but now, in

---

6   Virgil, *Eclogues* 4.7, tr. Kershaw, S.

addition to him and Maximianus, the two *Augusti*, there were to be two *Caesares*: C. Flavius Valerius Constantius (aka Constantius I Chlorus) and C. Galerius Valerius Maximianus ('Galerius'). Constantius I Chlorus and Galerius, who were both Illyrians with solid military credentials, were essentially deputies and heirs to Maximianus and Diocletian respectively. The arrangements were cemented by marriage alliances: Constantius I Chlorus was already married to Maximianus' daughter Theodora, while Galerius wed Diocletian's daughter Valeria (see Genealogy Table 5). The plan was that the *Caesares* would ultimately take over as *Augusti*, and nominate *Caesares* in their turn. An excellent sculptural representation of the tetrarchs and what they stood for currently stands in St Mark's cathedral in Venice.[7] Made from Egyptian porphyry, it shows the four men in military dress, embracing one another in a manly way and emanating good old-fashioned Roman virtue:

> They were indeed four rulers of the world: brave, judicious, affable and exceedingly generous, all of one mind toward the commonwealth, showing great restraint before the Roman Senate, moderate, friends of the people, deeply revered, grave and devout.[8]

The religious aspect of the regime was underpinned when Diocletian and Galerius formed the *Iovii* dynasty descended from Jupiter, while Maximianus and Constantius I Chlorus became the *Herculii*, descended from Hercules.

Each tetrarch was allocated his own *comitatus*, *sacrum cubiculum*, troops and sphere of operation:

> The Empire was divided into four parts, and all those regions of Gaul which lie across the Alps [i.e., Gaul and Britain] were

---

7 It was probably first erected in Nicomedia, but found its way to Constantinople, where it came to be called *Philadelphion* ('Brotherly Friendship'). It was looted by Crusaders in 1204, and taken to Venice.

8 *Historia Augusta, Carus, Carinus and Numerian* 18.4, tr. Kershaw, S.

entrusted to Constantius, Africa and Italy [and Spain and the northern frontier provinces] to Herculius [i.e., Maximianus], the coast of Illyricum right across to the Strait of Pontus [i.e., the Danube territories] to Galerius: Valerius [Diocletian] retained the rest [i.e., the East and Egypt].[9]

One crucial consequence of this was that although Rome itself remained important ideologically, the city's position as the hub of the Empire was fundamentally changed. Each tetrarch resided wherever he happened to be ruling or fighting: Nicomedia, Treveri (modern Trier), Mediolanum, Sirmium, Antioch, Serdica (modern Sofia) and Thessalonica, not to mention Naïssus, Carnuntum and Aquileia. Emperors still invested a considerable amount of money on building projects in Rome, but they themselves visited the place ever more infrequently.

In an attempt to generate an administration that was more in tune with the needs of his subjects, and to curtail the power of individual governors, Diocletian embarked on a root-and-branch reform of the Empire's organization (See Map 6). At the local level the basic unit remained the city-district (*Civitas*), but above this some major changes took place. The provinces were reduced in size but increased in number to over one hundred. Lactantius says that this was 'to ensure that terror was universal',[10] but the goal was more probably to give Diocletian tighter fiscal, legal and administrative control. For instance, Africa now had seven provinces, Hispania six and Britain four: *Britannia Prima* in the West, including Wales, with its capital at Corinium (modern Cirencester); *Britannia Secunda* in the north, possibly with Eboracum as the capital; *Maxima Caesariensis* (probably named after Maximianus) in the south, with its centre at Londinium; and *Flavia Caesariensis* (named after Constantius I Chlorus) in the East, where the capital may have

---

9   Aurelius Victor, *de Caesaribus* 39.30, tr. Bird, H. W., *Aurelius Victor, De Caesaribus, Translated with an Introduction and Commentary by H. W. Bird*, Liverpool: Liverpool University Press, 1994.
10   Lactantius, *On the Deaths of the Persecutors* 7.4, tr. Fletcher, W., op. cit.

been Lindum (modern Lincoln). Rome's provinces were all governed by Equestrian *praesides*, apart from Asia and Africa, where Senatorial Proconsuls held sway. Italy was split into multiple units under Senatorial *correctors*. On the whole, these men ran the civil administration but seldom exercised military power. This was crucial: uncoupling the army from the civil service meant that governors didn't control soldiers, and military commanders couldn't control the ration and salaries of their troops, which greatly reduced the odds of a challenge to the Emperor coming out of the provinces.

Above the provinces came twelve districts called *dioceses* (sing. *diocesis*), each ruled by an Equestrian *vicarius* ('vicar') who represented one of the Praetorian Prefects. The *Britanniae*, for instance, made up one of the twelve *dioceses*, with its *vicarius* based at Londinium and responsible to the *Praefectus Praetorio* of Gaul at Treveri. The other *dioceses* were: *Galliae*, *Viennensis*, *Hispania*, *Africa*, *Italia*, *Pannoniae*, *Moesiae*, *Thraciae*, *Asianae*, *Pontica* and *Orientis*. The Praetorian Prefects were effectively the Emperor's second-in-command, with less military power but considerable financial, legislative and administrative responsibility. The city of Rome remained outside this system, governed by its *Praefectus Urbis* (Prefect of the City).

Such a system needed a bureaucracy to make it function properly (even if some modern interpreters feel it was ludicrously top-heavy and a significant factor in the ultimate demise of the Empire). For much of its history Rome had had a minuscule bureaucracy – a few hundred people at the very most – but the *Notitia Dignitatum* shows that after Diocletian's arrangements there were now tens of thousands of officials pushing pens and counting beans: a Tribune of the Swine Market in Rome; an Accountant of Private Property in Britain; the eunuchs of the *sacrum cubiculum* (the 'Emperor's Sacred Bedchamber'); ministries of finance (the *sacrae largitiones* – the 'sacred largesses' – and the *res privatae* – the 'private affairs'); the *quaestor sacri palatii* ('imperial secretary'), backed up by an entire *sacra scrinia* ('imperial secretariat'); the *agentes in rebus* (the imperial couriers between the court and the provinces, and possibly a kind of secret police); and so on. They were powerful people, all with their own staff and plenty of perks, at least if John the Lydian's tirade against John the Cappadocian, the Byzantine Emperor Justinian I's *Praefectus Praetorio*, is sound evidence:

> Even as naked pleasure girls were fondling him, other prosti-
> tutes would lead him on his way with rampant kisses, leaving
> him no option but to have sex there and then. Then, when he
> was spent, he would snatch sweet canapés and drinks from
> the outstretched hands of other catamites. So many and so
> sweet and frothy were the drinks, that, when he could no
> longer keep them down, he just vomited, like a mighty river
> that has breached its banks, flooding the whole house.[11]

No wonder a post in the imperial civil service became highly sought after.

The Army, the Economy and the Law

Our written sources also credit Diocletian with, or accuse him of, some of the most far-reaching reforms to the Roman army since Augustus' day. Lactantius speaks of him

> multiplying the armies, as each of the [tetrarchs] strove to
> have a far larger number of troops than any previous Emper-
> ors had had when they were governing the state alone.[12]

Under Diocletian the army's strength was increased to some sixty legions, but archaeological evidence shows that legionary fortresses were now much smaller, so estimating the overall size of the Roman army at this time is an inexact science, although

---

11   John the Lydian, *De Magistratibus Reipublicae Romanae* 3.65, tr. in Moorhead, S. and Stuttard, D., *AD 410: The Year That Shook Rome*, London: British Museum Press, 2010, p. 34.
12   Lactantius, *On the Deaths of the Persecutors* 7.2, tr. Fletcher, W., op. cit.

figures of around 350 000 to 400 000 men are commonly quoted. The old-school legions of around 5 000 high-quality infantrymen now metamorphosed into something more flexible. The legions, auxiliary cavalry *alae* and cohorts of this 'New Model Army' now functioned alongside other units sometimes vaguely designated *numeri* ('numbers') while the cavalry of the field armies were organized into *vexillationes*. Overall the army was now divided into a central mobile field force (*comitatenses*, 'companions') commanded by *magistri militum*, and static frontier garrisons (*ripenses* – riverside troops, referring to the Rhine and Danube – and *limitanei*, 'borderers') commanded by *duces* (Dukes, sing. *dux*). *Limitanei* who became permanently attached to one of *comitatenses* were designated *pseudocomitatenses*. There was a hierarchy descending from the imperial guards (the *scholae* and the *domestici*), down to the elite 'palatine' units (*palatinae*), the 'praesental' field armies (those 'in the presence of' the Emperor), the regional field armies, and the *limitanei*, who got less pay and fewer privileges than the *comitatenses*, but still seem to have operated pretty effectively as a rule.

The basic kit of the Roman infantry came to be trousers and a shortish, long-sleeved tunic, belted at the waist. Belt buckles and the brooches that fastened their cloaks served as the badges of the different ranks. Armour comprised a mass-produced helmet, scale or mail body armour rather like the medieval hauberk but with sleeves and a hood, plus a circular or oval shield sporting the regimental insignia. Offensive weaponry included a sword called a *spatha* (longer than the old *gladius*), various combinations of thrusting- and throwing-spears (the *spiculum* – rather like a *pilum* – *verutum* and *lancea*), and lead-weighted darts called *plumbatae* or *mattiobarbuli*. Archers, slingers and *manuballistae* (cart-mounted catapults) were also deployed. The cavalry arm featured heavily armoured *clibanarii* and *cataphracti*, especially in the East, as well as lighter armed *scutarii*, *promoti*, *stablesiani*, mounted archers and units of Moors and Dalmatians.

All this, especially the trousers and long swords, had a somewhat 'barbarian' flavour to it. The *duces* were often of non-Roman stock, as is shown by names like Fullofaudes, Duke of Britain; the *Notitia Dignitatum* calls the workshops that produced ornamented armour *barbaricaria*; the later imperial army also adopted the *draco*, a sort of windsock in the form of a dragon, which the Dacians on Trajan's Column used as a standard; the units of the field army started to assume somewhat 'barbarous', almost animalistic, titles; and the war cry, the *barritus*, was often, if mistakenly, said to have a barbarian origin.[13]

In addition to the deployments of troops, Diocletian shored up the frontiers by installing fortresses (*castella*) and small forts (*burgi*), reinforcing natural barriers and constructing military roads. Needless to stay, this was very expensive – so much so that it is thought that around 66 per cent of GDP went into maintaining the army – and with this in mind the tetrarchs set out to regularize the tax system. They opted for assessments based on income in kind. The fiscal value of everybody's property was calculated in terms of *iuga* (land units of varying size depending on their productivity) and *capita* ('heads', poll-tax calculations), although the terms are broadly interchangeable. An edict by Aurelius Optatus, the Prefect of Egypt, shows the measures being introduced:

> Accordingly, seeing that in this too they have received the greatest benefaction, the provincials should make it their business in conformity with the divinely issued regulations to pay their taxes with all speed and by no means wait for the compulsion of the collector.[14]

The whole system was backed up by a regular five-yearly census so that the government could budget properly for the future. This may have been economically effective, but like any hardline tax collection measure it was unpopular.

13　See, e.g., Ammianus Marcellinus 26.7.17; Speidel, M. P., *Ancient Germanic Warriors: Warrior Styles from Trajan's Column to Icelandic Sagas*, London and New York: Routledge, 2004, pp. 101 ff.

14　*P. Cairo Isidore* 1, tr. in Lewis, N. and Reinhold, M. (eds), op. cit., p. 419.

Diocletian also tried to confront problems to do with the coinage and inflation by minting well-struck gold coins at a standard rate of sixty coins to the *libra* (pound) of high-quality metal, and similarly good silver ones, some of which were marked XCVI (i.e., ninety-six coins to the *libra* of silver) to signify their worth. In 301 there was a reform in which most coins seem to have had their value increased by 100 per cent, presumably in an attempt to keep pace with inflation, and this was followed two months later by the well-known *Edictum de Maximis Pretiis* ('Maximum Price Edict'), which sought to prevent profiteering on foodstuffs, goods and services. For instance, wheat was not to exceed 100 *denarii* per army *modius*, barley 60 or salt 100; first-quality aged wine was capped at 24 *denarii* per *sextarius*, Pannonian beer at 4 and Egyptian beer at 2; pork was limited to 12 *denarii* per Italian pound, beef to 8, butter and second-quality fish to 16. In terms of wages, a farm labourer or sewer cleaner got no more than 25 *denarii* per day, a carpenter 50, a shipwright working on a seagoing vessel 60, and a wall painter 75. Vets got 6 *denarii* per animal for clipping and preparing hooves, barbers 2 per man, scribes 25 for 100 lines of best writing, teachers of arithmetic 75 per boy per month, teachers of Greek or Latin language and literature 200 per pupil per month, and an advocate 1 000 per case. Transgressions were punishable by death, at least in theory, but the law seems to have been both unpopular and ineffective:

> Diocletian [. . .] tried to fix by law the prices of goods put up for sale. Much blood was then shed over small and cheap items, and in the general alarm nothing would appear for sale; then the rise in prices got much worse until, after many had met their deaths, sheer necessity led to the repeal of the law.[15]

Inflation would soon be a problem once again.

One rather more successful process that occurred in

---

15 Lactantius, *On the Deaths of the Persecutors* 7.6 f., tr. Fletcher, W., op. cit.

Diocletian's reign concerned the codification of Roman law. The laws of Rome were effectively made up from the rulings that the various Emperors had made over the centuries, and in around 292 some sixteen books of these, dating back to the mid-second century, were published by a certain Gregorianus, who was perhaps Domitian's *magister libellorum* (Master of Petitions), in the *Codex Gregorianus*. It was then supplemented by the *Codex Hermogenianus*, published in 295 by another *magister libellorum* called Aurelius Hermogenianus, who was really the first lawyer to try to distil the law down to a small number of key principles from which solutions to issues could be worked out. The term *codex*, which originally means 'a paged book', came to designate a code in the sense of 'a collection of imperial laws'.

Challenges from Within and Without

Diocletian had to face direct challenges to his authority from inside the Empire. In 297 a revolt broke out in Alexandria led by L. Domitius Domitianus and Aurelius Achilleus (if the two men are not in fact one and the same), but Diocletian managed to suppress it after a long siege which he conducted in person. More concerning was the threat coming from Allectus in Britain. Having murdered the 'third Augustus' Carausius in 293,[16] he remained at large until Constantius I Chlorus mounted a seaborne invasion against him in 296. The *Praefectus Praetorio* Asclepiodotus eluded Allectus' fleet in a mist, landed on the south coast and defeated his army near Calleva Atrebatum (modern Silchester), while Constantius' forces sailed up the Thames and entered Londinium as liberators. The Bibliothèque nationale de France has a superb solid gold medallion that was struck at Treveri to commemorate the event. It depicts the conquering hero approaching the gates of the city and being greeted by a kneeling female personification of London (the only pictorial representation of Roman London yet to be found)

16   See above, p. 294.

while a warship full of soldiers sails up the Thames. Constantius is on the obverse along with the key message *REDDITOR LVCIS AETERNAE* ('the Restorer of Eternal Light'); the light of Roman civilization shines over Britain again; the unity of the Empire is restored.

The tetrarchs certainly had to fight their corners, but they did so with some success: Constantius I Chlorus prevailed in fierce strife against the Alemanni; Maximianus triumphed over the Quinquegetani in Africa; and Diocletian and Galerius conquered the Bastarnae, the Iazyges and the Carpi, and then settled large numbers of them on Roman soil. In the East the new Persian king, Narses, resurrected Shapur I's imperialist ambitions and incited uprisings by the Blemmyae in Egypt and the Saracens in the Syrian desert. Diocletian dealt with the Egyptian problem easily enough, but an invasion of Armenia, Osrhoene and part of Syria by Narses was more problematical. Galerius initially suffered a defeat near Carrhae, but then comprehensively destroyed Narses' forces in 298, captured Ctesiphon, reinstalled the pro-Roman (and later Christian) Tiridates III in Armenia, extended Rome's possessions beyond the Tigris, and most importantly secured peace in the region for several decades. In a results-based world, the tetrarchy was doing very nicely.

The Great Persecution

To commemorate his victory over Narses, Galerius commissioned a triple arch, which was integrated into his palace complex at Thessalonica. Its sculptural panels depict Galerius subduing Narses in hand-to-hand combat, and elsewhere winged Victories place wreaths on the heads of the two *Augusti*, who sit enthroned above two figures that may represent heaven and earth, while female captives are brought to them. Their two *Caesares* and various supporting gods complete the image. This is illuminating: maintaining the *pax deorum*, the peace of/with the gods, was one of any Emperor's key jobs. The Romans felt strongly that piety guaranteed the security of the State, and conversely there was zero tolerance for any religious subversiveness that might alienate the gods.

Symptomatic of this mindset is Diocletian's *Edict Against Manichaeism*. Manichaeism had been founded by a Babylonian prophet called Mani in the middle of the third century. The cult offered redemption, and would become an important religion in due course, but for now it was persecuted by both the Persian and the Roman authorities. In around 297 the tetrarchs wrote to the Proconsul of Africa. They were concerned that 'the accursed customs and perverse laws of the Persians' might 'infect men of a more innocent nature, namely the temperate and tranquil Roman people':

> They lure on many others to accept the authority of their erroneous doctrine. But the age-old religion [ought not to] be disparaged by a new one. For it is the height of criminality to re-examine doctrines once and for all settled and fixed by the ancients [. . .] Now, therefore, we order that the founders and heads be subjected to severe punishment: together with their abominable writings they are to be burned in the flames. We instruct that their followers, and particularly the fanatics, shall suffer a capital penalty, and we ordain that their property be confiscated.[17]

It was in a similar context to this that Diocletian unleashed the Great Persecution against the Christians in 303. According to Lactantius, the trigger was a sacrifice at which the *haruspices*, who checked out the entrails of sacrificial victims, could not find any favourable omens and blamed the Christians who were present. Yet for Diocletian to take an anti-Christian stance seemed odd, given that he had no prior form for this and that his wife, Priscia, was Christian (or at least well disposed to Christians), and Lactantius makes Galerius the driving force

---

17 *Comparison of Mosaic and Roman Law* 5.3, tr. in Lewis, N. and Reinhold, M. (eds) , op. cit., p. 549.

behind the events, under the influence of his pagan-fundamentalist mother. To confirm that he was doing the right thing, Diocletian sent a *haruspex* to the oracle of Apollo at Didyma. The question is not recorded, but the answer was explicit: persecute the Christians. An indirect report of the consultation also appears in a letter written by the Emperor Constantine, who was eighteen years old at the time, and must have relied on a rather convoluted oral tradition:

> About that time it is said that Apollo spoke from a deep and gloomy cavern, and through the medium of no human voice, and declared that *the righteous men* [i.e., the Christians] on earth were a bar to his speaking the truth, and accordingly that the oracles from the tripod were fallacious. Hence it was that his priestess, letting her locks flow down and driven by madness was lamenting this evil among men.[18]

Constantine and his informants wrongly thought Apollo's response came from Delphi; there was no oracular cave at Delphi or Didyma; contrary to popular belief the priestess did not go into a frenzy;[19] and no one at Delphi or Didyma ever claimed that the oracular words came directly from the god himself. As with many second-hand reports about oracles, this all looks very circumstantial.

On 23 February 303, at the Roman festival of the Terminalia, the church at Nicomedia was ransacked, and the next day the first *Edict Against the Christians* was published. Its precise wording is not preserved, although it probably sounded rather like the *Edict Against Manichaeism*, and Eusebius gives us the gist:

---

18   Constantine, *ap.* Eusebius, *Life of Constantine* 2.50, tr. Richardson, E. C., in Schaff, P., and Wace, H., *The Nicene and Post-Nicene Fathers of the Christian Church, Second Series, Vol. I, Eusebius Pamphilus: Church History, Life of Constantine, Oration in Praise of Constantine*, Edinburgh: T & T Clark, 1890.
19   See Kershaw, S., op. cit, 2010., pp. 151 ff.

An imperial decree was published everywhere, ordering the churches to be razed to the ground and the Scriptures destroyed by fire, and giving notice that those in places of honour would lose their places, and domestic staff, if they continued to profess Christianity, would be deprived of their liberty. Such was the first edict against us. Soon afterwards other decrees arrived in rapid succession, ordering that the presidents of the churches in every place should all be first committed to prison and then coerced by every possible means into offering sacrifice.[20]

When Diocletian fell seriously ill in 304, Galerius issued another Edict that forced Christians to choose sacrifice or death. After Diocletian retired, the process was continued by Maximinus Daia, Galerius' Caesar, who issued further Edicts in 306 and 309, until Galerius made a deathbed repentance in 311, stopped the persecution and granted Christians legal recognition.[21] Maximinus Daia made one last attempt at a pagan revival in 311–312:

Who is so obtuse as not to see that the benevolent concern of the gods is responsible for the fertility of the earth, for keeping the peace, and defeating unrighteous enemies, for curbing storms at sea, tempests and earthquakes, which have only occurred when the Christians with their ignorant and futile beliefs, have come to afflict almost the whole world with their shameful practices.[22]

Ultimately the Emperor Constantine put a stop to this. Christianity was simply becoming too well-established in both the rural and the urban environments, particularly in the East, and the horrendous violence was also alienating many pagans who did not necessarily harbour the prejudices that their rulers did.

Saints George, Sebastian, Erasmus (Elmo), Vitus and

20   Eusebius, *Church History* 8.2, tr. Williamson, G. A., in Eusebius: *History of the Church*, London: Penguin Classics, 1989.

21   Lactantius *On the Deaths of the Persecutors* 33.11–35.1; 24.9; 8.14.1; Eusebius, *Church History* 8.16.1; 17.1–11; 8.14.1. See below, p. 309.

22   Eusebius, *Church History* 9.7.8–9, tr. Williamson, G. A., op. cit.

Catherine are all associated with Diocletian's persecution, along with perhaps as many as 3 500 other victims. Eusebius escaped, though, and wrote eloquently and emotionally about the events in his *Church History*. In fact, the Edicts were not consistently enforced: in Italy Maximianus was zealous to start with, but soon backed off, while in Gaul Constantius I Chlorus just went in for some desultory church destruction, if that. Nevertheless, the Great Persecution was incredibly distressing, and etched itself very deeply into the Christian psyche.

Power Struggles and the Rise of Constantine

Diocletian had always intended that the *Augusti* should abdicate, and once he and Maximianus had celebrated twenty years of rule, that is what happened. On 1 May 305, they gave up their powers (Maximianus rather unwillingly), to be replaced by their *Caesares* Galerius and Constantius I Chlorus. Since Diocletian had no direct heirs, the question of who would become the new *Caesares* was sensitive. There were dynastic options in the persons of Maximianus' son Maxentius and Constantine, Constantius' illegitimate son by Helena, a Bithynian barmaid (or, in British legendary tradition, an Essex girl). [23] But Diocletian had other ideas. He opted instead for Flavius Valerius Severus, an Illyrian friend of Galerius, as Caesar to Constantius in the West, and C. Galerius Valerius Maximinus Daia, as Caesar to his uncle Galerius in the East. With Constantius controlling Britain, Gaul and Spain, Severus in possession of Africa, Italy and Pannonia, Galerius ruling Asia Minor west of the Taurus Mountains, and Maximinus in charge of the other Asiatic provinces and Egypt, Diocletian retired to his humungous fortified palace at Spalato (modern Split, in Croatia), where he remained, contentedly growing vegetables, until his death.

Our sources make it very difficult to establish a clear political and chronological picture of the events of the next few years,

---

23   See Harbus, A., *Helen of Britain in Medieval Legend*, Cambridge: D.S. Brewer, 2002.

but it is clear that in 306 Constantius I Chlorus returned to Britain to command a major onslaught against the Picts in the north. He secured Galerius' permission to allow his son Constantine to accompany him, but died at Eboracum shortly after his victory. Constantine, who had probably been born around 273 at Naïssus in Moesia Inferior, was immediately proclaimed Augustus. This transgressed the ethos of the tetrarchy. An Augustus was supposed to be replaced by his Caesar (Severus was first in line), but Constantine informed everyone about his 'forced' elevation, moved across into Gaul, cemented his popularity with his troops by defeating the Alemanni and the Franks and throwing their kings to wild beasts in the arena, and waited for the other Augustus Galerius' reaction.

The uncertainty now gave an opportunity for Maximianus' son Maxentius to throw his hat into the ring by exploiting some unrest in Rome, getting himself nominated as *Princeps* (an old-fashionedly vague designation) and bringing his father Maximianus out of retirement. Galerius' response was to make Severus march on Rome, but Maximianus, who was now calling himself Augustus as well, pushed Severus back to Ravenna and captured him. Severus was duly put to death. Maxentius now joined the expanding list of *Augusti* as well.

Needing to bolster himself against the predictable forthcoming backlash from Galerius, Maxentius turned to Constantine. In return for reciprocal acknowledgements of Augustus status, Maxentius gave Constantine his sister Fausta in marriage. Galerius got as far as Interamna but did not have the wherewithal to storm the walls of Rome, so he had to back off. Maxentius must then have been appalled to find that is own father had tried to talk Constantine into attacking both himself and Galerius. Constantine was not prepared to do this, so Maximianus had to do his own dirty work: he went to Rome, but when he ripped Maxentius' purple robe from his shoulders the soldiers intervened. Maximianus sloped off to Constantine; Maxentius maintained control of Rome.

With the tetrarchic system in tatters, Galerius sought a diplomatic solution by asking Diocletian to chair a conference at Carnuntum that was held in November 308. Maximianus also attended, but Maxentius was excluded and outlawed. Diocletian preferred his green fingers to the imperial purple, but he did talk Maximianus into retiring. Licinianus Licinius, an experienced general and comrade of Galerius, succeeded Severus as the junior of the two *Augusti*, and was given Italy, Africa and Spain, despite the fact that Maxentius actually controlled them; Maximinus Daia carried on as Caesar as before; and Constantine was relegated to Caesar of Gaul and Britain. However, the egos of the two *Caesares* were not satisfied by this, and Galerius was forced into making them *Augusti* quite soon afterwards.

So now there were four *Augusti*: Galerius based at Thessalonica; Licinius at Sirmium; Constantine at Treveri, and Maximinus Daia at Antioch. Just to make things interesting there was also Maxentius claiming to be Augustus and the ex-*vicarius* of Africa doing the same under the grandiose title of Imperator Caesar Lucius Domitius Alexander Pius Felix Invictus Augustus. Gradually, though, various contenders fell by the wayside. In 310 a series of intrigues ended with Maximianus dead, and Constantine, if not directly responsible, at least pleased about it. The following year one of Maxentius' Praetorian Prefects dispatched Domitius Alexander, and Galerius died horribly:

> Without warning, suppurative inflammation broke out round the middle of his genitals, then a deep-seated fistular ulcer: these ate their way incurably into his inmost bowels. From them came a teeming indescribable mass of worms, and a sickening smell was given off; for the whole of his hulking body, thanks to overeating, had been transformed even before his illness into a huge lump of flabby fat, which then decomposed and presented those who came near with a revolting and horrifying sight.[24]

---

24 Eusebius, *Church History* 8.16, tr. Williamson, G. A., op. cit.

Galerius attributed this to the wrath of God for persecuting the Christians, repented just before he died, and issued an *Edict of Toleration*. Lactantius wanted to portray Galerius' fellow persecutor Diocletian as meeting a similarly exemplary fate, and says that he starved himself to death in 311 or 312, although Diocletian may in fact have lived longer. Constantine, meanwhile, was looking in a different direction for divine backing, and started to put forward the notion that his father, Constantius I Chlorus, was descended from Claudius II Gothicus, while an anonymous panegyric from 310 talks of him having a vision:

> You saw, Constantine, I believe, your own Apollo, accompanied by Victory, offering you a laurel crown, signifying three decades of rule.[25]

Constantine's coins now start to show Sol Invictus, the sun god, with whom Apollo was identified: he was moving away from his Herculean roots.

Events were moving towards their climax. Constantine came to an accommodation with Licinius, while Maximinus Daia threw in his lot with Maxentius. As Licinius and Maximinus Daia cancelled each other out in the East, Constantine took a huge risk and bore down on Maxentius in Italy, but he offset his numerical disadvantage by acting decisively. Having crossed the Alps, he scored a victory near Augusta Taurinorum (modern Turin) over a force that included some formidable *clibanarii*, received the surrender of Mediolanum, and again defeated Maxentius' forces at Verona. At Rome Maxentius prepared to resist a siege, but for some reason he had a change of heart and decided to settle things in open combat. On 28 October 312 he led his men out over the Tiber across the Pons Milvius (Milvian[26] Bridge) for a battle that would decide the future of Europe.

---

25 *Panegyrici Latini* VII [6].21, tr. Mynors, R. A. B., op. cit. The three decades were symbolized by the figure XXX.
26 Also interchangeably spelled Mulvius/Mulvian.

14

Christianity Ascendant: Constantine and his Successors (312–364)

And while [Constantine was] praying with fervent entreaty, a most marvellous sign appeared to him from heaven, the account of which it might have been hard to believe had it been related by any other person. But since the victorious emperor himself long afterwards declared it to the writer of this history, when he was honoured with his acquaintance and society, and confirmed his statement by an oath, who could hesitate to believe the evidence?
Eusebius, *Life of Constantine* 1.28[1]

Making an assessment of Constantine I the Great is essentially a leap of faith, whichever way one jumps. Many of the sources present pure unadulterated glorification of him, while others are vitriolic in their hatred, and, since Constantine is so crucial to the history of the Church, much modern commentary is determined, overtly or otherwise, by the author's attitude towards Christianity. Even the neutrals can be biased.

'With This be Victorious'

As Maxentius' troops prepared for the final showdown, they might have noticed something weird about their enemies'

---

1 Tr. Richardson, E. C., op. cit.

equipment. Their shields were sporting a symbol that looked like a letter X with a P superimposed on it – the chi-rho symbol of Christianity (the Greek characters *Chi* (X) and *Rho* (P) are the first two letters of 'Christ'). Constantine, the devotee of Sol Invictus, had shifted in his religious allegiances once again:

> Constantine was directed in a dream to mark the heavenly sign of God on the shields of his soldiers and thus to join battle. He did as he was ordered and with the cross-shaped letter X, with its top bent over, he marked Christ on the shields.[2]

That, at least, is how Lactantius, writing a couple of years later, narrates the event. However, Eusebius makes no mention of the shield logo or the dream in his account in his *Church History*, and in his *Life of Constantine*, completed shortly after the Emperor's death, he provides a rather different and more elaborate version than Lactantius', which places the event at an unspecified time before the battle:

> [Constantine] said that at about midday [. . .] he saw with his own eyes, in the sky above the sun, the sign of the cross, along with the words: 'With this, be victorious'.[3]

That night, said Constantine, Christ appeared to him in a dream and told him to make a copy of the celestial sign, and use it as protection against the enemy. Eusebius later saw the result:

> A long gilded spear with a horizontal bar formed the sign of the cross. At the top was a circlet of gold and costly jewels, in the centre of which was the symbol of our Saviour's name [the chi-rho symbol]. From the crossbar of the spear hung a royal banner, richly embroidered and shimmering with

---

2   Lactantius, *On the Deaths of the Persecutors* 44.3–6, tr. Fletcher, W., op. cit.
3   Eusebius, *Life of Constantine* 1.28, tr. in Moorhead, S. and Stuttard, D., op. cit, p. 41.

precious stones, all lavishly stitched with gold thread. It is impossible to describe its beauty – or its effect on those who saw it. The banner was square. On its upper part, beneath the sign of the cross and immediately above the embroidered panel, it bore a half-length portrait [*ikon*] of the devout emperor with his children.[4]

This new standard came to be known as the *Labarum*.

There are clearly discrepancies between the accounts, and the question of exactly what Constantine really saw, if anything, is hard to answer, as is that concerning whether we should regard the vision described by the panegyric writer of 310[5] as the same as this one. Recent speculation suggests that the vision could have been a 'solar halo phenomenon', created when sunlight is refracted through ice crystals in the upper atmosphere and forms 'light pillars' or ring haloes around the sun.[6] But what really mattered from the Roman perspective was that the vision came from the sun, to which Constantine had hitherto been deeply devoted. It is highly likely that, initially at any rate, he saw a very close link between the Christian God and Apollo and Sol Invictus. He certainly continued to put Sol on his coins and monuments for some years after the battle, ordered military units to pray to the sun as the 'one god and bringer of victory', and passed a law in 321 establishing the *dies solis* ('day of the sun', i.e., Sunday) as a day of rest for those working in cities.

The Battle of the Milvian Bridge turned on an attempt by Maxentius to lure Constantine onto a collapsible bridge of boats that he had constructed over the Tiber. The first part of the ploy

---

4   Ibid. 1.31.

5   See above, p 310.

6   See Weiss, P., 'The Vision of Constantine,' *Journal of Roman Archaeology* 16 (2003), 237–59; Drake, H. A., 'Solar Power in Late Antiquity', and Long, J., 'How to Read a Halo: Three (or More) Versions of Constantine's Vision', in Cain, A. and Lenski, N., (eds.), *The Power of Religion in Late Antiquity*, Farnham and Burlington: Ashgate Publishing Ltd., 2009, pp. 215 ff.

was executed perfectly, but as Maxentius conducted his withdrawal across the bridge, it gave way. Sculptures on the Arch of Constantine at Rome show Maxentius' heavily armoured men floundering in the water whilst Constantine's men pick them off from the bank. In the carnage that followed, the Praetorian Guard were wiped out, and when the drowned corpse of Maxentius was recovered from the river its head was lopped off and paraded round the streets of Rome, before being sent to Carthage. The regime change was complete.

Constantine reassured the Senate that he would exercise clemency, and pretty swiftly declared himself Christian, although his conversion still remains shrouded in mystery. He affirmed his faith quite publicly by having a statue of himself set up depicting him holding 'a lofty spear in the figure of a cross', and an inscription that read:

> By this sign of salvation, the true mark of valour, I saved your city and freed it from the yoke of the tyrant.[7]

However, the inscription on the Arch of Constantine, which was dedicated in 315, carefully sidesteps any direct allusion to Christ, and speaks of the 'prompting of Divinity' (*instinctu Divinitatis*).[8] Neither was he baptized straight away, although this was quite normal, since the possibility of committing a mortal sin was greatly reduced if you left it as late as possible. In any case, it would be wrong to imagine Constantine as a particularly saintly man: he was held responsible for the deaths of both his wife Fausta and his son Crispus, and pagan writers attributed his conversion to Christianity to guilt over this. His nephew, the Emperor Julian, wrote a satire in which the pagan gods refused Constantine admission to heaven on the grounds that his military successes were insignificant, and that he was a

---

7   Eusebius, *Life of Constantine* 1.40, tr. in Jones, A. H. M., *Constantine and the Conversion of Europe*, London: Macmillan, 1948, p. 83. Jones rightly raises the issue of whether Eusebius translated the inscription correctly.
8   *CIL* 6 1139.

'chef and a hairdresser', whereupon he was forced to seek refuge with Christ, who was offering forgiveness through baptism to 'whoever is corrupt, stained with blood, abominable and disgusting'. Because Constantine was polluted with his family's blood, he was only too happy to become a Christian.[9]

Modern opinion sometimes attributes Constantine's conversion to cynical self-interest, but this seems unconvincing. Christianity was a minority religion in the Empire as a whole, particularly in the West, the countryside, and among the Senate, and it is notable that once Constantine had made his decision he stuck rigidly to it. He may have felt that monotheism would dovetail nicely with Diocletian's totalitarian ideology of Empire, but that does not necessarily count against his piety: 'sincerity is not determinable by historical method; it is, in any case, not incompatible with a belief that consequential action may have political advantage'.[10] His conversion looks genuine enough: Christ now had his 'thirteenth apostle'.

The Senate now acknowledged Constantine as the senior Augustus, with precedence over Maximinus Daia, who still controlled Asia Minor from his palace at Nicomedia. Constantine then made a deal with Licinius at Mediolanum in February 313, which they cemented with a marriage between Licinius and Constantine's sister Constantia. Then they effectively won over the Eastern Christians, currently being persecuted by Maximinus, by issuing the Edict of Milan, which guaranteed religious tolerance. From that day forth, at least in theory, no Christian could be persecuted for his or her faith.

The Church did well under Constantine: clerics were granted exemption from civic liturgies and from taxation, although rich people were barred from holding clerical office; bishops acquired jurisdiction between Christian litigants; Christian celibacy and virginity were accommodated by

9 Julian, *Caesares* 328d–329d; 335a f.; 336a f.
10 Davis, R. P., *s.v.* 'Constantine I' in Hornblower, S. and Spawforth, A., *The Oxford Classical Dictionary,* 3rd revised edn., Oxford: Oxford University Press, 2003.

revoking the penalties on childless couples that dated back to Augustus' time;[11] the branding of slaves on the face was prohibited, since they were also created in God's image; crucifixion was also banned, although burning at the stake became a common alternative; and there was an energetic programme of church building that ultimately included St Peter's at Rome and the Church of the Holy Sepulchre in the Holy Land, which tradition associated with Constantine's mother, Helena, who was said to have discovered the True Cross during the construction work.

However, rather than showering Constantine with gratitude for all this, the Church started to cause him immense hassle. As the historian Ammianus Marcellinus later said,

> No wild beasts are such dangerous enemies to man as Christians are to one another.[12]

No sooner had the pagans stopped persecuting them, than the Christians started persecuting one another. An early flashpoint came at Carthage in a dispute over whether to allow those who had complied with Diocletian's orders to hand over the scriptures to be priests and bishops. The followers of a man named Donatus, the 'Donatists', adopted a hard line on this: they wanted the 'lapsed' clergymen excluded; the Orthodox were more conciliatory. Essentially, the argument was about who would become the official Church in Africa. A Church Council ruled against the Donatists, but they would not accept the judgement, and Constantine had to intervene. However, when he convened an Ecumenical Council, the Council of Arles of 314, which endorsed the Church Council decision, the Donatists again refused to accept its ruling. This

---

11   *Theodosian Code* 8.16.1 (320 CE). See above, p. 51.
12   Ammianus Marcellinus 22.5, tr. Hamilton, W., *Ammianus Marcellinus: The Later Roman Empire (AD 354–378), Selected and translated by Walter Hamilton with an Introduction and Notes by Andrew Wallace-Hadrill*, London: Penguin Books, 1986.

put Constantine in an impossible position: he couldn't face punishing his fellow Christians himself, so he simply condemned them as 'impious criminals' and passed the buck to God.

Constantine's Christian Empire

Back on the terrestrial plane, Maximinus Daia, the junior Augustus, found himself out on a limb. He relaxed his persecutions and crossed the Hellespont into Licinius' territory, but found himself defeated near Adrianople (Hadrianopolis, sometimes called Hadrianople – modern Edirne in Turkey) in April 313. Having lost hope, he committed suicide at Tarsus in the summer. The Empire was down to two *Augusti*: Licinius and Constantine.

Constantine was definitely the senior, and probably the more ambitious, of the two, and any possibility of lasting harmony diminished when Constantine's wife Fausta gave birth to a son, Constantinus, in the spring of 316 (see Genealogy Table 6). With dynastic ambitions, Constantine attacked Licinius later that year, and defeated him at Cibalae (modern Vinkovci in Croatia. See Map 7) in Pannonia and again at Campus Adriensis near Adrianople, appropriating the dioceses of Pannonia and Moesia in the process. Then, however, they patched up their differences, and on 1 March 317 they were both confirmed as *Augusti* and designated three new *Caesares* from among their respective infant sons: Constantine nominated Crispus (from his first marriage to Minervina) and Constantinus (aka Constantine II, by Fausta), while Licinius' son born to Constantia in 315, also called Licinius, completed the trio. The recently deceased Diocletian had established the tetrarchy to prevent precisely this sort of dynasty-building, and the reality of the situation meant that only one dynasty would prevail. Constantine soon moved ahead in that contest when the fecund Fausta gave birth to two more sons, Constantius II (317) and Constans (320 or 323), plus two daughters, Constantina and Helena.

The boundary between Constantine and Licinius' respective

blocs was established at the frontier of the *diocesis* of Thracia, where it remained until 324. Yet there were fundamental differences between the two *Augusti*, with Constantine favouring the Christians and Licinius resuming perfunctory persecutions, and the final conflict came when Constantine took the offensive, won a victory at Adrianople on 3 July 324, and then besieged Licinius at Byzantium. The city was duly captured, and Licinius abdicated, having been defeated again at Chrysopolis on the Bosporus. He was executed in 325, and his son was eliminated the following year. Constantius II replaced the younger Licinius as Caesar. Constantine was sole Augustus, and had established his dynasty. But in an episode that the anti-Constantine authors interpret as evidence of his innate nastiness, his son Crispus and wife Fausta also perished and incurred *damnatio memoriae*:

> Crispus' stepmother Fausta was madly in love with him but did not easily get him to go along. She then announced to his father that he [Crispus] loved her and had often attempted to do violence to her. Therefore, Crispus was condemned to death by his father, who believed his wife. But when the Emperor later recognized the truth he punished his wife too because of her licentiousness and the death of his son. Fausta was placed in an overheated bath and there found a violent end of her life.[13]

The story has too much in common with the Greek mythical tale of Phaedra, or the biblical story of Potiphar's wife, for it to ring true. An interesting interpretation is that Fausta was pregnant by Crispus (willingly or not) and died in her bath attempting to induce an abortion.[14] So Constantine should perhaps be blamed for inept PR in failing to cover up this sordid domestic mess, but not for murder.

---

13   Zonaras, *Epit.* 13.2.38–41, tr. Pohlsander, H. A., 'Crispus: Brilliant Career and Tragic End', *Historia* 33 (1984), p. 101. Crispus' name is erased on *CIL* 2 4107, 3 7172, 5 8030, 9 6838a, 10.517; both of them are erased on *CIL* 678.
14   Woods, D., 'On the Death of the Empress Fausta', *Greece and Rome* 45.1 (1998), 77.

On the world stage, Constantine proceeded to mark his victory over Licinius in the most extraordinary way by establishing Constantinople (Constantinopolis = 'Constantine City'), the 'New Rome'. The project got under way in 324 on the site of Byzantium, and Constantinople was dedicated on 11 May 330. In an excellent strategic location, it had its own Senate, free food and cheap wine handouts for its populace – a smart move by its rulers, given that 'the common people, desperate for its unrestricted consumption, are often moved to stage violent disturbances'[15] – and was decked out with the finest monuments available: the serpent column from Delphi (which still stands in the Hippodrome); Phidias' chryselephantine statue of Zeus of Olympia, one of the Seven Wonders of the Ancient World, whose bearded image ultimately became the model for the face Jesus in Byzantine art, replacing his hitherto clean-shaven, androgynous Apollo-like image; and (so it was said) the Palladium from Troy, which Aeneas had taken to Italy, but which was now buried under a 50-metre-high porphyry column surmounted by a statue of Constantine in the guise of Apollo. Under its legendary tutelary powers, Constantinople flourished.

On the whole, Constantine was sensible to acknowledge his responsibilities to his pagan subjects. In 325 he told an assembly of bishops:

> You are bishops (*episkopoi*) whose jurisdiction is within the Church: I also am a bishop (*episkopos* = 'supervisor'), ordained by God to overlook whatever is external to the Church.[16]

Some pagan temples were closed, but Constantine seemed happy enough for a new one to be constructed at Hispellum (modern Spello) in Italy and dedicated to the Imperial family. He promulgated a law forbidding sacrifice (the Eucharist had

15 Ammianus Marcellinus 14.6.1, tr. Hamilton, W., op. cit.
16 Eusebius, *Life of Constantine* 4.24, tr. Richardson, E. C., op. cit.

superseded it), and although the law no longer survives, his son Constantius II passed a similar one that refers to it:

> Let superstition cease. Let the madness of sacrifices be exterminated, for if anyone should dare to celebrate sacrifices in violation of the law of our father, the deified Emperor [i.e., Constantine], and of this decree of Our Clemency, let an appropriate punishment and sentence immediately be inflicted on him.[17]

But sacrifice didn't stop, and in any case Constantine had some rather more immediate problem-solving to do within the Christian community.

Now that Christianity was officially the religion of Rome, its hierarchy bickered over issues like Church property, patronage and the date of Easter. Significantly, in 325 the Church engaged in a deeply divisive dispute, known as the Arian Controversy. The problem was a fundamental one concerning the nature of the Trinity: were the Father, the Son and the Holy Ghost of *one and the same* substance (*homoousios* in Greek), or, as the Alexandrian theologian Arius contested, were they of *similar* substance (*homoiousios*)? Was Christ secondary to the Father, and had there been a time when he had not existed? That extra Greek letter 'i' made one massive iota of difference: if God was too dominant, he might look Jewish; if Christ was too human, he would look like a Greek mythological hero; if Christ was 'too divine', he might not seem to have sacrificed very much for mankind; but how could Jesus forgive mankind's sins if he were not completely divine?

Constantine convened the Church's first Ecumenical Council at Nicaea, where he and over 250 bishops from all over the Empire thrashed out the problem. It seems that Constantine favoured the homoousian solution, and this was adopted in the Nicene Creed:

---

17   *Theodosian Code*, 16.10.2, 341 CE, tr. in Cameron, A., *The Later Roman Empire: AD 284–430*, London: Fontana, 1993, p. 74.

We believe in one God the Father Almighty, Maker of all things visible and invisible; and in one Lord Jesus Christ, the only begotten of the Father, that is, of the substance [*ousias*] of the Father, God of God, light of light, true God of true God, begotten not made, of the same substance [*homoousion*] with the Father, through whom all things were made both in heaven and on earth.

All but five bishops concurred, but this lack of unanimity resulted in two recalcitrant bishops being anathematized, and Arius being exiled to Illyria. Yet the 'Arian heresy' refused to go away. Christianity had discovered sectarianism.

Constantine's Secular Empire

On the secular front, Constantine forged ahead with many of the policies that Diocletian had initiated. Military and civil careers became truly independent of one another, and Praetorian Prefects and *vicarii* acquired purely civilian functions. A new corps of guards (the *scholae*) replaced the Praetorians, and elsewhere in the armed forces a much clearer distinction was made between the field army (*comitatenses*) – whose commanders, the *Magister Equitum* (Master of Horse) and the *Magister Peditum* (Master of Infantry), were directly answerable to the Emperor – and the frontier troops (*limitanei*). The number of barbarian soldiers seems to have increased, especially in the higher ranks, and some 40 000 Goths were recruited to defend Constantinople, whose palace guard was made up mainly of Germans.

Constantine's frontier policy was robust, especially on the Rhine and the Danube, where a stone bridge protected by forts on the north bank was constructed at Oescus (near modern Pleven in Bulgaria) in 328, to match the one previously built at Colonia Agrippinensis in 310 to panegyrical approval:

Furthermore by building the bridge at Agrippinensis you defy the remnants of the defeated tribe and compel them never to abandon their fears but to be in constant terror, and to keep outstretched their hands in submission.[18]

However, in concert with these bellicose measures, Constantine stationed more and more troops close to or in cities, leading his pro-Diocletian pagan critics to accuse him of denuding the frontier defences and allowing the barbarians 'unhindered access to the Roman empire'.[19] By taking soldiers from where they were needed, and stationing them where they weren't, it was argued, Constantine allowed discipline to slip and the troops to go soft, and so was personally responsible for the Fall of the Roman Empire.

A government overhaul saw the *Magister Officiorum* (Master of the Offices) take control of the *scrinia* and the *agentes in rebus*; the *Quaestor Sacri Palatii* became the chief legal adviser, and the post was subsequently held by various prominent lawyers; the Counts of Finance (*Comes Sacrarum Largitionum* and *Comes Rei Privatae*) dealt with any income and expenditure not controlled by the Praetorian Prefects; the Praetorian Prefects themselves were increased in number and given jurisdiction over the prefectures of Gaul, Italy, Illyricum and the East, with the *vicarii* of the *dioceses* answering to them. Constantine's *consistorium* (council), which functioned as both a general council and a supreme court, would normally be made up of the highest civil and military officers of the imperial court (the *comitatus*) as permanent members, augmented by *comites* (Counts, sing. *comes*), who served as special commissioners.

The *comites* now became a third tier, just below the Senatorial and Equestrian orders, in Rome's already deeply class-conscious hierarchy. Both Senators and plebs could become a *Comes* at one of three levels: *ordinis primi*, *secundi* and *tertii*. The Equestrian order was divided into its grades of the *egregii*, *perfectissimi* (*vicarii*, *duces*, provincial governors) and

---

18   *Panegyrici Latini* [VI], 13.1–5, tr. Mynors, R.A.B, op. cit.
19   Zosimus, *New History* 2.34.

eminentissimi (Praetorian Prefects). Constantine greatly expanded the Senatorial order by elevating many Equestrians to Senatorial rank, and waiving the obligation to reside in Rome or even attend meetings of the Senate. Under Diocletian the Senatorial order had originally been made up purely of the *clarissimi* ('most shining'), 500 or so members of Rome's elite families, but as time went on 'grade inflation' set in, and extra honorific levels had to be created: the *spectabiles* ('notables'), *illustres* ('the honourable') and *gloriosi* ('the glorious'). Eventually, the rank of *clarissimus* became a meaningless title, and the end result was that the Equestrian order became so devalued that it pretty well disappeared: 'The fourth century witnessed the transformation of the old "orders", still closely linked to birth and wealth, into a service aristocracy, in which rank depended on office.'[20] Within the system there was, of course, plenty of 'corruption', which Constantine could do little about, although those kinds of judgement are often determined by the norms of the society making them: third-century Romans would have been puzzled by many things that the Parliamentary Commissioner for Standards now regards as sleazy.

Diocletian had introduced laws regulating the freedom of movement of *decuriones* (town councillors) and *coloni* (tenant farmers). The *decuriones* were personally liable for the taxes levied from the local population, and frequently tried to evade these responsibilities by taking refuge in the army, bureaucracy or clergy. This was no longer allowed. Constantine also introduced legislation that prevented *coloni* leaving their estates:

> Any person whatsoever in whose possession a *colonus* belonging to another is found not only shall restore said *colonus* to his place of origin but shall also assume the capitation tax on him for the time [that he had him]. As for the *coloni* themselves, it will be proper for such as contemplate flight to be bound with chains to a servile status, so that by virtue of such

---

20   Cameron, A. M., op. cit, p.104.

condemnation to servitude they may be compelled to fulfil the duties that befit free men.[21]

The Empire's tenant farmers were being transformed into hereditary serfs.

Inflation continued to be a problem, although the loot from Licinius' treasury, confiscations from the pagan temples and new taxes that were levied from merchants and craftsmen (the *chrysargyron*, or 'gold-and-silver tax') and from Senators offset this to a degree. Enforcement was rigorous:

> When this tax had to be paid, weeping and wailing were heard throughout the city, because beatings and tortures were in store for those who could not pay owing to extreme poverty. Indeed mothers sold their children and fathers prostituted their daughters under compulsion to pay the exactors of the *chrysargyron*.[22]

This did allow Constantine to issue a new gold coin called the *solidus* (seventy-two to the *librum*), which held its value very well, but the revenues were still insufficient to generate an economic recovery, and the rest of the coinage continued to depreciate.

There was little 'Christian spirit' in Constantine's social legislation, especially when it came to women. On the one hand, adultery by the woman immediately justified, and indeed necessitated, divorce by the husband, but on the other, a law of 331 stated that she was not allowed to sue for divorce 'because of her own depraved desires' (for instance, if her husband was an alcoholic, gambler or adulterer), but only if she could prove that he was 'a murderer or a preparer of poisons or a disturber of tombs'. Otherwise she was to lose her dowry, 'down to a

---

21   *Theodosian Code* 5.17.1 (332 CE), tr. in Lewis, N. and Reinhold, M. (eds), op. cit., p. 437.

22   Zosimus, *New History* 2.38, tr. Ridley, R. T., *Zosimus: New History*, Sydney: Australian Association for Byzantine Studies, 1982.

hairpin', and be deported to an island.[23] Even more hard line is a law of 326 concerning the abduction of an unwilling girl:

> Since often the watchfulness of parents is frustrated by the stories and wicked persuasions of nurses, this punishment shall first of all threaten them (the nurses), whose service is proven to have been hateful and whose talk is proven to have been bought: the opening of their mouth and throat, which brought forth destructive encouragements, shall be closed by the swallowing of molten lead.[24]

On the other hand, there was a growing trend towards more humane treatment of slaves. Constantine was concerned, for instance, about slave families being split up when someone's property was divided:

> For who could tolerate children being separated from their parents, sisters from their brothers, and wives from their husbands? Therefore, anyone who has separated slaves and dragged them off to serve under different owners shall be compelled to restore such slaves to single owners [but receive compensation]. And care should be taken that from now on no complaint shall continue throughout the provinces concerning the separation of slaves' loved ones.[25]

Constantine's Baptism and Death

In the author's collection is a Roman copper alloy *nummus* of Constantine that was minted at Treveri in 322. On the reverse side is a globe on an altar, and the words *BEATA TRANQVILLITAS* ('blessed peace'). In some ways these are

---

23   *Theodosian Code* 3.16.1 (331 CE).
24   Ibid. 9.24.1, (326 CE), tr. in Evans Grubbs, J., *Women and the Law in the Roman Empire: A Sourcebook on Marriage, Divorce and Widowhood*, Abingdon: Routledge, 2002, p. 181.
25   Ibid. 2.25.1 (325 or 334 CE), tr. Kershaw. S.

the keywords of the final phase of Constantine's reign. He worked hard on securing his dynasty. In 333 the two *Caesares*, Constantine II and Constantius II, were augmented by Constantine's fourth son Constans, and in 335 he appointed his nephews, Hannibalianus and Dalmatius, as 'King of Kings and of the Pontic Peoples' and Caesar (in charge of Thrace, Macedonia and Achaea) respectively. His hope must have been, somewhat optimistically, that these blood-related co-rulers would happily cooperate after his death. Admittedly the 'blessed peace' was disturbed from time to time: there were campaigns on the Rhine in 328/9, against the Goths in 332 and versus the Sarmatians in 334, although tens of thousands of the latter were then resettled south of the Danube; an attempted usurpation by Calocaerus on Cyprus ended with him being captured and burned alive in 334; in 336 Constantine recovered part of Dacia; and when the Persian Shah Shapur II started to threaten Rome's Eastern borders Constantine sent Hannibalianus and Constantius II to deal with him.

A diplomatic rapprochement with Shapur II proved elusive, however, so Constantine put together an expedition to conquer and Christianize Persia, during which he intended to be baptized in the River Jordan. However, he fell ill on the way, and his baptism took place near Nicomedia. Ironically, this was performed by Bishop Eusebius of Nicomedia, who was an Arian. Constantine died on 22 May 337. His body was taken to Constantinople and his sarcophagus placed in the Church of the Holy Apostles. He had set the world on a new path:

> Constantine, sitting amongst the Christian bishops at the oecumenical council of Nicaea, is in his own person the beginning of Europe's Middle Age.[26]

---

26 Baynes, N. A., in *Cambridge Ancient History*, Cambridge: Cambridge University Press, 1939, vol. 12, p. 699.

The Heirs of Constantine

If Constantine had unwittingly started the Middle Ages, there would still be a lengthy period of overlap with the Roman era. The immediate aftermath of his death saw too many *Caesares* and not enough *Augusti*: the *beata tranquillitas* was over. There were a few months of uncertainty, during which the army eliminated any potential Augustus who was not one of his sons: Hannibalianus, Dalmatius, plus all the male descendants of Constantius I Chlorus and Theodora, with the exception of Gallus (aged twelve) and Julian (aged six).

Constantine's three surviving sons now divided the Empire between themselves. Constantine II became Augustus of the West, Constantius II of the East and Constans of Italy, Africa and Illyricum. Inevitably, though, they fought for supremacy. In 340 Constantine II, who was the senior Augustus, tried to take Italy from Constans, but got killed near Aquileia in the process. Peace then broke out between the two remaining brothers for a decade or so, but during that time Constans lost the confidence of his troops, and in January 350 he was overthrown and killed in a coup staged by Flavius Magnus Magnentius, a military commander who originated from a community of German *laeti* in Gaul.

Constantius II had been preoccupied with aggression from the Shapur II, but now he marshalled his troops to deal with Magnentius. First, though, he cemented his dynastic position by having his sister Constantina marry his cousin Gallus, who was elevated to Caesar. On the way to confront Magnentius, Constantius II dealt with another commander called Vetranio, whose troops had proclaimed him Emperor in Pannonia in March 350. Constantius II and Magnentius came together at Mursa (modern Osijek in Croatia), near Sirmium on the Danube. In a titanic tussle fought on 28 September 351, Constantius II emerged victorious, but with such ghastly loss of life that the combined casualties 'were sufficient for any foreign wars and [. . .] might have provided many a triumph and much security'.[27] Magnentius escaped to Gaul. There he appointed his brother Decentius as his Caesar, but Constantius II had persuaded/bribed King Chnodomar of the Alemanni to harass them from across the Rhine, and when he brought his rivals to battle at Mons Seleuci, near Gap, he emerged triumphant again. The losing generals took their own lives in August 353.

Magnentius had been a pagan sympathizer, and after his demise Constantius II introduced a whole raft of anti-pagan measures, including the deeply symbolic removal of the Altar of Victory from the Senate House in 357, as well as outlawing soothsaying, astrology and divination:

> The curiosity of all men for divination shall cease in perpetuity. Whoever should refuse to comply with these orders shall suffer capital punishment struck down by the sword of vengeance.[28]

On the other hand, Christian clergy and their sons were to be exempt from compulsory public service and received tax breaks, Bishops could not be tried in secular courts, and Christian prostitutes could only be bought by Christians. Constantius II is often described as an Arian, although he tried to resolve the lingering disputes left after the Council of Nicaea. The argument had become even more polarized between the homoousians and Arian fundamentalists called anomoeans (Greek *anomoios* = 'unlike'), who not only denied the consubstantiality of Christ, but held that he was of a nature different to that of God. Constantius II's efforts to promote a kind of semi-Arianism, which rejected the consubstantiality of Christ but accepted that he was like the Father, made very little headway. He is simply remembered as a heretic.

---

27   Eutropius, *Breviarium* 10.12, tr. Bird, H. A., op. cit.
28   *Theodosian Code*, 9.16.4 (357 CE), tr. Kershaw, S.

Constantius II was, nevertheless, sole ruler of the Roman Empire. The last of the great Roman historians, Ammianus Marcellinus, a military officer from Antioch whose lively, informative, but not always impartial work becomes our prime source for events between 354 and 378, presents him as long-bodied, short-legged, always 'making a mountain of mischief out of a molehill of evidence', 'excessively influenced by his wives and his shrill eunuchs and his court officials', and capable of 'a cruelty which surpassed that of Caligula, Domitian and Commodus'.[29] But whatever his looks and personality, he certainly had plenty to worry about:

Everywhere [Constantius II] saw the Roman empire being dismembered by barbarian incursions: the Franks, Alemanni and Saxons had already taken forty cities on the Rhine and left them in ruins [. . .] The Quadi and Sarmatians had very boldly overrun Pannonia and Upper Moesia; and the Persians were continually harassing the East, whereas previously they had been inactive for fear of being attacked by Gallus Caesar.[30]

Gallus had turned out to be a cruel Caesar, and his wife Constantina hadn't helped:

She was a Fury in mortal form, incessantly adding fuel to her husband's rage, and as thirsty for human blood as he.[31]

Gallus was also inept, over-fond of gladiatorial shows and prone to roaming the streets at night asking everybody what they thought of the Caesar, and so Constantius II arranged for his 'disappearance' by having him recalled to Mediolanum and beheaded in 354. This left Constantius II needing personally to

29 Ammianus Marcellinus 21.16.11, 21.16.16, 21.16.8, tr. Hamilton, W., op. cit.
30 Zosimus, *New History* 3.1, tr. Ridley, R. T., op. cit.
31 Ammianus Marcellinus 14.1,2, tr. Hamilton, W., op. cit.

get to grips with both the Rhine and Danube barbarians and Shapur II. With that in mind he dragged Julian away from his studies at Athens to become Caesar at Mediolanum on 6 November 355. Julian had influential backing in the shape of Constantius II's childless second wife Eusebia, 'a woman of outstanding beauty and excellence of character [and] kindness of heart',[32] and wrote a *Speech of Thanks* to her that remains the earliest example that we have of an official speech of praise exclusively for an imperial woman. Julian's marriage to the Emperor's sister Helena further secured his status.

Rome's Empire had not faced such a sustained barbarian threat for around sixty years: Ammianus Marcellinus describes how the Alemanni penetrated deep into Gaul, and narrates at first hand a frightening situation where Silvanus, a general of Frankish origin who was supposed to be confronting the Alemanni, declared himself Augustus at Colonia Agrippina. This 'struck Constantius like a thunderbolt', and Ammianus, who fortified his courage by quoting Cicero, was part of a delegation sent to Silvanus that managed to bribe some troops of suspect loyalty into butchering him. Constantius II played his part too, conducting operations against Alemannic tribes from his base at Mediolanum in 355 and 356, and then dealing with threats to Pannonia and Upper Moesia from the Sarmatians, Quadi and a group called the Limigantes, who Ammianus said were Sarmatian serfs, from an HQ at Sirmium down to 359. He returned there 'like a conqueror'.[33]

In between those campaigns Constantius II made his one and only visit to Rome, in 357:

> A double line of standards went before him, and he himself was seated on a golden car gleaming with various precious stones, whose mingled radiance seemed to throw a sort of shimmering light [. . .] The Emperor's person was

---

32   Ibid. 21.6.4.
33   Ibid. 17.13.28.

surrounded by purple banners woven in the form of drag-
ons and attached to the tops of gilded and jewelled spears;
the breeze blew through their gaping jaws so that they
seemed to be hissing with rage, and their voluminous tails
streamed behind them on the wind. On each side marched
a file of men-at-arms with shields and plumed helmets,
whose shining breastplates cast a dazzling light. At intervals
were mailed cavalrymen, the so-called Ironclads, wearing
masks and equipped with cuirasses and belts of steel; they
seemed more like statues polished by the hand of Praxiteles
than living men.[34]

But for his part Constantius II was amazed, dazzled and
amused by Rome, her people, traditions and monuments: the
buildings of the baths 'as big as provinces', the amphitheatre
'with its top almost beyond the reach of human sight', the
Pantheon 'spread like a self-contained district under its high
and lovely dome', and, most impressive of all, the Forum of
Trajan. Awestruck, he

complained of the weakness or malice of common report,
which tends to exaggerate everything, but is feeble in its
description of the wonders of Rome.[35]

The new Caesar Julian also turned out to be a complete star.
He recovered Colonia Agrippina, which had been taken by
barbarians, and, although according to Ammianus he was
outnumbered by more than two to one, his disciplined Roman
infantry absorbed the wild onslaught of a coalition of Alemanni
led by Chnodomar and his nephew Serapio, and registered a
crushing victory near Argentoratum (modern Strasbourg) in
357. He then took the offensive against the Franks across the

34　Ibid. 16.10.6 ff.
35　Ibid. 16.10.17. See also Edbrooke, Jr., R. O., 'The Visit of Constantius II to
Rome in 357 and Its Effect on the Pagan Roman Senatorial Aristocracy', *The
American Journal of Philology*, 97.1, 1976, 40–61.

Rhine, and generally restored the damage inflicted on Gaul by Magnentius' usurpation and the pro-Constantius II barbarians.

Julian's success was a little too spectacular for Constantius II's liking. Jealous and worried, he sent orders for some of Julian's troops to be redeployed to the East, but their response was to elevate their leader to the rank of Augustus, and to do so in the Germanic manner by raising him aloft on an infantry shield. Whether this was carefully orchestrated or improvised ad lib, it was clearly not a situation that Constantius II was prepared to countenance. However, before he could marshal his army away from the campaign against Shapur II and hurl the Roman world into yet another civil war, he died at the age of forty-four at Mopsucrene, a road station between Tarsus and the Cilician Gates, on 3 November 361 (see Map 8). Rome probably had no inkling of the extraordinary bombshell that Julian was about to drop.

Julian the Apostate: 361–363

Julian 'came out'. He was pagan. The responses to this are uncompromising, be they ancient or modern, or for or against him:

> A pretentious, pseudo-intellectual, anti-Christian bigot whose ambitions greatly exceeded his limited abilities.[36]

> Though it has been my constant endeavour to sing the praises of this hero, yet have I ever found my words fall far short of the greatness of his performances.[37]

---

36   Woods, D., review of Tougher, S., *Julian the Apostate*, Edinburgh: Edinburgh University Press, 2007, in *Classics Ireland* 14 (2007) p. 141 ff.
37   Libanius, *Funeral Oration Upon the Emperor Julian*, 123, tr. King, C. W., *Julian the Emperor: Containing Gregory Nazianzen's Two Invectives and Libanius' Monody with Julian's Extant Theosophical Works*, London: George Bell and Sons, 1888.

As the younger son of Julius Constantius, one of Constantine's half-brothers, Julian had probably only survived because of his tender years when his father had been eliminated to make way for Constantine's sons in 337.[38] His early education had taken place at Macellum in Cappadocia, Nicomedia, Pergamum, Ephesus and Athens, and he was taught/influenced by an eclectic selection of influential thinkers, including the Arian Bishop Eusebius, the future bishops Basil of Caesarea and Gregory of Nazianzus, a Christian eunuch called Mardonius and, perhaps most importantly, the neo-Platonist philosopher Maximus of Ephesus.

Neo-Platonism was a kind of reinvented version of Platonic philosophy, but it also placed a strong emphasis on theurgy – a kind of magic that was believed to promote the union of the human and the divine – and Julian got to hear about Maximus' talents:

> He burned a grain of incense and recited to himself the whole of some hymn or other, and was so highly successful in his demonstration that the image of the goddess [Hecate] first began to smile, then even seemed to laugh aloud. We were all much disturbed by this sight, but he said: 'Let none of you be terrified by these things, for presently even the torches which the goddess holds in her hands shall kindle into flame.' And before he could finish speaking the torches burst into a blaze of light.[39]

Julian went to Ephesus and sought out Maximus, who was the prime mover behind his 'conversion'/'apostasy' from Christianity to paganism, which Julian himself dated to 351:

> For you will not stray from the right road if you heed one who till his twentieth year walked in that road of yours [i.e.,

---

38 See above, p. 327.
39 Eunapius, *Sophists* 435, tr. Wright, W. C., *Lives of the Philosophers and Sophists*, Cambridge, MA: Harvard University Press, 1921.

Christianity], but for twelve years now has walked in this road I speak of, by the grace of the [pagan] gods.[40]

However, he wisely kept pretty quiet about it at the time:

To frustrate any opposition and win universal goodwill he pretended to adhere to the Christian religion, from which he had secretly apostatized. A few only were in his confidence, and knew that his heart was set on divination and augury and all the other practices followed by the worshippers of the old gods.[41]

His opportunity to reveal his true beliefs came with Constantius II's death, after which he made his dramatic announcement:

The gods command me to restore their worship in its utmost purity, and I obey them, yes, and with a good will.[42]

Ammianus Marcellinus gives us more details:

[He] directed in plain and unvarnished terms that the temples should be opened, sacrifices brought to their altars, and the worship of the old gods restored. To make this ordinance more effective he summoned to the palace the Christian bishops who were far from being of one mind, together with their flocks, who were no less divided by schism, and warned them in polite terms to lay aside their differences and allow every man to practise his belief boldly without hindrance.[43]

Requiring the bishops to espouse religious toleration was a classic example of 'divide and conquer':

---

40   Julian, *Letter* 47, 434d, tr. Wright, W. C., *The Works of the Emperor Julian with an English translation by Wilmer Cave Wright*, vol III, London: Heineman, 1913.
41   Ammianus Marcellinus 21.2, tr. Hamilton, W., op. cit.
42   Julian, *Letter* 8, 415d, tr. Wright, W. C., op. cit., written at Naissa to Maximus late in 361.
43   Ammianus Marcellinus, 22.5, tr. Hamilton, W., op. cit.

His motive in insisting on this was that he knew that toleration would intensify their divisions and henceforth he would
no longer have to fear unanimous public opinion.[44]

But that was as far as he went. The 'god-fearing' pagans were
to receive positive discrimination, but there were to be no tetrar-
chic-style persecutions: he said that he did not wish 'the
Galileans' (Christians) to be put to death or unjustly beaten,
and he was proud of his record on this. However, he did ban
Christians from teaching rhetoric or grammar. The syllabus for
this was pretty well 100 per cent Classical Greek, and Julian felt
that it was 'absurd that men who expound the works of these
writers should dishonour the gods whom these men honoured'.[45]
This was an emotive issue, since these authors were a central
part of many people's cultural heritage, whether or not they
were Christian. Equally controversial was his projected rebuilding of the Temple at Jerusalem. This was an act of blatant
effrontery to Christian sensibilities. Since the establishment of
Constantine's Church of the Holy Sepulchre, Jerusalem had
become a major Christian pilgrimage centre, and the Christians
hated the idea of pagan sacrifices taking place on the Temple
Mount again. So there was widespread rejoicing when the
project was abandoned after 'repeated and alarming outbursts
of fireballs near the foundations made it impossible to approach
the spot', and several workmen were burned to death.[46]
Nevertheless, the old gods went on the warpath in the good
old Roman manner as Julian invaded Persia in what might be
seen as a 'war of national reconciliation' against Shapur II.
Setting off from Constantinople in May 362 he arrived in Antioch, where he spent the rest of the year assembling his forces.
Unfortunately, the presence of large numbers of troops in the
city caused grain shortages, high prices and discontent, and not

44   Ibid. 22.5.
45   Julian, *Letter* 36, 423a, tr. Wright, W. C., op. cit. Cf. Ammianus Marcellinus
22.10; 25.4.
46   Ammianus Marcellinus, 23.1.

just among the Christians. The population ridiculed Julian's goatee beard and satirized him as a monkey, dwarf and 'the axe-man' because of the number of sacrifices he made; he hit back with a derisory speech entitled the *Misopogon* ('Beard-hater'). He had given them some money to make sacrifices:

> Accordingly, I hastened thither [. . .] thinking that I should enjoy the sight of your wealth and public spirit. And I imagined [. . .] the sort of procession it would be [. . .] beasts for sacrifice, libations, choirs in honour of the gods, incense and the youth of the city surrounding the shrine.[47]

But Antiochenes had blown the money on chariot racing, and when he entered the shrine he simply met a priest who told him,

> I have brought with me from my own house a goose as an offering to the god, but the city this time has made no preparations.[48]

Julian hit the campaign trail under sunny skies on 5 March 363 with 65 000 men, including Ammianus Marcellinus. Things went well up to and including an engagement outside Ctesiphon where Julian's 'Homeric tactics'[49] prevailed. But the Roman high command decided not to besiege the city, lost their focus about their objectives, made some serious errors, which included burning the boats of their river-going fleet, and started to retreat. As the Sasanians were harassing the Romans on 23 June, Julian forgot to put on his breastplate, leaving him undefended against a cavalry spear thrown, as Ammianus Marcellinus

---

47 Julian, *Misopogon* 361d–362a, tr. Wright, W. C., *The Works of the Emperor Julian with an English translation by Wilmer Cave Wright*, vol II, London: Heineman, 1913.

48 Ibid. 362b.

49 Ammianus Marcellinus, 24.6.

says, 'by no one knows whom'.[50] Various other sources spin the story to suit their pro- or anti-Julian agendas: the unknown warrior can be a Saracen (fighting on either the Persian or the Roman side), a Persian or a Roman, and can be Christian or pagan. In any case, the wound was fatal. A few hours later, in his tent, Rome's last pagan Emperor died in the style of Socrates, engaged in deep discussion with philosophers. History was depicted by the victors in the form of a relief at Taq-e Bostan in north-west Iran, on which Julian's body, recognizable by his thin features and goatee beard, is trampled by Shapur II.

Christianity Back on Track

Whether Julian could ever have restored paganism to the Roman Empire is one of history's great counter-factual questions, but it seems an unlikely prospect, as is nicely illustrated by the tale of his supposed attempt to revive the sanctuary of Apollo at Delphi. He sent Oreibasios to consult the Oracle there, only for the priestess to prophesy her own demise:

> Go tell the king – the carven hall is felled,
> Apollo has no cell, no prophetic bay
> Nor talking spring; his cadenced well is stilled.[51]

Julian's quirky style of paganism never really belonged to the mainstream. He was not in tune with many of the intellectuals of his day, let alone with the rural and urban lower classes where pagan practice was still at its most resilient. Yet the spear that killed Julian did not kill paganism: upper-class and educated families at Aphrodisias in Caria and Heliopolis in Syria were

---

50 Ibid. 25.3.
51 Quoted by both the *Artemii Passio* 35 (Philostorgius *Historia Ecclesiastica* 7. p. 77) and Georgius Cedrenus, *Historiarum Compendium* 1 p. 532, Bekker. Tr. Jay. P., in *The Greek Anthology and Other Ancient Epigrams: A Selection of Modern Verse Translations Edited with an Introduction by Peter Jay*, Harmondsworth: Penguin, 1973.

still pagan in the sixth century, and pagan worship carried on in the countryside, often side by side with Christianity. Nevertheless, every ruler of Rome from now on would be Christian.

The last of Rome's pagan Emperors was also the last of Constantine's surviving male relatives. He had not appointed a Caesar, and he had no heir of his own blood:

> Julian was so spectacularly and incorruptibly chaste that after the loss of his wife he never tasted the pleasures of sex.[52]

So the army commanders held an emergency meeting at which they selected 'a passable candidate' as Emperor.[53] This was Flavius Iovianus ('Jovian') the *protector domesticus* (senior staff officer). He was a moderate Christian, and no reprisals were taken against the pagans, although he did revoke the law that forbade Christians teaching grammar and rhetoric. Jovian managed to extricate the Roman forces by negotiating a treaty with Shapur II under which he ceded large tracts of Galerius' conquests from the end of the previous century (notably Nisibis) and vacated Armenia. But as he was heading for Constantinople early in 364, he was found dead in his bed at Dadastana, a border town between Galatia and Bithynia. Ammianus Marcellinus reports three uninvestigated theories: he was overcome by the noxious smell of fresh plaster in his bedroom; he was suffocated by fumes from a large fire; or it was just indigestion brought on by overeating.[54] And so 'this dreadful period of uncertainty came to a sad end'.[55]

---

52   Ammianus Marcellinus, 25.4.1, tr. Hamilton, W., op. cit.
53   Ibid. 25.5.
54   Ibid. 25.10.
55   Ibid. 26.1.

15

The East–West Divide (364–395)

During this time, when the bolts of our frontiers were unfastened, bands of armed barbarians were pouring forth like glowing ashes from Mount Etna.

Ammianus Marcellinus[1]

Brothers in Arms: Valentinian and Valens

The response to Jovian's death in 364 was not instantaneous. Several possible candidates were considered and rejected, before, by 'divine inspiration',[2] the choice fell on a Pannonian soldier from a humble background whom we know as Valentinian I. Rome was Emperor-less for over a week until the chosen one was able to join the army at Nicaea, where they acclaimed him as Augustus. They had installed an energetic and decisive disciplinarian who was noted for his religious tolerance, even though he could be cruel, greedy, envious and grasping. Less than a month later, Valentinian I had appointed his rather indecisive, boorish, visually impaired, bow-legged, Arian-fundamentalist brother Valens as co-Emperor.

As winter turned to spring, the two brothers moved to Naïssus, where they came to an arrangement to divide the military commanders, troops and court officials between them. They then made a highly symbolic parting:

---

1 Ammianus Marcellinus, 31.4.9, tr. Kershaw, S.
2 Ibid. 26.1.4.

Valentinian departed to Mediolanum, Valens to Constantinople.[3]

This was a key moment. Now, for the first time, the two parts of the Roman Empire were truly separate, although Valentinian could pull rank if he needed to. They took the consular robes on 1 January 365, which was the normal protocol at the beginning of a new reign.

Valens was immediately confronted by a serious challenge to his position. As ever, anyone who could garner the support of a sufficiently powerful or venal group of army officers could orchestrate a coup, and Julian's pagan relative Procopius did just that. Yet although he played the dynastic card, personally carrying Constantius II's little daughter in his arms, it turned out to be a real shambles:

> No purple robe was available, and he was dressed in a gold-spangled tunic like a court official, though from the waist downwards he looked like a page. He wore purple shoes and carried a spear, with a shred of purple cloth in his hand. Altogether he was a grotesque object such as might suddenly appear on the stage in a satirical farce.[4]

Yet Procopius won enough backing to secure the control of Constantinople and make inroads into the provinces of Bithynia and Hellespont. In the end defections by his own officers and men caused his defeat in battles at Thyatira in Lycia and Nacolia in Phrygia in 366. Procopius was captured and beheaded, but the whole sorry affair proved that the new Valentinian dynasty could take nothing for granted.

Reprisals followed, and as time went on Valens acquired quite a reputation for savagery. There were vicious persecutions of pagans at Antioch, and on the pretext of eradicating sorcery Valens managed to exterminate practically all the best-known

---

3   Ibid. 26.5.4.
4   Ibid. 26.6.15, tr. Hamilton, W., op. cit.

non-Christian philosophers in the Eastern part of the Empire, including Maximus of Ephesus, the man who had turned Julian onto theurgy. One interesting example of the use of magic that Valens so feared was the case of Patricius and Hilarius, who had used a divining device similar to one found in excavations at Pergamon. Amidst prayers and incense they constructed a tripod out of laurel twigs and covered it with a round metal dish engraved with the letters of the Greek alphabet. A ring suspended by a thread was set swinging from it, and would jump to indicate the answer to whatever question was asked. When the consultants enquired who would be the next Emperor, it indicated ΘΕΟ (THEO), which was taken to refer to a Gaulish official called Theodorus. When Valens heard about this the result was torture and beheadings, yet it wasn't just pagans who suffered. The Arian Valens also directed his venom onto Nicaean bishops, and Rome's Eastern flank ended up riven by incessant religious intrigue.

Over in the West, Valentinian was being lauded for his statesmanlike qualities:

> Even his harshest critic cannot find fault with his unfailing shrewdness in matters of state, especially if he bears in mind that it was a greater service to keep the barbarians in check by frontier barriers than to defeat them in battle.[5]

Such a policy entailed recruiting barbarians and provincials in Gaul to ensure that Rome's armies were at full strength, alongside the construction and/or refurbishment of forts, lookout stations and bridgeheads along the Rhine. However, it was never easy for Valentinian to keep tabs on all the goings-on in his Empire, and devious local factions or officials could make the most of this, which is precisely what Romanus, the *Comes* of Africa, did in 363–4. When a tribe called the Austoriani raided Lepcis Magna, he responded with military assistance, but then demanded 4 000 camels from the hapless locals. They refused.

---

5 Ibid. 29.4.1.

So he abandoned them to the Austoriani. The citizens of Lepcis complained to Valentinian I; Romanus was defended by his own supporters; Valentinian could not decide between the two sides, and promised an inquiry; the Austoriani kept attacking Lepcis; Romanus still did nothing; Valentinian I dispatched a tribune called Palladius to pay the African army and report back; Romanus threatened to frame Palladius for embezzling the money; Palladius told the Emperor that the citizens of Lepcis had nothing to complain about; Valentinian I swallowed the whole story; and Romanus got away with it.

In Italy itself Valentinian I developed a life-threatening illness in 367. Various schemes were hatched to find a successor, but he duly made a full recovery and immediately made his eight-year-old son Gratian Augustus (with the approval of the troops). He was the first of the 'Child Emperors', and Ammianus Marcellinus was quick to acknowledge the significance of this:

> No one before had taken a colleague with power equal to his own except the Emperor Marcus [Aurelius], who made his adopted brother Verus his partner without any inferiority of status as an Emperor.[6]

There were also ever-increasing tensions between the Emperor and the Senate, which came to a head in a reign of terror orchestrated particularly by the Pannonians Maximinus of Sopianae and his friend Leo. They conducted a series of trials and executions of men and women of mainly senatorial rank who were accused of magic or sex crimes. Valentinian equated these 'offences' with treasonable activity, and allowed the use of torture even against those who were hitherto exempt from it: Ammianus Marcellinus' catalogue of the atrocities committed is both comprehensive and distressing.

It may have been that Valentinian I's actions at Rome were driven by fears of conspiracy. However rational or otherwise

---

6   Ibid. 27.6.16.

these may have been, in 367 he had to face the very real *Barbarica Conspiratio* ('Barbarian Conspiracy') in Britain, although the term itself is something of a misnomer, since there was never any inclusive sense of Germanic or Celtic identity among the various barbarian tribes. In the far north of Britain were people that the Romans called *Picti* ('Picts'). However, *Picti* is not the name of an ethnic group. It means 'the Painted Men', and was a general name by which the Romans, in a typical piece of 'barbarian stereotyping', referred to all the tribes north of Hadrian's Wall. How the Picts differed from neighbouring British tribes, if at all, is unclear, although they appear to have spoken a P-Celtic language like the Britons. However, because they left no written records, we have no idea what they called themselves, although Irish sources refer to them as 'Cruithne', which is a Q-Celtic version of a P-Celtic word like Pritani – Britons (*Britanni* in Latin). Ammianus Marcellinus says that two Pictish tribes, the Dicalydones and Venturiones, had banded together with the warlike Attacotti and the Scotti from Ireland, and had overrun Hadrian's Wall. Meanwhile, Saxons and Franks had killed the Count of the Saxon Shore and overwhelmed Fullofaudes, the Duke of Britain. However, these barbarians were not attempting, or even contemplating, conquest of the Empire, and in any case Valentinian I's *Comes Rei Militaris*, Theodosius the Elder, quashed the revolt, as well as dealing with another uprising by a chieftain named Firmus in Africa.

Back in the East, meanwhile, Valens had a score to settle with the Goths, 3 000 of whom had supported Procopius in 365. He invaded their territory from Marcianopolis (modern Devnya in Bulgaria) in Lower Moesia, and after building a fort at Daphne, bridging the Danube, harassing the Greuthungi and forcing Athanaric, the *Iudex* ('Judge', i.e., Head of the Royal Clan) of the Tervingi to flee, he made them sue for peace.[7] It was actually

---

7   The Greuthungi and Tervingi are both Gothic peoples, the former variously spelled Grauthingi, Greothingi, Greothyngi, Gruthungi or Grouthingoi, and also called Ostrogothi or Austrogoti by ancient writers; the Tervingi, whose name could be derived from the Gothic *triu* (= 'tree'), can also be referred to as Thervingi or Visi.

the disruption of their trade, rather than military defeat, that hit the Goths hardest, and having conducted a cost-benefit analysis of the conflict, both sides were ready to negotiate. In 369 Athanaric and Valens met on boats in the middle of the Danube and agreed that the Goths should be allowed to trade at just two crossing points on the river, and that Gothic chieftains would no longer be subsidized by Rome:

> No one saw gold coin counted out for the barbarians, countless talents of silver, ships freighted with fabrics or any of the things we were in the habit of tolerating before, enjoying the fruits of peace and quiet that was more burdensome than the incursions, and paying yearly tribute, which we were not ashamed to do, although we refused to call it by that name.[8]

Subsequently there was internal warfare among the Goths as a chieftain called Fritigern challenged the humiliated and presumably discredited Athanaric with the support of Roman *limitanei*.

Valentinian I was somewhat less sanguine in his dealings with the barbarians. He campaigned successfully against the Alemanni, Sarmatians and Quadi, but in the end it was the barbarian 'attitude problem' that killed him. In 375 some envoys of the Quadi approached him seeking peace, and on the advice of his *Magister Militum* Equitius, they were allowed to make their case. They initially blamed foreign brigands for their hostile behaviour, but then they referred to a 'wrongful and untimely' attempt by the Romans to build a fort across the Danube. Valentinian I was so livid about this that he suffered a seizure and collapsed:

> He tried to speak or give some order; this was clear from the gasps that racked his sides, and from the way in which he ground his teeth and made movements with his arms as if he

---

8   Themistius, *Oration* 10.135, tr. Moncur, D., in Heather, P. J. and Matthews, J. F., *The Goths in the Fourth Century*. Liverpool: Liverpool University Press, 1991, p. 40.

were boxing. Finally, he could do no more. His body was covered with livid spots, and after a long struggle he breathed his last.[9]

The succession issue needed to be settled quickly, and the power of the generals as 'Emperor-makers' was made clear when Equitius and the Frankish Merobaudes, the main generals of the Western armies, summoned Valentinian I's ambitious Arian widow Justina and her four-year-old boy to Aquincum (modern Budapest), where the latter was declared Augustus as Valentinian II (see Genealogy Table 6). Neither Valentinian II's teenaged half-brother Gratian in the West nor Valens in the East was consulted about this – they just had to accept it as a fait accompli. The child 'governed' Illyricum under Gratian's guardianship, Merobaudes' military expertise and his mother's influence, and this arrangement seemed to keep everyone grudgingly content. Valentinian I's advisers, including his old *Magister Equitum* Count Theodosius the Elder, were eliminated, while Gratian, basing himself at Mediolanum, installed his tutor, the witty, original and occasionally mildly erotic poet D. Magnus Ausonius as *Praefectus Praetorio*, and also fell under the influence of St Ambrose, the recently appointed Bishop of Mediolanum.

The Huns and the Goths

Over in the East, Valens had been making some reasonably successful interventions in Armenia when, from the Roman perspective, all hell broke loose on the Danube. However, from the trans-Danubian viewpoint, hell came in the shape of nomadic horsemen of debatable, but probably central Asian, origin: the Hunni ('Huns').

The very moment they are born, they make deep cuts in their children's cheeks, so that, when hair appears in the course of

---

9   Ammianus Marcellinus, 30.6.6, tr. Hamilton, W., op. cit.

time, its vigour might be checked by these furrowed scars
[. . .] They have squat bodies, strong limbs, and thick necks,
and are so prodigiously ugly and bent that they might be two-
legged animals, or the figures crudely carved from stumps
which are seen on the parapets of bridges [. . .] They live on
the roots of wild plants and the half-raw flesh of any sort of
animal, which they warm by placing it between their thighs
and the backs of their horses [. . .] They wear clothes made
out of linen or the skins of field mice sewn together; and,
once they have put on some shabby shirt, they will not take it
off again or change it until it has rotted away [. . .] On their
heads they wear round hats made of skins, and goatskins on
their hairy legs [. . .] They are virtually joined onto their
horses, which are tough but deformed [. . .] Whatever they do
by day or night, buying or selling, eating or drinking, they do
on horseback, even leaning over their horses' narrow necks to
sleep [. . .] They are totally ignorant of the difference between
right and wrong, their speech is shifty and obscure, and they
are under no constraint from religion or superstition.[10]

Their fanaticism and unorthodox battle tactics made them
even more frightening:

They are lightly armed and so fast and unpredictable that
they will scatter suddenly and gallop here and there chaoti-
cally, inflicting untold slaughter [. . .] They can fire missiles
from far off, arrows tipped not with the usual arrowheads but
with sharp splintered bones, which they attach onto the shafts
with extraordinary skill. They fight close-to without any fear
for their own lives; and while the enemy is busy watching out
for sword-thrusts, they catch him with lassoes made out of
plaited cloth, so that his limbs get all entangled and he cannot
walk or ride.[11]

---

10   Ibid. 31.2.2 f., tr. in Moorhead, S. and Stuttard, D., op. cit, p. 54 f.
11   Ibid. 31.2.7 f.

Much of this is classic Roman stereotyping: the further removed from the Mediterranean a people was, the weirder and wilder it was thought to be: out to the north-east were the Vidini and Geloni who clothed themselves with the skins of their dead enemies; the Agathyrsi who painted themselves blue; the cannibal Melanchlaenae ('Black-cloaks') and Anthropophagoi ('Man-eaters'); the Amazons; and worst of all the Huns, who the sixth-century historian Jordanes says were descended from Gothic witches.[12] As Guy Halsall has cogently argued,

> Roman depictions of barbarians are not part of a dialogue between 'us' and 'them' ('we are like this whereas *you* are like that') but between 'us' and 'us', between Romans ('*we* are [or, more often, ought to be] like this because *they* are like that').[13]

A similar process can be seen in the derogatory use of 'the Hun' for the Germans in British propaganda during the First World War, which has its origin in an address made on 27 July 1900 by Kaiser Wilhelm II to German soldiers bound for China:

> Just as a thousand year ago, the Huns under their King Attila gained a good reputation that lives on in the historical tradition, so may the name of Germany become known in such a way in China that no Chinaman will ever again dare to cast even a sideways glance at a German.[14]

Why the Huns were on the move is not known. Writers at the time painted a picture of them driving other peoples before them, but the reality may not be quite so clear-cut, and it could have been that changing economic conditions in the area between the rivers Tanais (Don) and the Danastius (Dniester) were a factor. Nevertheless, the ancient accounts say that they caused various tribes to

---

12　Jordanes, *Getica* 24.121–2.

13　Halsall, G., *Barbarian Migrations and the Roman West, 376–568,* Cambridge: Cambridge University Press, reprinted with corrections, 2009, p. 56.

14　*Weser-Zeitung,* July 28, 1900, second morning edition, p. 1, tr. Kershaw, S.

flinch away from them in the direction of the Roman Empire as they moved south-eastwards from the steppes, displaced the Alani, who were themselves no pushover, from north of the Caucasus, vanquished the Ostrogoth realm of Ermanaric, and smashed Athanaric's Visigoth army as they kept on coming across the river valleys of the Tanais, Borysthenes (Dnieper) and Danastius (see Map 8). The various displaced populations started to encroach closer to the Danube and the Rhine. The Goths' powers of resistance had not been helped by the prior defeats of Athanaric and the Greuthungi by Valens, and when they were now assaulted by the Huns, the 'greater part of the people' (Ammianus Marcellinus is vague about who exactly they were) deserted Athanaric and, under Alavivus and Fritigern, fled to the Danube, where in 376 the people whom Ammianus Marcellinus calls the Tervingi begged Valens to grant them safe haven within the Empire.

How many people there were, and what sort of threat they really posed, are questions that we cannot answer definitively. The Romans certainly regarded them as an innumerable horde, and Ammianus Marcellinus quotes Virgil to make his point:

> If you wish to know their number, go and tot up the grains
> Of sand that are whirled around by a sand-storm in the Sahara.[15]

Most modern scholarly analysis rejects this, and current guesses average out at about 15 000 to 20 000 warriors plus their dependants. This ought not to have been an insuperable force for Rome's armies to deal with, but Valens, who was still campaigning against the Sasanians, played his hand differently: he granted their request. Ever since its earliest days, Rome had welcomed immigrants – one of the Roman Empire's key strengths had always been an ability to assimilate outsiders – and Valens' hope was that they would provide an important military resource, cultivate the land, and increase his tax revenue. So they were to be allowed into Thrace.

---

15   Virgil, *Georgics* 2.105 f., tr. Day Lewis, C., op. cit.

The Romans even helped to ferry the Goths across; Ammianus Marcellinus saw the consequences with 20/20 hindsight:

> Diligent care was taken that no future destroyer of the Roman state be left behind, even if he were smitten with a fatal disease.[16]

The crossing was a chaotic fiasco, and if the immigrants were supposed to be disarmed on the other side, the job was not well done. To make matters worse, the Roman commanders Lupicinus and Maximus treated them disgracefully. Things reached their nadir when, entirely predictably, food started to become scarce, and the rate of exchange became one dead Roman dog for one Gothic slave. Around the same time, the Greuthungi crossed the Danube without Roman authorization, and the two Gothic contingents came together at Marcianopolis, which is where the Roman commanders were based. Here Lupicinus invited Fritigern and Alavivus to a lavish dinner and noisy floor-show, but refused to allow the starving masses into the city to purchase food; when fighting broke out, the Romans had Fritigern and Alavivus' bodyguard butchered; Fritigern was allowed to return to his people to calm them down; instead he hurried away to 'set in motion the various incitements that lead to wars'.[17] The Romans had missed a golden opportunity: as allies, the Goths could have been the source of strength that Valens had hoped for; as enemies, they would ultimately bring Rome down.

The Goths now lived up to their 'stereotypical barbarian' image: they burned and pillaged; they defeated Lupicinus; they received reinforcements from Gothic contingents in the Roman army; they ravaged Rome's Balkan provinces; they got penned in north of the Haemus mountains, but repelled a Roman attack

---

16 Ammianus Marcellinus, 31.4.5, tr. Rolfe, J. C., *Ammianus Marcellinus with An English Translation*, vol. 3, Cambridge, MA.: Harvard University Press, 1940.
17 Ibid. 31.5.7.

by forming their wagons into a laager at Ad Salices (in the modern Dobruja) in 377; they broke out again aided by some Huns and Alani; and the storm of destruction resumed, 'as if the Furies were putting everything in motion'.[18]

Valens had to respond, and he needed help. He sent Gratian, but he was preoccupied with tribal movements in the West, and in February 378 he had to engage with a large force of Alemanni who crossed the Rhine on the ice, and although he drove them back over the river and restored order in his sphere of influence, the operations cost valuable time.

Having disentangled himself and his *comitatenses* from the conflict with the Sasanians, Valens moved westwards to Adrianople (see Map 8). Here he was the victim of erroneous intelligence: there were far more Goths there than he had been led to believe. But Valens was irked by, and jealous of, the reports of his nephew's military success, and so he decided to engage without waiting for Gratian to arrive. However, before he could do this, Fritigern sent a deputation led by a Christian priest, which proposed peace in exchange for a Gothic homeland in Thrace. 'Loyalty for land' would become a Gothic mantra over the next decades, but the Roman response would always be the same: outright rejection.

Valens would be the last Roman Emperor personally to lead his men into battle for two centuries. He did so on a hot sunny day in August 378, and made his men march 8 Roman miles to get at the enemy. Fritigern's warriors had set light to the surrounding countryside, formed their wagons into the customary circle, and were raising their uncanny war cry. As the Romans deployed for battle, another Gothic peace mission was rejected because Valens felt the envoys were of too low rank. The delays were suiting Fritigern anyway, since he was waiting for reinforcements led by Alatheus and Saphrax, and he sent yet another envoy who proposed an exchange of hostages and a personal parley with Valens. This seemed reasonable to the

---

18   Ibid. 31.10.1, tr. Kershaw, S.

Romans, but as their chosen emissary headed for the Gothic ramparts, Fate intervened.

Some Roman soldiers launched an unauthorized attack; the Goths, having now been joined by Alatheus, Saphrax and some Alani, struck back with a devastating cavalry charge; the Romans rallied; the main battle lines collided; the Roman left wing drove the Goths back to their laager, but became isolated and 'collapsed like a broken dyke'; the Roman infantry became so compacted that they could not wield their swords effectively; the dust cloud that was thrown up meant that no one could see or avoid incoming missiles; the Goths overwhelmed the Roman baggage trains; and in the end the Romans could not organize an orderly retreat. Ammianus Marcellinus called it the biggest military defeat in Roman history since Hannibal had won the Battle of Cannae nearly 600 years before. Casualty estimates vary between 10 000 and 20 000, and Valens' body was never recovered. Various accounts of his death became current. In one he was simply killed outright by an arrow, in another he did not die instantly, but was taken to a fortified farmhouse, which was surrounded by Goths who burned the house and everyone in it.

The Goths continued to indulge their appetite for plunder, although they were denied the richest of rewards when they were repulsed from the walls of Adrianople. Roman Emperors generally travelled with large amounts of gold bullion in their baggage-trains, but on this occasion Valens had left the treasure inside the city. A Gothic sortie against Constantinople was also beaten back. The Goths were overawed, partly by the city's mighty fortifications and the cultural splendours inside them, and partly by Rome's Saracen allies, one of whom, clad only in a loincloth, hurled himself into the midst of the Gothic forces, slit a man's throat, put his lips to the wound and sucked out the gushing blood. Such barbarity even appalled Rome's barbarian foes. However, Fritigern's Goths did occupy Thrace and Illyricum, driving a wedge between the Roman Empire's Eastern and Western halves.

Theodosius I

Ammianus Marcellinus concluded his history by describing how a large number of Goths who had enrolled in the Roman army were treacherously massacred in order to protect the Eastern provinces. Thereafter, events become quite difficult to piece together, but it is clear that Gratian responded decisively to the disaster at Adrianople. If that defeat had been Imperial Rome's Cannae, she now needed a latter-day Scipio Africanus, and Gratian's choice to fulfil this role was the thirty-two-year-old son of the recently deceased Count Theodosius the Elder – Theodosius I. He was of proven military competence, and, like Gratian, embraced the Nicene Creed. He acceded to the purple as co-Augustus on 19 January 379 and took charge of Rome's Eastern end, along with the *dioceses* of Dacia and Macedonia.

Theodosius I was fortunate that the death of King Sapor II in 379 inaugurated a period of internal instability in Persia that kept the two powers from fighting one another for some time. In 386 they signed a treaty dividing Armenia between them, although when this was depicted on the base of the obelisk of Theodosius I, which still stands in the Hippodrome in Istanbul, it shows a Roman military victory. Peace with Persia freed Theodosius I to concentrate on the Goths, who might not have had the ability to capture cities, but were still able to take over the whole of Thrace, make incursions into Greece, and create an environment where city dwellers and garrisons were terrified of leaving fortified areas. They also devastated Pannonia, where, in 380, Gratian agreed to let some of them settle on vacant lands under their own chiefs.

On 11 January 381 Athanaric showed up in Constantinople, having been expelled in a dispute among his own tribespeople, although he died a fortnight later. The tide now started to turn Rome's way. Gratian's barbarian generals Bauto and Arbogastes ('Arbogast') expelled the Goths from Macedonia and Thessaly, and Illyricum was cleared by

September 382, paving the way for an accord to be reached in October. At the beginning of 383 Theodosius I celebrated his victory and Themistius delivered a speech to his court, *A Thanksgiving for the Peace*:

> We have seen their leaders and chiefs, not making a show of surrendering a tattered standard, but giving up the weapons and swords with which up to that day they had held power, and clinging to the [emperor Theodosius I's] knees [. . .] At present their offences are still fresh, but in the not too distant future we shall have them sharing our religious ceremonies, joining our banquets, serving along with us in the army and paying taxes with us.[19]

Many modern works refer to a *foedus* ('treaty') of 382, and regard it as a watershed in Roman history, the first time a semi-independent non-Roman group had been settled on Roman territory. Yet it has been pointed out that no source prior to Jordanes in the mid-sixth-century ever mentions a *foedus* with the Goths: rather, the Romans had narrowly prevailed in a difficult war, knew how vulnerable their Danube defences were, and so were prepared to grant the Tervingi land in exchange for peace. Theodosius I and Gratian allowed the Tervingi and some of the Greuthungi to settle as a group on the Empire side of the Danube in the provinces of Thracia and Dacia Ripiensis. It was, at least superficially, a win–win situation.

Religious and Political Divisions

Theodosius I and Gratian also had some spiritual battles that they wanted to win. Contracting a potentially life-threatening illness had prompted Theodosius I to get baptized at an early

---

19 Themistius, *Orations* 16, 210b-c, tr. in Heather, P. J. and Moncur, D., *Politics, Philosophy and Empire in the Fourth Century: Themistius' Select Orations*, Liverpool. Liverpool University Press, 2001.

point in his reign, and on 27 February 380 he issued an Edict to the people of Constantinople:

> It is our will that all peoples ruled by our Clemency shall prac-tise that religion which the divine Peter the Apostle transmitted to the Romans [. . .] We shall believe in the single Deity of the Father, the Son, and the Holy Spirit, under the concept of equal majesty and of the Holy Trinity. We order that those persons who follow this rule shall embrace the name of Catho-lic Christians. The rest, however, whom we judge demented and insane, shall [. . .] be smitten first by divine vengeance and secondly by the retribution of our hostility, which we shall assume in accordance with divine judgment.[20]

To help secure this orthodox dominance, Theodosius I fired Constantinople's Arian bishop Demophilus, and replaced him with the pro-Nicene Gregory of Nazianzus, who was influential when over 200 Eastern bishops convened for the 'First Council of Constantinople' in 381. This became recognized as the Second Ecumenical Council, and it formally proscribed Arianism:

> No place for celebrating their mysteries, no opportunity for practising the madness of their excessively obstinate minds shall be available to the heretics [. . .] The name of the One and Supreme God shall be celebrated everywhere; the observance, destined to remain forever, of the Nicene faith [. . .] shall be maintained. The poison of the Arian sacrilege [. . .] shall be abolished even from the hearing of men.[21]

All non-adherents to the Nicene Creed were to be banned from entering churches or holding assemblies in towns. They

20   *Theodosian Code* 16.1.2 (380 CE), tr. in Lewis, N. and Reinhold, M. (eds), op. cit., p. 614 f.
21   *Theodosian Code* 16.5.6 (381 CE), tr. in Lewis, N. and Reinhold, M. (eds), op. cit., p. 615.

were to be 'driven away from the very walls of the cities, in order that the Catholic churches throughout the whole world may be restored to all orthodox bishops who hold the Nicene faith'.[22] However, the one area where these measures could not penetrate was among the Goths. Bishop Ulfila ('Little Wolf'), who produced a Gothic translation of the Bible, had been important in their conversion, but his translation has homoiousian traits (he renders the Greek 'identical to God' as 'similar to God'). The Goths duly passed this on to various other Germanic peoples: the sackers of Rome would, in the end, be Arians.

The Edicts from Constantinople were issued in the joint names of Theodosius I, Valentinian II and Gratian, the latter of whom allowed Pope Damasus and his chief adviser Bishop Ambrose to take a hard line against the Arians, while he himself became very proactive in repressing paganism. Gratian cancelled the privileges of the pagan priests and the Vestal Virgins, and had the Altar of Victory removed from the Senate House at Rome again.[23] The Senators, notably the *Praefectus Urbis* Q. Aurelius Symmachus, protested and reminded him that as *Pontifex Maximus* he had a duty of care to pagan rites, whereupon Ambrose wrote to him in no uncertain terms:

> Since, then, most Christian Emperor, you should bear witness of your faith to the true God, along with enthusiasm for that faith, care and devotion, I am surprised that certain people have come to harbour expectations that by imperial edict you might restore their altars to the pagan gods and also provide funds for the celebration of pagan sacrifices.[24]

Gratian's riposte to the Senate was to renounce his office on the grounds that it was wrong for a Christian to hold it.

---

22   Ibid.
23   Julian had put it back after Constantius II had removed it. See above, p. 328.
24   Ambrose, *Epistula* 17.3, tr. Croke, B. and Harries, J., *Religious Conflict in Fourth-Century Rome*, Sydney: Sydney University Press, 1982, p. 30.

Gratian's uncompromising stance towards Arians and pagans alienated a large constituency of people who were very tenacious in their beliefs. To make matters worse, although he had a decent military track record, he was still quite young and had an 'innate tendency to play the fool',[25] while his passion for hunting invited comparisons with Commodus. Neither did the fact that he appeared in public dressed in full Gothic costume shortly after the Battle of Hadrianople endear him to his troops. Allegations of favouritism towards barbarian troops further fanned the flames of discontent, and when he moved the Western court from Treveri to Mediolanum in 380, he effectively loosened his control over Gaul. To make matters worse, when Theodosius I proclaimed his son Flavius Arcadius co-Augustus early in 383 without asking Gratian's permission, it looked like he was being sidelined by the East. Usurpation was on the cards.

In 383 the inevitable happened. The Roman army in Britain, which was manfully fighting off barbarian attacks from the north, rebelled and elevated Magnus Maximus ('Great the Greatest'), who was probably the *Dux Britanniarum*, to the purple. In later times he entered Welsh legend in the story of *Mabinogion*, and *The Dream of Macsen Wledig*, and prior to his departure for mainland Europe he seems to have minted coins at Londinium, which depicted a winged Victory hovering over the two Emperors (of which he was going to be the Western one). When he crossed into Gaul, Gratian was deserted by his troops (led by his general Merobaudes) at Paris (recently named as such after the Gallic Parisii tribe) and fled to Lugdunum. There he was betrayed by the governor and killed on 25 August.

Magnus Maximus and Theodosius I had some things in common: both were Spaniards, and both were highly orthodox. Magnus Maximus assumed control over Britain, Gaul and Spain from his capital at Treveri for the next five years, and began negotiating with Theodosius I and Valentinian II, who was currently in Mediolanum, to try to get them to recognize

---

25   Ammianus Marcellinus, 31.10.19.

him as their colleague. Theodosius I did acknowledge Magnus Maximus as co-Augustus, but Valentinian II, or more correctly Bishop Ambrose, who was acting on Valentinian II's behalf, dug his heels in. Magnus Maximus' terms would have relegated Valentinian II to the junior side of a father/son relationship (he was just twelve years old), and the arrangement was clearly unacceptable to his advisers. The only solution would be a military one.

In 387 Magnus Maximus invaded northern Italy. His success forced Valentinian II, accompanied by his mother Justina and sister Galla, to head east to Thessalonica. This presented Theodosius I with a dilemma he could not shirk. Should he keep faith with Magnus Maximus, who was stronger than Valentinian II, Nicene and Spanish; or should he support his family, despite the fact that Valentinian II was very much under the thumb of Justina, who was not just an Arian, but also even prepared to court pagans and African Donatists to bolster her son's position? To some surprise, he chose the family option. Zosimus explained why:[26] Theodosius I had recently lost his first wife Aelia Flacilla, who had been a model of Christian piety and charity. Justina now offered him her daughter Galla, who was extremely attractive on two counts: (1) she was stunningly beautiful; (2) she was (convolutedly) related to Constantine the Great. Her double allure was too much for Theodosius I, particularly when Justina promised that her family would become orthodox. So he marched against Magnus Maximus. His onslaught was so unexpectedly swift that he caught Magnus Maximus completely unprepared. Having won victories in the Balkans, he descended on Aquileia, where Magnus Maximus was captured and executed in 27 August 388.

Theodosius I, who now ruled both East and West, installed himself at Mediolanum until mid-391. Maximus' family and close associates were duly put to the sword, but the defeated soldiers were integrated into Theodosius I's armies. The obelisk

---

26 Zosimus, *New History* 4.34.

of Theodosius I now in the Hippodrome at Istanbul partly cele-brates his victory over Magnus Maximus, and its base has relief carvings showing him, Valentinian II, and his two sons Arcadius and Honorius. For now, Arcadius represented him as Augustus of the East, while Valentinian II was reinstated at Treveri under the watchful eye of the Frankish *Magister Militum* Arbogast.

From here on in, Theodosius I's battles would be for the soul of the Roman Empire, and his main sparring partner would be Bishop Ambrose. An early trial of strength came in late 388 when a mob led by the Bishop of Callinicum in Mesopotamia (modern al-Rakka in Syria) burned down the local synagogue. Ambrose was outraged when the Emperor ordered it be recon-structed at the incendiaries' expense: how, he asked, can a Christian Bishop build a 'home of perfidy, a home of impiety, in which Christ is daily blasphemed', without violating his faith?[27] Theodosius revoked his decision. A more serious dispute between the Bishop and the Augustus broke out in 390. Buth-eric, the Gothic garrison commander at Thessalonica, had imprisoned a celebrity charioteer for an attempted homosexual rape. This sparked a riot in which Butheric was killed, followed by retaliation by Theodosius I's troops. The church historian Theodoret reports that seven thousand people lost their lives in lawless and indiscriminate acts of murder, cut down like ears of wheat at harvest time.[28]

Although Theodosius I had backtracked on his initial venge-ful decision, his messengers arrived too late to prevent the massacre. A Roman Emperor ordering Goths to slaughter Roman citizens was a shocking new development, and Ambrose refused to give Theodosius I Holy Communion until he had done some eight months of penance – the so-called penance of Milan.

All this may have influenced Theodosius I's decision to issue an Edict against pagan sacrifice and cult on 24 February 391:

---

27   Ambrose, *Epistolae* 60.16.1101 ff.
28   Theodoret, *Church History* 5.17.3.

No-one shall pollute himself with sacrificial offerings; no-one shall slaughter an innocent victim; no person shall approach the sanctuaries, shall wander all over the temples, or revere images created by mortal labour, lest he become guilty by divine and human laws.[29]

A second decree in July[30] extended these provisions to Egypt, and on 8 November 392 his much longer third and final decree went further:

No person at all, of any class or order whatsoever [. . .] shall sacrifice an innocent victim to senseless statues in any place at all or in any city. He shall not, through more secret wickedness, venerate his household god with fire, his *genius* with wine, his *Penates* with fragrant essences [. . .] If any one should dare to immolate a victim for the purpose of sacrifice, or to consult the entrails, he shall be reported in accordance with the example of a person guilty of high treason.[31]

This hit the Senate particularly hard. They came from a centuries-old tradition where pagan priesthoods and public offices were inseparable, so conversion to Christianity would entail abandoning their cultural heritage. For them, Christianity was about much more than faith.

The year 392 saw another curious event. Valentinian II was found hanged at Vienna (modern Vienne in France). Arbogast said it was suicide, but others suspected foul play. Certainly the swift appointment of a Christian but pagan-sympathetic rhetorician called Flavius Eugenius as his successor has a whiff of conspiracy about it, and the new Augustus had the backing of many Senators. Theodosius I knew that this was not only a threat to him, but, by association, to Christianity itself. He

---

29   *Theodosian Code*, 16.10.10, tr. Kershaw, S.
30   Ibid. 16.10.11.
31   Ibid. 16.10.12. tr. in Lewis, N. and Reinhold, M. (eds), op. cit., p. 612.

rejected all of Eugenius' efforts to secure his recognition, and made the situation clear by elevating his younger son Honorius to the rank of Augustus, before mobilizing a formidable army to take on the usurper in 394.

Theodosius I included large numbers of Goths in his army, and not just in the rank and file. Among his commanders was a talented, loyal and brave fighter by the name of Alaric ('Lord of All'). The armies came together at the River Frigidus (modern Vipava in Slovenia) on 5 September 394. Each side made its religious affiliations clear: Eugenius set up a statue of Jupiter, and images of Hercules adorned his banners; Theodosius led his troops under the Christian *labarum*. Unusually for an ancient battle, the fighting lasted two days. During the intervening night Theodosius I supposedly prayed for a storm, and had his prayers granted:

> Such a fierce wind arose as to turn the weapons of the enemy back on those who hurled them. When the wind persisted with great force and every missile launched by the enemy was foiled, their spirit gave way, or rather it was shattered by the divine power.[32]

Eugenius was captured and executed; Arbogast escaped but committed suicide; but Christian historians felt that the most high-profile casualty was paganism itself.

Theodosius I had little time to enjoy the fruits of victory: he died at Mediolanum in January 395, leaving his elder son Arcadius as Augustus in the East, and his *Magister Utriusque Militiae* ('General in Command of Cavalry and Infantry') Flavius Stilicho as regent for Honorius in the West. His death marks the moment when the Roman Empire irrevocably split in two.

---

32   Rufinus, *Historia Eremitica* 9.33, tr. Cameron, A., op. cit. p. 76.

16

The Sack of Rome (395–411)

The fall and ruin of the world will soon take place, but it seems that nothing of the kind is to be feared as long as the city of Rome stands intact. But when the capital of the world has fallen [. . .] who can doubt that the end will have come for the affairs of men and the whole world?

Lactantius, *Divine Institutes* 7.15[1]

January 395: A Divided Empire with Child Emperors

Julius Caesar famously began his *Gallic Wars* by saying that 'all Gaul is divided into three parts'; some four and a half centuries later, on the death of Theodosius I, the Roman Empire was formally divided into two parts, and so it would remain until 476, when it would be reduced to just one. The Byzantine Empire is sometimes regarded as beginning at this point, although people living at the time would probably not have seen it that way.

The contemporary historian Eunapius describes the state of play in January 395 like this:

It is recorded that Theodosius' sons [Arcadius in the East; Honorius in the West] succeeded him as Emperor. But if one were to give a truer picture of what happened (and truth is, after all, the purpose of history), they took the title of

---

1 Tr. in Lewis, N. and Reinhold, M. (eds)., op. cit., p. 628.

Emperors, while in reality total power lay with Rufinus in the East and Stilicho in the West.[2]

Arcadius was in his late teens and just on the verge of being able to rule in his own right, but for now the *Praefectus Praetorio* Flavius Rufinus held the reins of power. In a change to the fourth-century model of itinerant *Augusti*, Arcadius and his court stayed at Constantinople.

In Mediolanum the most powerful individual was the half-Vandal general Stilicho. He had been born great – he was a talented commander and an intelligent statesman – and was now having greatness thrust upon him. He had already been married to Theodosius I's niece Serena for over ten years, and when the Emperor breathed his last, Stilicho announced that his dying wish was that he, Stilicho, should not only be regent for the eleven-year-old Honorius in the West, but also for Arcadius in the East. In the *Oration on the Death of Theodosius*, Bishop Ambrose explicitly endorsed Stilicho's claim, as did Stilicho's Alexandrian Greek poetical spin-doctor Claudian. This was tantamount to seeking authority over the entire Roman world, and the Eastern court was having none of it. The inevitable conflict now produced the rise of Alaricus ('Alaric') the (Visi)goth.

Alaric the Visigoth and Stilicho the Half-Vandal

Alaric's origins and status are hard to pinpoint: Claudian claims that he was born on an island in the Danube; he was now in his mid-twenties and had married the sister of the Gothic leader Athaulph; and he certainly held Roman offices, but what their specific titles were is often unclear. When, or indeed whether, he became King of the Goths is a difficult question. Some Roman sources call him *rex* (King), although, at different points in his career, Greek ones use *phylarkhos* (tribal chieftain), *hegemon* (leader) and *tyrannos* (tyrant/king), while some sources quite

---

2   Eunapius, *fr.* 62, tr. Wright, W. C., op. cit.; cf. Zosimus, *New History* 6.1–4.

pointedly give him no title at all. It is similarly tricky to establish the precise nature of his forces, their activities and their demands; although what seems to have mattered most at the time was that they were simply thought of as 'the Goths'. The designation *Visi*, as in 'Visigoths', does not appear until the *Notitia Dignitatum*.

Alaric's first move was to lead his Goths out of Italy into Thrace and Macedonia and cause chaos there before menacing Constantinople. Rufinus may have tried to buy Alaric off, and Stilicho was told to return the contingents that had marched west during River Frigidus campaign of 394 to their bases in the East. He complied and sent them back under the *Comes Rei Militaris* Gaïnas. But Gaïnas may have had secret instructions:

> The Emperor was persuaded to come out before the city. Rufinus, the city prefect, accompanied him. But, once Gaïnas and his men had prostrated themselves and received due welcome from the Emperor, Gaïnas gave the signal. All at once they surrounded Rufinus, falling on him with their swords. One sliced off his right hand, another his left, while another cut off his head and ran off singing a victory song.[3]

The main beneficiary of this incident was not Stilicho but a eunuch named Eutropius who was the *Praepositus Sacri Cubiculi*, and who had already arranged Arcadius' marriage to Aelia Eudoxia, the daughter of a Frankish general called Bauto, who was perhaps Arbogast's father.

> When Eutropius saw that the Emperor was intrigued by his account of the girl, he showed him a painting of her, which increased Arcadius' enthusiasm even more, and persuaded him to choose her for his wife.[4]

---

3 Zosimus, *New History* 5.7.5–6, tr. in Moorhead, S. and Stuttard, D., op. cit, p. 72.
4 Ibid. 5.3.3, tr. Ridley, R. T, op. cit.

Eutropius is one of antiquity's most colourful characters, and his power led him to become a bizarre role model:

> Even some who were already grown men, craving to be eunuchs and yearning to become Eutropiuses, disposed of both their sense and their testicles that they might enjoy the condition of Eutropius.[5]

Claudian had a field day with him in his lengthy poem *Against Eutropius*:

> His pallor and cadaverous appearance disgusted his masters, and his anaemic face and emaciated form repelled all who met him, frightening the children, sickening everyone who dined with him, shaming fellow-slaves, an ill-omen to any who crossed his path.[6]

Yet Eutropius manipulated the court politics to become the dominant figure in Constantinople; Gaïnas became *Magister Militum* in Thrace; Alaric didn't have the resources to take Constantinople, so he chose a softer target and went on the rampage in Greece (395–396), where he sacked Athens; Stilicho intervened in the Peloponnese, which he tried to detach from the East, but Alaric, to whom Eutropius granted the title of *Magister Militum per Illyricum* around now, fought him off and moved into Illyricum out of Greece. According to Zosimus, Stilicho, who had been declared a public enemy by Eutropius, had allegedly become diverted by luxury, comic actors and shameless women, but a more important distraction was Gildo, Africa's *Magister Utriusque Militiae*, who at Eutropius' bidding caused huge worry in Italy by diverting the grain supplies to Constantinople.

---

5 Eunapius, *fr.* 897, tr. in Moorhead, S. and Stuttard, D., loc. cit.
6 Claudian, *Against Eutropius* 121 ff., tr. in Moorhead, S. and Stuttard, D., op. cit., p. 73. See Long, J., *Claudian's* In Eutropium: *Or, How, When, and Why to Slander a Eunuch*, Chapel Hill and London: University of North Carolina Press, 1996.

However, Stilicho knew that Rome still trumped Constantinople, and by some smooth diplomacy he got the Senate to make Eutropius the public enemy and declare war on Gildo. Gildo was ultimately defeated by his brother Mascazel, who held a grudge against him, but Stilicho still had Mascazel drowned, just to be on the safe side: Zosimus says he laughed as Mascazel was swept away by the current.

> From now on, the hatred between Eutropius and Stilicho was no longer hidden. Everyone was talking about it [. . .] Stilicho married his daughter Maria to the emperor Honorius, while Eutropius kept Arcadius like a fattened animal.[7]

Stilicho became the new hard man, and he now focused his attention northwards. Britain and Gaul had both suffered withdrawals of troops from the time Magnus Maximus had made his bid for glory in 383, and the units that had been withdrawn had also suffered high rates of attrition, particularly at the Battle of the Frigidus. Magnus Maximus may have tried to devolve responsibility for local policing in Britain onto some urban-based tribal leaders (many Welsh genealogies claim him as an ancestor under his Cymric name Macsen Wledig), and, rather oddly, at this period metalwork associated with Rome's regular army is only found south of a line roughly from the Severn estuary to Yorkshire, which may suggest a strategic withdrawal. It is also possible that Saxon mercenaries were introduced into Britain around this time (Rome's central government could not afford to fund mercenaries itself), at least if the *superbus tyrannus* ('proud tyrant') of Gildas' *On the Ruin and Conquest of Britain* refers to Magnus Maximus and not the semi-legendary Vortigern ('High King') whose rule began in 426 and resulted in the establishment of the royal house of Gwynedd (if this is fact and not later legend). The presence of the mercenaries in the south-east zone may be archaeologically visible in the

---

7 Zosimus, *New History* 5.12.1, tr. Ridley, R. T., op. cit.

distribution of distinctive belt-buckles that were used as military status-badges.

So, on behalf of Honorius, Stilicho moved in and checked the seaborne invasions into Britain in 396–398, although his success was probably less spectacular than Claudian suggests when he puts these words into the mouth of Britannia:

> Next spoke Britannia, veiled with the skin of a wild beast of Caledonia, her cheeks tattooed, her blue cloak sweeping over her footprints like the surge of Ocean: 'I too,' she said, 'when neighbouring tribes were destroying me – I too was fortified by Stilicho, when the Scotti set all Ireland astir, and [the sea] frothed with the enemy's oars. His was the care which ensured I should fear not the spears of the Scotti, nor tremble at the Picti, nor watch all along my shore for the arrival of the Saxons with the shifting winds.'[8]

Claudian also tells us that the Eastern court made Alaric their *Magister Utriusque Militiae* in 399. Crucially, this allowed Alaric access to supplies via legitimate Roman military channels. Yet at the same time the Eastern court was not without its problems. Eutropius had done well against some Huns invading Asia Minor and had been elevated to the rank of *Patricius* (the Empire's senior honorific title) and made Consul in 399, but the Gothic *Comes* Tribigild had also rebelled and caused disturbances in the same region.

Eutropius detailed Gaïnas to sort Tribigild out, but instead he made a pact with his fellow Goth and also got Arcadius to dismiss and then execute Eutropius. Gaïnas' ascendancy was short-lived, though. His attempts to impose himself by military force backfired in the summer of 400. He occupied Constantinople, but when he demanded a Catholic church for his Arians he was opposed by Ioannes Khrysostomos (John Chrysostom),

---

8   Claudian, *de Consulatu Stilichonis*, 2.250 ff., tr. in Mann, J. C. and Penman, R. G. (eds), op. cit.

the Patriarch of Constantinople, and the people of the city slaughtered 7 000 of his Gothic troops. Arcadius used Fravitta, another Goth who was *Magister Militum per Orientem*, to subdue the remainder of Gaïnas' troops, and the fugitive Gaïnas himself was killed by a Hun called Uldin or Uldes (the first named Hunnic leader that we know of). January 401 saw his severed head paraded through Constantinople, and in the same month Aelia Eudoxia, who was becoming more and more the political mistress of the East, was elevated to *Augusta*. Fravitta, however, was murdered shortly after his success. Public opinion was turning decidedly anti-Gothic.

This situation affected Alaric badly. His standing under Rufinus, Eutropius and his fellow Goth Gaïnas was undermined by the summer uprising of 400, and regime change at Constantinople may have meant he lost his military command. This in turn meant he was deprived of official resources to feed and pay his men. So he invaded Italy late in 401. Stilicho was not expecting this. He was currently sorting out frontier issues in Raetia, where a Gothic king called Radagaisus had violated the Empire's borders. The Western court relocated to Ravenna, which was better fortified than Mediolanum, but their fears were allayed when Stilicho managed to hold Alaric off in battles fought at Pollentia (modern Pollenzo) on Easter Day 402, where Alaric's wife and family were taken prisoner, and some months later near Verona.

The decisiveness of Stilicho's victories is often overplayed, particularly by the coinage, which shows Honorius trampling a Goth, and by Claudian: Stilicho was not in a position to destroy Alaric at this stage, and instead he probably returned Alaric's family and let the Goths withdraw to Pannonia. Alaric himself drops off our sources' radar until 405, and it remains unclear whether he held an official command or acted independently. For his part Stilicho altered his strategy and started using Goths as his allies as he attempted to wrest Illyricum away from the Eastern Empire. The Goths eventually moved back to their former possessions in Epirus, which put pressure on Thessalonica.

For Stilicho's nineteen-year-old boss Honorius, it was celebration time. His generalissimo's successes against Alaric called for a triumph and in 404 as he rode into Rome. It was a glittering occasion. Claudian said that the women of Rome ogled the bejewelled Honorius, who was as handsome as the god Bacchus with his rosy cheeks and fine shoulders:

> The roar of the adoring multitude [. . .] rises up like thunder from the hollow bowl of the arena, reverberating round the seven hills to echo back as one the name 'Honorius'.[9]

The Emperor was careful to pay due deference to the Senate and their pagan sympathies: they still had some power and influence, both in the minds of the people and in terms of the constitution, and although Honorius was Christian, he nevertheless poured a libation to river god Tiber. It may have been just a gesture, but it was not an empty one.

It is entirely understandable that Stilicho's focus on internal politics made him pay less attention to the barbarians outside the Empire than he should have done. Now, any future plans that he might have been formulating had instantly to be put on hold, because Radagaisus reappeared on the scene, leading an army that his contemporaries numbered at 200 000 or even 400 000. His position might have come under threat in the face of the dominance of the Huns, and he was probably seeking either a safe haven in the Empire or a swift military success that would generate enough prestige and booty to reassert his position in *barbaricum*. Either way, he was disappointed: Stilicho deployed thirty units of the Roman field army, plus some allied Huns and Alani, surrounded him near Ticinum in Liguria, and captured and executed him on 23 August 406. Some 12 000 of Radagaisus' warriors were drafted into the Roman

---

9   Claudian, *Panegyric on Honorius' 6th Consulship* 611 ff., tr. Platnauer, M., *Claudian with an English Translation by Maurice Platnauer*, vol. 2, London: Heinemann, 1921.

army, and so many others were enslaved that the price of slaves in Italy plummeted.

No sooner had Stilicho made his triumphant return to Ravenna than he was apprised of a series of usurpations in Britain. Two Britons, Marcus and Gratianus, had been raised to the purple only to be assassinated in swift succession before the army elected a soldier called Flavius Claudius Constantinus (Constantine III). This was possibly a response to the lack of protection that the province was receiving from the central authorities, but it soon became more than a local issue. Channelling his more illustrious namesake, who had also been proclaimed in Britain, he renamed his sons Constans and Julian, and then took the decision to sacrifice Britain in order to save Gaul.

The effect of Constantine III's withdrawal of the Roman army from Britain can be seen from a letter written by Honorius a few years later, in 410 (if its reference to the people of *Brittia* is indeed to Britannia, and not Bruttium in Italy, and if Zosimus has not confused Bolonia in Italy with Boulogne in Gaul, both of which were called Bononia by then), which tersely instructs its inhabitants to see to their own defence: the raising of local forces would not be considered an act of rebellion. But with no Counts, Dukes, *vicarii*, governors or generals left, there was little that they could do. So, letter or no letter, the Britons ejected the Empire's officials and ruled themselves. But the island was denuded of its field army because Constantine III had taken it across the Channel to confront yet another barbarian menace, which historians call 'The Great Invasion'.

On New Year's Eve 405,[10] an enormous force of Silingi and Hasdingi Vandals (from Silesia in modern Poland, and the border with Dacia respectively), Suevi and Alani had crossed the Rhine. Gibbon propagated a myth that they crossed the

---

10   There is dispute over the date: 31/12/406 is also given: Prosper of Aquitaine's *Chronicle* can be read either way; Zosimus implies it was 31/12/405; Orosius says the attack happened in 408. See Kulikowski, M., 'Barbarians in Gaul, usurpers in Britain', *Britannia* 31 (2000), 325–45.

river when it was frozen, although no ancient source corroborates this. The Franks put up some stiff resistance and slew the Vandal king, but were unable to hold out. The Christian Bishop Orientius later wrote that 'all of Gaul smoked as a single funeral pyre'.[11] As the invaders swept onwards (their itinerary is not clear, but Moguntiacum, Borbetomagus (modern Worms), Remi (Reims) and Treveri were all overrun – see Map 8), the British army stepped in. Constantine III secured most of Gaul and then won over Spain. Honorius' relatives Didymus and Verenianus tried to dislodge him from Spain, but Constantine III's general Gerontius defeated, captured and executed them, and Constantine III's son Constans was placed in charge there.

For once Stilicho acted too slowly. In 408 he dispatched a Gothic officer called Sarus to stop Constantine III. However, choosing Sarus was an inexplicably bad decision, and despite some initial success he soon retreated back to Italy, while Constantine III took the area around Arelate (modern Arles). Constantine III would subsequently seek recognition from Honorius, who would send him an imperial robe – an unequivocal acknowledgement that he was indeed his fellow Emperor.

Alaric suffered a temporary crisis when his daughter Maria died, thereby severing his familial ties with Honorius (she had married the Emperor in *c.*398), but a swiftly arranged wedding between the Emperor and Maria's sister Thermantia put things back on track. Alaric saw other opportunities too. He vacated Epirus and moved to Noricum, which gave him two good options: he could menace Italy, with or without Constantine III's collaboration; or he could block the Alpine passes and keep Constantine III out. From this position of strength Alaric demanded an exorbitant 4 000 pounds of gold for 'services rendered' in Illyricum, and sought permission to take his army into Pannonia, which would presumably have become a Gothic homeland. Honorius remained intransigent, though, and the Senators at Rome, who would be the ones to find the gold,

---

11   Orientius, *Commonitorium* 2. 184, tr. Kershaw, S.

initially voted to resist. Stilicho persuaded them otherwise, however, leading Lampadius famously to shout, 'That is not peace, but a bargain of servitude!' before taking refuge in a church.[12]

Just to complicate matters, the Eastern Emperor Arcadius died on 1 May 408, leaving Honorius' seven-year-old nephew, Theodosius II, as successor. Stilicho saw the new situation in the East as a good opportunity to assert his authority over the Balkan region. So he made a deal with Alaric in which Alaric would attack Constantine III, freeing himself up to take control of the succession in the East. However, Stilicho's plans all came crashing down when Honorius' *Magister Officiorum*, the eunuch Olympius, started falsely to allege that Stilicho was plotting to overthrow Theodosius II and to install his own son, Eucherius, in his stead. In fairness, Stilicho had already made some moves in this direction by betrothing Eucherius to Arcadius and Honorius' half-sister Galla Placidia, but the troops at Ticinum (modern Pavia) swallowed Olympius' extreme conspiracy theory and slaughtered a number of Stilicho's supporters. Stilicho headed for Ravenna, but when Sarus defected to Olympius and massacred his Hunnic bodyguards in a night-time stealth attack, he could only flee and take refuge in a church in Ravenna. At daybreak on 22 August 408 Olympius' henchmen, led by Heraclianus, caught up with him. There, Stilicho was lured out with a promise that he was only going to be arrested, and was promptly executed.

Olympius immediately instigated a reign of anti-Stilicho terror: senior figures in the administration were publicly tortured in Ravenna to try to make them confess that Stilicho had been plotting to overthrow Honorius, and when they didn't they were clubbed to death; Honorius divorced Thermantia and sent her back to her mother Serena in Rome; Stilicho's son, Eucherius, still engaged to the Emperor's half-sister Galla Placidia, was

---

12 Zosimus, *New History* 5.29.9, tr. Kershaw, S. The Latin is elegant: *non est ista pax sed pactio servitutis.*

assassinated; Stilicho's brother-in-law Bathanarius was relieved of his post as commander of Africa, which was reassigned to Heraclianus; and Honorius' soldiers proceeded to massacre thousands of barbarian men, women and children in Italy, which induced some 30 000 survivors to look to Alaric for protection and vengeance.

The Sack of Rome (410)

Alaric had an axe to grind. He had no formal command, his legitimacy was shaky, and his 4 000 pounds of gold was still unpaid. So once more he struck camp and headed for Italy. But this time his itinerary took him to Rome itself. The Senate panicked. They accused Stilicho's widow Serena of having treacherous contact with Alaric, and following a meeting of the Senate in late 408, they asked her cousin and former foster daughter Galla Placidia, who was also the ex-fiancée of Serena's son Eucherius, to endorse a death sentence. She did.

However, strangling Serena was not the solution: Alaric was strangling Rome. By October 408, he had the city surrounded and controlled Portus at the Tiber mouth. Rome was starving. Jerome relates that new mothers had to eat their newborn babies, 'so that the belly received again what a short time before it had given forth',[13] and with famine came disease. The pagans blamed the Christians for this: Rome had ruled the universe when the old deities were honoured, but now Christianity had supplanted them, and just look at what had happened. Honorius was still at Ravenna, and so the Roman Senate held crisis talks and decided to negotiate. But their two envoys, one of whom, Ioannes, was on amicable terms with Alaric, got the tone completely wrong. They told him that Rome was indeed ready to make peace, but she was also well prepared for war, and not afraid of Goths. Alaric had the perfect riposte:

---

13   Jerome, *Letter to Principia* 1.121, tr. in Moorhead, S. and Stuttard, D., op. cit., p. 97.

He said that he would not end the siege unless he got all the gold in the city; and all the silver too; not to mention any movable property that there might be in Rome; and all the barbarian slaves. When one of the ambassadors asked, 'If you take all this, what will you leave us?', Alaric replied, 'your lives'.[14]

The Senators backed down.

Alaric said he was prepared to accept 5 000 pounds of gold, 30 000 pounds of silver, 4 000 silk tunics, 3 000 scarlet-dyed skins and 3 000 pounds of pepper, and a Senator named Palladius tried to work out how much each Senator should contribute. But he couldn't balance the books and it came to the point where he had to order the melting down of gold and silver statues of the gods. This was traumatic, particularly the destruction of the statue of *Virtus* (Manliness/Courage):

When it was taken away, such bravery and virtue as the Romans possessed went with it.[15]

Meanwhile, the Senate sent envoys to Ravenna to tell Honorius what was happening, and Alaric added an offer of his own: if Honorius would ratify the treaty, give him land and provide hostages, the Goths would not just make peace, but join with Rome against her enemies. Honorius said that he accepted the terms, and Alaric was stupid enough to believe him.

Alaric granted a seventy-two-hour suspension of hostilities, but the hostages never arrived. On the contrary, news filtered through of grand celebrations at Ravenna in honour of Honorius' eighth consulship. The Senate dispatched three of its most accomplished diplomats, including a certain Priscus Attalus, to Ravenna to discover what was going on, and to get Honorius to give Alaric the land and the hostages. Unfortunately, Olympius

---

14   Zosimus, *New History* 5.40.3, tr. Ridley, R. T, op. cit.
15   Ibid. 5.41.7.

refused to endorse any deal that had the slightest hint of his old nemesis Stilicho's policy of cooperation with Alaric, and so Honorius didn't deliver. Instead, he sent the ambassadors back, having appointed one of them, Caecilianus, as Prefect of Rome, and made Priscus Attalus *Comes Sacrarum Largitionum* (Finance Minister). He also summoned five legions from Dalmatia to go to Rome under a commander named Valens, who naively allowed his force to be ambushed by Alaric: 6 000 soldiers set out; just 100, including Valens and Priscus Attalus, made it to Rome.

The Senate could hardly believe what had happened. They sent a second deputation to Honorius, which included Pope Innocent I and probably Priscus Attalus as well, and needed special permission and an escort from Alaric to make the journey. By now, though, the court at Ravenna was in chaos, a situation that wasn't helped by the fact that Alaric's brother-in-law Ataulf (Ataulfus to the Romans; Athavulf , 'Noble Wolf', to the Goths) was now in Italy bringing reinforcements. Honorius mobilized the Italian garrisons and dispatched Olympius and 300 Huns to make a pre-emptive strike against Ataulf. The Huns made a successful night raid, but in the cold light of day they realized how heavily outnumbered they were. Returning to Ravenna, Olympius knew his days were numbered, and so he fled to Dalmatia.

At Ravenna, Honorius kept hold of Pope Innocent I, but sent Priscus Attalus back to Rome, having promoted him to *Praefectus Urbis* and also appointed a pagan barbarian called Generid to the military command in Dalmatia and the provinces northeast of the Alps. At this point, though, Honorius was faced with a mutiny by his garrison, which left Ravenna cut off by both land and sea. But instead of dealing with the problem directly, Honorius hid. Into the breach stepped a character called Iovius, who dealt with the mutinous troops and sought ratification of the treaty with Alaric. The Goth and his brother-in-law said no to Iovius' offer of a meeting at Ravenna, but were happy to convene at Ariminum (modern Rimini). Alaric again asked for money and a homeland in Histria and Venetia as well as Dalmatia and the two Noricums (see Map 6). Unfortunately, Iovius also claimed that Alaric wanted Stilicho's title of *Magister Utriusque Militiae*, but the court at Ravenna did not want to be reminded of Stilicho, and they handled the negotiations in an incredibly crass way. Iovius was in Alaric's tent when their response was read out: under no circumstances would Honorius bestow any honour whatsoever on Alaric.

With relations at a very low ebb, Iovius slunk back to Ravenna and promised never to make peace with Alaric. Alaric headed for Rome, but then thought twice about it. Peace and a homeland were still his preferred options, and he was prepared to modify his demands. He would settle for just

the two Noricums, which lie at the furthest reaches of the Danube for they are regularly under attack and pay little in the way of tax. In addition, he would be content with however much corn the Emperor saw fit to give him on an annual basis. Forget about the gold; instead there would be friendship and military alliance between Alaric and the Romans.[16]

Rome's future might have been very different had Iovius not stuck to his promise. Alaric did go to Rome, where he arranged to be invited into the city and to address the Senate. His plan was simple. He would appoint the next Emperor of the West, for which there was a shortlist of one: Priscus Attalus. On 4 November 409 the new Augustus delegated the day-to-day running of the State to the Senate, and control of the army to Alaric as *Magister Utriusque Militiae*, with Ataulf as commander of the household cavalry. As an indication of the new regime's ambitions, Attalus Priscus' new coins showed the personified Rome seated on a throne holding Victory on a globe, and carried the legend *INVICTA ROMA AETERNA* ('Unconquerable Eternal Rome').

---

16 Ibid. 5.50.2–3.

If Rome were to remain unconquerable she would need grain, but the supply from Africa was being controlled by Honorius' ruthless henchman Heraclianus. Alaric wanted to send an army to eliminate him once and for all, but instead Priscus Attalus sent an envoy called Constans to open negotiations at Carthage.

Meanwhile, Alaric and Priscus Attalus marched to Ariminum, where Iovius made a proposal on Honorius' behalf: Priscus Attalus could become co-Augustus. But with Constantine III already strutting about in the purple robe that Honorius had sent him the previous year, a triple-Emperor solution was not an option. Instead, Priscus Attalus made Honorius an offer: he could step down, retire to wherever he liked, and live like an Emperor for the rest of his days. However, Iovius put a spanner in the works by inserting the condition that, prior to his exile, Honorius should be symbolically mutilated in one limb, most likely his right hand, the fingers of which were usually extended in a gesture symbolizing his legitimacy when any Emperor spoke. This was not acceptable to Priscus Attalus, who said that it was not customary to mutilate an Emperor who had resigned willingly, any more than it was to Honorius. However, while Honorius was weighing up the pros and cons of a life of left-handed leisure, a fleet from the East arrived surreptitiously in Ravenna carrying about 4 000 troops that had been sent from Constantinople by Honorius' nephew Theodosius II. But for Iovius, this was too little too late. He defected to Priscus Attalus, and was replaced by the eunuch Eusebius, who was Honorius' *Praepositus Sacri Cubiculi*. Eusebius was quickly supplanted by the general Allobichus, who had Eusebius clubbed to death in Honorius' presence.

Any benefit that this may have brought to Alaric was quickly offset by news of the abject failure of Constans' trip to Africa: he had been killed, and Heraclianus had imposed a grain embargo on Rome. So Alaric and Iovius decamped to Rome, where an emergency meeting of the Senate decided in favour of Priscus Attalus' proposal that a Roman army should be sent to

Africa, rather than a Gothic one as Iovius had suggested. Alaric was livid. He vented his wrath on Priscus Attalus' cavalry commander Valens, who was executed for treason, and it is unlikely that he was surprised when the African expeditionary force was defeated. At this point Alaric raised the siege of Ravenna, which seemed futile, while Honorius exploited the contrast between Heraclianus' bounty and Attalus' food shortages to win over soldiers to his side. The people of Rome were reduced to seeking the legalization of cannibalism: 'Put a price on human flesh!' they chanted.[17]

Alaric badly needed to get rid of Priscus Attalus. He started to negotiate with Honorius, and the two came to an agreement to end the hostilities. Alaric took Attalus Priscus with him to the signing ceremony, plus Honorius' half-sister Galla Placidia as insurance, and when the two sides convened outside Ravenna Alaric's men relieved Attalus Priscus of his imperial regalia, and duly delivered them to Honorius. Peace should have broken out at this point, but there were other players who had vested interests in it not doing so. One such person was Sarus, the Goth who had betrayed Stilicho, who was now in Ravenna. He loathed Alaric, and just as the negotiations were being wrapped up he attacked his camp with 300 warriors. Alaric assumed that this was Honorius' doing. His dream of a Gothic homeland had turned into a diplomatic nightmare. He decided to destroy Rome.

On 24 August 410 Alaric's Goths entered the Eternal City. The Romans traced their ancestry back to the mythical Trojans, and now they experienced the sack of Troy all over again. According to Procopius, the 'Trojan Horse' of 410 was either a group of 300 of Alaric's finest warriors who dressed up as slaves, infiltrated the city, and opened the Salarian gate, or it was a woman called Proba, from the well-to-do family of the Anicii, who was motivated by pity for Rome's starving populace. If we believe some Christian sources (Alaric and his Goths were

---

17   Ibid. 5.6.11.

Christian), the city was sacked in a gentle and caring sort of way: God had sanctioned the capture of Rome; the Goths were doing His will; so they must be seen to be acting within God's laws. The contemporary historian Orosius saw the hand of God at work, describing a storm in which the most famous places in the city, even though they had been spared by the Goths, were destroyed by thunderbolts,[18] and certainly some of Rome's most famous landmarks, like the imperial palaces and the mausoleums of Augustus and Hadrian, were devastated, although by human agency. But we are also told that Alaric ordered that anyone sheltering in a church was to be spared, and individual stories of clemency abound, such as that of the treatment of an old nun who was in possession of the sacred vessels of the apostle Peter. Rather than suffering rape and pillage, she became the focus of a festive, hymn-singing procession to St Peter's that was protected by the merciful Goths and escalated into a huge Romano-Gothic carnival.

On the other hand, a radically different story probably gives a more accurate picture of the sack. A wealthy octogenarian lady called Marcella, who had dedicated her life to God, given away most of her inherited wealth and founded what is sometimes regarded as the first convent in the history of the Church, saw her institution violated by the Goths. A letter written by St Jerome to Marcella's pupil Principia, who was there at the time, relives the terror for her:

> They say that, when the soldiers burst into her house, she received them with equanimity. When asked for the gold and hidden treasure, she pointed to her old worn tunic as a sign of her poverty. But they did not believe that she had really chosen the path of poverty. They say that, even when she was being beaten with clubs and whips, she felt no pain, but lay face down before them; and begged through her tears that you, Principia, might not be taken from her; nor that your

---

18   Orosius, *History Against the Pagans* 7.39.

youth might mean you would suffer what her old age meant that she had no need to fear. Christ softened their hard hearts and, amidst those bloodstained swords, piety found a place. The barbarians escorted both you and Marcella to the Basilica of the Blessed Paul, that it might be your place of refuge, or your tomb.[19]

Marcella died of her injuries in Principia's arms, just one victim of innumerable atrocities. Even St Augustine writes of Romans being put to death in a 'hideous variety of cruel ways', bodies left unburied in the streets, arson, pillage, rape, people-trafficking and enslavement.[20] Jerome tells of a woman who fell into the hands of the notorious Heraclianus:

To him, nothing was sweeter than wine or money. He claimed to serve the meekest emperor [Honorius], while being himself the cruellest of all tyrants [. . .] 'From mothers' arms he snatched their daughters-in-law betrothed', and sold noble girls in marriage to Syrian businessmen – the most grasping of any in the human race.[21]

Both pagans and Christians reflected on the events. For the former, it was obvious that Rome fell because she had spurned her old gods, who reciprocated by spurning her. St Augustine explained their response:

If Rome had not been saved by its gods, it is because they are no longer there; as long as they were there, they kept the city safe.[22]

---

19   Jerome, *Letter to Principia* 13, tr. in Moorhead, S. and Stuttard, D., op. cit., p. 129 ff.
20   Augustine, *City of God* 1.7 ff., tr. Dods, M., in Schaff, P., *The Nicene and Post-Nicene Fathers of the Christian Church, First Series, Vol. 2,* Edinburgh: T & T Clark, 1890.
21   Jerome, *Letter to Demetrias*, 7, tr. in Moorhead, S. and Stuttard, D., op. cit., p. 129 ff. The quotation comes from Virgil, *Aeneid* 10.79.
22   Augustine, *Sermon* 296.

But Augustine, who had been Bishop of Hippo (modern Bone in Algeria) since 395, also wrestled with the problem that these events posed for Christians: Rome was now a Christian city, so where was God when it was sacked? And, what's more, sacked by Christians. His answer was expounded in his monumental *De Civitate Dei (City of God)*, written between 413 and 426.

Neither was it just Goth v Roman or pagan v Christian. The inhabitants of Rome pursued old personal vendettas amidst the chaos. All in all it had been an apocalyptic event. Jerome reflected:

> Who could believe that after being raised up by victories over the whole world Rome should come crashing down, and become at once the mother and the grave of her peoples?[23]

Honorius could not get his head round what had happened. A story grew up that when one of his eunuchs, presumably the keeper of his poultry, told him that Rome was no more, he made a famously misguided comment:

> 'And yet it has just eaten from my hands!' For he had a very large cock, Rome by name; and the eunuch comprehending his words said that it was the city of Rome which had perished at the hands of Alaric.[24]

Honorius then followed it up with an even more notorious quip, to the effect of, 'Oh, that's a relief!'

---

23 Jerome, *In Ezekiel*, III *Praef.*, tr. in Ward-Perkins, B., *The Fall of Rome and the End of Civilization*, Oxford: Oxford University Press, 2005, p. 28.
24 Procopius, *History of the Wars of Justinian* 3.2.26, tr. Dewing, H. B., in *Procopius with an English Translation by H. B. Dewing in Six Volumes, II, History of the Wars, Books III and IV*, London: Heinemann, 1916.

The Death of Alaric

From Alaric's perspective he had undoubtedly traumatized most of the Roman world by sacking Rome, but it had done him very little good politically. Having spent three days in the city, he moved on: there were no grain supplies coming in from Africa, so he decided to go there to get them. With a convoy that also included Galla Placidia and Attalus Priscus he moved south into Campania and thence to Rhegium at the toe of Italy, but rough seas prevented him crossing to Sicily, and at that point he became seriously ill. With their leader confined to a wagon, the Goths headed north, but early in 411, at Consentia in Bruttium, Alaric died.

> His people mourned him with the greatest devotion. Near the city of Consentia, the life-giving waters of the River Busentus tumble down from the foot of the mountain. After diverting the river from its course, his people gathered a workforce of captives [. . .] to dig a grave for Alaric in the middle of the river bed. At the centre of this pit, they buried their leader, surrounded by many treasures. Then they turned back the waters of the river to flow along its old course. So that no one should ever know exactly where Alaric was buried, they killed everyone who had dug his grave.[25]

Nobody has found Alaric's tomb, and no one has dug up the treasure.

---

25   Jordanes, *Getica* 30.158, tr. Davis, W. S., *Readings in Ancient History, Illustrative Extracts from the Sources, II, Rome and the West*, Boston, New York and Chicago: Allyn and Bacon, 1913.

17

Roman Empresses, Barbarian Kings
(411–450)

> *It was obvious to everyone that, if the Roman Empire had
> shunned luxury and embraced war, there was nothing in all
> the world it could not have conquered and enslaved. But God
> has infected man's nature with a lethal characteristic, like the
> poisonous gall in a lobster or thorns upon a rose.*
>
> Eunapius, 55.5–9[1]

Good Thing/Bad Thing; Fall/Transformation

By giving his magnum opus the brilliant title *The History of the
Decline and Fall of the Roman Empire*, Edward Gibbon exerted
a huge influence on the way Roman history would be perceived.
Rome's historical trajectory could become a warning, or a
model, or both, although there is no 'one size fits all' response
to the events that unfolded after the death of Alaric the Goth.
There are those who regard the demise of the Roman Empire
as 'a Bad Thing', synonymous with the end of education, liter-
acy, high-quality architecture, sophisticated economics and
the rule of written law; but conversely there are those who see
it as 'a Good Thing', turning a decadent, effete, corrupt, slave-
owning autocracy into a manly proto-democracy of free
peasants and ultimately a world in which human beings

---

1   Tr. Blockley, R. C., *The Fragmentary Classicising Historians of the Later Roman
Empire: Eunapius, Olympiodorus, Priscus and Malchus*, Liverpool: Cairns, 1983.

attained a much higher degree of equality. Current academic trends reflect current social values, and both Gibbon's idea of the 'Fall of the Roman Empire' and, to a degree, the idea of 'the barbarian invasions' have become extremely unfashionable. Academics prefer fifty shades of grey to black-and-white distinctions, and much discussion centres on the *transformation* of the Roman *world*, rather than the *fall* of the Roman *Empire*. Yet whether you subscribe to the 'transformation thesis' or not, and however you answer the question, 'Did Rome really fall?', there is no doubting that the mere idea that it might have done still has a deep resonance: *Are We Rome? The Fall of an Empire and the Fate of America* is one recent book title that plugs into the way that Roman history can fire the imagination and instil fear.[2]

Anyone seeking a single cause for the downfall/transformation of Rome will probably be disappointed, and even fixing a date can be problematical, since the process could easily be extended beyond 476, after which there were no more Roman Emperors in the West, until Mehmet II the Conqueror's sack of Constantinople in 1453. There is enormous disagreement as to whether Rome was assassinated, (accidently) committed suicide, or died at all, and literally hundreds of 'causes of death' have been put forward: environmental problems, disease, decadence, dysgenic breeding, war, slavery, manpower shortages, lead poisoning from the pipes, impotence caused by hot water in the baths, 'race-suicide', Christianity, pacifism, economic stagnation, conflicts between discipline and liberty, the centralization of power, the problems of dynastic succession, migrants forcibly stripping Rome of her tax base, inept foreign policy and inadequate frontier defence represent just a small sample of the topics presented for discussion.[3]

---

2   Murphy, C., *Are We Rome? The Fall of an Empire and the Fate of America*, Boston and New York: Mariner Books, 2008.

3   See Demandt, A., *Der Fall Roms*, Beck: Munich, 1984, whose last page gives a list of over two hundred reasons that have been suggested to explain Rome's demise.

The Post-Alaric Aftershocks

As the waters of the River Busentus closed over Alaric's grave in 411, his brother-in-law Ataulf assumed the leadership of the Goths and ran amok in Italy:

> Like a plague of locusts, [he] stripped all Italy bare of anything that still remained, not merely private wealth, but public too; and there was nothing that Honorius could do to stop him.[4]

Nevertheless, Honorius would not capitulate, and so early in 412 Ataulf changed his approach and marched into Gaul.

The Gallic situation was very unsettled. The Suevi, Vandals and Alani who crossed the Rhine in 405/6[5] had moved through the province into Spain, which itself was trying to decide whether to back Constantine III or stay loyal to Rome. Initially it had opted for Constantine III, but his forces had got embroiled in some convoluted local power struggles and he had been forced to dispatch a delegation to Spain to sort out the situation. Unfortunately, his general Gerontius, who commanded the occupying forces, had misread Constantine III's intentions: suspecting his own life to be in danger, he had 'retaliated' by proclaiming his follower (or possibly his son) Maximus as Augustus. These rebels had taken the offensive and killed Constantine III's son Constans in the process in late 410/early 411, although, with some help from Geoffrey of Monmouth's *History of the Kings of Britain*, Constans found his way into medieval British legend as the brother of King Arthur's father Uther Pendragon and himself King of Britannia, albeit as a puppet of Vortigern.

For their part, once they had perpetrated the requisite amount of devastation, the Vandals, Suevi and Alani had divided the Spanish provinces between themselves by lot. Gerontius

---

4   Jordanes, *Getica* 31.159, tr. Davis, W. S., op. cit.
5   See above, p. 369 f.

and Maximus had effectively acknowledged this barbarian acquisition of political control over Roman territory, and Orosius makes the startling assertion that some Romans preferred to live in poor freedom under the barbarians than as subjects of Roman taxation.

While this was going on, Constantine III was holed up in Arelate, where, as a result of Gerontius' defection, he found himself under siege in about May 411. Then Honorius' general Flavius Constantius (who was nothing to do with the Emperors Constantius I and II) had arrived on the scene with a much larger army. From Honorius' perspective, Maximus was just as much a usurper as Constantine III, and if he wanted to get rid of the latter, he would have to deal with the former. Sandwiched between two hostile armies, Gerontius and Maximus were deserted by their own men and hounded into Spain by Honorius'. Maximus escaped into historical obscurity (unless he is the same Maximus who was paraded in chains at Honorius' thirtieth-year celebrations in 422), while Gerontius was run to ground in a fortified house with his wife Nunchia and a faithful Alan *thegn*. Having beheaded his wife and the Alan at their request, Gerontius failed three times to kill himself with his own sword, and so used a dagger instead.

None of this had really helped Constantine III, however. In fact, things had got even worse, because Iovinus, a Gallo-Roman Senator, had been proclaimed Emperor at Moguntiacum with the backing of the kings of the Burgundiones and Alani in 411. With the situation looking utterly bleak, Constantine III had doffed the purple robes that Honorius had once sent him, become a monk, and taken refuge in a church. Sadly for him, this proved a futile gesture: he and his son Julian were apprehended and sent off to Ravenna, but they were dead before they got there. Constantine III's head received rather more than a monk's tonsure, and ended up displayed alongside Constans' on the walls of Carthage.

This, then, was the situation that Ataulf walked into in Gaul in 412. On Priscus Attalus' advice, he backed the man that he thought would be the winner: Iovinus. But not for long. Ataulf discovered that his old adversary Sarus, the wrecker of the peace talks with Alaric, had now fallen out with Honorius and was about to join up with Iovinus. Ataulf couldn't resist the opportunity for vengeance, so he waylaid Sarus' twenty-eight men with 10 000 of his own. The pursuit ended with Sarus being lassoed and killed. This duly alienated Iovinus, who proclaimed his brother Sebastian as co-Emperor without seeking Ataulf's approval. So the Goth simply switched his allegiance to Honorius. According to St Jerome, Ataulf 'strove to turn his back on war and to promote peace',[6] although that clearly did not preclude defeating and capturing Iovinus in battle at Valentia in 413. His head was sent to Carthage where it made a neat trio with those of Constantine III and Constans.

If the severed heads of Honorius' enemies were intended to act as a deterrent, they failed. As the controller of the African grain supply, Heraclianus' loyalty had been crucial to Honorius' survival, but now Flavius Constantius had started to purge Stilicho's enemies. The eunuch Olympius had already had his ears lopped off before being clubbed to death, and the fact that Heraclianus was Stilicho's killer put him in a dangerous position. So he cut off Italy's grain before invading the peninsula in 413. The expedition soon ended in failure and Heraclianus' death, but its ramifications were significant and centred on a woman who becomes one of the key figures of the period: Galla Placidia (see Genealogy Table 6).

Galla Placidia

Judging by images on coins, Galla Placidia possessed all the qualities that a Roman Empress should: good looks, charisma and expensive tastes in clothes, while Jordanes writes of her 'nobility, beauty and chaste purity'.[7] Ataulf was still holding her

---

6   Quoted by Orosius, *Histories Against the Pagans* 7.43.4 ff., tr. Kershaw, S.
7   Jordanes, *Getica* 31.160, Cf. Orosius 7.40.2; 7.43.

hostage, but now he was asked to return her. Flavius Constantius tried to exert some extra leverage by withholding grain supplies to the Goths, whereupon Ataulf went on the warpath in southern Gaul. Clearly Galla Placidia was going nowhere. Flavius Constantius, meanwhile, was granted all of Heraclianus' property in Africa and a consulship, but all the honours and riches in the world could not assuage his jealousy when Ataulf married his prisoner at (probably) Narbo (modern Narbonne) in January 414. The wedding was astonishing, and his gifts to her included fifty good-looking youths clad in silk, each bearing plates laden with gold and with jewels from Alaric's sack of Rome. Priscus Attalus sang the epithalamium.

Flavius Constantius still lusted after Ataulf's bride and all her potential fringe benefits. He succeeded in souring the relationship between Ataulf and Honorius, who authorized him to blockade Gaul's Mediterranean ports. Ataulf's response was to elevate Priscus Attalus to the purple for a second, but ultimately equally unsuccessful, time. The Goths abandoned Priscus Attalus once Flavius Constantius got control of Gaul, and after his capture he was displayed in what turned out to be the last triumph ever celebrated in Rome:

> Honorius ordered Attalus to stand on the first step of the tribunal [. . .] He cut off two fingers from his right hand, the [thumb?] and forefinger. Then he banished him to the island of Lipara, doing nothing more to harm him, but rather ensuring that he had all the necessities of life.[8]

Priscus Attalus didn't get to enjoy his island life for long. He died in 415, by which time Ataulf had also expired. Flavius Constantius had forced the Goth to cross the Pyrenees into

---

8   Philostorgius, *Ecclesiastical History* 12.5.2, tr. Walford, E., *The Ecclesiastical History of Sozomen: comprising a history of the church from AD 324 to AD 440 translated from the Greek: with a memoir of the author. Also, the Ecclesiastical history of Philostorgius as epitomized by Photius, Patriarch of Constantinople; translated by Edward Walford,* London : Henry G. Bohn, 1855. Cf. Orosius 7.42.10.

Spain, where he took Barcino (modern Barcelona), but Ataulf must still have felt confident for the future, since Galla Placidia had given birth to a son whom they called Theodosius after his mother's father. Since Honorius was childless, this made Ataulf the sire of the potential heir to the throne of the West. But sadly Theodosius died in infancy (there is no suspicion of foul play), and his father followed shortly afterwards (there is a great deal of suspicion).

Ataulf was assassinated by one of his own men. Jordanes names the perpetrator as Everulf, whom Ataulf habitually mocked for being short, although other sources call him Dubius, motivated by revenge for Ataulf killing his former master who was 'king of a part of the Goths'. This could refer to Ataulf's old enemy Sarus, whose brother Singeric (also rendered Sigeric or Sergeric) emerged as the prime beneficiary:

> Through treachery in force, rather than by lawful succession, Singeric became king. He killed Ataulf's children by his first marriage, tearing them by force from the arms of Bishop Sigesarus. And out of malice against Ataulf, he ordered that his queen, Placidia, be made to walk in front of his horse, with the rest of the prisoners, in a procession of some 12 miles from the city.[9]

Singeric didn't last long, though. He was murdered and replaced by a certain Wallia, and the Goths were again reduced to starvation by Flavius Constantius. This got so bad that the Vandals started selling them grain at the exorbitant rate of one gold *solidus* per *trula* ('spoonful'), and calling them by the derogatory nickname *truli* – 'the Spoonies' – as a result. Now, at last, Galla Placidia was returned to the Roman court, and an indication of her high value is that her ransom was enough wheat to feed a quarter of a million people for about three weeks.

---

9   Olympiodorus, *fr.* 26, tr. Blockley, R. C., op. cit.

As part of the Galla Placidia settlement, Wallia also agreed to provide military service to Honorius, and his first assignment was to campaign against the Alani and Vandal Silingi in Baetica and Lusitania. This he did with some success. In 417 and 418 he harassed the Silingi, killed the Alan King Addax in 418, and forced the survivors to seek refuge with the Hasdingi Vandals in Gallaecia. Flavius Constantius then rewarded Wallia's Goths with a permanent residence, albeit not an independent kingdom, in Aquitania in southern Gaul in 418 or 419. However, Wallia did not live to see the great dream of a Gothic homeland within the Roman Empire realized, since he died a few months after the agreement was made. So it was his successor, Alaric's grandson Theoderic I (also called Theoderid), who saw the arrangements through. From the Roman viewpoint, one major downside of giving up territory to Goths, Suevi, Burgundiones, Alani and Vandals, and abandoning Britain, was that they lost large amounts of tax revenues.

Galla Placidia's return also gave Flavius Constantius the opportunity he had yearned for. He sought her hand in marriage. Unfortunately, his passion was not reciprocated, and one can perhaps see why:

> In public processions, Constantius was sullen and morose. He had bulging eyes, a thick neck, and massive head. When riding, he slumped over his horse's neck, looking shiftily from side to side.[10]

We are told that he was good fun at parties, though. But Gallia Placidia dug her heels in until Honorius had to force her to marry her unwelcome admirer on 1 January 417. Their marriage is portrayed as truly miserable, but it did fulfil one of its most important functions: the couple had two children, a girl called Honoria, and a boy, born in July 419, who would come to rule Rome as Valentinian III. That same year Flavius

---

10 Olympiodorus, *fr.* 23, tr. Blockley, R. C., op. cit.

Constantius held office as Consul for the third time, and in February 421 he became co-Augustus alongside Honorius as Constantius III, while his spouse took the title of Augusta. The Eastern Emperor Theodosius II was unhappy at these promotions and refused to acknowledge Constantius III, who started to plan a campaign against him. But things never got further than that: Constantius III died of pleurisy before the year was out, leaving the Western Empire in better shape than it had been for some time, but also clearing the way for an ugly political aftermath.

In Spain, general Castinus had deployed the Gothic army against the Vandals in Baetica, but when he had all but forced them to surrender he was defeated thanks to some unspecified Gothic treachery. He also had a major disagreement with his co-commander and protégé of Galla Placidia, Bonifacius ('Boniface'), who crossed over to Africa and started to build a power base there. The Augusta, meanwhile, started to become rather too close to her half-brother Honorius for the rumour-mongers' liking. Amid allegations of incest their relationship deteriorated, and by the spring of 423 Galla Placidia and her children found themselves in exile in Constantinople at the court of Theodosius II.

Everything changed, though, on 27 August 423. Shortly after Honorius had celebrated his thirtieth year as Augustus, he died from dropsy (pulmonary edema, perhaps), leaving Galla Placidia's four-year-old son Valentinian III as his heir. The boy was made Augustus on 23 October, but was immediately challenged when John, the *primicerius notariorum* (Chief Palace Notary), declared himself Emperor of the West. John faced robust opposition from Bonifacius in Africa, but could count on the support of Castinus and a general called Flavius Aetius, who allegedly deployed 60 000 Huns (in his youth he had spent time among them as a hostage). Theodosius II rejected John's attempts to reach an accommodation, and in 425 he dispatched a seaborne task force under Ardabur, and a land-based one under Candidianus and Ardabur's son Aspar. When the

Theodosians gained the upper hand, John was betrayed by his troops and duly decapitated at Aquileia; Flavius Aetius persuaded the Huns to return back over the Danube (no doubt sped on their way by a pay-off from Galla Placidia), received a pardon, switched sides and performed sterling work against difficult Goths and Franks for the rest of the 420s; the six-year-old Valentinian III was reinstated as Augustus, and his mother Galla Placidia became one of the world's most powerful women.

The late 420s saw a Vandal revival in Spain (Andalusia is still named after them), to the extent that they were attacking the Balearic Islands and plundering Rome's province of Mauretania Tingitania in North Africa. After their king, Gunderic, died and was succeeded by his brother Gaiseric they embarked on a hugely significant enterprise: in the month of May of some year between 427 and 429[11] Gaiseric organized them into eighty groups of a thousand people, and ferried them across the Strait of Gibraltar into Africa. St Augustine would be one of the high-profile casualties of their advance, killed in the siege of the city of Hippo in 430.

A major incursion of Vandals would naturally have been of great concern to Galla Placidia's African-based supporter Bonifacius, but his main worries centred on the court at Ravenna. Somehow Galla Placidia had been convinced that he was plotting against her, and when he took Flavius Aetius' advice not to obey her orders to return to Italy, this simply confirmed her suspicions. Still, a Gothic commander called Sigisvult managed to smooth things over, which allowed Bonifacius to confront the barbarians. He was defeated, however, and by 434 the Vandals, having also overpowered an Eastern Roman force under Aspar, had been officially granted the two Mauretanias and Numidia.

Meanwhile, the power struggles at Ravenna moved to another level as Flavius Aetius' machinations brought about the death of

---

11 Victor of Vita, *History of the Vandal Persecution* 1.2. The date of the crossing is problematical: see Mathisen, R. W., 'Sigisvult the patrician, Maximinus the Arian and political stratagems in the Western Roman Empire, *c.*425–507,' *Early Medieval Europe* 8 (1999), 177, n. 6.

Galla Placidia's *Magister Militum Praesentalis* Flavius Felix, and his own promotion to *Magister Utriusque Militiae*. To give him his due, Flavius Aetius turned out to be a highly effective commander, but his success provoked a backlash from Bonifacius, who also received support from Aspar. Bonifacius and Flavius Aetius contested a battle near Ariminum in 432 in which the former could have claimed victory, had he not died of his wounds. Flavius Aetius used another awesome force of Huns to expel Boniface's son Sebastian. This effectively gave him total dominance over Galla Placidia and Valentinian III, and from 433 he remained unchallenged as *Magister Utriusque Militiae* until his death twenty-one years later.

Theodosius II, Pulcheria and Eudocia in Constantinople

Flavius Aetius was Emperor of the West in all but name, but almost the opposite has been said of Theodosius II in Constantinople, who 'reigned rather than ruled'[12] from 408 to 450. Orphaned and made Emperor at the age of seven, he was described by Priscus of Panion as an unwarlike, cowardly man who secured peace with cash rather than by force of arms, and whose every action was under the influence of eunuchs.[13]

However, other sources focus on the education he received from his fiercely ascetic, strong-minded, Christian older sister Aelia Pulcheria. In the past, influential Roman women like Livia and her ilk had achieved much of their influence through sex, marriage and their children, but Pulcheria exploited her virginity to gain power:

> The Divine Power which is the guardian of the universe, foresaw that the Emperor would be distinguished by his piety, and therefore determined that Pulcheria, his sister, should be

12   Jones, A. H. M. and Liebeschuetz, W., s.v. 'Theodosius (3) II', in Hornblower, S. and Spawforth, A., *The Oxford Classical Dictionary*, 3rd revised edn., Oxford: Oxford University Press, 2003.
13   Priscus of Panion *fr*. 3.

the protector of him and his government. The princess was not yet fifteen years of age [in 414 when she became Augusta], but had received a mind most wise and divine above her years. She first devoted her virginity to God [. . .] After quietly resuming the care of the State, she governed the Roman Empire excellently and with great orderliness.[14]

It might be closer to the truth to say that Theodosius II's *Praefectus Praetorio* Anthemius ran the show down to 414, followed by the Master of Offices Helion from 414 to 427, but Pulcheria's decision to devote herself to the cult of the Virgin Mary, irrespective of her true religious convictions, was a shrewd political move – any attack on her was by association an attack on the Mother of God – and her influence is noted by contemporary Church historians:

[Theodosius II] made the palace into nothing so much as a monastery (*asketerion*). He and his sisters used to rise at dawn and sing antiphonal hymns to the divinity. He knew the holy books by heart and could carry on discussions of the sacred texts with the bishops he met like a long established priest.[15]

A tradition (which modern scholarship treats with caution) has it that Pulcheria was also instrumental in finding her brother the perfect bride: an orphaned Athenian girl called Athenais who was highly educated in astronomy, geometry, Greek and Latin literature and philosophy, as well as being stunningly beautiful, witty and intelligent:

A pure young thing, with slim and graceful figure, a delicate nose, skin as white as snow, large eyes, charming features, blonde curly tresses and dancing feet.[16]

---

14   Sozomen 9.1, tr. Dods, op. cit.
15   Socrates 7.22.4, tr. Dods, op. cit.
16   Malalas, *Chronichon Paschale* a. 420 (p. 577 f.), tr. Holum, K., *Theodosian Empresses: Women and Imperial Dominion in Late Antiquity*, Berkeley and London:

Such loveliness was marred only by her paganism, but she was persuaded to be baptized, and assumed a new Christian name: Aelia Eudocia (Greek *eudokia* = the Approval of God). The wedding took place on 7 June 421, and by the time Eudocia was made Augusta in 423 she had already borne Theodosius II the first of their three children, Licinia Eudoxia (see Genealogy Table 6). Aelia Eudocia, too, would come to wield great influence.

Pulcheria was not averse to courting ecclesiastical controversy. Her mother Aelia Eudoxia had carried on a perpetual feud with John Chrysostom and had even banished him twice, and now Pulcheria became the centre of some strongly divisive issues herself. There was already something of a power struggle between the Sees of Antioch, from where Nestorius, the current Bishop of Constantinople, originated, and Alexandria, where Cyril, whose fanatical monks had possibly perpetrated the murder of the pagan female mathematician and philosopher Hypatia in 415, was Bishop. Pulcheria and Nestorius had a fractious relationship that came to a head over whether the Virgin Mary should be called *Theotokos* ('Mother of God'), which was the view of Pulcheria and the majority, or, as Nestorius espoused, *Khristotokos* ('Mother of Christ'). It was the kind of problem that had ramifications for the entire vexed issue of the nature of Christ, and in 431 Theodosius II convened an Ecumenical Council at Ephesus (a strong centre of the veneration of Mary) where Cyril's uncompromising theological onslaught resulted in Nestorius' deposition and exile. Having disposed of her nemesis, Pulcheria received adulation from the crowds at Constantinople:

Long live Pulcheria! It is she who has strengthened the faith! [. . .] Long live the orthodox ones![17]

University of California Press, 1982, p. 114.

17 *Acta Conciliorum Oecumenicorum*, 1.1.3.14, tr. Holum, K., op. cit., p. 170.

However, Nestorius didn't disappear without a struggle, and neither did the Christological problems, which polarized into positions known as Monophysitism, which maintained that Christ's nature was single and indivisible yet both human and divine at the same time, and Nestorianism, which stressed the disunion between his Godhead and manhood.

After Cyril's death in around 444, Theodosius II convoked a Second Council of Ephesus in 449 under the presidency of his successor Dioscurus. This was a brutally violent meeting, and was described by St Leo as a *latrocinium* ('Robber Council'), a name by which it is still known.

At Theodosius II's court, rivalry started to develop between his wife and his sister, and, given the forceful personalities involved, this made his domestic and political life very awkward. There was even an anecdote, which greatly amused the courtiers, about Pulcheria once tricking her gormless brother into making Eudocia a slave. However, Eudocia's overall status shot up when Galla Placidia's son Valentinian III, now eighteen years old, married her daughter Licinia Eudoxia, thereby unifying the houses of the East and West: the commemorative coinage depicted Valentinian III and Theodosius II holding an orb to symbolize the united Empire. As the happy couple honeymooned by touring the Empire, perhaps spending some newly minted coins, which carried the legend *FELICITER NVPTIIS* ('Happy Wedding'), the mother-of-the-bride boosted her piety ratings by making a pilgrimage to Jerusalem and returning to Constantinople with the holy relics of St Stephen, although it was Pulcheria who finally deposited them in the church of St Lawrence.

Unlike her offspring's, Eudocia's 'honeymoon period' did not last long. The palace eunuch Chrysaphius managed to wheedle his way into Theodosius II's confidence. He engineered the removal of the highly cultured Cyrus of Panopolis, who, assisted by Eudocia's patronage, had become *Praefectus Praetorio* of the East. Known for replacing Latin as the language of administration and issuing his edicts in Greek, Cyrus had also introduced street lighting to Constantinople, but now he was exiled to Phrygia. Chrysaphius also played off Eudocia and Pulcheria against one another: Pulcheria stepped out of the public gaze, and in 443 Eudocia was accused of adultery with Theodosius II's old friend Paulinus, the *Magister Officiorum*. According to the sixth-century Greek chronicler John Malalas, Eudocia was betrayed by a large Phrygian apple. Theodosius II had given this to her as a present, but when Paulinus, unaware of this, then showed the same apple to the Emperor, his suspicions were aroused, particularly since Eudocia had said that she had eaten it. Theodosius II concluded that his love-gift was doing the rounds in a rather unhealthy way, and Paulinus was executed. Eudocia fled to Jerusalem, where she wrote some decent literature and performed good works for the last eighteen years of her life. Her old enemy Nestorius tried to besmirch her reputation by arguing that her downfall was divine retribution for her heretical views, but other Christian authors regarded Nestorius as the heretic, the charges as scurrilous fabrication, and Eudocia as wise, chaste, spotless and perfect.

If all this palace intrigue leaves an impression of a chaotic administration, it should also be acknowledged that Theodosius II achieved some significant successes during his reign, notably the codification of all Roman laws issued since 312. This was published in the *Codex Theodosianus* ('Theodosian Code'), which came into force on 1 January 439. On 23 December of that year the Senate of Rome formally received it, shouting 'Well spoken', and voicing their approval twenty or thirty times after each clause was read out.

Theodosius' foreign policy was pretty effective too: relations with Persia were amiable enough, apart from a brief spat in 421–422 when Roman forces backed some Christians in a conflict with some Zoroastrian fire-worshippers; fleets were sent to Africa to address the threat from Gaiseric and his Vandals from Africa in 431 and 441, albeit with little success; the defences on the lower Danube were maintained; and the *Praefectus Praetorio* Anthemius oversaw the addition of a powerful outer ring of land walls to Constantinople's mighty fortifications, to which Cyrus of Panopolis added the sea walls prior to his exile. The most difficult problem was the Huns, whose King Rua, and subsequently his successor Attila, demanded tribute and devastated the Balkans and Thrace whenever they felt the payments were insufficiently generous. Predictably the price of peace escalated: 350 pounds of gold per annum in 422; 700 in 434; and 2 100 in 443. Nevertheless, it was probably worth it:

> The Romans complied with all Attila's instructions, and treated them as the command of their master. For not only were they taking precautions not to engage in a war against him, but they also were afraid that the Persians were preparing war, and that the Vandals were disturbing the peace at sea, and that the Isaurians were inclined to engage in brigandage, and the Saracens were mounting raids into their Eastern Empire, and that the tribes of Ethiopia were in rebellion. For this reason they swallowed their pride and obeyed Attila, but tried to prepare for military action against the other peoples, gathering their forces and appointing commanders.[18]

However, looking at the big picture, these were relatively minor distractions, especially compared with the struggles that were unfolding in the West, and in reality Theodosius II's reign probably represented the most settled period the East had enjoyed since the second century. The Seven Sleepers of Ephesus, who are said to have awoken during his reign, experienced the situation at first hand, and were pleasantly surprised to find the Cross placed above Ephesus' city gate, delighted to hear people swearing by the name of Christ, impressed to see a great church, and bemused by the reaction that their coins with a pagan Emperor's portrait caused in the market.

---

18 Priscus of Panion, *fr.* 10, tr. in Mitchell, S., *A History of the Later Roman Empire AD 284–641: The Transformation of the Ancient World*, Oxford: Blackwell, 2007, p. 105.

On 28 July 450, Theodosius II died as a result of a riding accident. This placed Pulcheria in a tricky situation, since her brother had not produced a male heir. Nevertheless, she succeeded in acting as de facto ruler of the Empire until a successor could be found. After about a month she and the *Magister Militum* Aspar settled on a Thracian military officer called Flavius Marcianus ('Marcian'). This meant that the fifty-one-year-old Pulcheria had to compromise one of her most deeply held convictions and agree to get married. However, in order for her not to have to violate her vow of chastity, Marcian promised not to violate her. On 25 August 450 she crowned him as the new Augustus.

The man at the top of Marcian and Pulcheria's elimination list was Chrysaphius. Most sources simply say that Pulcheria handed him to another of his bitter enemies, Jordanes, who put him to death, but Malalas introduces chariot racing into the story. Apparently, Chrysaphius had been head of the Green faction, whereas Marcian was a fan of the Blues. Following some scuffles between rival gangs of hooligan supporters, Marcian ordered Chrysaphius to explain what was going on, but as the eunuch made his way to the tribunal he was stoned to death by an angry mob who resented the high taxes levied to pay the tribute to Attila the Hun.

Flavius Aetius, Vandals and Huns

Over in the West, the situation facing Valentinian III in 434 was that Galla Placidia was overseeing the life of the court at Ravenna, arbitrating various disputes, building churches and trying to manipulate powerful generals and control difficult children, while Flavius Aetius was in overall control, presiding over Italy, the recently pacified provinces north of the Alps, the West's Balkan provinces, Africa Proconsularis and Byzacena, Narbonensis, Viennensis, and perhaps the frontier zone from the mouth of the Loire to the northern edges of the Alps. But large swathes of Rome's former territories were no longer under his sway: Britain was completely out on a limb and fell prey to Picti, Scotti, Angles, Saxons and Jutes; the Rhine frontier had collapsed; northern Gaul had fallen outside Roman administration; the Goths in Aquitania II and Novempopulana may have been in revolt; the situation in Spain looked rather like that in northern Gaul, with a large kingdom of Suevi allying itself to the Visigoths of Theodoric I, who were settled around the Garonne; and the Vandals now had official control of Numidia and the Mauretanias. Essentially Flavius Aetius was caught in a vicious circle of three 'T's: loss of territory meant loss of tax revenue, which meant less money for troops. There was still a pretty effective regular Roman army, but this would need to be bolstered by barbarian allies from outside the Empire if he were to realize his ambitious plans to restore the West.

Gaul was the first area on his list. He recovered the strategically crucial cities of Arelate and Narbo from the Goths in 436, pushed some Frankish tribes back across the Rhine (or incorporated them as *foederati*, tribes subsidized by Rome in return for them supplying warriors to fight her armies), and destroyed the Burgundian kingdom of King Gundigar on the middle Rhine, an episode that later inspired the Nibelungen saga. The defeated Burgundiones were settled in Sapaudia (modern Savoy), while the Alani were established in Aureliana Civitas (modern Orléans). Flavius Aetius also brought to heel a number of rebellious local leaders whom the Ravenna government called Bagaudae. The famous *gemitus Britannorum Agitio ter consuli* ('groans of the Britons to Agitius, three times Consul') could belong in this context too, since 'Agitius' is usually held to be Flavius Aetius, and his third consulship fell in 446. The Britons groaned that:

> The barbarians drive us to the sea, the sea drives us back to the barbarians; death comes by one means or another: we are either slaughtered or drowned.[19]

---

19   Gildas, *De Excidio et Conquestu Britanniae* 1.20, tr. Kershaw, S.

Military intervention in Britain was out of the question, but St Germanus of Auxerre made his second visit to the island, perhaps in 446–447. His first visit in 429 had been to combat a heresy known as Pelagianism. Despite being ridiculed by Jerome as a 'stupid idiot stuffed with Scottish porridge [. . .] like a mountain of fat'[20] and therefore prone to a weak memory, Pelagius was a well-educated man who rejected the idea that man's capacity for good is most effective when his will is surrendered as a vehicle for the divine will, and would not accept that the weakness of their natures makes human beings entirely dependent for salvation on the grace or favour of God. On the contrary, he believed that the exercise of pure human will can give people control over their own salvation. In theological terms, Pelagius' viewpoint amounts to a denial of original sin and Christian grace, so Germanus was keen to stamp it out. But whilst confronting Pelagianism, Germanus also defeated some Picti and Saxons in the 'Alleluia victory', where he baptized the British fighters, and taught them to shout 'Alleluia' at the moment of attack, which apparently so terrified their adversaries that victory was inevitable. So clearly Germanus was a good choice of ambassador in 446, for his military, civil and religious leadership qualities, and Pelagianism did not take hold.

The second item on Flavius Aetius' 'to-do list' was Spain, where all went well initially. In the first half of the 440s the *Magister Utriusque Militiae* Asturius had success in Tarraconensis, as did his son-in-law Merobaudes, after which a third *Magister Utriusque Militiae* called Vitus led an army through Carthaginiensis and Baetica. So far so good, but the Suevi counter-attacked, and their leader Rechila defeated Vitus and reasserted Suevic control. When Rechila died in August 448, his successor Rechiar joined forces with one of the Bagaudae, who went under the name of Basilius ('Emperor'), and not only wreaked havoc in Spain, but also visited Alaric's grandson

---

20   Jerome, *In Jeremia* I and III, *Praef.*, tr. Kershaw, S.

Theoderic I in Gaul and married one of his daughters. This was very worrying to the Romans.

Across the Straits of Gibraltar the situation was even more alarming. In 439 Gaiseric's Vandals seized Carthage in a surprise attack (most of the inhabitants were watching the races at the hippodrome, we are told). This was a real game-changer: one of the Mediterranean's premier cities was now under firm barbarian control; Rome's grain supply was at risk; Sicily was under threat; and Constantinople's access to the Eastern Mediterranean was inhibited. So in order to focus on this problem, the Romans struck a landmark treaty with the Goths in 439, which essentially granted them a sovereign (or at the very least, semi-sovereign) state within the borders of the Roman Empire. Then in 440 Gaiseric attacked Sicily; Theodosius II sent a naval expedition to the Western Mediterranean in 441, but this was not done with any real conviction, since he was already preoccupied with Persia and the Huns; and in 442 the Empire signed a treaty with the Vandals that acknowledged their control over Numidia, Byzacena and Proconsularis, and though the less attractive Mauritanian provinces were returned to the Romans, the Spanish situation precluded them exercising any effective government there either. Although some modern scholarship has tried to rehabilitate the Vandals' image, Christian sources portray their activities in Africa as utterly terrifying. Nevertheless, Gaiseric softened his approach in the mid-440s, when his son Huneric was betrothed to Valentinian III's five-year-old daughter Eudocia, despite the fact that he was already married to a daughter of Theoderic I of the Goths. Gaiseric marked the new betrothal by accusing Theoderic I's daughter of trying to assassinate him, cutting off her nose and ears, and sending her back to her father.

By the time that Marcian succeeded the late Theodosius II in Constantinople in 450, it was hard to judge whether Flavius Aetius' regime was a success, but in that year some unexpectedly bizarre developments pushed events in a new direction. At the sharp end of a curious love triangle was Galla Placidia's daughter (and Valentinian III's older sister), the thirty-two-year-old Honoria. Honoria had a chequered past. When she had fallen pregnant at the age of sixteen, her lover Eugenius had been executed and Honoria had been sent off to live with her hyper-chaste cousin Pulcheria in Constantinople. When she was finally allowed back to Ravenna (stripped of her rank of Augusta), a suitably admirable but low-key husband was found for her in the shape of Herculanus Bassus. Honoria clearly had aspirations of marrying someone much more exciting, and she rebelled from her family in the most extreme way imaginable: she wrote a letter explaining her predicament, enclosed her ring with it, and gave it to her eunuch Hyacinthus with instructions to deliver it to Attila the Hun.

Attila couldn't believe his luck. He had just made a peace deal with Constantinople, and was already refocusing on the West. As far as he was concerned, Honoria's missive was tantamount to a marriage proposal, and he demanded that Valentinian III should give her to him, along with her share of what he called the 'sceptre of Empire' – i.e., half of the Western Roman Empire. Ravenna responded that it had no intention of doing this, and that in any case females did not hold the 'sceptre of Empire'. This gave Attila the excuse that he needed to declare war, on the (spurious) grounds that he was defending the honour of his 'bride'. Obviously Theodosius III rejected Attila's demands. The go-between Hyacinthus was duly tortured and beheaded, while Honoria was delivered to Galla Placidia for punishment. Galla Placidia simply insisted that Honoria marry Herculanus Bassus – presumably a fate worse than death.

This was Galla Placidia's last contribution to the story of Rome. On 27 November 450 she died in her early sixties from unknown causes. She had built a mausoleum for herself in Ravenna, but she was not buried there. Recent research has suggested that the find on 25 June 1458 of a marble sarcophagus containing two silver-coated wooden caskets holding the bodies of an adult and a child, along with 7.25 kg of cloth-of-gold and an inscribed cross, could be the remains of Galla

Placidia and Theodosius, her infant son by Athaulf. The items were discovered at the chapel of St Petronilla on the Vatican Hill, which had previously been Honorius' mausoleum. Honorius' wife Maria (the daughter of Stilicho and Serena) was buried there, and the literary sources tell us that Theodosius was reinterred in a silver coffin by Galla Placidia in 450 following the transfer of his body from Spain to Rome. It is an enticing inference to interpret the adult body found lying next to the child as that of Galla Placidia.[21]

While Galla Placidia rested for all eternity, Attila the Hun went on the rampage. Rome's days were numbered.

---

21 See Johnson, M. J., *The Roman Imperial Mausoleum in Late Antiquity*, Cambridge: Cambridge University Press, 2009, pp. 167–71; Freisenbruch, A., *The First Ladies of Rome: The Women Behind the Caesars*, London: Jonathan Cape, 2010, p. 311 f.

18

The End of Rome in the West
(450–476)

While the Colisaeus stands, Rome shall stand.
When the Colisaeus falls, Rome shall fall,
When Rome falls, the world shall fall.
Attributed to the Venerable Bede

The Survival of Rome in the East: 450 Onwards

While the Roman regime in the West was trying to stop itself
from imploding, the new Eastern supremo Marcian was immediately faced with two equally daunting challenges: dealing with
Attila the Hun and reconciling the feuding Christian factions
within his own realm.

Early in his reign (451) he convened an Ecumenical Council
at Chalcedon. This was done with the grudging assent of Pope
Leo I 'the Great', and sought to rectify the shambolic outcome
of the Second ('Robber') Council of Ephesus of 449. The vehe-
ment Monophysitism versus Nestorianism disagreement about
the nature of Christ was still raging,[1] and so the Council of
Chalcedon issued the 'Chalcedonian Definition' or 'Chalcedonian Creed', in order to get things absolutely clear:

> We [. . .] teach people to confess one and the same Son, our
> Lord Jesus Christ, the same perfect in Godhead and also

---

1   See above, p. 395.

perfect in manhood; truly God and truly man, of a reasonable soul and body; consubstantial with the Father according to the Godhead, and consubstantial with us according to the Manhood; in all things like unto us, without sin; begotten before all ages of the Father according to the Godhead, and in these latter days, for us and for our salvation, born of the Virgin Mary, the Mother of God, according to the Manhood; one and the same Christ, Son, Lord, only begotten, to be acknowledged in two natures, inconfusedly, unchangeably, indivisibly, inseparably.[2]

In reality the judgement merely led to the so-called Monophysite schism between those who accepted the Second Council of Ephesus and those who accepted the Council of Chalcedon, and the issue remained a thorn in the side of Eastern Emperors for centuries.

The Council had less difficulty when they passed a decree known as the 'canon 28', which dealt with the rivalry between Alexandria and Constantinople: henceforth, as the New Rome, the See of Constantinople would have equal privileges with Rome, and be second in eminence and power to the Bishop of Rome. Pulcheria received great public acclaim as a 'New Helena' for her part in all of this, and when she died in July 453 aged fifty-four, there was an enormous public outpouring of grief.

As far as foreign policy was concerned, Marcian benefited from the settlement of Rome's differences with Persia, and his approach to Attila became much more uncompromising. And it needed to be, because the Huns were still a formidable proposition. Ever since Attila and his brother Bleda had succeeded to the kingship in the 430s they had wreaked havoc in Rome's Balkan territories on an unprecedented scale. In addition to harassing the East and extorting money from Constantinople,

2   See Kelly, J. N. D., *Early Christian Doctrines*, 5th edn., London: Continuum, 1977, p. 340.

Attila had murdered Bleda in 445 and overrun Pannonia. Attila's political heartland came to be the area north of the Danube that had once been occupied by the Tervingi, but by the late 440s the tentacles of his power were stretching far beyond there. Unlike the Goths, the Huns had no interest in securing a permanent residence inside the Empire and regarded blackmail and extortion as completely acceptable. Marcian, however, did not. He took steps to recover the Balkans, and he stopped paying them off. The policy bore fruit: Attila simply decided that the West was a softer target, which allowed Marcian a breathing space to establish a modicum of peace and prosperity throughout his own realm. Attila's death in 453 eased the pressure still further, and the money that was once paid to the Huns was used to make tax cuts.

Marcian died, allegedly of gangrene, in 457, leaving a healthy treasury surplus. His intended successor was his son-in-law Procopius Anthemius, but the scheming Alan *Magister Militum* Aspar engineered the accession of the Dacian Leo I. According to Constantine Porphyrogenitus he was raised aloft on the shields of his soldiers in a gesture that recalled the practice of the Germanic troops who elevated Julian to the purple in 360, and was crowned by the ever-increasingly powerful patriarch of Constantinople.[3] Procopius Anthemius would duly become Emperor of the West on Leo I's say-so in 467, but if Aspar was looking to become the power behind the throne, he would be thwarted by Leo I's equally Machiavellian machinations. The Emperor recruited a bodyguard of Isaurian tribesmen (Isauria is a mountainous part of southern Asia Minor), who were intimately involved in the murder of the 'dynasty of Aspar and his sons' in the palace in 471. Leo I also married off his daughter Ariadne to a leading Isaurian called Tarasikodissa. This man won Leo I's confidence, was promoted from *Comes Domesticorum* to *Praefectus Praetorio* of the East, and assumed the Greek name Zeno.

---

3   Constantine Porphyrogenitus, *De Ceremoniis* 1.91.

On the world stage, Leo I tried to deal with the Vandal menace by sending an armada against them in 468, but this was a complete failure. Then in 474 he made an attempt to gain control over the Western Empire by sending Julius Nepos, the commander of the Balkan army and a relative by marriage of his wife Verina, to take over from Glycerius, who had ascended the Western throne in 473.[4] Again this came to naught: Leo I died in February 474; his young successor Leo II died in November; and Julius Nepos returned to the Balkans after a brief tenure of power lasting into 475.[5]

Zeno, who had been appointed as the protector of Leo II, assumed sole control of the Eastern Empire from 474 to 491. He repelled Goths and usurpers, including Leo I's widow Verina's brother Basiliscus, who was proclaimed at Constantinople in 475. Verina contributed to the usurpation's initial success, and Zeno was exiled for a time while Basiliscus and his son Marcus ruled together, but their heretical religious beliefs soon got them into difficulties, and Zeno was able to make a comeback. He has the distinction of being the Eastern Roman Emperor when the last Emperor of the West was deposed. The Eastern Roman Empire had effectively become the Byzantine Empire, and a new era was coming into being.

Attila the Hun

As the Eastern Roman Empire was heading off into its Byzantine future, the West was struggling to cope with Attila. Brandishing Honoria's letter,[6] he gathered his warriors, crossed the Rhine, destroyed Divodurum Mediomatricum (modern Metz) and several other cities, and arrived at the Loire. He was held at bay at Aureliana Civitas, which gave Flavius Aetius a breathing space to garner the support of various Gauls and Aquitanian

4 See below, p. 419f.
5 See below, p. 420.
6 See above, p. 402.

Visigoths, the latter brought onside by a Gallic noble called Avitus. Valentinian III's decision to betroth his daughter Eudocia to the Vandal Gaiseric's son Huneric, and Gaiseric's mutilation of the Gothic leader Theoderic I's daughter,[7] might have made a Gothic alliance with Flavius Aetius an unlikely proposition, but when Gaiseric allied himself with Attila, Theoderic I took a pragmatic approach and linked up with the Romans, possibly as the lesser of two evils. Flavius Aetius was also joined by a Frankish faction, some Alani and several contingents of northern Gallic Bagaudae, who started to be called by the more respectable name of Aremoricani once they were on the Roman side. He may also have been able to deploy some of the former Rhine *limitanei* and maybe some remnants of the old British *comitatenses*.

Flavius Aetius' multi-ethnic army forced Attila to back off, and finally engaged with him at the Battle of the Catalaunian Fields (known to the ancient authorities as *Campus Mauriacus*), which modern scholarly consensus places midway between Troyes and Châlons-sur-Marne (see Map 8). Prosper of Aquitaine described the incalculable slaughter; Hydatius numbered the dead at 300 000; the *Gallic Chronicle of 511* spoke of innumerable cadavers; Theoderic I was killed in action; but crucially Attila got the worse of things and retreated to Pannonia.

The victorious army was too badly weakened to give chase, however, and by the following year Attila was attacking Italy with fresh forces. Flavius Aetius was powerless to keep him out. Aquileia, Mediolanum and Ticinum all fell but, rather unexpectedly, Attila did not press on and sack Rome. Legend has it that Pope Leo I talked him out of it (he certainly asked him to withdraw, although he may have paid him off); another version says that the Huns thought that there was a curse on anyone who sacked Rome (look at Alaric, they said); or Attila's forces may have been suffering from malaria or dysentery, which

---

7   See above, p. 401.

commonly affected armies in Italy at that time; or the Eastern Roman army may have attacked Attila's trans-Danubian heartland. In any case, Attila headed back across the Danube, where, in 453, he met a slightly bizarre and unheroic end. Having indulged in some serious drinking after another marriage to a Gothic princess, he had a nosebleed that choked him while he was sleeping.

Attila had been the glue that held the whole Hunnic project together, and his unexpected death was an enormous bonus for Rome. The Germanic tribes began to gain the ascendancy over the Huns, and they smashed Attila's heirs in a huge battle in Pannonia:

> And so the bravest nations tore themselves to pieces. For then, I think, must have occurred a most remarkable spectacle, where one might see the Goths fighting with pikes, the Gepidae raging with the sword, the Rugi breaking off the spears in their own wounds, the Suevi fighting on foot, the Huns with bows, the Alani drawing up a battle line of heavy-armed and the Heruli of light-armed warriors.[8]

The Hunnic survivors asked to be allowed to enter the Eastern Roman Empire, and their request was granted. From here on we see the rise of the Ostrogoths. The nomenclature was first used by Claudian in 392, when they were connected with the Greuthungi, but now they became the dominant Germanic group in the Balkan area. The term Ostrogoths is now used to demarcate them from the Visigoths who were settled in Aquitaine, but in reality neither group actually used those designations, even though some Italian Goths used Ostrogotha as a personal name.

---

8 Jordanes, *Getica* 50.261, tr. Mierow, C. C., *The Gothic History of Jordanes*, Princeton, NJ: Princeton University Press, 1915.

The Fall (or Transformation) of Rome in the West: 453 Onwards

Attila had probably been the greatest threat to the Western Empire since Hannibal in the third century BCE, but Rome's man of the moment did not get to enjoy the fruits of victory for long. Rather like a latter-day Scipio Africanus, Flavius Aetius campaigned effectively in Spain, bringing parts of Carthaginiensis back under Roman rule, and using Frederic, the brother of the new Gothic king, Theoderic II, to subdue some Bagaudae in Tarraconensis. Yet just like Scipio Africanus, Flavius Aetius became entangled in political intrigues, although his end was more violent, hacked down by Valentinian III in person on 21 September 454.

The Greek tragedian Aeschylus often explored the themes of vengeance in his plays: 'The one who acts must suffer,' say the Chorus of two of his plays,[9] and so it was now as things descended into a cycle of vendetta. Flavius Aetius' officials were purged, but on 16 March 455 two of his bodyguards, possibly Huns but with the Gothic names of Optila and Thraustila, avenged their master's death:

> Valentinian rode in the Field of Ares [Campus Martius] with a few bodyguards and the followers of Optila and Thraustila. When he had dismounted from his horse and proceeded to archery, Optila and his friends attacked him. Optila struck Valentinian on his temple and when turned around to see the striker he dealt him a second blow on the face and felled him.[10]

It is not beyond the bounds of possibility that there was another motive, and that Optila and Thraustila were put up to

---

9 Aeschylus, *Agamemnon* 1564; *Libation Bearers* 313. See Kershaw, S., op. cit., 2010, pp. 166 ff.
10 John of Antioch *fr.* 201.4–5, tr. Gordon, C. D., in *The Age of Attila: Fifth-Century Byzantium and the Barbarians*, Ann Arbor: University of Michigan Press, 1960, pp. 52–53.

this by Petronius Maximus, a wealthy Senator whose wife had been raped by Valentinian III and may have committed suicide as a result. On the other hand, Petronius Maximus might simply have wanted the throne for himself, since he now bribed his way into power and cemented his position by marrying Valentinian III's widow Licinia Eudoxia, whose elder daughter Eudocia was offered to his son Palladius. The problem with the latter arrangement was, of course, that Eudocia was already betrothed to Gaiseric's son Huneric.

The great Anglo-Saxon scholar the Venerable Bede (673–735) later expressed his view that the Roman Empire came to an end with Valentinian III's murder, but that does not seem to be the way that people at the time saw things. There were certainly plenty of problems, but there were also plenty of people who fought tooth and nail to keep the Roman Empire alive. In Spain, the Suevi broke their treaty and ravaged Gallaecia. Closer to home, Licinia Eudoxia emulated her sister-in-law Honoria's tactics for escaping an unhappy marriage by appealing to Gaiseric. This in turn presented Gaiseric with the possibility of getting hold of Huneric's fiancée Eudocia, so he set sail for Rome.

The arrival of the Vandal fleet off Ostia caused panic, in the midst of which Petronius Maximus was hacked down by some imperial slaves on 22 May 455. His dismembered body was thrown into the Tiber, and Gaiseric now perpetrated another sack of Rome. This one lasted for fourteen days and was far more destructive even than Alaric's:

[Gaiseric] took everything from the palace, even the bronze statues. He even led away as captives surviving Senators, accompanied by their wives; along with them he also carried off to Carthage in Africa the empress Licinia Eudoxia, who had summoned him; her daughter [Galla] Placidia [the Younger], the wife of the patrician Olybrius, who then was staying at Constantinople; and even the maiden Eudocia. After he had returned, Gaiseric gave the younger Eudocia, a maiden, the daughter of the empress Eudoxia, to his son Huneric in marriage, and he held them both, the mother and the daughter, in great honour.[11]

Huneric's marriage to Eudocia was crucial: she was the granddaughter of Theodosius II, and from Gaiseric's perspective, any legitimate male offspring would be the heirs to the Western Roman Empire.

Once Gaiseric had returned to Africa and Rome had been well and truly vandalized (in both the literal and the figurative senses – this was how the Vandals got the reputation that their tribal name still perpetuates), the question remained: who would rule the West? An ambassador of Petronius Maximus' called Avitus, who came from a Gallic senatorial family, was currently at the court of the Gothic king, Theoderic II. There he was declared Emperor. Backed by the Gallic nobility and the army of Theoderic II and his brother Frederic, Avitus entered Italy and took the throne. He sought recognition from Marcian in the East, but it is not clear whether this was forthcoming.

Marcian was not at the top of Avitus' agenda, however. Gaiseric was. When diplomatic overtures proved unproductive, Majorian and Flavius Ricimer, the commanders of the Italian army, fought the Vandals in Sicily with some success. Majorian was a young man, perhaps of Egyptian descent, whose father had been a financial official under Flavius Aetius, while Ricimer was the grandson of Vallia, who had taken over from Athaulph as ruler of the Visigoths between 415 and 418. For his part, Avitus set his sights on Africa. The omens were good. On 1 January 456 the young poet Sidonius delivered the customary panegyric, and talked up the benefits that Avitus would bring to Rome:

> He will restore Libya to you a fourth time in chains [. . .] it is easy to feel sure even now of what he can do by waging war,

---

11   Malchus, *Chron.* 366, tr. Blockley, R. C., op. cit.

how he shall, time and again, bring nations under your yoke
[. . .] Lo, this prince of riper years shall bring back youth to
you whom child-princes have made old.[12]

Avitus paid his Visigothic troops with money raised by selling
bronze fittings stripped from public buildings to metal-
merchants, and focused initially on Spain. There the Suevi
under Rechiar were making attacks on Carthaginiensis and
Tarraconensis and abducting large numbers of prisoners. So
Avitus sent in the Visigoths:

Theodoric, king of the Goths, entered Spain with a massive
army of his own, at the will and behest of the emperor Avitus.[13]

On 5 October 456, the Suevi were comprehensively
defeated at the Battle of the River Urbicus. Rechiar fled; the
Visigoths invaded Gallaecia and sacked Rechiar's capital; and
Rechiar was subsequently captured and killed. But all this
fighting only created chaos throughout the Iberian Peninsula,
primarily because Avitus had to deal with more pressing
issues in Italy.

The Vandals always had the option of cutting off or restrict-
ing Italy's grain supplies:

When Avitus was emperor of Rome there was famine at the
same time. The mob put the blame on Avitus and compelled
him to dismiss from the city of the Romans his allies who had
entered with him from Gaul.[14]

With Italy denuded of Avitus' troops, Ricimer and Majorian
rebelled. Avitus faced them on the battlefield at Placentia on 17

---

12 *Carmina* 7.587–598, tr. Anderson, W. B., *Sidonius; with an English translation,
introduction and notes by W. B. Anderson*, Cambridge, MA: Harvard University
Press, 1936.
13 Hydatius, *Chronicle* 173, tr. Kershaw, S.
14 John of Antioch *fr.* 202: tr. Gordon, C. D., op. cit., p.116.

October 456, but was defeated. His life was spared, and Bishop Eusebius of Mediolanum used an innovative method of deposing him: he made him into a Bishop. Avitus seems to have lived until 457, when he may have been 'removed' by Majorian.

The uncertainty in the West was compounded by the fact that the Eastern Emperor Marcian died shortly after Avitus. His successor Leo I appointed Majorian as *Magister Utriusque Militiae* in February 457; the Italian army proclaimed Majorian Emperor in April; and he seems to have received formal recognition in December.

Majorian managed to rule until 461. He was a genuinely talented Emperor, and he needed to be. He beat off an Alemannic attack on Raetia, a Vandal raid on Campania, and quelled rebellions in Gaul by the Burgundiones and by some supporters of Avitus in Narbo. A Gallic officer called Aegidius was influential in restoring the Gallic situation; while in 458 Majorian went to Gaul in person and handled the diplomatic settlement with some aplomb. So with Gaul reintegrated into the Empire, Majorian turned his attention to the extremely confused situation in Spain, where a Gothic army loyal to Avitus was on the rampage, various factions were fighting over what was left of the Suevic kingdom and Bagaudae were making their unwelcome presence felt. However, when Theoderic II moved into Gaul he ended up defeated by Majorian's army, commanded by Aegidius, at Narbo, and he had come to terms before 459 was out.

Majorian clearly did not envisage the decline and fall of the Roman Empire. His successes had given him the opportunity to focus solely on the Vandals, and if he could secure a successful outcome against them he could then concentrate on re-establishing Roman government elsewhere. So he moved into Spain in May 460, appointed Nepotianus as *Magister Militum* alongside Theoderic II's general Sunieric, gathered a fleet at Cartagena, redeployed his general Marcellinus from Dalmatia to Sicily, and spurned Gaiseric's offer of a peace settlement. The Vandal then poisoned the wells in Mauretania – Majorian's

Africa corps would have to transit that region in order properly to get to grips with him – and hit back with a highly effective surprise attack on the Roman fleet at Cartagena. That put paid to Majorian's plans, and he signed a treaty with Gaiseric under which he accepted 'shameful', but unspecified, terms. However, no Roman Emperor could afford that kind of setback, and no sooner had he set foot on Italian soil than he was apprehended by Ricimer and executed on 2 August 461.

A power vacuum ensued, at the end of which Ricimer played Emperor-maker and installed an Italian Senator called Libius Severus (sometimes called Severus III), who assumed power on 19 November 461. We know nothing about Libius Severus' pre-imperial career, and he made little impact as Augustus. Spain drops off our historical radar, too, apart from some contemporary accounts of raiding by the Suevi in Gallaecia and Lusitania from the local Bishop Hydatius. Libius Severus' problem seems to have been that hardly anyone accepted the legitimacy of his rule: Aegidius (who assumed the title King of the Franks), the Dalmatian warlord Marcellinus and Gaiseric all refused to acknowledge him. Indeed, Gaiseric had plans of his own: he now wanted Valentinian III's daughter Galla Placidia the Younger's husband Olybrius to take the purple (the marriage links would then mean that Gaiseric's son Huneric would be the brother-in-law of the Emperor). Adopting an aggressive stance, he took Sardinia and Sicily, and no one could do anything to curtail his widespread seaborne raids, although Emperor Leo I at Constantinople did get him to agree to release Placidia and Eudoxia (for a large ransom).

Inside Libius Severus' regime, Theoderic II was looking powerful. In practice he commanded the Roman troops in Spain, and the Emperor badly needed his services, particularly in light of the nagging problem posed by the disloyalty of the Gallic army on the Loire under Aegidius. So in exchange for military support, Libius Severus, gave Narbonne to Theoderic II in 462. The strategic implications of this were enormous, since any Roman army wanting access to Spain, or indeed to Africa via the Straits of Gibraltar, would now have to pass through Gothic territory first. Gundioc, the king of the Burgundiones, was named in Aegidius' stead as *Magister Militum* in Gaul, and he may have married Ricimer's sister. It was Aegidius who initially got the upper hand, though, and in 463 he defeated the Goths near Aureliana Civitas and killed Theoderic II's brother Frederic. Aegidius then sought to hammer out a deal with Gaiseric, but this came to nothing when he was killed, either in an ambush or by poison. The Frank Childeric I now assumed the most powerful position north of the Loire, and together with a *Comes* Paulus of Civitas Andecavorum (modern Angers), who may have been an ex-officer of Aegidius, he fought Saxons coming from Britain, who were led by a certain Adovacrius (Eadwacer), often, though almost certainly incorrectly, identified with Odoacer, the future king of Italy.

After Libius Severus died on 15 August 465 there was a period of almost two years during which the Western throne was unoccupied. Ricimer and the Senate at Rome asked the Eastern Emperor Leo I to step in, and he installed Procopius Anthemius as Caesar. This eminent aristocrat had family links to both the Constantinian and Theodosian dynasties (he was Marcian's son-in-law), and a fine military track record in the Balkans to boot. He arrived in Rome in 467 at the head of an army of Eastern troops and backed by a fleet commanded by Marcellinus. Any potential opposition from Ricimer was defused when Procopius Anthemius offered him his daughter Alypia in marriage, and the Caesar was duly elevated to Augustus on 14 April 467. With this competent man on its throne, fully endorsed by Constantinople and allied to the Emperor-maker Ricimer, the West could face the future with a modicum of optimism.

As usual, the Vandals were public enemy number one. Procopius Anthemius' offensive options were a seaborne assault into their territory from the north, a land-based attack from Libya, which was still part of Rome's Eastern Empire, or some combination of the two. He opted to make use of his Eastern connections, and a plan was formulated whose ambition was matched by its vast expense: 64 000 pounds of gold and 700 000 of silver. But the cost-benefit analysis made it a gamble worth taking, and in 468 a mighty armada of 1 100 ships was assembled to transport a formidable army to Africa under the command of Leo I's brother-in-law Basiliscus, while a land army under Heraclius, who was probably the Eastern *Comes Rei Militaris*, was to march simultaneously into Vandal territory. Marcellinus was to complete the offensive by invading Sardinia with a Western fleet.

All three prongs of the attack had initial success: Heraclius drove the Vandals out of the province of Tripolitania; Marcellinus captured Sardinia, and followed this up by driving the Vandals out of Sicily; and Basiliscus defeated one of Gaiseric's naval squadrons close to the island. Unfortunately for the Romans, rather than driving home his advantage, Basiliscus allowed Gaiseric to negotiate a five-day truce. The Vandal exploited this to assemble a fleet that included fireships, and when he unleashed them against Basiliscus' fleet, they caused pandemonium. Gaiseric's conventional vessels drove home the advantage, and the outcome was catastrophic for the Romans, with Sardinia and Sicily going back under Vandal control, and Marcellinus being assassinated. Ricimer could well have orchestrated Marcellinus' murder as he sought to eradicate any Eastern-backed rivals from Italy, but the main man fitting that description was still Procopius Anthemius, who, rather surprisingly, emerged relatively unscathed from the expedition's failure.

Procopius Anthemius had other interrelated worries aside from the Vandals, namely Gaul and Ricimer. The relationship with Ricimer became particularly awkward when a character called Romanus had tried to poison Procopius Anthemius but been thwarted and then executed for sorcery. The problem was that Romanus had been a friend of Ricimer's, and a stand-off then ensued in which Ricimer installed himself at Mediolanum with 6 000 men, and Anthemius, backed by the SPQR, based himself at Rome. For the time being, however, the two just conducted a rather crass war of words: Procopius Anthemius told Ricimer that he wished his daughter hadn't married a 'skin-clad barbarian'; Ricimer dismissed the Emperor as a Galatian or a 'Little Greek' (*Graeculus*). Bishop (later Saint) Epiphanius of Pavia tried to mediate.

Meanwhile in Gaul, Theoderic II had been killed by his brother Euric just after Procopius Anthemius' accession. Euric's relations with the new Emperor seem to have been amicable enough to include possibly playing a role in the ill-fated anti-Vandal offensive, but things turned sour when Arvandus, the *Praefectus Praetorio* of Gaul from 464 to 469, was accused of treason. The allegation was that he had incited Euric to rebel against Procopius Anthemius and was planning to take over Gaul in concert with the Burgundiones, although the reason he had contacted Euric was partly because, for reasons that remain obscure, a substantial army of hostile Britons had turned up on the Loire commanded by a man named Riothamus. The plot was betrayed when an incriminating letter from Arvandus to Euric was intercepted:

> This seemed to be a document sent to the king of the Goths [Euric], urging him not to make peace with the Greek Emperor [Leo I], demonstrating that he ought to launch an attack on the Britanni north of the Loire, stating firmly that the Gallic provinces should be divided with the Burgundiones according to the law of the nations, and very many other mad things in the same manner, such as might rouse an aggressive king to fury, a pacific one to shame.[15]

At the same time there seems to have been a deterioration in the détente between the Goths and the imperial court, and worries that their position was under threat may have underpinned Euric's decision to rebel.

Arvandus was lucky to suffer exile rather than death, while

15	Sidonius, *Epistulae* 1.7.5, tr. in Mitchell, S., op. cit., p. 176.

Procopius Anthemius sent his son Anthemiolus over the Alps to confront Euric in a military operation that could have been designed to link up with Riothamus' Britons. Anthemiolus was also prepared to negotiate, but his overtures were not sufficiently attractive to Euric, who opted for war, even though it meant fighting on two fronts. His confidence was justified, though, since Anthemiolus was defeated and killed, Riothamus' army was crushed, the defeated British survivors sought refuge among the Burgundiones, and Euric's troops took Avaricum (modern Bourges).

Euric's success was good news for Ricimer, who now laid siege to his 'Little Greek' foe in Rome. But Procopius Anthemius was not a soft touch. When he had held out for four months, Ricimer proclaimed Olybrius Augustus of the West, which may have been a sop to Gaiseric, given Olybrius' position as Huneric's brother-in-law. We also hear that around this time an Ostrogothic leader called Videmer invaded Italy. Whose side he was on is not clear, but he died before he could influence events in any significant way. In the end, however, persistent siege operations forced Rome to capitulate. Procopius Anthemius' escape attempt involved dressing up as a beggar outside the Church of Santa Maria in Trastevere, but it failed, and he was captured and beheaded by Ricimer's nephew, the Burgundian prince Gundobad, on 11 July 472.

Ricimer's triumph might have been sweet, but it was short. Just over a month after Procopius Anthemius' death he died coughing up blood. Olybrius expired soon afterwards, also from natural causes, and an interregnum followed that lasted until March 473, when Gundobad took on Ricimer's Emperor-maker role and appointed Glycerius, the *Comes Domesticorum*, as Emperor in the West. Glycerius perhaps appointed Videmer's son, also called Videmer, as *Magister Militum* in Gaul, but if he did the outcome was totally unsatisfactory, since somehow or other his men ended up as part of Euric's army. This was a damaging failure, especially since Glycerius' appointment had never been acceptable to Leo I in the East, who sent his preferred nominee, Julius Nepos, to replace him.[16] By the time Julius Nepos and his army landed in Italy, Zeno had replaced Leo I as the incumbent in Constantinople, but Julius Nepos carried out his mission anyway. Glycerius capitulated meekly and Gundobad decided there was no point in backing a loser, and went off to secure his position as King of the Burgundiones, who in due course came back into the imperial fold.

Zeno's handling of relations with the Vandals took the heat off Julius Nepos somewhat, especially when the new Eastern Emperor signed a treaty that allowed Gaiseric to keep possession of all of his territorial acquisitions in return for ending the persecution of Catholics and releasing Roman prisoners. This agreement concluded what is sometimes referred to as the 'Fourth Punic War', even if equating the Vandals with the third- and second-century BCE Carthaginians is stretching historical veracity a little.

The removal of the Vandal menace allowed Julius Nepos a little breathing space, but the pressures on him and his dominions were simply too great. When Euric's Goths overran Provence it took the Burgundiones, three Gallic bishops and the concession of Clermont to get them to withdraw. Julius Nepos did attempt to exert some degree of control over Gaul, and with this in mind he gave the command to Orestes, a Pannonian officer who had served at Attila's court. Unfortunately for Julius Nepos, Orestes, with the Italian army in tow, rebelled against him in August 475. Julius Nepos fled to Dalmatia where, in 480, he was murdered, doubtless in an act of revenge, at the instigation of Glycerius, who was now the Bishop of Salona.

The Last Western Emperor

Orestes installed his own son Romulus Augustulus ('Little Augustus') as what would turn out to be the last ruler of Rome's Empire in the West. For what it was worth, that Empire now only comprised Italy and southern Provence, and Romulus

---

16   See, p. 407.

Augustulus was not recognized by Zeno in Constantinople anyway. Yet even this tiny realm proved too difficult to administer. Orestes lost the loyalty of his troops, who instigated a mutiny under their German commander Odoacer in August 476. Orestes was killed at Placentia, but Romulus Augustulus was not even worth putting to death. He was placed under house arrest, given a living allowance, and may have established a monastery in Campania with his mother. Odoacer assumed control, but the Western Empire didn't need an Emperor any more, and when Zeno refused to legitimize him on the technicality that Julius Nepos still reigned in Dalmatia (which he did until he was assassinated in 480), simply took the title of *Rex* (King) instead, and governed from Ravenna, not Rome.

There is considerable irony in the fact that her last Emperor carried the names of Rome's first king, Romulus, and her first Emperor Augustus, albeit in the diminutive. But the irony extends further. Although the Western Roman Empire became transformed into medieval Europe, the Eastern Empire lived on in the form of the Greek-speaking Byzantine Empire, still based in Constantinople, until the city fell to the Ottoman Turks under Mehmet II the Conqueror in 1453. In 1462 Mehmet II visited what he thought was the site of Troy, now under his sway, and his reaction was fascinating:

> Allah has stored up for me [. . .] the right to avenge this city and its people. I have subdued their enemies, pillaged their cities and made them the 'spoils of the Mysians.' For it was the Greeks [. . .] who ravaged this city in the past, and whose descendants [i.e., the Byzantines] have now, after so many years, paid me the penalty for their hubris against the peoples of Asia.[17]

By sacking Constantinople, Mehmet II was claiming to have avenged the sack of Troy by the Greeks, and therefore, because

---

17 Critoboulus of Imbros, 4.11.5, tr. Kershaw, S. 'Spoils of the Mysians' is a proverbial phrase meaning 'a prey to everybody.'

the Romans traced their lineage back to the Trojans, he might be said to have done so on Rome's behalf. Yet for all the scholarly dispute about whether Rome 'fell' or was 'transformed', there is perhaps a third option. In the first book of Virgil's *Aeneid*, Jupiter had prophesied the future of the Roman race:

> For the empire of these people I impose neither limits of space nor time: I have given them power without end.[18]

Odoacer's barbarian-style coronation in 476 might seem to belie that prophetic vision, yet, as T. S. Eliot very pertinently wrote,

> We are all, so far as we inherit the civilization of Europe, still citizens of the Roman Empire, and time has not yet proved Virgil wrong.[19]

Culturally Rome never fell; her history is our present; and all roads lead from, rather than to, Rome. In the Eternal City Goethe mused that

> Everywhere else one starts from the outside and works inward; here it seems to be the other way round. All history is encamped about us and all history sets forth from us. This does not apply only to the history of Rome, but to the history of the whole world.[20]

And today the people who still admire the awe-inspiring relics scattered all over Rome's former dominions are not so much looking at the ruins of a great civilization, but at the foundations of another.

---

18   Virgil, *Aeneid* 1. 278 f., tr. Kershaw, S.
19   Eliot, T. S., 'Virgil and the Christian World', in *On Poetry and Poets*, London: Faber & Faber, 1959, p. 13.
20   Goethe, J. W., *Italienische Reise*, 1816–17, tr. Auden, W. H. and Meyer, E. in *The Italian Journey*, London: Collins, 1962, p. 137.

Bibliography

Africa, T. W., 'The Opium Addiction of Marcus Aurelius,' *Journal of the History of Ideas*, 22 (1961), 9–102.

Barrett, A. A., *Caligula: The Corruption of Power*, New Haven: Yale University Press, 1990.

Barrett, A. A., *Agrippina: Sex, Power, and Politics in the Early Empire*, New Haven: Yale University Press, 1996.

Barrett, A. A. (ed.), *Lives of the Caesars*, Oxford: Blackwell, 2008.

Baynes, N. H., *The Historia Augusta: Its date and purpose*, Oxford: Clarendon Press, 1926.

Beard, M., *Pompeii: The Life of a Roman Town*, London: Profile Books, 2008.

Beckman, M., *The Column of Marcus Aurelius: The Genesis and Meaning of a Roman Imperial Monument*, Chapel Hill: University of North Carolina Press, 2011.

Bennett, J., *Trajan Optimus Princeps. A Life and Times*, London and New York: Routledge, 1997.

Berry, J., *The Complete Pompeii*, London: Thames & Hudson, 2007.

Birley, A. R., *Marcus Aurelius: A Biography*, London: Routledge, 2nd edn., 1987.

Birley, A. R., *Septimius Severus: The African Emperor*, New Haven: Yale University Press, rev. edn., 1988.

Birley, A. R., *Hadrian, The Restless Emperor*, London: Routledge, 1997.

Boardman, J., Griffin, J. and Murray, O., (eds.), *The Oxford History of the Roman World*, Oxford and New York: Oxford University Press, 1986.

Boatwright, M. T., *Hadrian and the City of Rome*, Princeton, NJ: Princeton University Press, 1987.

Boatwright, M. T., *Peoples of the Roman World*, Cambridge: Cambridge University Press, 2012.

Boethius, A., *The Golden House of Nero*, Ann Arbor: University of Michigan Press, 1960.

Bowersock, G. W., *Roman Arabia*, Cambridge, MA: Harvard University Press, 1983.

Bowman, A. K., Garnsey, P., Rathbone, D. (eds.), *The Cambridge Ancient History, Volume XI, The High Empire, AD 70–192*, Cambridge: Cambridge University Press, 2nd edn., 2000.

Brauer, G. C., *The Young Emperors, Rome, AD 193–244*, New York: Thomas Y. Crowell, 1967.

Braund, D., *Rome and the Friendly King: The Character of the Client Kingship*, London: Croom Helm, 1984.

Breeze, D. J., *The Northern Frontiers of Roman Britain*, London: Batsford, 1982.

Brown, P., *The Making of Late Antiquity*, Cambridge, MA, and London: Harvard University Press, 1978.

Brunt, P. A., 'The *Lex de Imperio Vespasiani*', *Journal of Roman Studies* 67 (1977), 95–116.

Bryant, E. E., *The Reign of Antoninus Pius*, Cambridge: Cambridge University Press, 1895.

Butler, O. F., *Studies in the Life of Heliogabalus*, New York and London: Macmillan, 1908.

Cain, A. and Lenski, N., (eds.), *The Power of Religion in Late Antiquity*, Farnham and Burlington: Ashgate Publishing Ltd., 2009.

Cameron, A., *The Later Roman Empire: AD 284–430*, London: Fontana, 1993.

Campbell, J. B., *The Emperor and the Roman Army, 31 BC–AD 235*, Oxford: Clarendon Press, 1984.

Cary, M. and Scullard, H. H., *A History of Rome Down to the Reign of Constantine*, New York: St Martin's Press, 3rd edn., 1975.

Champlin, E., *Fronto and Antonine Rome*, Cambridge, MA: Harvard University Press, 1980.

Chisholm, K. and Ferguson J. (eds.), *Rome: The Augustan Age*, Oxford: Oxford University Press, 1981.

Coarelli, F., Foglia, A. and Foglia, P., *Pompeii*, New York: Riverside Book Co., 2002.

Cooley, A. and M. G. L., *Pompeii: A Sourcebook*, London: Routledge, 2004.

Collins, R. H. J., *Early Medieval Europe 300–1000*, London: Palgrave Macmillan, 3rd edn., 2010.

Croke, B. and Harries, J., *Religious Conflict in Fourth-Century Rome*, Sydney: Sydney University Press, 1982.

Dando-Collins, S., *Legions of Rome: The Definitive History of Every Imperial Roman Legion*, London: Quercus, 2010.

Darwall-Smith, R. H., *Emperors and Architecture: A Study of Flavian Rome*, Brussels: Latomus, 1996.

Davies, P. J. E., *Death and the Emperor: Roman Imperial Funerary Monuments from Augustus to Marcus Aurelius*, Cambridge: Cambridge University Press, 2000.

De la Bédoyère, G., *Roman Britain: A New History*, London: Thames & Hudson, 2006.

Drinkwater, J. and Elton, H., *Fifth-century Gaul: A Crisis of Identity?*, Cambridge: Cambridge University Press, 1992.

Dudley, D. and Webster, G., *The Roman Conquest of Britain*, London: Batsford, 1965.

Duggan, A., *He Died Old: Mithradates Eupator King of Pontus*, London: Faber and Faber, 1958.

Earl, D., *The Age of Augustus*, New York: Crown Publishers, 1968.

Esmonde-Cleary, S., *The Ending of Roman Britain*, London: Batsford, 1989.

Evans Grubbs, J., *Women and the Law in the Roman Empire: A Sourcebook on Marriage, Divorce and Widowhood*, Abingdon: Routledge, 2002.

Feldherr, A. (ed.), *The Cambridge Companion to the Roman Historians*, Cambridge: Cambridge University Press, 2009.

Ferguson, J., *The Religions of the Roman Empire*, Ithaca, NY: Cornell University Press, 1970.

Freisenbruch, A., *The First Ladies of Rome: The Women Behind the Caesars*, London: Jonathan Cape, 2010.

Galinsky, K., (ed.), *The Cambridge Companion to The Age of Augustus*, Cambridge: Cambridge University Press, 2005.

Garnsey, P. and Humfress, C., *The Evolution of the Late Antique World*, Cambridge: Orchard Academic, 2001.

Garzetti, A., *From Tiberius to the Antonines: A History of the Roman Empire, AD 14–192*. Tr. Foster, J. R., London: Methuen, 1974.

Gibbon, E., *The History of the Decline and Fall of the Roman Empire*, London: Strahan & Cadell, 1776–1788.

Goffart, W., *Barbarians and Romans AD 418–585: The Techniques of Accommodation*, Princeton, NJ: Princeton University Press, 1980.

Goldsworthy, A., *The Complete Roman Army*, London: Thames & Hudson, 2003.

Goldsworthy, A., *The Fall of the West: The Slow Death of the Roman Superpower*, London: Weidenfield & Nicolson, 2009.

Grainger, J. D., *Nerva and the Roman Succession Crisis of AD 96–99*, Milton Park: Routledge, reprinted with corrections, 2004.

Grant, M., *The Roman Emperors: A Biographical Guide to the Rulers of Rome, 31 BC–AD 476*, New York: Scribner's, 1985.

Grant, M., *The Antonines: The Roman Empire in Transition*, London and New York: Routledge, 1994.

Grant, M., *The Severans: The Changed Roman Empire*, London and New York: Routledge, 1996.

Griffin, M. T., *Nero: the End of a Dynasty*, London: Routledge, 1984.

Halsall, G., *Barbarian Migrations and the Roman West, 376–568*, Cambridge: Cambridge University Press, reprinted with corrections, 2009.

Halsberghe, G. H., *The Cult of Sol Invictus*, Leiden: E. J. Brill, 1972.

Hammond, M., *The Antonine Monarchy*, Rome: American Academy in Rome, 1959.

Hammond, N. G. L. (ed.), *Atlas of the Greek and Roman World in Antiquity*, Park Ridge, NJ: Noyes Press, 1981.

Hanson, W., *Rome's North West Frontier: the Antonine Wall*, Edinburgh: Edinburgh University Press, 2nd edn., 1986.

Harnecker, J., *Arminius, Varus and the Battlefield at Kalkriese: An Introduction to the Archaeological Investigations and their Results*, Bramsche: Rasch Verlag, 2004.

Haynes, H., *Tacitus on Imperial Rome: The History of Make-Believe*, Berkeley and Los Angeles: University of California Press, 2003.

Heather, P. J., *The Goths*, Oxford: Blackwell, 1996.

Heather, P. J., *The Fall of Rome: A New History*, London: Macmillan, 2005.

Heather, P. J. and Matthews, J. F., *The Goths in the Fourth Century*, Liverpool: Liverpool University Press, 1991.

Heather, P. J. and Moncur, D., *Politics, Philosophy and Empire in the Fourth Century: Themistius' Select Orations*, Liverpool: Liverpool University Press, 2001.

Hekster, O., *Commodus: Emperor at the Crossroads*, Amsterdam: J.C. Gieben, 2002.

Holum, K., *Theodosian Empresses: Women and Imperial Dominion in Late Antiquity*, Berkeley and London: University of California Press, 1982.

Honoré, T., *Emperors and Lawyers*, Oxford: Clarendon Press, 2nd edn., 1994.

Hopkins, K. and Beard, M., *The Colosseum*, London: Profile Books, updated paperback edn., 2011.

Icks, M., *The Crimes of Elagabalus: The Life and Legacy of Rome's Decadent Boy Emperor*, London and New York: I. B. Tauris, 2011.

Johnson, M. J., *The Roman Imperial Mausoleum in Late Antiquity*, Cambridge: Cambridge University Press, 2009.

Jones, A. H. M., *Constantine and the Conversion of Europe*, London: Macmillan, 1948.

Jones, A. H. M., *The Later Roman Empire. A Social, Administrative and Economic Survey*, Oxford: Basil Blackwell, 1964.

Jones, B. W., *The Emperor Titus*, London: Croom Helm, 1984.

Jones, B. W., *The Emperor Domitian*, London and New York: Routledge, 1992.

Jones, P. and Sidwell, K., *The World of Rome: An Introduction to Roman Culture*, Cambridge: Cambridge University Press, 1997.

Kershaw, S., *A Brief Guide to the Greek Myths*, London: Robinson, 2007.

Kershaw, S., *A Brief Guide to Classical Civilization*, London: Robinson, 2010.

Kyle, D. G., *Spectacles of Death in Ancient Rome*, London & New York: Routledge, 1998.

Lambert, R., *Beloved and God. The Story of Hadrian and Antinous*, New York: Viking, 1984.

Lenski, N. E. (ed.), *The Cambridge Companion to the Age of Constantine*, Cambridge: Cambridge University Press, 2006.

Lenski, N. E., *Failure of Empire: Valens and the Roman State in the Fourth Century AD*, Berkeley and Los Angeles: University of California Press, 2002.

Lepper, F. A., *Trajan's Parthian War*, Oxford: Oxford University Press, 1948.

Lepper, F. and Frere, S., *Trajan's Column. A New Edition of the Cichorius Plates*, Gloucester: Alan Sutton, 1988.

Levick, B., *Claudius*, New Haven: Yale University Press, 1990.

Levick, B., *Vespasian*, London and New York: Routledge, 1999.

Lewis, N. and Reinhold, M. (eds.), *Roman Civilization: Selected Readings Edited by Naphtali Lewis and Meyer Reinhold, Volume II, The Empire*, New York: Columbia University Press, 3rd edn., 1990.

Liebeschuetz, J. H. W. G., *Continuity and Change in Roman Religion*, Oxford: Oxford University Press, 1979.

Long, J., *Claudian's* In Eutropium: *Or, How, When, and Why to Slander a Eunuch*, Chapel Hill and London: University of North Carolina Press, 1996.

Luttwak, E. N., *The Grand Strategy of the Roman Empire from the First Century AD to the Third*, Baltimore: Johns Hopkins University Press, 1976.

Macdonald, W. L., *The Pantheon: Design, Meaning and Progeny*, Cambridge, MA: Harvard University Press, 1976.

MacDonald, W. and Pinto, J., *Hadrian's Villa and its Legacy*, New Haven and London: Yale University Press, 1995.

MacMullen, R., *Corruption and the Decline of Rome*, New Haven and London: Yale University Press, 1988.

Mann, J. C. and Penman, R. G. (eds.), *LACTOR 11: Literary Sources for Roman Britain*, London: London Association of Classical Teachers, 2nd.edn., 1985.

Mattern, S. P., *Rome and the Enemy. Imperial Strategy in the Principate*, Berkeley: University of California Press, 1999.

Matthews, J., *Western Aristocracies and Imperial Court AD 364–425*, Oxford: Clarendon Press, 1975.

Mayor, A., *The Poison King: The Life and Legend of Mithradates, Rome's Deadliest Enemy*, Princeton, NJ: Princeton University Press, 2010.

McCrum, M. and Woodhead, A. G., *Select Documents of the Principates of the Flavian Emperors Including the Year of Revolution*, Cambridge: Cambridge University Press, 1961.

McGing, B. C., *The Foreign Policy of Mithridates VI Eupator King of Pontus*, Leiden: E. J. Brill, 1986.

Meijer, F., *Emperors Don't Die in Bed*, London and New York: Routledge, 2004.

Merrills, A. H. (ed.), *Vandals, Romans and Berbers: New Perspectives on Late Antique North Africa*, Aldershot and Burlington: Ashgate Publishing, 2004.

Millar, F., *The Emperor in the Roman World*, Ithaca: Cornell University Press, 1992.

Millar, F., *The Roman Near East, 31 BC–AD 337*, Cambridge, MA, and London: Harvard University Press, 1993.

Millar, F. and Segal, E. (eds.), *Caesar Augustus, Seven Aspects*, Oxford: Clarendon Press, 1984.

Mitchell, S., *A History of the Later Roman Empire AD 284–641: The Transformation of the Ancient World*, Oxford: Blackwell, 2007.

Moorhead, S. and Stuttard, D., *AD 410: The Year That Shook Rome*, London: British Museum Press, 2010.

Murphy, C., *Are We Rome? The Fall of an Empire and the Fate of America*, Boston and New York: Mariner Books, 2008.

Nicolet, C., *The World of the Citizen in Republican Rome*, Berkeley and Los Angeles: University of California Press, 1980.

Opper, T., *Hadrian: Empire and Conflict*, London: British Museum Press, 2008.

Parker, H. M. D., *A History of the Roman World from AD 138 to 337*, 2nd edn., revised with additional notes by B. H. Warmington, London: Methuen, 1958.

Peddie, J., *Invasion: The Roman Conquest of Britain*, New York: St. Martin's Press, 1987.

Perowne, S., *Hadrian*, London: Hodder and Stoughton, 1960.

Perowne, S., *Caesars and Saints*, London: Hodder and Stoughton, 1962.

Perowne, S., *The Caesars' Wives – Above Suspicion?*, London: Hodder and Stoughton, 1974.

Pollard, N. and Berry, J., *The Complete Roman Legions*, London: Thames & Hudson, 2012.

Potter, D. S., *The Roman Empire at Bay AD 180–395*, London and New York: Routledge, 2004.

Potter, D., *Emperors of Rome: Imperial Rome from Julius Caesar to the Last Emperor*, London: Quercus, 2007.

Price, S. R. F., *Rituals and Power: The Roman Imperial Cult in Asia Minor*, Cambridge: Cambridge University Press, 1984.

Raaflaub, K. A. and Toher, M. (eds.), *Between Republic and Empire: Interpretations of Augustus and his Principate*, Berkeley: University of California Press, 1990.

Ramsey, J. T. and Licht A. L., *The Comet of 44 BC and Caesar's Funeral Games*, Chicago: Scholars Press (Series: APA American Classical Studies, No. 39.), 1997.

Richardson, L., *A New Topographical Dictionary of Ancient Rome*, Baltimore: Johns Hopkins University Press, 1992.

Richlin, A., *The Garden of Priapus. Sexuality and Aggression in Roman Humor*, New Haven and London: Yale University Press, 1983.

Rohrbacher, D., *The Historians of Late Antiquity*, London and New York: Routledge, 2002.

Rossi, L., *Trajan's Column and the Dacian Wars*, tr. Toynbee, J. M. C., London: Thames & Hudson, 1971.

Rossini, O., *Ara Pacis*, Milan: Electa, new expanded edn., 2008.

Rubin, Z., *Civil War Propaganda and Historiography*, Brussels: Latomus, 1980.

Rutherford, R. B., *The Meditations of M. Aurelius: A Study*, Oxford: Clarendon Press, 1989.

Saddington, D. B., *The Development of the Auxiliary Forces from Caesar to Vespasian (49 BC–AD 79)*, Harare: University of Zimbabwe, 1982.

Scarre, C., *Chronicle of the Roman Emperors: The Reign by Reign Record of Imperial Rome*, London: Thames & Hudson, 1995.

Scullard, H. H., *A History of Rome from 133 BC to AD 68*, London and New York: Methuen, 5th edn., 1982.

Seager, R., *Pompey: A Political Biography*, Oxford: Basil Blackwell, 1979.

Shenton, J. A., *As the Romans Did: A Source Book in Roman History*, New York and Oxford: Oxford University Press, 1988.

Shahîd, I., *Rome and the Arabs: A Prolegomenon to the Study of Byzantium and the Arabs*, Dumbarton Oaks: Harvard University Press, 1984.

Smallwood, E. M., *Documents Illustrating the Principates of Nerva, Trajan and Hadrian*, Cambridge: Cambridge University Press, 1966.

Smallwood, E. M., *Documents Illustrating the Principates of Gaius, Claudius and Nero*, Cambridge: Cambridge University Press, 1967.

Smith, R. R. R., Ilgım, M. and Özgüven, H., *Aphrodisias Sebasteion Sevgi Gönül Hall*, Istanbul: Yapı Kredi Publications, 2008.

Southern, P., *Domitian: Tragic Tyrant*, Bloomington: Indiana University Press, 1997.

Southern, P., *Empress Zenobia: Palmyra's Rebel Queen*, London and New York, Continuum, 2008.

Southern, P., *Ancient Rome: The Empire 30 BC–AD 476*, Stroud: Amberley Publishing, 2011.

Speidel, M. P., *Ancient Germanic Warriors: Warrior Styles from Trajan's Column to Icelandic Sagas*, London and New York: Routledge, 2004.

Speidel, M. P., *Emperor Hadrian's Speeches to the African Army: A New Text*, Mainz: Verlag des Römischen-Germanischen Zentralmuseums, 2006.

Swain, S., *Hellenism and Empire. Language, Classicism and Power in the Greek World, AD 50–250*, Oxford: Clarendon Press, 1996.

Syme, R., *Tacitus*, Oxford: Oxford University Press, 1958.

Syme, R., *The Roman Revolution*, Oxford: Clarendon Press, reprinted from corrected sheets of the First Edition, 1956.

Syme, R., *Ammianus and the Historia Augusta*, Oxford: Clarendon Press, 1968.

Talbert, R., *The Senate of Imperial Rome*, Princeton, NJ: Princeton University Press, 1984.

Tougher, S., *Julian the Apostate*, Edinburgh: Edinburgh University Press, 2007.

Toynbee, J. M. C., *The Hadrianic School*, Cambridge: Cambridge University Press, 1934.

Varner, E. R., *Mutilation and Transformation:* Damnatio Memoriae *and Imperial Roman Portraiture*, Leiden: E. J. Brill, 2004.

Vogel, L., *The Column of Antoninus Pius*, Cambridge, MA: Harvard University Press, 1973.

Wallace-Hadrill, A., *Suetonius: The Scholar and His Caesars*, London: Duckworth, 1983.

Ward-Perkins, B., *The Fall of Rome and the End of Civilization*, Oxford: Oxford University Press, 2005.

Warmington, B. H., *Nero: Reality and Legend*, London: Chatto & Windus, 1969.

Webster, G., *The Roman Imperial Army of the First and Second Centuries*, London: Black, 3rd edn., 1985.

Wellesley, K., *The Long Year: AD 69*, London and New York: Routledge, 3rd edn., with a new introduction by Barbara Levick, 2000.

Wells, C., *The Roman Empire*, London: Fontana Press, 2nd edn., 1992.

Whitmarsh, T., *The Second Sophistic*, Oxford: Oxford University Press, 2005.

Williams, C. A., *Roman Homosexuality*, Oxford: Oxford University Press, 2nd edn., 2010.

Yavetz, Z., *Plebs and Princeps*, Oxford: Oxford University Press, 1969.

Zanker, P., *The Power of Images in the Age of Augustus*, translated by Alan Shapiro, Ann Arbor: University of Michigan Press, 1988.

Index